Nonverbal Communication in Close Relationships

"Looking at a wide variety of nonverbal behavior, Nonverbal Communication in Close Relationships: What Words Don't Tell Us considers the ways in which nonverbal signaling and decoding function within close relationships. With a world-class array of contributors, the book convincingly shows that it's often not what we say, but how we act nonverbally that determines the course of human relationships."

—Robert S. Feldman, *Senior Advisor to the Chancellor Professor, Department of Psychological and Brain Sciences, University of Massachusetts*

"The list of authors contributing to this work includes some of the world's top researchers in the field of nonverbal communication."

—Robert Rosenthal, *University Professor and Distinguished Professor of Psychology at the University of California, Riverside*

"This perceptive book gathers two dozen top experts on nonverbal communication to uncover why love looks not only with the eyes, but also with the mind, and why a lover's ear will hear the lowest sound but can also sometimes sense too much, from the neurochemical symphony to the interactional synchrony, from flirting to courting to touching, thus providing unmasked cues to key movements of social life. Excellent innovative scholarship."

—Howard S. Friedman, Ph.D., *Distinguished Professor, University of California, Riverside*

"This volume brings together world experts, as well as new voices, to address the many aspects of nonverbal communication in close relationships. The content is a perfect companion to courses in nonverbal communication, interpersonal relationships, or the psychology of close relationships and belongs on the library shelves of leading scholars in these areas."

—Judee K. Burgoon, *Professor of Communication, Center for Identification Technology Research, University of Arizona*

Robert J. Sternberg • Aleksandra Kostić
Editors

Nonverbal Communication in Close Relationships

What words don't tell us

palgrave
macmillan

Editors
Robert J. Sternberg
Department of Psychology
College of Human Ecology
Cornell University
Ithaca, NY, USA

Department of Psychology
University of Heidelberg
Heidelberg, Germany

Aleksandra Kostić
Faculty of Philosophy
Department of Psychology
University of Niš
Niš, Serbia

ISBN 978-3-030-94491-9 ISBN 978-3-030-94492-6 (eBook)
https://doi.org/10.1007/978-3-030-94492-6

This Palgrave Macmillan imprint is published by the registered company Springer Nature Switzerland AG.
The registered company address is: Gewerbestrasse 11, 6330 Cham, Switzerland

Preface

Almost all of us have been in situations in which a person's words said one thing and their actions said another. Maybe they told us how much they loved us but could not look us in the eye. Or perhaps they told us that we could trust them, but their actions belied their words. When people's words say one thing, but their actions say another, most of us have learned that we should rely on the nonverbal signals rather than the verbal ones. For a variety of reasons, it is easier to fake words than nonverbal signals or actions.

The goal of this book is to convey to readers what the secret language of close relationships is—the nonverbal signals, which often conflict with verbal ones—about how someone feels about someone with whom they are in a close relationship—whether as a romantic partner, a friend, an employer, a leader, or whatever.

In this book we provide an up-to-date compendium of knowledge on the secret language of close relationships, namely, nonverbal routes of communication. In such relationships, as everyone learns sooner or later, the usefulness of words can be somewhat limited, because people (a) mean different things by the same words, (b) mean the same thing by different words, (c) sometimes find it hard to express their feelings in words, and (d) lie. Nonverbal signals therefore often provide the best means of communication. This book helps decode those signals.

This book potentially has an exceptionally wide audience because of the topic. Whereas some topics appeal only to individuals who specialize in that topic, nonverbal communication in close relationships is potentially interesting and relevant to everyone. We believe that the book is relevant to academics in the fields of close relationships, nonverbal communication, and social psychology in general. The book also should be of interest to students in those fields. But the book also has special relevance to practitioners as well, because therapists and counselors deal on a daily basis with people who have problems in their close relationships. Being well aware of the nonverbal language of such relationships can help these professionals better serve their clients. And even the clients themselves—and laypeople interested in close relationships—can benefit both from learning how better to convey their love nonverbally and from learning if they are making mistakes that may be conveying messages they do not wish to convey.

The book has 14 chapters in all.

In Chap. 1, "Interpersonal Oculesics: Eye-Related Signals of Attraction, Interest, and Connection," Jonathan M. Bowman and Benjamin L. Compton consider nonverbal signals that emanate from the eyes. The authors point out that the eyes are a source of both intentional and unintentional messages and that these messages can convey approach toward another, avoidance of another, or anything in-between these two extremes.

In Chap. 2, "Communication and Communal Emotions in the Learning of Love," Ross Buck discusses the origins and development of human bonding, including parental, filial, and sexual bonding. He contrasts the emotions of gratitude, respect, elevation, appreciation, and trust ("GREAT emotions") with the emotions of loneliness, ostracism, shunning, exclusion, and rejection ("LOSER" emotions). The former are associated with love, and the latter with lack of love or failed love. These latter emotions can lead to admiration for charismatic, authoritarian leaders and rejection of perceived outsiders, a problem facing many countries today, including the United States. Often, these "LOSER" emotions are hidden behind a thin religious or ideological veneer that barely covers the negativity underneath.

In Chap. 3, "The Role of Nonverbal Communication in Leadership Skills," Mirjana Franceško and Jasmina Nedeljković discuss nonverbal communication in the context of leader-follower relations. Their goal is to construct an instrument for assessing beliefs about a leader and leadership. They are particularly interested in measurement of the significance of nonverbal communication in a particular setting, what this significance is in comparison with verbal signals, and leaders' knowledge of the nonverbal symbols that they can and do use.

In Chap. 4, "The Look of Love: Evolution and Nonverbal Signs and Signals of Attraction," Mark G. Frank, Anne Solbu, Zachary R. Glowacki, Zena Toh, and Madison Neurohr examine the nonverbal signals related to interpersonal attraction and also consider the evolutionarily derived reasons for them as well as their meanings. They also look at features of people's faces that we find to be attractive and the relations of these features to generalized desirable features of individuals, such as health, fertility, and dominance. They further examine the nonverbal signals that signify attention, trust, and commitment.

In Chap. 5, "Love Signals and the Reproductive Force," David B. Givens and John White relate nonverbal signals to reproductive forces. They believe that the reproductive force in humans is a powerful motivator of behavior. It shows up in people's overall demeanor, their facial expressions, their gestures, and in their nonverbal communication with each other. On this view, we can understand nonverbal communication better if we seek to understand it in terms of how it contributes to reproduction.

In Chap. 6, "The Verbal and Nonverbal Communication of Romantic Interest," Terrence G. Horgan, Judith A. Hall, and Melissa J. Grey consider early courtship and the signals people emit to show their interest in a romantic relationship. They compare the romantic signals that men and women emit to show romantic interest. They further consider the romantic signals sent in same-sex courtships and relationships.

In Chap. 7, "Misunderstood Nonverbal Cues in Close Relationships: The Contributions of Research Over Opinions," by Amy S. Ebesu Hubbard, we learn how easy it is for nonverbal communication in close relationships to be misinterpreted. Often, people's nonverbal skills do not match their verbal ones, so they encode or decode the wrong signals. Misunderstandings can arise in many areas of relationships, including but not limited to interest in forming a relationship, sexual interest and consent, and understanding of what constitutes the partner's cultural norms. It thus is important for partners in close relationships to be sure that the signals they are sending or receiving are those that are truly intended.

In Chap. 8, "What Words Don't Tell Us: Nonverbal Communication and Turmoil in Romantic Relationships," Diana K. Ivy and Shane A. Gleason claim that nonverbal cues reveal a kind of truth about relationships that verbal communication often obscures. They are especially interested in how nonverbal cues display both turmoil and turbulence in relationships. In particular, they look at cues emanating from touch/affection, proxemics, eye behavior, vocalics, and dyadic synchrony.

In Chap. 9, "Negative Emotions, Facial Clues, and Close Relationships: Facing the End?" Aleksandra Kostić, Marija Pejičić, and Derek Chadee note, as have others, that nonverbal communication reveals feelings in a way that verbal communication does not, whether because words are used to hide feelings or because words obscure feelings. Decoding of nonverbal communication is very important in relationships, both to preserve them and to make them better. Often, negative expressions serve as a warning that something is wrong and thus can serve as a first step toward improving a relationship.

In Chap. 10, "Love in the Time of COVID-19: What We Can Learn about Nonverbal Behavior from Living with a Pandemic," Valerie Manusov makes five major points. The first is that nonverbal cues are essential in sending messages in close relationships. Second, the same messages can be communicated in various ways, both verbally and nonverbally. Third, nonverbal communication, like verbal communication, follows fixed rules. Fourth, touch is important in communication, especially in times of a pandemic when so much about relationships is limited. Fifth, nonverbal communication can change over time and place. Finally, empathy and compassion are critical to successful relationships.

In Chap. 11, "Nonverbal communication: From good endings to better beginnings," Stephen Nowicki and Ann van Buskirk suggest that relationships proceed in cycles. They can have multiple beginnings and multiple endings. In other words, a relationship is not a straight line passing through time but rather a cycling process that can be at various stages at various times, sometimes moving forward, sometimes seeming to move backwards, but cycling along rather than simply moving from beginning to end. On their view, there can seem even to be multiple relationships with the same person, with each new relationship building upon but ultimately superseding the earlier ones.

In Chap. 12, "The Functions and Consequences of Interpersonal Touch in Close Relationships," Martin S. Remland and Tricia S. Jones analyze the emotional consequences of both touch and deprivation of touch. They also look at cultural factors and how, in various cultures, touch serves as a basis for understanding people's needs for intimacy and closeness of various kinds. Their analysis is at multiple levels: biological, social, and cultural. They also examine how the Age of the Internet, where so many relationships can become remote ones, affect people, given their need for touch and physical closeness.

In Chap. 13, "Nonverbal Skills in Relationships: Too Little or Too Much May Be a Bad Thing," Ronald E. Riggio and Alan Crawley suggest that there is not always a linear relationship between skills and success, especially as this principle applies to nonverbal communicational skills. In particular, they suggest that too high a level of nonverbal skill can be detrimental, just as too low a level can be. They analyze in particular three skills—expressivity, sensitivity, and control—seeking to understand what the optimal levels of these skills are.

In Chap. 14, "Nonverbal Communication in Relationships as a Link between Affect and Social Intelligence," Robert J. Sternberg seeks to summarize the main takeaway messages of the book as a whole. He notes that nonverbal communication is an important feature of close relationships. Indeed, nonverbal communication often is more important than verbal communication. Nonverbal communication forms a language, just as do the symbols of verbal communication. Nonverbal communication involves both encoding and decoding, which are distinctive but related abilities. Nonverbal abilities have some degree of domain-specificity. It also is often transmitted preconsciously and unintentionally. We often are not aware of the messages we are transmitting. But sometimes, when people are aware of what they are doing, they try to manipulate nonverbal communication to make it appear as though a signal that is communicated intentionally is unintentional. And finally, nonverbal signals may contradict both each other and verbal signals.

As you can see, the book covers a very wide range of psychological phenomena regarding nonverbal communication. We hope you enjoy reading it!

Ithaca, NY, USA Robert J. Sternberg
Niš, Serbia Aleksandra Kostić

Contents

List of Contributors

Jonathan M. Bowman University of San Diego, San Diego, CA, USA

Ross Buck University of Connecticut, Storrs, CT, USA

Derek Chadee ANSA McAl Psychological Research Centre, The University of the West Indies, St. Augustine, Trinidad

Benjamin L. Compton University of Washington, Seattle, WA, USA

Alan Crawley Universidad del Salvador, Buenos Aires, Argentina

Amy S. Ebesu Hubbard Department of Communicology, University of Hawai'i at Mānoa, Honolulu, HI, USA

Mirjana Franceško Department of Psychology, Faculty of Legal and Business Study dr Lazar Vrkatić, Union University, Belgrade, Serbia

Mark G. Frank University at Buffalo, State University of New York, Buffalo, NY, USA

David B. Givens Center for Nonverbal Studies, School of Leadership Studies, Gonzaga University, Spokane, WA, USA

Shane A. Gleason Department of Social Studies, Texas A&M University-Corpus Christi, Corpus Christi, TX, USA

Zachary R. Glowacki University at Buffalo, State University of New York, Buffalo, NY, USA

Melissa J. Grey Monroe County Community College, Monroe, MI, USA

Judith A. Hall Northeastern University, Boston, MA, USA

Terrence G. Horgan Department of Psychology, University of Michigan, Flint, MI, USA

Diana K. Ivy Department of Communication & Media, Texas A&M University-Corpus Christi, Corpus Christi, TX, USA

Tricia S. Jones Communication and Media, Temple University, Philadelphia, PA, USA

Aleksandra Kostić Faculty of Philosophy, Department of Psychology, University of Niš, Niš, Serbia

Valerie Manusov Department of Communication, University of Washington, Seattle, WA, USA

Jasmina Nedeljković Department of Psychology, Faculty of Legal and Business Study dr Lazar Vrkatić, Union University, Belgrade, Serbia

Madison Neurohr University at Buffalo, State University of New York, Buffalo, NY, USA

Stephen Nowicki Department of Psychology, Emory University, EU, Atlanta, GA, USA

Marija Pejičić Faculty of Philosophy, Department of Psychology, University of Niš, Niš, Serbia

Martin S. Remland Department of Communication and Media, West Chester University of Pennsylvania, West Chester, PA, USA

Ronald E. Riggio Kravis Leadership Institute, Claremont McKenna College, Claremont, CA, USA

Anne Solbu University at Buffalo, State University of New York, Buffalo, NY, USA

Robert J. Sternberg Department of Psychology, College of Human Ecology, Cornell University, Ithaca, NY, USA
Department of Psychology, University of Heidelberg, Heidelberg, Germany

Zena Toh University at Buffalo, State University of New York, Buffalo, NY, USA

Ann van Buskirk Emory University, EU, Atlanta, GA, USA

John White Dublin City University, Dublin, Ireland

List of Figures

List of Photos

1

Interpersonal Oculesics: Eye-Related Signals of Attraction, Interest, and Connection

Jonathan M. Bowman and Benjamin L. Compton

Introduction

Although overused media tropes about people experiencing "love at first sight" after their "eyes met across a crowded room" are pervasive, many people may underestimate the importance of the oculesic code of eye-related nonverbal behaviors. Focusing exclusively on the meanings that are encoded by the eyes—and decoded about the eyes—the range of possible nonverbal messages are far more significant than many laypersons and even scholars are likely to realize. After all, popular discussions about the use of eyes in communication seem to focus exclusively on the role of eye contact, missing other key elements of oculesic behaviors that may in fact impact our ability to send and receive relational messages using our

J. M. Bowman (✉)
University of San Diego, San Diego, CA, USA
e-mail: bowman@sandiego.edu

B. L. Compton
University of Washington, Seattle, WA, USA

R. J. Sternberg, A. Kostić (eds.), *Nonverbal Communication in Close Relationships*,
https://doi.org/10.1007/978-3-030-94492-6_1

eyes. Whether conveying attention or interest to a partner or indicating affection or threat, the possible impact of eye-related behaviors must not be overlooked in the context of close relationships.

Oculesic Structures

To be clear, there are actually three main types of eye behaviors used in *sending* messages. At the same time, the eyes can be used in an almost infinite number of applications for *receiving* nonverbal and verbal messages from both intentional and unintentional interaction partners (Bowman, 2020). After all, the eyes have been said to account for the majority of social information, with up to 80% of our social information being sight-based (Morris, 1985). Because visual cues encompass the majority of other nonverbal codes, the three oculesic behaviors mostly focus on the intentional and unintentional *sending* of messages from a structural perspective.

Gaze The most common way to understand active messaging in a situation requires an individual to look in the direction of the other person(s) who might be sending messages. This act of one person looking at one or more other people is called *gaze.* It is one of the quickest ways to gain important demographic and cultural information about the person being viewed (Bowman, 2020). When an individual is gazing at another, they are often observing and interpreting a variety of markers of information—including but not limited to the perceived gender and age of the individual in addition to making guesses about their racial, economic, and even sometimes religious identities as well. In initial interactions, this gaze can also provide important information that may lead to attraction and interest, whether platonic or sexual in nature (Bowman, 2019). Gaze can even serve as a sort of indicator of attraction, in that people often look in the direction of people or things that they find pleasing or attractive and can even reinforce those feelings of pleasure or attractiveness through extended gaze (Shimojo et al., 2003). Not all gaze is positively valenced, however, and the experience of unwanted or prolonged gaze can create discomfort or lead to negative evaluations of a known or unknown other, a phenomenon which we will discuss in the fifth section of this chapter. Clearly, even the one-sided gaze of an individual toward an interaction partner influences the nature of the communal experience of messaging and the overall tenor of the situation. Mutual Gaze and Eye Contact When two people are gazing in the direction of one another's eyes, they are engaging in a specific form of visual regard known as *mutual gaze* (Jongerius et al., 2020). When both parties become aware of their shared mutual gaze, we typically refer to the experience of individuals having experienced *eye contact* (Argyle & Cook, 1976; Bowman, 2020). This shared experience of eye contact has multiple impacts upon both parties, with eye contact serving not only as an indicator of possible attraction but also as a social function which increases one's own attraction to an interaction partner (Jarick & Bencic, 2019). That is, using eye contact with a potential or current romantic partner may not only indicate your own attraction but also increase your own attraction to that other person. The idea that our eyes are mostly used to perceive information about the social world dramatically misrepresents the importance of eye contact in influencing one's own attraction to a potential mate. Eye Movement The third main category of oculesic structures involves the way that we move our eyes while in interaction with others. While eye movements are normal as one changes the focus of attention across varied people and objects within a particular context, one can also engage in social signaling where the eyes are used functionally in the same manner as gestures. Consider, for example, a situation where an individual has gone shopping with roommates and has bought a birthday cake as a surprise for their partner. If the partner walks into the room where the day's purchases are laid out on the counter, the roommate may widen his or her eyes to gain the speaker's attention, and then use their eyes to "point" in the direction of the cake to make sure that they cover it up before it is seen. In such a case, the friend has used their eyes to "flag down" their conversation partner and focused that partner's attention in the needed direction. Thus, an oculesic (eye-related) nonverbal behavior can approximate a kinesic (motion-related) nonverbal behavior in function (if not in structure). Pupil Dilation The final category of oculesic structures is also about the physical motion of the eye, but in this case focusing on the widening or narrowing of the pupils. Interestingly, the widening or dilating of the pupil is often an unintentional indication of physical attraction, with an individual's pupils dilating more when viewing attractive individuals of that individual's preferred sex (Rieger & Savin-Williams, 2012). In addition, individuals may subconsciously perceive pupil dilation as a possible indicator of attraction, unknowingly responding by becoming more attracted to a potentially available partner who they have subconsciously discovered may fancy them (Hess, 1965). That is, the very physiological response that displays attraction to a potential partner may in fact unwittingly induce attraction in that same partner (Tombs & Silverman, 2004). At the same time, however, recent research has begun exploring the impact of attraction on pupil constriction, noting that brief constriction may occur when viewing an attractive partner (Liao et al., 2021) and demonstrating that the movement of pupils is much more nuanced than is the relatively stable finding that pupil dilation leads to increased attraction.

Multiple Meanings of Eye-Related Behaviors Before getting into some of the specific functions of these oculesic structures, it must be noted that the range of structural behaviors for the eyes is relatively limited compared to, say, the nonverbal code of physical appearance. For example, physical appearance can include a range of nonverbal characteristics and behaviors like perceptions of age/sex/race, body shape, height, apparel and artifacts, viewable physical ability, and general physiognomy like hair color and texture, facial structure, and skin color among many others. Oculesic nonverbal behaviors typically involve the ways that one moves and directs one's eyes toward or away from others. As a result, while humans have established many norms for encoding and decoding eye behavior, these movements must often be processed as a gestalt in conjunction with myriad other nonverbal cues (Burgoon et al., 1996). As a result, one can use additional contextual nonverbal cues to easily distinguish between the eye contact associated with a sexual advance (e.g., mutual gaze, smile, licking of lips, and emphasis of bodily sex-based difference) as compared to the eye contact associated with a threat of harm (e.g., mutual gaze, scowl, furrowed brow, and striking of a fist into a palm). While all these other features help distinguish between the oculesic dialectic of interest and threat, the intense, prolonged, unbroken stare may be structurally very similar despite the highly discrepant functional intents. That is, there is often *polysemy*—multiple meanings associated with a specific nonverbal oculesic behavior—that makes it relatively difficult to interpret based solely on a limited channel alone (Manusov & Harvey, 2011).

Given the polysemous nature of oculesic structures, we will explore some of the functional aspects of our use of eyes in close relationships. Despite the exhortation of the often-misattributed proverb, "the eyes are the window to the soul," in fact, the eyes can tell us some interesting information about an individual's attitudes toward the people around them, especially useful in the context of close relationships. Oculesic behaviors can result in feelings of both platonic and romantic attraction. Oculesic behaviors can demonstrate interest in others while also maintaining the interest of an interaction partner. Oculesic behaviors can aid in the creation and maintenance of intimacy and affection through connection. Finally, as aforementioned, oculesic behaviors can lead to a variety of antisocial responses as well, ones which can lead to the deterioration of a relationship or even cause harm to an interaction partner. Clearly, the way that we use our eyes have multiple implications for our close relationships across the entirety of the relational lifespan, able to send multiple messages despite a rather limited set of possible structures.

Attraction

One of the most obvious uses of the eyes involves the observation of one's surroundings and the subsequent gleaning of important social and contextual information. Essentially, we use our eyes to look around us and figure out what is going on. At the same time, we assign valences—positive, neutral, or negative attitudes or feelings—to the objects and especially the people that we observe. Those things which are positively valenced (or evaluated favorably) can be said to be attractive to the observer, and that attraction is incredibly important in the formation of close relationships (Berscheid & Reis, 1998). At the same time, one's use of the eyes can also serve to indicate to others those things to which one is attracted. As a result, oculesic behaviors can both promote and indicate attraction. In this section, we will talk about the nature of attraction as experienced in a one-sided manner. That is, the implications associated with one-sided observations of others like those found in simple gaze. In our next section, we will focus more on the impact of mutual gaze on interest between interaction partners who share a close relationship.

Initial Attraction

During the initial impression-forming stages of relationships, we gain much of our information about one or more individual(s) simply by looking in their direction and evaluating both their appearance and their behaviors (Duran & Kelly, 1988). During the earliest stages of relational development, observations are made before any significant interaction has occurred, serving as a gatekeeper to help both parties determine whether future interaction is beneficial (Bowman, 2019; Knapp & Vangelisti, 2005). Put simply, as we look in the direction of a potential interaction partner (whether that partnership is potentially platonic or romantic) we observe their physical appearance to find information about their physical and social characteristics, in part to determine the compatibility that we might have with one another (Bowman, 2019). If you are interested in sports, you might look at a possible friend in order to determine if they would make a good gym buddy or running partner or maybe even be interested in joining your softball team. You might also observe the way that the other person behaves, looking to see if they appear to be relatively similar to yourself and also perhaps seem to be of good humor or attentive to others. Observed physical features like muscle tone and body fat would then combine with some observed interpersonal behaviors like a broad smile and an open body orientation to determine whether that person might be a good fit for future sport-based interactions.

The same process occurs as we look for potential romantic partners, searching for physical features that we find attractive and/or interesting while also looking for the ways of behaving that meet the needs we have decided are important for a potential romantic encounter. For some, they may be attracted to a tall dark and handsome partner, somewhat aloof and dripping with cool. Others may be most interested in a more androgynous individual who appears open, warm, caring, and affectionate. The very things that we observe in these initial interactions are sorted to allow us to quickly determine the potential for additional engagement with one another (Finkel & Eastwick, 2009; Knapp & Vangelisti, 2005). To be sure, however, one must clarify that the attraction resulting from the oculesic behaviors we are discussing have to do with the observation of characteristics about a relatively unknown other. This is different from the interest that emerges with a known other (discussed in the next section). Even more significantly, this is different from the one-sided looking behaviors known as surveillance, a set of oculesic practices that can be much more sinister in nature, relying on differences in power and efficacy to gain information about another individual (Marwick, 2012).

Oculesic Indicators of Attraction

One can also observe a variety of indicators which may be perceived as indicators of individual attraction, behaviors which may not necessarily be intentional and which may not always be exclusively representative of attraction. Two of these indicators of attraction are directly related to oculesic behaviors, including the dilation of one's pupils and the use of one-sided gaze.

Pupil Dilation As discussed earlier in this chapter, people may interpret dilated pupils of another individual as an indication of attraction (Hess, 1965). While this is a valid assumption grounded in research, there also exist other reasons for pupil dilation that can somewhat muddy the waters. For example, it is possible to observe dilated pupils on individuals under the influence of prescription or recreational pharmaceuticals of certain sorts (Bowman, 2020; Larsen & Waters, 2018). At certain times throughout human history, larger pupils have been associated with facial attractiveness in women (Couch & Koeninger, 2016; Tombs & Silverman, 2004) and there have been recorded attempts of persons regularly using small doses of poisons to achieve this dilated pupil appearance in order to capitalize on such trends (Hess & Petrovich, 1987). Similarly, people may experience temporary pupil dilation upon viewing *objects* that they find pleasing or attractive, which can also account for potential misunderstandings associated with physical attraction (Gump, 1962;

Kuraguchi & Kanari, 2021). Larger pupils themselves are more likely to be seen as "cute" and are linked with a desire to protect and nurture among adults (Sternglanz et al., 1977). Scholars also note that other emotional experiences may include (as a side effect) similar changes in pupil dilation (Hess & Petrovich, 1987) so it is quite possible that this indicator of attraction is not as robust as people likely subconsciously perceive. Gaze Somewhat surprisingly, the very act of looking in the direction of someone or something may also be seen as an indicator of attraction. After all, humans spend more time looking at people or things that they find attractive than they do at those people or things that they find unattractive (Shimojo et al., 2003). As a result, gaze can be seen not only as a way of discovering social information about an attractive individual, but also as a de facto way to indicate that one considers someone else to *be* an attractive individual (Bowman, 2020). Perhaps unsurprisingly, the trope of a young person staring off in the direction of an unrequited love—to the obvious amusement of friends and classmates who are able to ascertain an attraction-based motivation—finds itself actually grounded in regular human behavior. People do in fact stare at the people and things that they find attractive or pine after. This positive valence for one-sided gaze is well-demonstrated, showing not only that gaze is an indicator of attraction but that it can also be a contributor towards attraction. Indeed, across the course of the life span scholars have found a robust preference for direct gaze from both humans and primates (Simpson et al., 2019). When that previously one-sided gaze is observed and reciprocated, the resulting mutual gaze may be seen as a component of shared interest rather than simple individual attraction—as we discuss in this next section. Interest

Once attraction has been established through gaze, individuals may continue to engage in more interaction-based oculesic behaviors—such as eye contact or mutual gaze—to signal romantic or sexual interest in another individual. Extended eye contact is often seen as an approach signal, used socially as an invitation to initiate interaction (Givens, 1978; de Weerth & Kalma, 1995). In the process of courtship, once an individual has determined one's attraction to another through gaze and observation, they likely will then pursue signaling their own interest while simultaneously attempting to decode whether there is mutual interest.

Initiation of Interaction

Apart from those few individuals blessed with an excess of self-confidence, most individuals prefer some assurance that the apple of their eye is at least somewhat expressing reciprocal interest. One of the primary nonverbal indicators of this interest is expressed through eye contact. When it comes to initiating interaction, individuals often rely on reciprocity to gauge whether another is mutually interested (Burgoon et al., 1995). Such *reciprocity* occurs when an individual reacts to another's behavior by mirroring or displaying similar behavior. Imagine one is hanging out with friends at a bar on a Friday night, and during their evening, their friend informs them that an attractive person at the end of the bar keeps glancing in one's direction. Over the course of the next ten minutes, one may begin to gaze toward the attractive person, whereupon they engage in prolonged eye contact on numerous occasions. Fortunate for both parties, eye contact can express confidence and assertiveness and is perceived as an indicator of self-esteem (Droney & Brooks, 1993). Assured that this attractive person might be gazing with romantic or sexual interest, one feels as though there is enough evidence to confidently approach the attractive person at the end of the bar to pursue additional interaction.

Eye contact is not expressed as an exclusive nonverbal signal in the approach decision-making process, however. Studies have found that eye contact coupled with smiling tends to increase whether an individual might decide to approach another (Walsh & Hewitt, 1985). Given the polysemous nature of eye behavior (Manusov & Harvey, 2011), in our previous example, the attractive person's gaze might have not been a message of romantic or sexual interest, but instead the result of some other issue. Perhaps the gazer thought one was someone they knew, or maybe they believed that one was dressed in a peculiar way. For that matter, it is even possible that the attractive person at the end of the bar was bored and simply looking at everyone in the bar as a form of entertainment or even trying to determine who might have been their blind date for the evening. Most individuals might not deem the presence of a solitary nonverbal behavior as enough evidence to confidently determine mutual interest, but the combination of eye behavior and other nonverbals like facial expressions can add confidence or even certainty. Many of these behaviors exist, and other studies focused on gender have found that eye contact combined with space-maximizing movements (e.g., stretching, extending limbs), intrasexual touching, and less closed-body postures (e.g., crossed arms, crossed legs) were indicators that men were more likely to approach women (Renninger et al., 2004) in these polysemous contexts.

Flirting

Once an individual has determined attraction and interest and approached someone, the two persons might engage in flirting behavior. Flirting is when an individual expresses romantic or sexual attraction to another, receives such an expression of attraction, or attempts to decide if the feelings of attraction are mutual (Hall, 2013). Although one might be tempted to rely solely on eye contact alone to determine mutual attraction, flirting is a much more nuanced interaction than being limited to just one nonverbal behavior. While the eyes can't solely provide a guaranteed assurance of interest, the eyes might allow one to differentiate between romantic and social intrigue. That is, both gazing toward one another's eyes and using extended eye contact might help individuals discern platonic interactions from flirtatious interactions (England et al., 1996).

During a flirtatious interaction, the quantity and quality of oculesic behavior is very much dependent on the individuals involved and their idiosyncratic preferred flirting styles. Overall, flirtatious glances (i.e., gazes that involve an eyebrow raise with a smile, which may or may not involve mutual look) have been linked with physical attraction within the first three minutes of interaction, whereas one-sided or mutual gazing was linked with physical attraction between the subsequent four to nine minutes of interaction (Hall & Xing, 2015). In other words, when an individual is attracted to another, they tend to first engage in flirtatious glances toward the other and then as the interaction progresses it relies more on gazes that are subsequently absent of those eyebrow or facial movements.

Research has argued that there is more than one "type" of flirting style that can be applied to individuals when interacting with novel others within initial interactions (Hall & Xing, 2015). Depending on an individual's preferred flirting tendencies, the use of flirtatious glances and/or gazing might be enacted more during initial interactions with a potential partner. For example, individuals who prefer creating an intense emotional connection with a potential partner (i.e., sincere flirts) tend to engage in flirtatious glances within the first few minutes of an interaction compared to the average individual (ibid.). On the other hand, individuals who prefer to flirt purely for fun without the desire for long-term commitment (i.e., playful flirts) tend to use more flirtatious glances after the first few minutes of interaction compared to the average individual. One explanation for this might be that sincere flirts might prefer to begin interaction with subtle behavior, such as more coy and flirtatious glances, and then begin to engage in direct behavior (e.g., asking questions seeking intimate disclosure, partaking in active listening behaviors, etc.) following initiation of interaction as a means to signal sincere interest (ibid.). Of course, not all individuals flirt specifically to create intimate connection, but once an intimate relationship has been established the use of eye contact can continue to build connection—as discussed in this next section.

Connection

Not only do nonverbal oculesic behaviors serve to demonstrate and induce attraction and/or interest depending on the nature of the relationship, but also some of these eye-related behaviors can serve to establish and maintain perceptions of connection between two or more individuals. Within the context of an established relationship, it would be difficult to understate the significance of mutual gaze—or the lack of this reciprocal behavior—for the vast majority of relationships. Indeed, the popular tropes that emphasize the abilities of couples to communicate "with just one look" is widespread and trusted, perhaps unsurprising since humans have their earliest experiences with interpersonal connection as a result of the mutual gaze they experience as an infant with a caregiver or trusted adult (Brooks & Meltzoff, 2014).

Intimacy

Scholars have identified multiple forms of intimacy over the course of studying human relationships (e.g., emotional intimacy, sexual intimacy, recreational intimacy, among others; Schaefer & Olson, 1981) and yet a key foundational element of intimacy is the sense of connection to one's partner (whether romantic, platonic, and/or familial). The experience of shared mutual gaze (i.e., eye contact) within the context of a significant relationship is one of the most robust elements of nonverbal intimacy and immediacy behaviors (Bowman, 2019). Indeed, the linkage between partner gaze and the experience of emotional connection are borne out at even the most basic chemical level in our bodies (Denes, 2012).

This use of eye contact is so foundational to what it means to connect with other humans on a deeper level that partners even interpret gaze avoidance (covered later in this chapter) or gaze directed at an extradyadic individual to be seen as an indicator of a potential relational threat by a partner (Guerrero et al., 1995). To regularly look at a partner and to share eye contact with a partner is a key part of intimate communication. Indeed, when trying to simulate a sense of connection between a human and an anthropomorphic robot, programmers consider the importance of oculesics in trying to foster and build connections between the two (Kim & Kwon, 2010).

Maintenance Part of keeping an established relationship between individuals at the desired level of connection involves engaging in relational maintenance behaviors (Bowman, 2019; Bowman, 2020). These behaviors include a variety of nonverbal intimacy cues for nonverbal codes across the body, and yet the importance of eye contact is one of the most-discussed nonverbal indicators in popular culture (perhaps alongside perceptions of the importance of sex). Indeed, immediacy behaviors like eye contact are strongly related to those positive behaviors in a relationship that are predictive of long-term relational satisfaction (Hinkle, 1999). Clearly, people who are skilled at keeping a relationship at a desired state are also fluent in nonverbal expressions of connection like eye contact. At the same time, eye contact is not just one of those behaviors that can demonstrate connections in the same manner that sexual intimacy can signal the intact nature of a relationship or that relationship's health. Members of healthy relationships that are sexually active may also need to use oculesic behaviors in addition to *and as part of* sexual intimacy behaviors. Indeed, researchers have even begun exploring the importance of eye contact as essential to relational maintenance even during specific relational moments, such as during the brief period following immediately post-coitus; the importance of meaningful oculesic behaviors proving to be a component of one of the more obvious (but less scrutinized) moments of shared connection within an established relationship (Denes et al., 2017).

Clearly, the use of one's eyes can serve to increase the salience of the relationship that two people share with one another. The use of affectionate gaze and eye contact serve to indicate and promote both interest and intimacy, two important components of successfully maintained romantic relationships. Not all oculesic behavior need be serious and intense, however; in fact, just the opposite. Eye contact can be seen as one of many flirting behaviors used within an established relationship to signal connection and to reinforce perceptions of shared commitment with one another (Frisby & Booth-Butterfield, 2012). Those same nonverbal oculesic expressions of attraction and interest that proved essential to the establishment of a relationship may also prove to be core components that keep a relationship in working order moving forward. However, not all oculesic behaviors are necessarily intended to promote a relationship's establishment or to maintain that relationship successfully. In the next section, we'll explore some of the ways that humans might use their eyes in antisocial contexts which bring harm or detriment to both known and unknown others.

Antisocial Contexts

While eyes can serve the function of bringing together two strangers or strengthening a nascent bond between two lovers, oculesic behaviors may instead function to create anxiety or miscommunication between two parties (Argyle & Cook, 1976). Much of this chapter has focused on eye contact as an intentional and positive experience, yet often behaviors such as a one-sided look or mutual gaze might result in negative consequences, especially in situations in which two or more individuals may not desire to be the recipient of another's gaze. *Gaze avoidance,* for example, occurs when one person intentionally avoids another's eyes (von Cranach & Ellgring, 1973). Unlike *gaze omission,* where a person unintentionally fails to look at an interlocutor, gaze avoidance is an intentional act where an individual actively avoids either making eye contact or gazing toward an interlocutor's facial region. There might be many reasons why an individual might actively avoid making eye contact with another, yet in the realm of intimate communication, it might come down to what unsolicited eye contact might communicate.

Misperception

On average, men tend to oversexualize women's nonverbal behaviors as compared to women's perception of men's behaviors, including but not limited to behaviors such as interpersonal touch, conversational distances, adornments, and quantity of eye contact (Abbey & Melby, 1986; Koukounas & Letch, 2001). This oversexualization is only enhanced under certain circumstances involving courtship behaviors or alcoholic intake (Farris et al., 2008). For example, when Tyler arrives at a nightclub with his friends, he makes eye contact and smiles at many women that he encounters. As the night progresses and Tyler consumes progressively more alcohol, he might begin to tell his friends that there are a lot of women at the club that are sexually interested in him. By the end of the night, when Tyler is attempting to order his last drink from the bartender, he asks the bartender if she'd like to go home with him after her shift—and is ultimately denied the ability to order any more alcohol at the nightclub for the evening. As Tyler's alcohol intake increased, so too did his misguided perception that any woman who participated in mutual gaze was intentionally sending sexual courtship messages.

However, it should be noted that not all men are likely to oversexualize eye contact with women. Kowalski (1993) found that men's belief in traditional sex roles (i.e., men as sexually aggressive and women as submissive) was likely to predict whether or not those men gave sexual connotations to women's nonverbal cues. That is, men who rejected traditional sex role stereotypes were no more likely to perceive women's nonverbal behaviors (e.g., eye contact) as sexual in nature.

Dominance

One's attempt to enact a one-sided look in order to engage in eye contact might be met with gaze avoidance, and such a situation can result in this failed attempt at mutual gaze being perceived as an oculesic threat. The threatening stare is a display cue that is universally understood as a signal of dominance (Ellyson & Dovidio, 1985), which can result in an increase in anxiety for the recipient of the gaze (Drummond & Bailey, 2013). Research has found that consistent and prolonged gaze is perceived as more threatening and dominant when used by men and/or when used by individuals who are perceived in high-status positions (Le Poire & Burgoon, 1994; Tang & Schmeichel, 2015). Interestingly, humans tend to be very effective at detecting when they are being looked at (Conty et al., 2006), so the very act of gaze avoidance might not necessarily allow an individual to avoid the potential feeling of anxiety when being the target of what is perceived to be an aggressive stare.

Using Tyler from our earlier nightclub example, consider a scenario where a young woman is very friendly and smiled at Tyler and each of his friends as they joined the dance floor. Mistaking the initial friendly eye contact as a signal of sexual interest, Tyler may turn his attention toward the young woman and stare in her direction over the next short while. If this young woman notices and avoids this one-sided gaze behavior, she may begin to feel uncomfortable and worried that Tyler might engage in more intrusive nonverbal behaviors on the dance floor like unwanted touching. As a result, this young woman may quickly head to the bathroom with a friend and avoid Tyler for the rest of the evening.

The Case of the "Male Gaze"

While not all looking behaviors by men are problematic, the aforementioned oversexualized misperception of nonverbal cues combined with a threatening stare of dominance has resulted in the widespread notion generally referred to as the *male gaze,* an antisocial oculesic behavior gaining much attention in society as of late. This term derives in part from the finding that heterosexual men tend to focus visual attention more on the body while heterosexual women tend to focus more on the facial region of potential mates (Hollet et al., 2021). Similarly, when these men are more appearance-focused (instead of personality-focused) they are more likely to focus specifically on gazing at a woman's chest and waist more than her face (Gervais et al., 2013), an experience which is understandably perceived as depersonalizing (and even dehumanizing). This focus on the female figure rather than the facial region—the physical feature primarily used to encode and decode identity and expression—can be used as an act of dominance, as well as an act of social control (Kleinke, 1986).

One explanation for this can be found in *objectification theory* (Fredrickson & Roberts, 1997), which argues that the objectification and sexualization of the female body (and the resultant forced gender roles and the suppression of women) is enacted through these objectifying gaze behaviors. Ultimately, this theory argues that a woman's personhood is reduced to her physical body, and society generally and men specifically are complicit in using visual inspection as a way to subjugate women (ibid.). As such, this gazing behavior ultimately becomes an act of power. Not surprisingly, men who hold more sexist views of gender roles are more likely to engage in gazing behavior and to believe this behavior is acceptable, and also more likely to (incorrectly) believe that women enjoy being the recipient of men's gaze as compared to men who do not believe in traditional gender roles and differences (Compton, 2016). While objectification theory focuses on women as the visual target of men, the theory has been used to explain the experiences of both lesbian and trans* individuals as well (Hill & Fischer, 2008; Lefebvre, 2020).

Consequences

Whereas mutual gaze can result in positive consequences noted throughout this chapter, unwanted gaze as a product of the male gaze can have very dire consequences for women. The very experience of *anticipated* male gaze can have major negative impact on women's anxiety around body shaming and social physique (Calogero, 2004). Similarly, when both men and women are the recipient of an objectifying gaze during a performance task (i.e., math quizzes), women were much more likely to score lower compared to men (Gervais et al., 2011), highlighting the prevalence of women's external physical characteristics being valued over their internal characteristics compared to men. Recent literature has replicated these negative findings on the impact of the male gaze on women, in regard to both self-objectification (Yilmaz & Bozo, 2019) and performance tasks (Guizzo & Cadinu, 2017).

Of course, not all one-sided looks are messages of dominance, and not all gazes toward women are of the objectifying nature. As mentioned earlier in the chapter, gazing can serve an important role in the courtship process (Givens, 1978). Clearly, individuals are biologically wired to gaze at each other for information gathering, but culture information or experiences can alter or intensify the impact of these oculesic behaviors. In other words, *nature* might cause an individual to look, but *nurture* might impact the frequency, duration, and location of that gaze. It is those latter characteristics of oculesic behaviors that influence perceptions of antisocial behavior in social relationships.

Conclusion

Over the course of the chapter, we have seen that the eyes can do many things in each stage of love and love seeking. Eyes can scan, inspect, peek, gaze, wink, seduce, check out, and function in many more manners that each might play a different role and purpose within the stages of courtship, connection, and maintenance of love. At the same time, these same oculesic behaviors can also run the risk of causing anxiety or harm to another in one's pursuit of love or connection. Given the polysemous nature of any nonverbal behavior (Manusov & Harvey, 2011), decoding another's eye behavior isn't as simple as previously thought. While most are unable to glean another's intentions with complete accuracy, the pairing of eye behavior coupled with other nonverbal indicators might better improve one's chances to accurately encode or decode any relational messages that one might send or receive. While the distinction between gazing at and checking out a relational partner might only be known to the message sender, it is often the recipient of these oculesic behaviors that experience the consequences, whether positive (e.g., experiencing relational intimacy) or negative (e.g., experiencing anxiety) in nature.

There is a robust literature on the important topics of oculesic nonverbal behaviors and their structures and functions within personal relationship contexts. At the same time, any topic with such near-universal importance need be further refined. Much of the extant research on courtship initiation was done prior to 2010, where in-person interaction was the primary source of meeting and finding potential mates. In the years since, online dating has become a prominent medium for individuals to find their next date or sexual partner. Given this paradigm shift in courtship behavior, one wonders what the impact might be for oculesic nonverbal behaviors during in-person situations. For example, an individual who spends hours every day perusing online dating apps might ignore or misinterpret prolonged eye contact from an unknown other in-person, given the relative ease with which conversations can occur in mediated spaces where one need not monitor such a multiplicity of nonverbal cues. Future research need explore the impact of mediated contexts on both the fluency with and dependency upon oculesic signals of attraction.

In addition, there is a need for greater understanding of nonheterosexual individuals and nontraditional relationships, both of which are severely understudied in mainstream oculesic research—as is the case with much social science research on relationship contexts. The transferability of research findings to individuals of all genders and sexualities can only help to strengthen our understanding of the impact of oculesic behavior across *all* relationship contexts, writ large. It is essential to consider the nonverbal signals of love characterized by eye contact, eye movement, gaze-related behaviors, and the structural and functional aspects of these oculesic behaviors in a way that reflects the diversity of an authentic, engaged society. Indeed, both intentional and unintentional messaging sent through the nonverbal oculesic channels are worth greater scrutiny and appreciation in the context of close interpersonal relationships regardless of description or difference.

References

Abbey, A., & Melby, C. (1986). The effects of nonverbal cues on gender differences in perceptions of sexual intent. *Sex Roles, 15*(5/6), 283–298.

Argyle, M., & Cook, M. (1976). *Gaze and mutual gaze.* Cambridge University Press.

Berscheid, E., & Reis, H. T. (1998). Attraction and close relationships. In D. T. Gilbert, S. T. Fiske, & G. Lindzey (Eds.), *The handbook of social psychology* (pp. 193–281). McGraw-Hill.

Bowman, J. M. (2019). *Interconnections: Interpersonal communication foundations and contexts.* Cengage Publishing.

Bowman, J. M. (2020). *Nonverbal communication: An applied approach.* SAGE Publishing.

Brooks, R., & Meltzoff, A. N. (2014). Gaze following: A mechanism for building social connections between infants and adults. In M. Mikulincer & P. R. Shaver (Eds.), *Mechanisms of social connections: From brain to group* (pp. 167–183). American Psychological Association.

Burgoon, J. K., Buller, D. B., & Woodall, W. G. (1996). *Nonverbal communication: The unspoken dialogue.* McGraw-Hill.

Burgoon, J. K., Stern, L. A., & Dillman, L. (1995). *Interpersonal adaptation: Dyadic interaction patterns.* Cambridge University Press.

Calogero, R. M. (2004). A test of objectification theory: The effect of the male gaze on appearance concerns in college women. *Psychology of Women Quarterly, 28*, 16–21.

Compton, B. L. (2016). *Characteristics of the male gazer: Application of ambivalent sexism theory and sociosexuality on male gazing behavior.* Unpublished master's thesis, University of Kansas, Lawrence.

Conty, L., Tijus, C., Hugueville, L., Coelho, E., & George, N. (2006). Searching for asymmetric in the detection of gaze contact versus averted gaze under different head views: A behavioral study. *Spatial Vision, 19*(6), 529–545.

Couch, L. L., & Koeninger, A. L. (2016). Attraction: The many factors that draw us to like, lust, and love. *Social Psychology: How Other People Influence Our Thoughts and Actions [2 volumes]*, 299.
de Weerth, C., & Kalma, A. (1995). Gender differences in awareness of courtship initiation tactics. *Sex Roles, 32*(11/12), 717–734.
Denes, A. (2012). Pillow talk: Exploring disclosures after sexual activity. *Western Journal of Communication, 76*(2), 91–108.
Denes, A., Dhillon, A., & Speer, A. C. (2017). Relational maintenance strategies during the post sex time interval. *Communication Quarterly, 65*(3), 307–332.
Droney, J. M., & Brooks, C. I. (1993). Attributions of self-esteem as a function of duration of eye contact. *The Journal of Social Psychology, 133*(5), 715–722.
Drummond, P. D., & Bailey, T. (2013). Eye contact evokes blushing independently of negative affect. *Journal of Nonverbal Behavior, 37*, 207–216.
Duran, R. L., & Kelly, L. (1988). The influence of communicative competence on perceived task, social, and physical attraction. *Communication Quarterly, 36*(1), 41–49.
Ellyson, S. L., & Dovidio, J. F. (1985). *Power, dominance, and nonverbal behavior*. Springer-Verlag.
England, K. L., Spitzberg, B. H., & Zormeier, M. M. (1996). Flirtation and conversational competence in cross-sex platonic and romantic relationships. *Communication Reports, 9*(2), 105–117.
Farris, C., Treat, T. A., Viken, R. J., & McFall, R. M. (2008). Sexual coercion and the misperception of sexual intent. *Clinical Psychological Review, 28*, 48–66.
Finkel, E. J., & Eastwick, P. W. (2009). Arbitrary social norms influence sex differences in romantic selectivity. *Psychological Science, 20*(10), 1290–1295.
Fredrickson, B. L., & Roberts, T. A. (1997). Objectification theory: Toward understanding women's lived experiences and mental health risks. *Psychology of Women Quarterly, 21*, 173–206.
Frisby, B. N., & Booth-Butterfield, M. (2012). The "how" and "why" of flirtatious communication between marital partners. *Communication Quarterly, 60*(4), 465–480.
Gervais, S. J., Holland, A. M., & Dodd, M. D. (2013). My eyes are up here: The nature of the objectifying gaze toward women. *Sex Roles, 69*, 557–570.
Gervais, S. J., Vescio, T. K., & Allen, J. (2011). When what you see is what you get: The consequences of the objectifying gaze for women and men. *Psychology of Women Quarterly, 35*, 5–17.

Givens, D. B. (1978). The nonverbal basis of attraction: Flirtation, courtship, and seduction. *Psychiatry: Interpersonal and Biological Processes, 41*(4), 346–359.
Guerrero, L. K., Andersen, P. A., Jorgensen, P. F., Spitzberg, B. H., & Eloy, S. V. (1995). *Coping with the green-eyed monster: Conceptualizing and measuring communicative responses to romantic jealousy*. Taylor Francis.
Guizzo, F., & Cadinu, M. (2017). Effects of objectifying gaze on female cognitive performance: The role of flow experience and internalization of beauty ideals. *British Journal of Social Psychology, 56*, 281–292.
Gump, R. (1962). *Jade: Stone of heaven*. Doubleday.
Hall, J. A. (2013). *The five flirting styles: Use the science of flirting to attract the love you really want*. Harlequin.
Hall, J. A., & Xing, C. (2015). The verbal and nonverbal correlates of the five flirting styles. *Journal of Nonverbal Behavior, 39*, 41–68.
Hess, E. H. (1965). Attitude and pupil size. *Scientific American, 212*(4), 46–55.
Hess, E. H., & Petrovich, S. B. (1987). Pupillary behavior in communication. *Nonverbal Behavior and Communication*, 327–348.
Hill, M. S., & Fischer, A. R. (2008). Examining objectification theory: Lesbian and heterosexual women's experiences with sexual- and self-objectification. *The Counseling Psychologist, 36*(5), 745–776.
Hinkle, L. L. (1999). Nonverbal immediacy communication behaviors and liking in marital relationships. *Communication Research Reports, 16*(1), 81–90.
Hollet, R. C., Rogers, S. L., Florido, P. M., & Mosdell, B. A. (2021). Body gaze as a marker of sexual objectification: A new scale for pervasive gaze and gaze provocation behaviours in heterosexual women and men. https://doi.org/10.31234/osf.io/bct3p
Jarick, M., & Bencic, R. (2019). Eye contact is a two-way street: Arousal is elicited by the sending and receiving of eye gaze information. *Frontiers in Psychology, 10*, 1262.
Jongerius, C., Hessels, R. S., Romijn, J. A., Smets, E. M., & Hillen, M. A. (2020). The measurement of eye contact in human interactions: A scoping review. *Journal of Nonverbal Behavior*, 1–27.
Kim, Y. M., & Kwon, D. S. (2010). A fuzzy intimacy space model to develop human-robot affective relationship. In *2010 world automation congress* (pp. 1–6). IEEE.
Kleinke, C. L. (1986). Gaze and eye contact: A research review. *Psychological Bulletin, 100*, 78–100.

Knapp, M. L., & Vangelisti, A. L. (2005). Relationship stages: A communication perspective. *Interpersonal Communication and Human Relationships*, 36–49.

Koukounas, E., & Letch, N. M. (2001). Psychological correlates of perception of sexual intent in women. *The Journal of Social Psychology, 141*(4), 443–456.

Kowalski, R. M. (1993). Inferring sexual interest from behavioral cues: Effects of gender and sexually relevant attitudes. *Sex Roles, 29*(1/2), 13–36.

Kuraguchi, K., & Kanari, K. (2021). *Enlargement of female pupils when perceiving something cute, except for female faces* (Version 1). Advance. https://doi.org/10.31124/advance.13727320.v1([]).

Larsen, R. S., & Waters, J. (2018). Neuromodulatory correlates of pupil dilation. *Frontiers in Neural Circuits, 12*, 21.

Le Poire, B. A., & Burgoon, J. K. (1994). Two contrasting explanations of involvement violations: Expectancy violations theory versus discrepancy arousal theory. *Human Communication Research, 20*(4), 560–591.

Lefebvre, D. (2020). *Transgender women and the male gaze: Gender, the body, and the pressure to conform.* Unpublished master's thesis, University of Calgary, Calgary. http://hdl.handle.net/1880/111822

Liao, H. I., Kashino, M., & Shimojo, S. (2021). Attractiveness in the eyes: A possibility of positive loop between transient pupil constriction and facial attraction. *Journal of Cognitive Neuroscience, 33*(2), 315–340.

Manusov, V., & Harvey, J. (2011). Bumps and tears on the road to the presidency: Media framing of key nonverbal events in the 2008 democratic election. *Western Journal of Communication, 75*(3), 282–303.

Marwick, A. (2012). The public domain: Surveillance in everyday life. *Surveillance & Society, 9*(4), 378–393.

Morris, D. (1985). *Bodywatching*. Random House Books.

Renninger, L. A., Wade, J. T., & Grammar, K. (2004). Getting that female glance: Patterns and consequences of male nonverbal behavior in courtship contexts. *Evolution and Human Behavior, 25*, 416–431.

Rieger, G., & Savin-Williams, R. C. (2012). The eyes have it: Sex and sexual orientation differences in pupil dilation patterns. *PLoS One, 7*(8), e40256.

Schaefer, M. T., & Olson, D. H. (1981). Assessing intimacy: The PAIR inventory. *Journal of Marital and Family Therapy, 7*(1), 47–60.

Shimojo, S., Simion, C., Shimojo, E., & Scheier, C. (2003). Gaze bias both reflects and influences preference. *Nature Neuroscience, 6*(12), 1317.

Simpson, E. A., Paukner, A., Pedersen, E. J., Ferrari, P. F., & Parr, L. A. (2019). Visual preferences for direct-gaze faces in infant macaques (Macaca mulatta) with limited face exposure. *Developmental Psychobiology, 61*(2), 228–238.

Sternglanz, S. H., Gray, J. L., & Murakami, M. (1977). Adult preferences for infantile facial features: An ethological approach. *Animal Behaviour, 25*, 108–115.

Tang, D., & Schmeichel, B. J. (2015). Look me in the eyes: Manipulated eye gaze affects dominance mindsets. *Journal of Nonverbal Behavior, 39*, 191–194.

Tombs, S., & Silverman, I. (2004). Pupillometry: A sexual selection approach. *Evolution and Human Behavior, 25*(4), 221–228.

von Cranach, M., & Ellgring, J. (1973). Problems in the recognition of gaze direction. In M. von Cranach & I. Vine (Eds.), *Social communication and movement: Studies on interaction and expression in man and chimpanzee*. Academic Press.

Walsh, D. G., & Hewitt, J. (1985). Giving men the come-on: Effect of eye contact and smiling in a bar environment. *Perceptual and Motor Skills, 61*, 873–874.

Yilmaz, T., & Bozo, Ö. (2019). Whose gaze is more objectifying? An experimental study of college women's state self-objectification, body shame, negative mood, and body dissatisfaction. *Mediterranean Journal of Clinical Psychology, 7*(2), 1–23.

2

Communication and Communal Emotions in the Learning of Love

Ross Buck

In this chapter I present a *developmental-interactionist* conceptualization of the emotion of love that offers a unified analysis following the general structure of *Emotion: A Biosocial Synthesis* (2014). The concept of emotion is difficult in scientific psychology because different aspects of emotional responding—subjectively experienced feelings, displays, and physiological responses—do not vary together in a simple way and therefore appear to violate an essential criterion of construct validity and throw doubt that emotions are "natural kinds" discoverable by science (Barrett, 2006). Also, a central aspect of emotion—subjective emotional experience—is not open to public observation, violating the verifiability criterion. Some have concluded that a general definition of the term "emotion" is impossible and can be useful only in the context of a given research program. This has led to fragmented approaches and conclusions that an integrative theory of emotion is impossible (Niedenthal & Brauer, 2012).

R. Buck (✉)
University of Connecticut, Storrs, CT, USA
e-mail: Ross.buck@uconn.edu

R. J. Sternberg, A. Kostić (eds.), *Nonverbal Communication in Close Relationships*,
https://doi.org/10.1007/978-3-030-94492-6_2

Defining Love

In defining emotion, I suggest an integrated definition as primary motivational-emotional systems (*Primes*), where motivation is the potential for behavior that is unseen and emotion is the *readout* of motivational potential in physiological responding (*Emotion I*), communicative display (*Emotion II*), and subjectively felt feelings and desires, or affects (*Emotion III*: See Buck, 1985). The latter do not vary together because they are associated with different functions and undergo different histories during social learning and development ("emotional education" Buck, 1983). The distinction has analogies with the distinction between matter and energy in physics: energy is never observed directly, but rather as its effects on matter: on heat, light, and force. Similarly, motivation is not seen directly, but as its effects on emotion: on physiological responding, display, and self-reported experience (see Buck, 1985, 2014).

A fundamental distinction of biological emotions is that arousal, approach-avoidance, and agonistic emotions are inherently *individualistic*, functioning to protect the individual; while prosocial emotions are inherently *cooperative*, functioning to preserve the species (Buck, 1999; Ross, 2021). Love clearly belongs in the latter category.

I see "love" to be a natural kind at two levels. First, it involves readouts of specifiable neurochemical systems associated with subjective emotional experience. A given feeling state at any point in time represents a variable symphony of feelings and desires, normally playing in pianissimo and unnoticed but occasionally rising in crescendo and dominating consciousness. Different neurochemical systems are analogous to individual instruments or sections of instruments (brass, woodwinds) contributing to the sound of the whole (Buck, 2014).

The nature of the neurochemical symphony associated with passionate love was summarized by Fischetti (2011). They include high levels of dopamine (DA), reflecting feelings of pleasure and activation; oxytocin (OT), reflecting attachment and trust; arginine vasopressin (AVP), reflecting attraction and sexual arousal, and cortisol (CORT), reflecting stress and alertness. Neurochemicals associated with sadness, fear, anxiety, and pain sensitivity are all low. Notably, serotonin (5-HT) is at a low level, reflecting tendencies toward insecurity, jealousy, aggression, and obsessional thinking. The symphony of more mature love may differ, for example not including low serotonin. One can imagine how different specific examples of love may be reflected in different levels of constituent neurochemicals interacting to yield varying yet related melodies of feelings and desires.

The second way that love and other biological emotions are natural kinds is that at the ecological level they involve communication—displays and preattunements to those displays (associated with co-evolved mirror neuron systems)—that operate at the ecological level of analysis. Unlike emotions displayed by pancultural facial expressions that function optimally at personal and social distances, displays of love involve touches, caresses, murmurs, scents/pheromones that function optimally at intimate distances (< 18 inches) too close for efficient facial communication (Hall, 1966).

Importantly, biological neurochemical systems and the ecological reality of emotion with respect to display and communication are separate but both "real" natural kinds open to objective observation and investigation. There has been a revolution in our ability to record, examine, manipulate, and image phenomena at the biological level associated with feelings, and a simultaneous revolution in our ability to image, measure, and time the fleeting nuance of display and expression, using for example high-speed computer analysis and inexpensive low-light video technology. This revolution has rendered the ephemeral permanent, allowing us objectively to examine the biology of subjective feelings and desires and the "body language" of nonverbal communication in human beings and other animals.

Love and Communication

Symbolic and Spontaneous Communication Displays and preattunements fulfill ecological functions that organize a species socially and take the phenomenon of emotion, and love, outside the individual body into the social-communicative environment. They involve a stream of *spontaneous communication* that is biologically based in its sending and receiving aspects, nonintentional, nonpropositional, and involving externally accessible *signs* of internal motivational-emotional states (Buck, 1984). This differs from symbolic communication that is learned and culturally patterned, intentional at some level, propositional, and involving symbols that have arbitrarily defined meaning (Buck, 1984; Buck & Van Lear, 2002).

The earliest communication, both phylogenetically and ontogenetically, is spontaneous. It occurs in the simplest creatures: for example, quorum sensing that underlies social organization in microbes. The peptide neurohormone gonadotropin hormone releasing hormone (GnRH) functions in erotic feelings in human beings and is a sexual pheromone in yeast (LeRoith et al., 1982). Developmentally, spontaneous communication is the foundation of *empathy*.

Love and Empathy *Empathy* is generally defined as the ability accurately to know the feelings and to understand the thoughts and perspectives of other persons (Cuff et al., 2016). It is widely accepted that empathy involves both emotional and cognitive aspects (e.g., Decety & Jackson, 2004; Telle & Pfister, 2016). Emotional and cognitive empathy are dependent on different neuroanatomical substrates and can be doubly dissociated neurologically, such that each is impacted independently of the other in studies of brain lesions (Shamay-Tsoory et al., 2009).

There is theory and evidence that early social responsiveness on the part of newborns is the origin of emotional empathy, and that cognitive empathy requires additional maturation. Murray and Trevarthen (1986) found that mothers and 3–12-week-old infants viewing a full-face, life size image of the other on a video screen allowing "eye contact" to be maintained, interact naturally when their interaction was played live and in real time, with exquisite sensitivity to the timing and form of the communicative behaviors of the other. They "appeared to be communicating naturally" (Murray & Trevarthen, 1986, p. 17). The simultaneous live video link allowed *mutual contingent responsiveness*: both mother and infant could respond spontaneously and synchronously "on-line" to the flow of the communicative behavior of the other. In the resulting *proto-conversation*, each directly, naturally, automatically, and unconsciously become attuned to the subjective state displayed by the other via co-evolved displays and preattunements. This is termed *primary intersubjectivity* (Trevarthen, 1979).

The smooth communication flow between mother and infant was dramatically disrupted when either was unexpectedly shown a playback of the partner's behavior instead of the live behavior. The physical stimulus was identical to that seen previously, but the playback made synchronizing and mutually contingent responding impossible. The infant displayed distress and looked away, the mother‘s characteristic high-frequency motherese baby-talk changed (Trevarthen & Aitken, 2001). Similarly, when an infant is happily interacting face-to-face with a responsive partner and the partner suddenly becomes unresponsive, displaying a "still-face," the infant often displays immediate distress and frantically attempts to reengage (Tronick, 1978).

Normally, the stage of primary intersubjectivity cements strong emotional bonds between infants and caregivers that are critical throughout life. With normal learning and social experience, it is succeeded by a stage of *secondary intersubjectivity* (approx. 9 months) characterized by infant and caregiver orienting to a third object, and by a stage of *tertiary intersubjectivity* (approx. 20 months). These stages are in turn succeeded by the attainment of mature *Theory of Mind* (ToM) on the part of the child, along with the cognitive skills of attribution and perspective-taking. This results in the maturation of the ability to accurately read the thoughts and intentions of others, or cognitive empathy. The successive stages of intersubjectivity in the development of empathy were conceived as successively larger dolls that contained a smaller doll in de Waal's Russian Doll theory of empathy (de Waal, 2007). Each successive stage hides the previous state, but in the model, each is dependent on the earlier states and ultimately dependent on primary intersubjectivity (de Waal & Preston, 2017).

The Biology of Love

Oxytocin and Arginine Vasopressin Love is associated with a variety of neurochemical systems as noted, with OT and AVP of particular interest. These peptide neurohormones diverged from the vasotocin molecule that organizes social behavior in reptiles and birds (Donaldson & Young, 2008; Moore, 1987). This evolutionary divergence coincided with the evolution of mammals, when the requirements of parental care diverged into protective and nurturing elements. Briefly, in most reptiles (e.g., lizards) the male establishes a nesting territory, defends it from intruders, and advertises for a mate. The female is attracted to the nest site and lays eggs which are fertilized. The eggs are hidden in the nest and the parents go their separate ways. The young are nourished by the egg and when hatched are for practical purposes miniature adults capable of independent survival: parental nurturance is not required. In contrast, mammals are defined by placental birth and feeding of the young after birth by mother's milk (Gore, 2003). The mammalian lifestyle involves incompletely developed young who cannot survive on their own. They are nurtured after birth by mother's milk and experience an extended period of socialization before reaching sexual maturity at puberty. The male role is organized by AVP, associated with androgens and testosterone (T) production, and is particularly involved in protection of the young. AVP promotes male-typical socio-sexual behaviors including aggressive behaviors (Koolhaas et al., 1990). Panksepp (1998, pp. 93–94) suggested that AVP may be a specific carrier for male dominance and persistence urges, and that the underlying subjective emotional correlate involves irritability and anger. In contrast, the female role is organized by OT, associated with prolactin and involved in lactation and uterine contractions of childbirth and the female sexual orgasm (Insel, 1992; Pert, 1997). OT is related to sexual behaviors in both males and females (Richard et al., 1991). Panksepp (1998) suggested that OT mediates subjective feelings of acceptance and social bonding (p. 93).

Rodents The vole is a mouse-size rodent of the genus *Microtus,* some species of which are relatively monogamous, forming lasting female-male bonds, and others of which manifest polygamous lifestyles. Prairie voles (*Microtus ochrogaster*) show monogamy as evidenced by selective and lasting partner preferences (pair bonds) activated by mating; living together, snuggling with their mate in side-by-side social postures within a common nest; and responding aggressively toward intruding voles, perhaps functioning to guard mate and territory. The male helps to build the nest and care for the young pups, spending almost as much time with the young as does the female. If separated from the nest, the pups become agitated and display ultrasonic distress calls and high stress response as evidenced by increases in cortisol (CORT). In contrast, closely related species—the meadow vole (*Microtus pennsylvanicus*) and montane vole (*Microtus montanus*)—show none of the signs of strong social bonding behaviors displayed by the prairie vole (Carter et al., 1997). They are nonmonogamous, nest independently, and breed promiscuously; with the males playing no parenting role. Even the females abandon their pups soon after birth, and the pups do not appear to be distressed by this abandonment.

OT and AVP are both critical to social bonding in the monogamous prairie vole. A female becomes sexually receptive when exposed to a chemical in the urine of a strange male (i.e., a male unrelated to her, avoiding incest). She will mate repeatedly: in the process the two form a monogamous pair bond, and soon become parents. If the bonded partner dies, a surviving prairie vole will often live alone rather than take a new mate (Carter et al., 1997; Insel & Young, 2001). OT is necessary and sufficient for the development of these pair bonds (Insel, 1992): an unbonded female exposed to an unrelated male and OT agonists becomes bonded without mating, while OT antagonists block bonding despite mating. Similarly, AVP is necessary and sufficient for bonding in the male prairie vole: AVP stimulates the formation of a partner preference even without mating, and AVP antagonists will prevent the formation of partner preferences even after mating (Insel & Young, 2001).

There also are brain differences distinguishing monogamous and nonmonogamous voles in the amount of brain area devoted to OT and AVP. Brain areas associated with OT are much larger in the prairie vole compared to the nonmonogamous montane vole (Insel et al., 1997). Similarly, the distribution of AVP receptors in the male brain is different, with the prairie vole having a relatively high density of AVP receptors (Young et al., 2001). Interestingly, Lim et al. (2004) found substantially increased partner preference formation in the promiscuous meadow vole by V1aR AVP receptor gene transfer into the ventral forebrain. It is theorized that this allows an animal to associate the partner more easily with reward, showing that a change in the expression of a single gene liked to love can profoundly alter complex social behavior and suggesting a potential molecular mechanism for rapid social evolution.

The role of OT in rodent social behavior has also been studied in rats and mice, which have been bred to lack genes necessary to produce OT (oxytocin knockout, or OTKO animals: Young, 2001). Such animals show deficits in a variety of social behaviors, including less distress by social isolation, lack of preference for their mothers, and lack of social recognition ("social amnesia"), which is reversed by injections of OT into the brain prior to social exposure. Ferguson, Aldag, Insel and Young (2001) demonstrated that OT receptor activation in the medial amygdala is both necessary and sufficient for social recognition in the mouse.

Oxytocin in Humans The role of OT in human attachment and love is of great interest. Both OT and AVP are released into the bloodstream during sexual intercourse and play important roles in complex human social behavior (Freeman & Young, 2011). Studies of central nervous system effects have demonstrated an impact of OT nasal spray on human social behavior using a placebo containing all ingredients except the active OT in both within and between subject comparisons (Guastella & MacLeod, 2012). OT or a placebo is administered in a double-blind study: that is, no one knows whether a given individual received OT or the placebo until after the completion of the study (Kosfeld et al., 2005). Importantly, participants are unaware of whether they had received OT, and its influence is seen as automatic, intuitive, and unconscious (Baumgartner et al., 2008).

The effects of OT have been examined using this methodology in studies by Ruth Feldman and colleagues (see Feldman, 2012 review). Feldman suggested three prototypes of human attachment: *parental love* between parent and infant, *filial love* between friends and comrades, and *romantic love* between sexual partners. She suggested that these prototypes share common brain mechanisms underpinned by OT in the promotion of *biobehavioral synchrony*: the temporal concordance of the biological and social behavior of interactants. Such synchrony is regarded as touching at a distance, and is a cardinal feature of mutual contingent responsiveness and primary intersubjectivity noted previously (Murray & Trevarthen, 1986).

Feldman (2012) argued that OT plays a key role in the motivation to bond, particularly in interaction with the DA reward system including the nucleus accumbens (NAcc); and she reported research involving the observation and micro-coding of human interaction behaviors including touching, eye contact, emotion display, and soft vocalization; assessing the coordination of these behaviors in parent-infant, filial, and sexual dyads. This research included longitudinal studies assessing long-term effects of early parenting styles. For example, plasma OT and cortisol (CORT) were assessed in mothers from the first trimester of pregnancy to one month after birth. Compared with women not in a romantic relationship, OT levels were higher, tended to be stable, and OT levels in the first trimester of pregnancy were associated with maternal bonding behaviors micro-coded during interaction with the infant, including gaze, the display of positive emotions, motherese vocalizations, and affectionate touch. The rise in OT from the first to the third trimester was also associated with maternal bonding behaviors (Feldman et al., 2007). Another study compared secure mothers who coordinated their behavior with that of the infant signals, and intrusive mothers who did not. Secure mothers showed activity in the left NAcc to films of infants, suggesting reward; while insecure mothers showed right amygdala activity, suggesting anxiety and stress. Also, brain activity of secure mothers was more organized, with significant correlations between OT, NAcc, and amygdala activation (Atzil et al., 2011).

Other studies involved OT and the behavior of fathers. One manipulated OT in fathers in a double-blind study using OT or placebo in nasal spray. Fathers inhaling OT showed longer infant engagement and more frequent touch, and infants in the OT condition had longer social gaze and toy engagement and increased Respiratory Sinus Arrhythmia (RSA), a measure of parasympathetic nervous system arousal associated with and readiness for social contact (Porges, 1995). Also, OT levels in the infant were raised when the father had inhaled OT, even though OT was not administered to the infant. Feldman concluded, "These findings are the first to demonstrate that OT administrations to a parent can lead to alterations in the physiology and behavior of an infant in ways that induce greater readiness for social contact" (2012, p. 7).

The Evolution of Love

Feldman (2012) noted that only 3–5% of mammalian species exhibit active paternal involvement in childcare, but there is evidence that such paternal involvement may have been a factor in human evolution long preceding the expansion of the brain. New fossil evidence about human evolution, and new techniques of measurement including genetic analyses, have produced increasingly detailed scenarios of human social evolution. Such scenarios can consider geological changes that created the environment in which human evolution occurred.

With the extinction of the dinosaurs over 65 million years ago, the Cenozoic era began, with a relatively constant climate of hot, wet, tropical rainforests and swamps covering much of the planet for nearly 60 million years. Early primates evolved from arboreal, nocturnal, insect-eating mammals. Their adaptation to the lush rain forest ecology included evolving efficient grasping hands, an omnivorous diet, binocular color vision, and good brains, and they likely lived in social groups organized by audio-vocal communication characteristic of forest-dwelling monkeys and apes today.[1]

About 12 million years ago, earth's climate became drier, and the rain forests shrank toward the equator, where they remain today. As rainforests were replaced by drier savannah and woodland, some monkey and ape species adapted to the difficult and dangerous new environment. They could not digest the grasses of the savannah like specialized herbivores; and lacked speed, strength, and natural weapons of specialized carnivores. Their color vision had a significant disadvantage on the savannah: it was less efficient in dark relative to the vision of powerful predators. However, they had the primates' efficient hands, binocular vision, good brain, probably an ability to make simple tools, and perhaps most important, social organization and communication.

The closest genetic relative of human beings is the chimpanzee, an ape whose ancestors remained in the rain forest while those of some baboons adapted to the savannah. Human ancestors were ground-dwelling apes

[1] The analysis is adapted and abridged from the account published in R. Buck (2014). *Emotion: A Biosocial Synthesis*. Cambridge, UK: Cambridge University Press.

that adapted to the savannah, so baboons can be considered our closest ecological relatives (Morris, 1967). One of the major differences between chimpanzees and baboons involves male and female relationships. Male and female chimpanzees rarely interact outside the relatively rare times when the female is in estrus and fertile. In contrast, male and female baboons often form long-term and even life-long "friendships" in which they stay physically close, move together, and groom one another (Smuts, 1987). A male is more likely to aid a female and her offspring if she is a friend. Male-female friendships persist through phases of the reproductive cycle when the female is not sexually available, including during pregnancy and lactation that can last up to two years. Also, as baboons lack sexual exclusivity, friendships persist despite any guarantee of paternity. In *The Naked Ape* (1967), Desmond Morris suggested that baboons form *pair bonds* to help enlist the support of the male in child-rearing, and that a similar phenomenon may have occurred during human evolution. Human ancestors that adapted to the new conditions included *Ardipithecus ramidus* and *Australopithecus afarensis*: Ardi and Lucy, respectively.

The Garden of Ardi and Lucy Human ancestors—*hominins*—separated from those of chimpanzees about 7 million years ago (the chimpanzee last common ancestor or CLCA). *A. ramidus*, known as *Ardi* stood about three feet tall. Her feet were adapted to grasping and tree-climbing rather than walking for long distances, but her pelvis, foot, and the angle of the foramen magnum indicate that she walked upright. Ardi had a small brain (300 to 350 cc.) like modern chimpanzees; but unlike chimpanzees her teeth lacked large canine teeth in males (Lovejoy, 2009). Their absence is significant because they are used in aggressive male-male competition, and with evidence that Ardi males are only slightly larger than females in body size, this suggests that Ardi was less aggressive that its chimpanzee-ancestor cousins and is consistent with Morris' (1967) hypothesis that hominin males may have contributed to parenting.

Ardi lived at least 1.2 million years, from relatively soon after the CLCA to 4.4 million years ago. The next major hominid species discovered was *Australopithecus*, who lived over an even longer span of time of nearly 3 million years: from over 4 to over 1 million years ago. The best-known representative is *A. afarensis*, who left strong evidence of bipedal gait. A 40% complete skeleton was discovered in 1974 and named *Lucy*. She stood 3 feet 7 inches tall, and her pelvis and leg bones functioned similarly to those of modern humans. Below the waist the body proportions of Lucy were more like a modern human than a chimpanzee, yet her brain remained relatively small (380–450 cc).

Ice and the Stone Age About 2.6 million years ago, the earth's climate changed; cycles of ice ages began in which ice sheets covered great areas of the globe. Lucy and her kind, after enduring for so long, disappeared. However, beginning about 2.3 to 2.4 million years ago, the genus *Homo* emerged roughly with the onset of the ice ages and includes modern human beings. A salient development in *Homo* was an increase in cranial capacity to 600 cc in *Homo habilis* and 850–1100 cc in *Homo erectus*, the latter figure overlapping with modern humans, *Homo sapiens*. This and evidence for the presence of Broca's area in the brain's left hemisphere suggest the capacity for articulate language in *H. erectus* (Leakey & Lewin, 1992). *H. erectus* migrated from Africa around 2 million years ago and dispersed throughout much of the world.

Homo sapiens—modern humans—probably originated between 200,000 and 150,000 years ago in Africa (Hetherington & Reid, 2010). They were and are distinguished from all other animals by propositional language, which afforded systems of behavior control and organization that do not exist in other animals (Buck, 1988).

It can be suggested that the basic motivational and emotional systems underlying human behavior, including love, attachment, and family life, evolved during the long period of the Garden of Ardi and Lucy, and that the evolution of human linguistic, intellectual, and complex cognitive capacities did not occur until the onset of severe selection pressures associated with climate changes associated with the onset of ice ages. If this is correct, the motivational and emotional systems laid down during the long Garden period are of great interest, even more so as we consider Morris' (1967) hypothesis that what evolved was an entirely new and different sort of love and bonding.

The Development of Love

Accounts of the development of intersubjectivity and of stages of parental, filial, and romantic love dovetail with Harry Harlow's (1971) account of socio-emotional development in rhesus monkeys. Harlow's work was based on his well-known studies of the impact of cloth-covered versus bare wire surrogate mothers on young monkeys. Monkeys raised on cloth-covered surrogates initially seemed to develop normally, but later showed severe social deficits. Observational studies of interactions between real monkey mothers and their infants distinguished three succeeding stages, each depending on the earlier. Initial interactions during the first three months involved intimate contact comfort and were the necessary conditions for the initial *parental affectional system*, reflected in high mother-infant contact and low punishment of the infant. Harlow suggested that this stage functioned to instill a basic sense of love and trust in other monkeys. Declining contact with the mother between three and six months, marked by increasing punishment and rejection by the mother of unrestricted contact and increasing motor skills, motivated interactions between peers. The growing youngster increasingly separated from the mother and interacted with age-mates, providing the necessary conditions for the *peer affectional system* stage characterized by rough-and-tumble play. These interactions were initially playful but got increasingly rough with age as puberty approached, and involved communicative displays, including threats, warnings, submissive behaviors, and immature courting, that apparently functioned to teach the youngster *how to use* the communicative displays and preattunements built into the species. This in turn provided the necessary conditions for learning and successfully managing the *sexual affectional system* that arrived with puberty and served as the communicative basis for adult social organization.

Harlow (1971) suggested that the parental affectional system involved the display, and likely experience, of emotions of love and distress on the part of the infant. The peer affectional system was initially characterized by evidence of fear, and increasingly anger, with age. The sexual affectional system featured adult emotions including sex and potentially deadly violence, which was tempered by communicative displays so that deadly violence was averted. Initial bonding was accompanied by love unblemished by the belligerent emotions of fear and anger that appeared in development as social learning experiences functioned to allow their moderation. Harlow suggested that the major socio-emotional events of these three affectional systems are mirrored in infancy, childhood, and adolescence in human beings. The maturation of fear is signaled by the appearance of fear of strangers at about 18 months and the maturation of anger by the common events of the "terrible twos" at 2½ to 3½ years.

Harlow's observations were supplemented by studies of family attachment by John Bowlby and colleagues in Britain at the Tavistock Clinic in London. The World Health Organization (WHO) commissioned Bowlby to write a report, *Maternal Care and Mental Health* (Bretherton, 1992). His central conclusion was that "the infant and child should experience a warm, intimate, and continuous relationship with his mother (or permanent mother substitute) in which both find satisfaction and enjoyment" (1953, p. 13), and he emphasized the necessity for society to support the caregiver-child relationship. A center of his interest was the intergenerational transmission of attachment patterns: that people who have themselves experienced secure attachment will tend to act in ways that transmit attachment security to their young (Bretherton, 1992). The fact that a father's OT levels can shape the infant's physiology and behavior suggests an epigenetic mechanism for the intergenerational transmission of attachment security. As Feldman concluded, "Behavioral coordination provides one channel through which parental OT shapes the infant's emerging neuropeptide organization and its ensuing life-time effects on social affiliation" (2012, p. 7). Unfortunately, it is also the case that neglect and abuse can tend to foster abuse and neglect in the next generation.

At Tavistock, Mary Salter Ainsworth developed the '*strange situation*' to document types of attachment (Ainsworth & Bell, 1970). Mothers and 12–18 months-old infants were observed during three-minute episodes where mother and infant were first alone and then joined by a stranger. The mother then left the infant with the stranger. Next, the mother returned and the stranger left, then the mother left the infant alone. Next, the stranger returned, and finally, the mother returned and stranger left. Infant behaviors measured included separation anxiety when the mother left, willingness to explore, anxiety in the presence of the stranger, and reunion when the mother returned. Three types of attachment were distinguished: *secure attachment* was demonstrated when the infants displayed stress when mother left, avoided the stranger when alone but was friendly when mother was present, and displayed happiness when the mother returned. *Insecure ambivalent attachment* was shown when infants displayed distress when the mother left, fear and avoidance of the stranger, and resisted contact when the mother returned, possibly pushing the mother away. Insecure ambivalent infants cried more and explored less than other attachment types. Finally, *insecure avoidant attachment* was shown when infants did not show distress when the mother left, did not fear the stranger, and did not show interest when the mother returned. Ainsworth and Bell (1970) suggested that the infant's behavior in the strange situation was determined by the behavior of the mother: secure attachment is associated with sensitive and responsive care; insecure ambivalent attachment is associated with inconsistent care; and insecure avoidant attachment is associated with unresponsive care.

The Social Psychology of Love

As previously discussed, biological emotions are seen to be based in primary motivational-emotional systems or Primes, each associated with specifiable neurochemical systems and, ultimately, with specifiable genes and genetic systems. Due to their similar functions, these modules are "packaged" ecologically by the forces of evolution into familiar primary emotions such as happiness, sadness, fear, and love.

Biological and Higher-Level Emotions A central proposition in Silvan Tomkins's (1962-1982, 1982) theory is that the affect mechanism is a separate assembly, a general motivational system, functioning to amplify other aspects of behavior. I suggest that this is not the case for the biological emotions: they each have motivational force built into the system. Indeed, I define them as involving a readout of motivational potential. However, Tomkins's notion of a separate affect system is useful in conceptualizing differences and similarities of biological and higher-level emotions. The essential difference is that the former can "stand alone" as it were: the complete Emotion I, II, and III package of arousal, display, and experience resides in the individual organism, although the proper functioning of this package requires social experience and communication as we have seen. In contrast, higher-level emotions involve biologically based affects, but these affects function as general motivational systems in Tomkins's sense, and the unique character of different higher-level emotions is determined externally, by events in terrestrial and social reality. For example, a child's general need for exploration can appear in the guise of curiosity in a novel situation, surprise in an unexpected situation, and dread in a frightening or uncertain situation (Buck, 2014). Similarly, a child's need for social attachment can appear in the guise of pride when the child is successful, in resentment when another child succeeds unfairly, and love in the presence of one's parent, child, friend, comrade, or lover.

Thus, higher-level emotions respond to specific ecological challenges in the terrestrial and social environments, and they exist relative to external stimuli or other persons, including situations involving events in memory and imagination. These challenges are packages of *ecologically fundamental interpersonal contingencies,* defined formally as *specific combinations of circumstances existent in the social-interaction environment with implications for the comparative well-being of self and others.* Critical architectures for higher-level social emotions are ecologically present over development as social affordances naturally present in the course of social interaction and communication, so that social emotions are discovered by the child and emerge naturally and spontaneously as self-organizing systems from architectures objectively present over development in the child's communicative interactions with parents and other adults, peers, and also media models. Unlike biological emotions higher-level emotions are not always "on," but they exist as potential until activated by those specific ecological challenges. And, while higher-level emotions involve a general biologically based affective readiness, they require experience over the course of development with the specific ecological challenges to become appropriately, effectively, and competently experienced and expressed.

Love exists at both levels, as a biological and higher-level emotion. First, love is a biological emotion associated with specifiable neurochemical modules that can, in principle, be manipulated directly by drug or gene alterations within the body, such as OT as we have seen. Second, love is always "on" as potential, albeit normally at low levels and unnoticed. Third, love emerges developmentally in an internally programmed maturational sequence which as we have seen is timed with its functions in the parental, filial/peer, and romantic/sexual affectional systems.

Love is based upon specifiable neurochemical systems that are the source of prosocial *attachment affects* that, when combined with ecological challenges in the form of combinations of interpersonal contingencies, produce higher-level social emotions. Attachment motives expose the child to people and events that evoke prosocial emotions: love, warmth, intimacy, bonding, caring, nurturance; as well as panic and despair associated with separation, isolation, and bereavement. Normal social development and bonding requires the initial "turning on" of attachment motives via contact comfort and later emancipation from parents. Early social deprivation, neglect, and abuse can lead to life-long attachment disorders. Attachment is gloriously displayed in rough and tumble play in the peer affectional system, where the affective seeds of adult behavior are sown and begin to take root.

The motivation arising from attachment has two aspects: a *need to be loved*, and a *need to follow/exceed the expectations of others* (Buck, 1988). A person is motivated to be esteemed and loved by others; and a person is motivated to conform, to do that which is expected and indeed to exceed expectations. Perceived challenges in the social environment involving social comparison can activate strong and persistent affective needs to be loved and esteemed. Individuals can themselves satisfy or fail to satisfy these affective needs; and they can compare themselves with other persons, *comparison others* (COs), who satisfy or fail to satisfy these needs for themselves. A consequence is that social emotions do not require complex cognitive processing—they can exist in social animals as well as human beings—because given attachment motives they emerge naturally and effortlessly from the ecology of social interaction. So, given basic attachment/bonding, social emotions play out within the natural logic of interaction, and function quite effectively in social animals.

Selfish Social Emotions Consideration of events in terrestrial and social reality that accompany attachment motives suggests two general sorts of social emotion: *selfish social emotions* involving social comparisons with other persons, and *communal social emotions* functioning to support bonding within groups. Selfish social emotions derive from the classic dominance-submission relationship, combining success and failure at satisfying these two fundamental social motives on the part of a person and CO as the ecologically fundamental interpersonal contingencies. The result is an array of eight such contingency combinations that can be related to common English labels for social emotions, as well as labels in other languages. All else equal, a relatively successful person (P) is likely to experience a social emotion labeled in English *pride* and/or *arrogance* and to have *pity* and/or *scorn* for the less fortunate comparison others (COs). Proud persons are relatively unlikely to experience *guilt, shame, envy*, or *jealousy*. On the other hand, relatively unsuccessful COs comparing themselves with a successful P, are relatively likely to experience *guilt* and/or *shame*, and *envy* and/or *jealousy* toward P in comparison These eight selfish social emotions are summarized in the Fig. 2.1a. The interdependence of these social emotions stems from the natural architectures of ecologically fundamental interpersonal contingencies based upon social comparisons of relative gain and loss, or success and failure. Because these combinations of contingencies are naturally interrelated, selfish social emotions themselves are interrelated so that one has implications for the others (Buck, 2014).

Communal Social Emotions Emotions facilitating within group bonding are of two sorts: *positive communal emotions* (GREAT emotions) supporting within-group bonding and *negative communal emotions* (LOSER emotions) resulting from the rejection and ostracism of those outside or opposed to the group.

The Achievement of Love and the GREAT Emotions The GREAT emotions are *Gratitude*, *Respect*, *Elevation*, *Appreciation*, and *Trust.* These emotions cement bonding of in-group members and define civility and dignity within the group, as summarized in the top of Fig. 2.1b. Following social rules fairly are the bases of civility and dignity. *Gratitude* involves

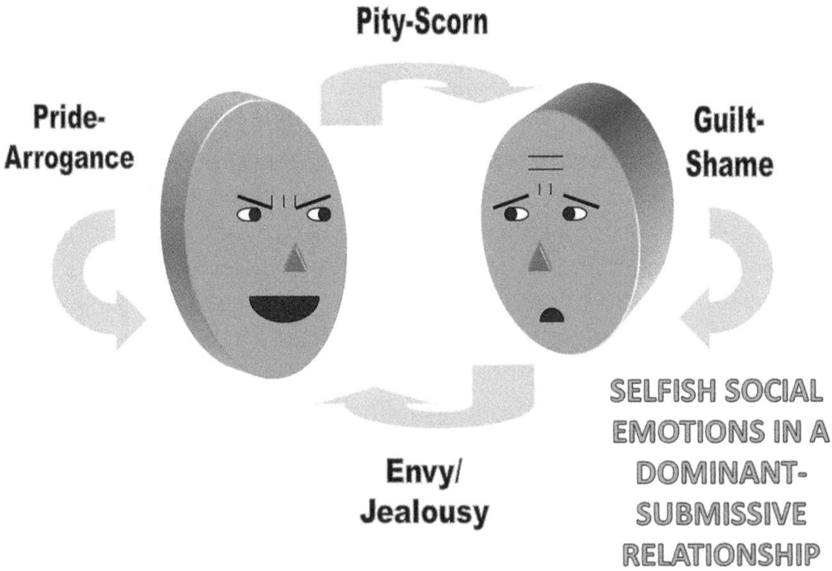

Fig. 2.1a Selfish social emotions

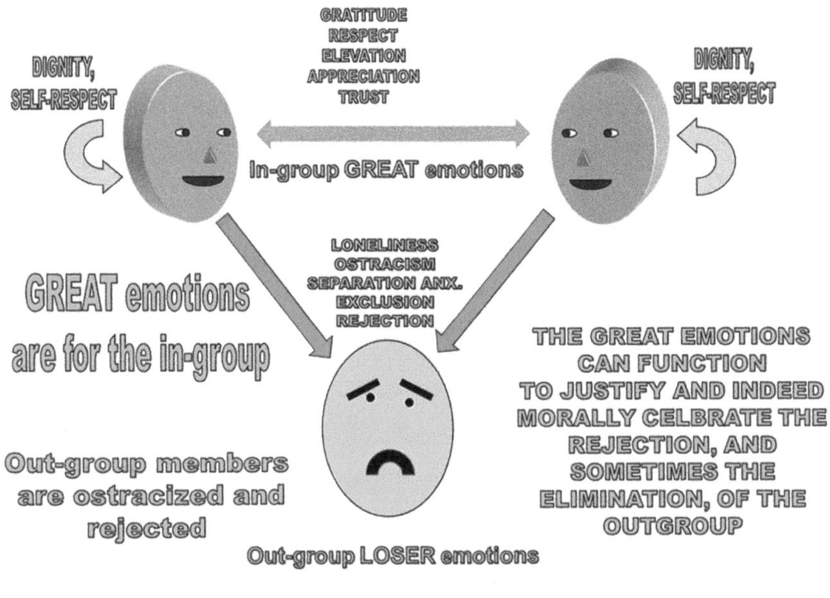

Fig. 2.1b Positive and negative communal social emotions: GREAT and LOSER emotions

acknowledging that a CO follows social rules fairly, resulting in a relationship of mutual *respect* in which each is *elevated* by the other. Following social rules fairly results in mutual *appreciation*, and the general expectation that the other will follow social rules fairly and act with civility is *trust*. These positive communal emotions are, in effect, given to the CO: we feel grateful for, trust, and so on, the CO. They ameliorate selfish social emotions, resulting in a perception of fairness and cooperation that supports and maintains the dignity, self-respect, and self-esteem of both self and CO.

The GREAT emotions underlie ingroup cohesiveness and are normally maintained by rituals of common politeness. We rarely notice this, but it is a powerful social mechanism operating unconsciously. As Moll et al. (2002) put it, "humans are endowed with a natural sense of fairness that permeates social perceptions and interactions. This moral stance is so ubiquitous that we may not notice...(this)...automatic tagging of ordinary social events with moral values" (p. 2730). The GREAT emotions foster accurate and positive mutual emotional communication, agreeableness, and emotional control, and relaxation; thereby buffering against stress and disease. The resulting communication supports empathy, intuition, rapport, and compassion.

Ostracism, the Loss of Love and the LOSER Emotions On the other hand, if someone acts impolitely and one feels *dis*respected, it is highly noticeable, painful, and unpleasant. An entirely different set of emotions is activated: the LOSER emotions of *Loneliness*, *Ostracism*, *Separation anxiety*, *Exclusion*, and *Rejection*. These are the negative communal emotions with effects opposite to those of the positive communal emotions that make separation so punishing.

The ecologically fundamental interpersonal contingencies relating to the positive and negative communal emotions were discovered by social psychologist Kipling Williams. On a visit to the shore, he noticed two men throwing a beachball back and forth to one another. On one occasion the ball came close to Williams, who threw it back. The two then included Williams in their game for a bit, then ignored him and threw to each other. Williams reported that he was surprised at how upset and disappointed he felt at being ignored and resolved to study the situation more closely. He and colleagues created an online version of the ball toss game called *Cyberball*, in which one interacted with two persons on a screen throwing virtual balls back and forth.

Cyberball was used to explore the effects of many variables on reactions to ostracism, and it was discovered that the negative effects were surprisingly strong and robust. People reacted badly even though they knew they were playing against a computer instead of people; and even though they were told that the other players were members of despised out-groups such as the Ku Klux Klan (Gonsalkorale & Williams, 2007). Even when ostracism paid—participants were charged money each time a ball was thrown to them—it still hurt to be ostracized (van Beest & Williams, 2006). Williams (2007) suggested that ostracism is detected crudely but rapidly, and that because of the role of pain in social attachment (Panksepp, 1998), ostracism is felt as psychic pain and recruits the pain mechanism directly, involving same neural architecture as physical pain. More specifically, ostracism activated areas of the dorsal anterior cingulate cortex (ACC) linked to the experience of pain, and the brain activity was related to self-reports in ways compatible with pain studies (Eisenberger et al., 2003).

The Dark Side of Love OT has been called the cuddle hormone, and indeed it seems to be when the relationship with the other is positive and secure. But if the other is regarded with anxiety or even as the foe of kith and kin, OT may increase fear, anger, and hostility. The LOSER emotions demonstrate a negative side of love: where love is actively withheld and replaced by its obverse, hatred. Insecure persons may generally regard others with suspicion and thus expect to be rejected, and there is evidence that OT can increase anxiety in insecure persons (Hazan & Shaver, 1987).

This suggests that it may be more broadly correct to regard OT as the *communication* hormone, with the valence and impact of the communication determined by the nature of the personal relationship. It is affectively positive to communicate with a friend but affectively negative to communicate with an enemy, so by increasing communication OT may have both, apparently contradictory, effects. One may inquire how a single molecule has this power, and the answer lies in the power of communication, particularly spontaneous emotional communication. Communication sculpts relationships with others from the first moments of life. It forms unshakable bonds of love between parent and infant, siblings and comrades, and lovers through the GREAT emotions, and at the same time it motivates hatred, schadenfreude, and xenophobia, resulting in the LOSER emotions. The self-described Proud Boys are, in fact, humiliated. These emotions of the unloved may motivate the submission to and admiration of strong leaders and social movements that promise acceptance, inclusion, and love. So, love, nurtured at mother's knee, is also at the root of fascism. This appears contradictory, but it is not. It *is* deeply ironic: a stubborn and persistent, and often tragic, aspect of humanity's social nature.

References

Ainsworth, M. D. S., & Bell, S. M. (1970). Attachment, exploration, and separation: Illustrated by the behavior of one-year-olds in a strange situation. *Child Development, 41*(1), 49–67.

Atzil, S., Hendler, T., & Feldman, R. (2011). Specifying the neurobiological basis of human attachment: Brain, hormones, and behavior in synchronous and intrusive mothers. *Neuropsychopharmacology, 36*, 2603–2615.

Barrett, L. F. (2006). Are emotions natural kinds? *Perspectives on Psychological Science, 1*(1), 28–58.

Baumgartner, T., Heinrichs, M., Vonlanthen, A., Fischbacher, U., & Fehr, E. (2008). Oxytocin shapes the neural circuitry of trust and trust adaptation in humans. *Neuron, 58*(4), 639–650. https://doi.org/10.1016/j.neuron.2008.04.009

Bowlby, J. (1953). *Maternal care and mental health*. The World Health Organization.

Bretherton, I. (1992). The origins of attachment theory: John Bowlby and Mary Ainsworth. *Developmental Psychology, 28*(5), 759–775. https://doi.org/10.1037/0012-1649.28.5.759

Buck, R. (1983). Emotional development and emotional education. In R. Plutchik & H. Kellerman (Eds.), *Emotion in early development* (pp. 259–292). Academic Press.

Buck, R. (1984). *The communication of emotion*. Guilford Press.

Buck, R. (1985). Prime theory: An integrated view of motivation and emotion. *Psychological Review, 92*(3), 389–413. https://doi.org/10.1037/0033-295X.92.3.389

Buck, R. (1988). *Human motivation and emotion*. Wiley.

Buck, R. (1999). The biological affects: A typology. *Psychological Review, 106*(2), 301–336. https://doi.org/10.1037/0033-295X.106.2.301

Buck, R. (2014). *Emotion: A biosocial synthesis*. Cambridge University Press.

Buck, R., & Van Lear, C. A. (2002). Verbal and nonverbal communication: Distinguishing symbolic, spontaneous, and pseudo-spontaneous nonverbal behavior. *Journal of Communication, 52*, 522–541.

Carter, C. S., Lederhendler, I. I., & Kirkpatrick, B. (Eds.). (1997). *The integrative neurobiology of affiliation. Annals of the New York Academy of Sciences* (Vol. 807). The New York Academy of Sciences.

Cuff, B. M. P., Brown, S. J., Taylor, L., & Howat, D. J. (2016). Empathy a review of the concept. *Emotion Review, 8*, 144–153. https://doi.org/10.1177/1754073914558466

de Waal, F. B. M. (2007). The 'Russian Doll' model of empathy and imitation. In S. Bråten (Ed.), *On being moved: From mirror neurons to empathy* (pp. 49–69). John Benjamins Publishing Company. https://doi.org/10.1075/aicr.68.06waa

de Waal, F. B. M., & Preston, S. D. (2017). Mammalian empathy: Behavioural manifestations and neural basis. *Nature Reviews Neuroscience*. https://doi.org/10.1038/nrn.2017.72

Decety, J., & Jackson, P. L. (2004). The functional architecture of human empathy. *Behavioral and Cognitive Neuroscience Reviews, 3*(2), 71–100. https://doi.org/10.1177/1534582304267187

Donaldson, Z. R., & Young, L. J. (2008). Oxytocin, vasopressin, and the neurogenetics of sociality. *Science, 322*, 900–904.

Eisenberger, N. I., Lieberman, M. D., & Williams, K. D. (2003). Does Rejection Hurt? An fMRI study of social exclusion. *Science, 302*(5643), 290–292.

Feldman, R. (2012). Oxytocin and social affiliation in humans. *Hormones and Behavior, 61*(3), 380–391. https://doi.org/10.1016/j.yhbeh.2012.01.008

Feldman, R., Weller, A., Zagoory-Sharon, O., & Levine, A. (2007). Evidence for a neuroendocrinological foundation of human affiliation: Plasma oxytocin levels across pregnancy and the postpartum period predict mother-infant bonding. *Psychological Science, 18*(11), 965–970. https://doi.org/10.1111/j.1467-9280.2007.02010.x

Ferguson, J. N., Aldag, J. M., Insel, T. R., & Young, L. J. (2001). Oxytocin in the medial amygdala is essential for social recognition in the mouse. *Journal of Neuroscience, 21*(20), 8278–8285. https://doi.org/10.1523/JNEUROSCI.21-20-08278.2001. PMID: 11588199, PMCID: PMC6763861

Fischetti, M. (2011). Your brain in love: Cupid's arrows, laced with neurotransmitters, find their marks. *Scientific American, 304*, 92.

Freeman, S. M., & Young, L. J. (2011). Oxytocin, vasopressin, and the evolution of mating systems in mammals. In E. Choleris, D. W. Pfaff, & M. Kavaliers (Eds.), *Oxytocin, vasopressin, and related peptides in the regulation of behavior* (pp. 128–147). https://doi.org/10.1017/CBO9781139017855.011

Gore, R. (2003). The rise of mammals. *National Geographic, 203*(4), 2–37.

Guastella, A. J., & MacLeod, C. (2012). A critical review of the influence of oxytocin nasal spray on social cognition in humans: Evidence and future directions. *Hormones and Behavior, 61*(3), 410–418. https://doi.org/10.1016/j.yhbeh.2012.01.002

Hall, E. T. (1966). *The hidden dimension*. Doubleday.

Harlow, H. F. (1971). *Learning to love*. Albion.

Hazan, C., & Shaver, P. R. (1987). Romantic love conceptualized as an attachment process. *Journal of Personality and Social Psychology, 52*(3), 511–524. https://doi.org/10.1037/0022-3514.52.3.511

Hetherington, R., & Reid, R. G. B. (2010). *The climate connection: Climate change and modern human evolution*. Cambridge University Press.

Insel, T. R. (1992). Oxytocin – A neuropeptide for affiliation: Evidence from behavioral, receptor autoradiographic, and comparative studies. *Psychoneuroendocrinology, 17*(1), 3–35. https://doi.org/10.1016/0306-4530(92)90073-G

Insel, T. R., Young, L., & Wang, Z. (1997). Molecular aspects of monogamy. In C. S. Carter, I. I. Lederhendler, & B. Kirkpatrick (Eds.), *Annals of the New York Academy of Sciences. Vol. 807. The integrative neurobiology of affiliation* (pp. 302–316). The New York Academy of Sciences.

Insel, T. R., & Young, L. J. (2001). Opinion: The neurobiology of attachment. *Nature Reviews Neuroscience, 2*(2), 129–136. https://doi.org/10.1038/35053579

Koolhaas, J. M., van den Brink, T. H. C., Roozendaal, B., & Boorsma, F. (1990). Medial amygdala and aggressive behavior: Interaction between testosterone and vasopressin. *Aggressive Behavior, 16*(3), 223–229.

Kosfeld, M., Heinrichs, M., Zak, P. J., Fischbacher, U., & Fehr, E. (2005). Oxytocin increases trust in humans. *Nature, 435*, 673–676.

Leakey, R. E., & Lewin, R. (1992). *Origins reconsidered: In search of what makes us human*. Doubleday.

LeRoith, D., Liotta, A. S., Roth, J., Shiloach, J., Lewis, M. E., Pert, C. B., & Krieger, D. T. (1982). Corticotropin and β-endorphin-like materials are native to unicellular organisms. *Proceedings of the National Academy of Sciences of the United States of America, 79*, 2086–2090.

Lim, M. M., Wang, Z., Olazábal, D. E., Ren, X., Terwilliger, E. F., & Young, L. J. (2004). Enhanced partner preference in a promiscuous species by manipulating the expression of a single gene. *Nature, 429*, 754–757.

Lovejoy, C. O. (2009). Reexamining human origins in light of *Ardipithecus ramidus*. *Science, 326*(2), 74.

Moll, J., de Oliveira-Souza, R., Eslinger, P. J., Bramati, I. E., Mourao-Miranda, J., Andreiulo, P. A., & Pessoa, L. (2002). The neural correlates of moral sensitivity: A functional magnetic resonance imaging investigation of basic and moral emotions. *Journal of Neuroscience, 22*, 2730–2736.

Moore, F. L. (1987). Behavioral actions of neurohypophysial peptides. In D. Crews (Ed.), *Psychobiology of reproductive behavior: An evolutionary perspective* (pp. 61–87). Prentice Hall.

Morris, D. (1967). *The naked ape*. Constable.

Murray, L., & Trevarthen, C. (1986). The infant's role in mother-infant communications. *Journal of Child Language, 13*, 15–29.

Niedenthal, P. M., & Brauer, M. (2012). Social functionality of human emotion. *Annual Review of Psychology, 63*, 259–285.

Panksepp, J. (1998). *Affective neuroscience: The foundations of human and animal emotions*. Oxford University Press.

Pert, C. B. (1997). *Molecules of emotion: Why you feel the way you feel*. Scribner.

Porges, S. W. (1995). Cardiac vagal tone: A physiological index of stress. *Neuroscience & Biobehavioral Reviews, 19*(2), 225–233. https://doi.org/10.1016/0149-7634(94)00066-A

Richard, P., Moos, F., & Freund-Mercier, M. J. (1991). Central effects of oxytocin. *Physiological Reviews, 71*, 331–370.

Ross, E. D. (2021). Differential hemispheric lateralization of emotions and related displays behaviors: Emotion-type hypothesis. *Brain Sciences, 11*, 1034–1061.

Shamay-Tsoory, S. G., Aharon-Peretz, J., & Perry, D. (2009). Two systems for empathy: A double dissociation between emotional and cognitive empathy in inferior frontal gyrus versus ventromedial prefrontal lesions. *Brain, 132*(3), 617–627. https://doi.org/10.1093/brain/awn279

Smuts, B. (1987). What are friends for? *Natural History, 96*(2), 36–45.
Telle, N.-T., & Pfister, H.-R. (2016). Positive empathy and prosocial behavior: A neglected link. *Emotion Review, 8*(2), 154–163. https://doi.org/10.1177/1754073915586817
Tomkins, S. S. (1962-1982). *Affect, imagery, consciousness* (Vol. 1–3). Springer.
Tomkins, S. S. (1982). Affect theory. In P. Ekman (Ed.), *Emotion in the human face* (2nd ed., pp. 353–395). Cambridge University Press.
Trevarthen, C. (1979). Communication and cooperation in early infancy: A description of primary intersubjectivity. In M. Bullowa (Ed.), *Before speech: The beginning of human communication* (pp. 321–347). Cambridge University Press.
Trevarthen, C., & Aitken, K. J. (2001). Infant intersubjectivity: Research, theory, and clinical applications. *Journal of Child Psychology and Psychiatry, 42*(1), 3–48. https://doi.org/10.1111/1469-7610.00701
Tronick, E. (1978). The infant's response to entrapment between contradictory messages in a face-to-face interaction. *Journal of the American Academy of Child Psychiatry, 17*, 1–13.
van Beest, I., & Williams, K. (2006). When inclusion costs and ostracism pays, ostracism still hurts. *Journal of Personality and Social Psychology, 91*, 918–928. https://doi.org/10.1037/0022-3514.91.5.918
Williams, K. D. (2007). Ostracism. *Annual Review of Psychology, 58*, 425–452.
Young, L. J. (2001). *Social deficits in oxytocin knockout mice*. National Institution of Child Health and Human Development/ACC 2001 Conference: Potential cellular and molecular mechanisms in autism and related disorders, Bethesda.
Young, L. J., Lim, M. M., Gingrich, B., & Insel, T. R. (2001). Cellular mechanisms of social attachment. *Hormones and Behavior, 40*(2), 133–138.

3

The Role of Nonverbal Communication in Leadership Skills

Mirjana Franceško and Jasmina Nedeljković

Introduction

Leadership is a kind of interaction, based on the mutual influence of the leader and the corresponding group members. The communication of actors who have different positions in the group forms the basis of group dynamics and is the most important mechanism of its functioning. *We define leadership as a kind of interaction between people whose roles differ in terms of influence, initiative, and responsibility, and whose ultimate function is to direct individual differences toward the common goal of the group*. Thus, leadership is a process that takes place through verbal and nonverbal transactions, primarily conditioned by the content of the group's activities and the joint activities of members, but also by the perception of "closeness" between them. The leader is a figure whose degree of influence, as well as level of initiative and responsibility, is greater and different in relation to other members of the group. Although the leader has a

M. Franceško (✉) • J. Nedeljković
Department of Psychology, Faculty of Legal and Business Study dr Lazar Vrkatić, Union University, Belgrade, Serbia

R. J. Sternberg, A. Kostić (eds.), *Nonverbal Communication in Close Relationships*,
https://doi.org/10.1007/978-3-030-94492-6_3

more visible transactional influence on others due to his/her central role, this does not signify that the influence of group members on the leader is nonexistent or that it has only a marginal role in group dynamics. The way group members interpret and understand a leader's verbal and nonverbal messages largely determines their motivation and willingness to accept and follow them. At the same time, it is important to emphasize that, in the process of leadership, changes in the role of the subject and object of social perception are very dynamic. The focus on one another in group functioning indicates the closeness of their relationships.

Nonverbal Behavior and Leadership

Over decades of research into nonverbal communication, numerous scholars have tried to define nonverbal communication, striving for the most adequate definition. As expected, these definitions have frequently differed from each other. This trend is also apparent in the results of a survey published in the book *Speak Without Words* (Serbian: *Govor bez reci*, Kostić, 2008). The survey's participants were leading researchers of nonverbal communication (Argyle, Gottman, Ginsberg, Ekman, Moore, Ellsworth, Camras, Bond, Keating, Craig, Laird, Pacori), who answered questions about the definition, origin, social role, practical implications, and perspectives of nonverbal communication. The analysis of their responses showed differences in their views and definitions of nonverbal communication. Some of them offered narrower points of view and some broader, while some insisted on interpreting the nature of this form of communication based largely on physiological, psychological, or cultural aspects. There were also those who favored narrower specifications, placing nonverbal means or nonverbal effects in the foreground, as well as various functions of nonverbal communication. There were also unexpected statements, such as that it is superfluous to search for definitions when scientists are currently and systematically researching intriguing phenomena of nonverbal behavior (Ellsworth & Ross, 1975). A significant number of researchers, however, have seemingly come to agree on relatively consistent defining aspects, concluding that nonverbal communication involves everything that does not belong to the semantic content of speech (Craig), or what can be called "non-linguistic communication" (Moore). Based on our examination of the results of this survey, we concluded that Argyle and Gottman were among those who had chosen a narrower way of defining nonverbal communication, insisting on the importance of exploring nonverbal elements that form sets of nonverbal signals (facial expression, gestures, touch, posture, gaze, and proxemic and paralinguistic communication), with both of them indicating a belief that nonverbal signals are carriers of important information and that it is necessary to develop the skill of accurately recognizing different signals, which in most situations ensures harmonious and quality communication with others. In contrast, Keating has emphasized the value of emerging nonverbal configurations and the effects caused by signals that have been broadcast (per Kostić, 2008).

For the purposes of examining the main topic of this chapter, the authors have chosen to recognize the definition offered by Paul Ekman as most appropriate (per Kostić, 2008). Ekman distinguishes between the term *nonverbal behavior* and the term *nonverbal communication*, indicating that nonverbal behavior is a broader and more appropriate term, as is its corresponding definition. Nonverbal behavior includes information that is obtained when we observe the movements of the face and body and when we listen to the manner of speech, as well as the tone and pitch, of a person or group of people who are objects of our perception. Thus, this term encompasses several aspects of the nonverbal sign system, including its informative and communicative functions.

Nonverbal behavior plays a highly significant role in all manners of human social interactions, as it conveys information about the temperamental, physical, and mental health, emotions, interpersonal attitudes, intentions, and expectations of the participants in an interaction. It is particularly noteworthy that participants in social interactions have been shown to trust more in nonverbal signs of behavior than in verbal communication, seeing these signs as highly informative and as appearing spontaneously and without control, and thus as more reliable than words. However, interaction participants may also emit, intentionally and consciously, various nonverbal signals to achieve current individual or group goals. Thus, one's spatial behavior, as well as the position of the body (posture), can convey information about an individual's desire to maintain distance and isolation from other participants in the interaction, sometimes creating an impression of being superior to them, while another member of the group may show affection for others, as well as fondness for their cooperation, by reducing spatial distance and touching an interlocutor. Such messages often communicate the will, intention, and current needs of a person. Body position and behavior in space (proxemic communication) are generally determined by the role and function of the participants in an interaction. Such communication represents a controlled, deliberate sending of certain nonverbal messages.

Social interaction through verbal or nonverbal communication channels, or through their combination, forms the basis of, and is key to, the functioning, duration, and survival of small and large groups. One of the ways to concretize the role of verbal and nonverbal transactions in group functioning is through precise analysis of the leadership process, which includes many interactive mechanisms. These mechanisms are particularly pronounced in small structured groups. Such groups are characterized by the mutual perception of members who, in the process of performing basic activities, come into frequent direct contact with one another—"face to face" communication. Direct interaction between members, their interdependence and influence on each other, generally determines the pace and success of performing tasks, as well as the quality of mutual relations within a small group.

Leadership is a construct whose topicality of study is constantly evolving. Every answer that authors, theorists, and researchers provide raises new questions. Therefore, it can be said that while leadership is one of the most examined phenomena in human behavior, it remains an undefined phenomenon about which many questions remain and for which explanations and solutions continue to be sought. Why is it so? One of the reasons lies in its complexity, which means that there are indeed a number of perspectives from which it is possible to approach the study of leadership. Certain authors (Bass, 1990; Bass & Bass, 2009; Stogdill, 1974; Yukl, 1998, 2006; Northouse, 2018) have tried, through their extensive efforts, to compile and establish a number of theoretical approaches and research results. However, the question remains: How could our current knowledge be classified into several approaches that would enable us to prioritize, direct our attention to, and examine specific segments of this complex phenomenon? Such classification could establish basic perspectives from which we could approach theoretical discussions and/or design research. Therefore, it is necessary to construct and embrace some kind of classification of views that would entail and possess the characteristics of both comprehensiveness and structure. A schematic approach enables easier navigation of a number of sources. At the same time, the challenge is to create a system of classification that not only recognizes the limits of differentiating the ways in which attempts to understand leadership are primarily approached, but also leaves open possibilities for supplementing certain segments that have been studied in other, separate approaches. We are of the opinion that approaching the subject from the point of view of such schematic models makes scientific knowledge sufficiently systematic and at the same time sufficiently open. This further implies that this approach is sufficiently understandable, yet also sufficient in its scope and context in seeking to attain insights into complex socio-psychological phenomena such as leadership. When additionally taking into account the complexity of nonverbal behavior, the appropriateness of employing the schematic approach from the very beginning of the study and understanding of leadership is heightened yet further, as each of the different approaches to leadership defines and implies a specific role and angle of studying this type of communication. Thus, the question arises: can we place and treat, and, if so, in what way, the issues of nonverbal behavior in a space defined by different approaches to leadership, which do not exclude each other but rather complement each other in a unique way?

In our earlier studies (Franceško, 2000, 2001, 2003; Franceško et al., 2009), we have singled out four categories of approaches to leadership. The first approach refers to the study of leadership from the point of view of the *characteristics*, *skills*, and *competencies* of a person who is the leader in a given group. The second category combines approaches that focus on *situational factors* and a recognizable *manner* of influencing or leadership *style*. The third category emphasizes regarding leadership from the point of view of group members' *interaction* with the leader. The final, fourth category, refers to the understanding of leadership as a *role in a group*. Each of these approaches will be the subject of broader elaboration. Yet, here, at the very beginning and in brief, instead of an introduction, we would point out the general angle from which it is possible to approach the analysis of nonverbal behavior in each of the above categories of examining leadership, respectively. For example, nonverbal behavior can be regarded a manifestation of a leader's personality traits, whether these are enduring traits and/or emotional and motivational experiences. In this light, knowing and applying the laws of nonverbal behavior is a kind of skill that increases the probability of accuracy in social perception. Relatedly, yet contrasting in orientation, the leader, by observing the nonverbal behavior of group members and their relationships, can largely be seen as establishing social context as one of the defining benchmarks of leadership, and thus it has gained the status of a significant situational factor of leadership. In the context of interaction, or the third approach in our categorization, group members are subjects who perceive the leader's nonverbal behavior. The complexity of the leader's role raises questions in the context of nonverbal behavior. One of the basic ones is the question of the significance of this role for the person in that position and, related to that, which aspects of that role will be given more importance in the leadership process. This kind of psychological experience certainly has its manifestations in nonverbal behavior, which thus becomes a powerful indicator for becoming familiar with and predicting leadership. Finally, consideration of the role of the leader includes consideration of complementary roles, that is, the behavior of group members. Hierarchical positions and related roles can be treated as factors in the manifestation of nonverbal behavior, but at the same time as factors of perception and interpretation (decoding) of signals from different positions of actors.

Studying leadership from the point of view of the personality traits of a person that leads is the oldest approach. The basic question is: What qualities predetermine a person to become a leader? In accordance with the development of scientific thought, the orientation of authors pursuing answers to this question have also changed. Initial attempts were focused on the search for one general exceptional trait that would predestine a person to become a leader in any group. This universalist orientation soon proved inappropriate, prompting authors to try to single out a set of traits that might set leaders apart. Based on theoretical assumptions and research results, numerous lists of leader-defining characteristics have emerged, yet they have often differed in the characteristics indicated, their number, and their significance for the leadership process, as well as in the justifications of their positions (Stogdill, 1948, 1974; Mann, 1959; Bass, 1990; Bryman, 1992; Judge et al., 2002; Zaccaro et al., 2004; Bass & Bass, 2009; Northouse, 2018; Yukl, 1998, 2006). From the numerous lists of traits of (successful) leaders, we single out one set defined by Yukl (1998, 2006). It is the authors' opinion that a distinct set of traits, or, more precisely, a series of characteristics of a successful leader, is both crucially informative and useful in the context of studying leadership and nonverbal behavior and Yukl's particularly astute set recognizes the following as desirable qualities of leaders: high energy potential and stress tolerance, self-confidence, an orientation toward the inner locus of control, emotional maturity, personal integrity, a socialized aspiration for power, a relatively high degree of orientation toward achievement, and a moderate need for affiliation. It can be said that these characteristics derive from each other by some logical sequence, making the structure congruent, which itself is a characteristic of a *mature person*. These distinct, yet synergized, characteristics imply a character of personal dispositions that are modified through various processes of socialization in terms of degree of expression, meaning, and content, and thus can become, and serve as, a kind of requisite, or prototypical, skillset for successful leadership.

In addition to this blueprint, and despite the differences in the lists of traits mentioned above, there are certain traits that stand out for their appearance in nearly all sets: intelligence, self-confidence, domination, initiative, achievement orientation, and social sensitivity. Common to all these characteristics is what they inherently signify, and the degree of significance they carry, in the manifestation of nonverbal signals of a leader, yet also in the perception and interpretation of nonverbal behavior of other people and group members. In essence, it is *social motivation* and the *emotional way of reacting* that dominate, that is, characteristics that are significantly manifested in nonverbal behavior, and emotional behavior in the leadership process has been specifically studied through the notion of emotional intelligence (Mayer et al., 2008; Caruso & Wolfe, 2004). This more explicitly explains the importance of the nonverbal behavior of the leader and group members, since this is one of the indicators of a person's emotional experience. At the same time, the aspect of the informativeness of the "message" is especially important, which is an integral part of the emotional experience in interpersonal relationships, both in regard to the person we regard as the subject (the sender, initiator, observer) and the person regarded as the object, whose reaction is perceived and interpreted.

With the situational approach and the interaction-based approach, the context of the examination expands. Leadership is considered within the group and its dynamics (Stogdill & Coons, 1957; Likert, 1961, 1967). The *relationship* between the leader and the members of the group, on an individual and group level, becomes one of the central topics of theoretical considerations and subjects of research. Thus, it opens up new perspectives for the study of nonverbal behavior within leadership.

In the situational approach, special attention is paid to situational leadership factors. It is a context that relativizes the meaning and influence of certain characteristics of a person in leadership for emergence and success in leadership. Numerous and strongly contrasting situational factors have been cited in the relevant literature. If we focus on studying leadership in parallel with nonverbal behavior, the intensity of the interpersonal relationship between the leaders and the members of the group gains special significance. This entails determining whether the nonverbal behavior of the leader and or group members is studied in small or large groups. The basis for distinguishing between these groups is the influence of group dynamics and culture on the social perception of members. The influence of these mechanisms, which also involves weighing and determining the cognitive and emotional schemes through which the nonverbal behaviors of members are interpreted, is often much more intense in small than in large groups. This further indicates that the study of nonverbal behavior in the leadership process outside the context of group dynamics, in our opinion, is not informative enough to yield the in-depth understanding of this issue which is sought.

Starting from the context characteristic of the situational approach and employing the definition cited above, leadership can be considered from the point of view of the role, leadership style, and interaction of group members with the leader.

In this context, the *role* is the expected and characteristic behavior that is related to a certain position in the group. It is always the result of objective or formal "requirements" and the individual characteristics of the bearers of a given role. The most general framework of individual differences can be considered the experience or meaning that the role of a leader has for a given person. The inclusion of more hierarchical positions in the group activates the instrumental significance of this role to meet some fundamental needs attributed to a leader, such as *power*, *achievement*, and *affiliations* with other people. The meaning that a leader attaches to his/her hierarchical position is consciously and/or unconsciously transmitted through verbal and nonverbal reactions. The second level of analysis, from the point of view of the role of the leader, refers to the distinguishing of its individual aspects. Almost all aspects of the role of the leader are directly or indirectly included and realized through social interaction. For example, Mintzberg (1973) singles out several aspects of the role of a leader, such as: interpersonal (figure of the boss, person who connects and leads), informational (observer, transmitter, speaker ...), and aspects of the role related to decision-making (negotiator, entrepreneur, problem solver...). According to Pettinger (1996), a leader is: an ambassador, a lawyer, a praiser, a defender, one who makes the rounds, who is a model, and who is always visible. Thus, the role of a leader includes various aspects of social perception whether it is the leader as the subject or object of such an assessment. If we add to this *success* in leading a given group, special emphasis must be placed on *accuracy in social perception*. Accurate assessment of group members, their reactions, and attitudes, assessed on the basis of both verbal and nonverbal cues, is one of the fundaments for successful leadership. Group members almost always have a certain inhibitory factor in verbally addressing a person in hierarchically higher positions, for one reason or another, and the capacity to interpret nonverbal cues that are subtler and for which there is less awareness or conscious control on the part of the cue-giver gains special value and represents one of the most important skills of successful leaders.

Leadership style has been defined as the way a leader behaves in a group that is characteristic of the person and which is manifested not only in his/her behavior in the same situations, but also in different, or novel, situations (Franceško, 2003). The very definition of this term explicitly entails the manifestation of behavior that involves nonverbal signals as an important factor. The idea of the concept of leadership style is to unite different manifest forms of behavior based on certain criteria. Numerous models of distinguishing leadership styles have been developed (Katz & Kahn, 1951; Cartwright & Zander, 1960; Likert, 1961; Blake & Mounton, 1964;) in which people-oriented and task-oriented dimensions are distinguished. Lewin (1951), in his research, singled out the autocratic, democratic, and "free" (laissez-faire) ways of leading. Numerous theories of leadership that have emerged in the last 50 years have their basis in these classic distinctions of leadership style. What we regard as important for understanding leadership style, as well as for studying nonverbal behavior within this type of interpersonal relationship, is the relationship between people-oriented dimensions and task-oriented dimensions and the styles of leadership established by Lewin. In the literature on leadership, being people-oriented is often equated with the democratic style, while being task-oriented with an autocratic style of leadership. It is the authors' opinion that the bases of these dimensions are grounded in their distinct criteria for differentiating and determining individual differences. The contrast in the dimensions of *people-orientation* and *task-orientation* is related to the *basic functions of the group* and the respective dimension indicates the degree to which the leader is oriented to fulfill them. At the core of autocratic and democratic leadership is the difference in the *way* the leader *influences* group members. The justification of the separation of these dimensions and their treatment as independent criteria for assessing leadership is confirmed by the results of some of our research (Franceško, 2000, 2001, 2003; Franceško et al., 2009). In the context of studying the nonverbal behavior of the leader, the autocratic-democratic leadership duality is especially interesting, because the influence of the leader on the members of the group is realized through verbal, but also nonverbal reactions. Nonverbal behavior is an integral part of issuing orders, of treating group members as those who should obey the leader, of punishing mistakes, of insisting on one's own principles and distance, and of trying to keep group members under constant control, all of which are characteristic forms of autocratic leadership behavior. Yet nonverbal behaviors are also embedded in the democratic style of leadership. While their expression may not be as obvious or energetic as in the autocratic approach, they are certainly an important indicator of the efforts of, and a tool for, democratically oriented leaders to motivate, educate, promote, reward, and involve group members in the decision-making process and the like. The motivational basis in the autocratic and democratic styles of governing is grounded in the respective differences in the degree, content, and function of power orientation, which are especially expressed in the perception and communication of actors in different hierarchical positions. Regarding the manner of measuring, nonverbal reactions are an important indicator of the presence of the degree of autocracy and democracy in leadership, when it is assessed based on the observation of the leader's behavior by educated observers and/or respective group members.

In the fourth approach to understanding the leadership phenomenon, the focus is on the *interaction of group members with the leader*. This means that group members are treated as subjects, and the leader as an object of social perception. The results of this direction of social perception are multifold, and are largely based on the acceptance of the leader, his/her authority, and thus the willingness of group members to follow him/her. Thus, the influence of group members is multidimensional. The very experiencing and interpretation of the verbal and nonverbal behavior of the leader act as motivating factors for the members of the group. On the other hand, the reactions of the members, their readiness to channel their activities along the directions of the leader, that is, the tasks of the group, are an important reference point for determining the leading of the group. In the social perception of the leader as an object, that is, of his/her verbal and nonverbal behavior, the assessments of the similarities and differences of the leader in relation to the members of the group change dynamically, which makes this psychological process very complex and layered. The leader must at the same time be perceived as "one of us," that is, a typical representative of the group (or one similar or identifiable with "most of us"), yet also as "the best of us." In each segment of assessment, which can be determined in different ways—in terms of characteristics, values, attitudes, motivational orientations, and emotional reactions or general forms of behavior, nonverbal forms of behavior are implicit. This further means that for each dimension of assessment, the question can be asked as to which segments of nonverbal behavior are the most informative in observation and whether they, as manifest indicators of the leader, are key benchmarks of these assessments. No less important is the question of universality, that is, the relativity of the meaning of the indicated assessments. In other words, the question arises as to whether the assessments of potential leaders based on their verbal and nonverbal behavior have universal meaning, or is it the specificity of a certain group's structure and dynamics that have a more dominant role in interpreting and attributing meaning to perceived signals.

Nonverbal Expression and Perception of Dominance and Submissiveness in a Small Group

Social interactions can be pictorially presented as two dimensions that are perpendicular to each other—the horizontal and vertical dimensions (Hall et al., 2005). The horizontal dimension of social interactions is characterized by kindness and warmth at one end of the dimension, and hostile behavior and aggression at the other end of the dimension. The vertical dimension is characterized by differences in power and dominance between group members who interact (Kiesler & Auerbach, 2003; Moskowitz, 1993; Tiedens & Jimenez, 2003). Given that the world we live in is hierarchically arranged in every form of social interaction, it is reasonable to expect that aspects of domination and power have an impact on our behavior. What, then, is domination exactly? According to Gifford (1991), domination is a very important interpersonal attitude that has the power to initiate, develop, and transform people's social relations. It can unite and divide the members of any group, making them cooperative or competitive. Skillfully employed dominance in leadership can ensure the satisfaction of individual and group needs, as well as the realization of individual and common goals. However, imposed, undeserved, and unaccepted domination by the members of the group can lead to splitting in the group or its disintegration.

According to Schmid Mast, a dominant person either possesses power or has a strong need to gain power. A dominant person usually tells others what to do but is rarely willing to accept the advice, suggestions, assessments, or orders of others. He/she speaks more than others and often interrupts the speech of others. The respective interlocutors see these tendencies as indicators of dominant behavior.

In defining dominance, we have chosen as more appropriate its broader definition (Ellyson & Dovidio, 1985), which assumes the existence of a characteristic interpersonal attitude that includes power and status. This may involve the privilege of accessing limited resources (for example, time, money), and/or the striving to obtain such privileges. This is often accompanied by a tendency to "master," that is, gain control over, other people and influence them (Ellyson & Dovidio, per Kostić 2008).

As already mentioned, the establishment of hierarchy, that is, domination, directly affects the organization of interpersonal behavior. Yet despite the importance of dominance and the relatively large number of studies demonstrative of its scientific interest to scientists, there still do not appear to be adequate integrative cases of reference research that indicate or confirm "closed" and reliably researched issues and/or those that are still "open," or unresolved, with many of these issues and questions that are unexplained, unexamined, or controversial remaining neglected in this area (Schmid-Mast & Cousin, 2013). It seems that we should start with basic questions such as: "How is domination expressed?" "What signs do people rely on in assessing domination?" "Are observers successful in interpreting the status or domination of others?"

The hierarchy of relationships in groups, including small groups, significantly affects the perception, reasoning, and behavior of participants in interactions in the dimension of domination-subordination. The results of research on conformism (Larsen et al., 1979) have shown that individuals' suspicion of their own judgment on an issue is directly proportional to the dominant status of the person dictating the social norm into which one is expected to fit.

Ethological studies of apes (per Keating, 1985) have focused the attention of certain researchers on two characteristic forms of facial behavior associated with dominance, in relation to subordination. On the upper part of the face, the eyebrows of the dominant apes would be lowered and pressed toward one another, while in subordinate individuals, the eyebrows would be arched and raised. Correspondingly, on the lower part of the face, the crucial difference was seen to stem from the presence or absence of a smile. Subordinate individuals were observed to make a "smile" of sorts, while for the dominant apes, movement of the facial muscles that stretch the lips was not noticed. This facial behavior has been reported in children (Camras, 1977) and in adults (Brannigan & Humphries, 1972). Opinions and findings on the use and influence of the gaze, or looking at a respective subject, in relation to the dimension of dominance-subordination have been mixed and at times contradictory. Namely, Mehrabian (1972) found that dominant persons look at their interlocutors less often, while Strongman and Champness (Strongman & Champness, 1968) reported that gazing intently at one's interlocutor is characteristic of dominant individuals, whose goal is to confuse and force the interlocutor to look away. Also, Michael Chance (1967), in studying dominance in animals, defined the phenomenon of "attention structure," which describes that the dominant individual keeps in focus the attention of the subordinate individual by determining the path they will move upon and the activities they will undertake on that path. Similar forms of leadership have been confirmed in humans. Such contradictory findings led Schmid Mast and Hall (2008) to conclude that the perception of dominance is actually based on a larger number of characters than the number that has been recorded in the expression of dominance. In this light, successful recognition of facial signs of dominance, that is, from the perspective of submissiveness, would be based on the careful recognition of relevant dynamic facial signs. However, the observer's assessment has also been shown to be based on his/her beliefs and expectations about which facial signs were related to dominance and which to submissiveness. Moreover, the characteristics of the social situation have also been indicated to influence assessments of dominance or subordination (Kostić et al., 2020).

Study of the Nonverbal Behavior of Leaders and Other Members in the Small Group Context

A deeper look into the nonverbal behavior of leaders and other members in small groups required the design and implementation of a study with the primary goal of singling out a set of nonverbal behaviors of actors in the transpiring of leadership processes in a small group. A specific observation protocol was constructed and applied over a period of time. The starting point was the view that leadership is a complex and dynamic interactive process which shapes forms of nonverbal behavior. This meant the highlighting of several indicators of nonverbal expression of leader dominance and of the corresponding reaction of small group members.

Protocol for Registering Nonverbal Signs of Domination and Power

Drawing upon the results of a large number of previous studies (Camras, 1977; Blurton Jones, 1971; Brannigan & Humphries, 1972; Grant, 1969; Birdwhistell, 1968; Keating et al., 1977; Schmid Mast & Hall, 2004; Barnes & Sternberg, 1989), a protocol was created for registering facial and other nonverbal signs of domination and signals of presented power in a small group. The protocol was constructed of two parts. The first part was comprised of data on the date of the observation, the position of the person in the work organization, as well as a brief description of the situation in which the observation was conducted. The second part of the protocol consisted of lists of facial signs, of features related to gaze, of positions of the head (upright and oblique), of vocal features, and of physical behavior and proxemic features of nonverbal behavior. The list of facial signs on the upper part of the face to be recorded (checked for) included the presence of: (a) lowered eyebrows; (b) eyebrows pressed together; and (c) lowered and drawn eyebrows, in the following forms; (a) raised eyebrows, (b) arched eyebrows, and (c) raised and arched eyebrows. From the characteristics of the observing person's gaze, we singled out: (a) strict looking into the eyes of the interlocutor; (b) turning the gaze to the side; and (c) looking down. On the lower part of the face, the frequency of smiling was checked for and recorded as occurring: often, occasionally, and not smiling. Vocal characteristics of speech which were examined and recorded, regardless of whether the communication was in the mother tongue or a foreign language, included the tone of speech, its pitch, the speed of speech, and pauses in speech. Physical and proxemic signs are described by the characteristics of the position of the body in space during face-to-face or telephone communication (the manner of sitting and moving). In evaluating the occurrence of such signs in the observational study, the sitting position could be described as: (a) upright; (b) reclining; or (c) leaning forward, while movement during communication could be reported as: (a) static standing; (b) moderately fast walking in both directions; or (c) the absence of movement or standing.

Design of the Study

The study was designed as a direct observation of nonverbal behavior in different situations to take place over a period of six to nine months. The sample of respondents consisted of employees in a highly successful private company—Live natural (Live natural, d.o.o., Niš, Serbia)—comprising five members, including the owner, who is also the head, and leader, of the company. In addition to the defined protocol established above, great attention was also paid to controlling variables in order to maintain objectivity in the observation, that is, to avoid any risk of transition into participant observation. For this reason, with the permission of the owner, arrivals were not announced and the time spent in observation was limited to three hours, regardless of the number of activities in the organization. In the first part of the research, the focus was on observing and qualifying the nonverbal behavior of the leader and the subordinates. After thusly assessing the trust of subordinates, the second part of the research was carried out, which involved the filling out of a questionnaire on interpersonal domination (Burgoon & Dunbar, 2006) by the subordinate employees, in which they assessed the leader.

What Was Confirmed and What Was Not?

The research lasted nine full months, during which 73 meetings were realized. The results of the provided questionnaire indicate that the subordinates assessed the leader as a person who is often consulted by others before making decisions, who has influence over others, who has pronounced skills in conducting conversations, and who is very successful in convincing others to behave in a desired way.

In addition to the above-mentioned behavioral correlates of the dominance of a leader who possesses substantial legitimate power, the following nonverbal signs of domination were noted in relation to the leading figure: constant mild frowning and smile control stood out as the dominant facial signs; regarding vocal characteristics of speech the most pronounced were: a commanding tone and moderately fast, soft, and short speech with rare pauses, the seeming function of which was to additionally direct the interlocutor's attention to communication. Nervousness was rarely registered in communication with subordinates. Dependent on the importance of the topic (problem) being discussed, the following were observed: the subordinate interlocutor would be interrupted by the leader while speaking, would be cut off abruptly in mid-sentence with the immediate suspension of communication (if the topic was deemed irrelevant), or the leader would be reading and replying to short messages on a cellphone during the conversation. Depending on the social context, eye contact was observed as direct, sometimes as threatening and provocative, or as completely disregarding (looking "through a subordinate"). Regarding postural signs, an upright posture and relaxed standing when there was no movement were observed. Spatial behavior was also observed as depending on the social context—the leader's leaning toward the interlocutor was noted only if there was seemingly a strong personal motivation to persuade. Otherwise, a relaxed spacing was noted—the leader's reclining in a chair with crossed legs so that the ankle of one leg was over the knee of the other leg.

The nonverbal behavior of subordinates was documented as being characterized by submissive pairings in terms of the facial signs of the upper and lower parts of the face: arched eyebrows and frequent smiling, more resembling grinning, or a silent, steady thin smile with the teeth visible, which subordinates seemed to use as a signal of reconciliation. In communication, there was noted: a "gathering" of oneself in the chair, expectantly waiting for a visual response, insecurity in verbal expression, and "relief" (long exhalation) after the conversation's end. Also, breaks in the vocalization of the subordinates in communication with the leader were observed as longer, likely in the function of avoiding possible consequences due to the words spoken. It was noted that subordinates raised the pitch of their speech when they felt threatened for some reason. Subordinates were also often documented as continuing to talk to themselves, or mutter, after the conversation with the leader was over.

The Role of the Nonverbal Behavior of the Leader in Motivating Subordinates

In addition to the general and largely confirmed signs of facial and bodily nonverbal behavior of the dominant person-leader, behavior in the function of increasing the motivation of subordinates to perform tasks was also registered. Seeming expectations of large business gains were observed as influencing the leader to mitigate his typical nonverbal behavior. When the situation appeared to require increased work motivation, a high level of flexibility and adaptability of nonverbal behavior toward subordinates was observed in the dominant person-leader. Depending on expectations, nonverbal behavior was seemingly adapted to each subordinate, which is in line with the findings of some studies into leaders' effectiveness regarding their nonverbal behavior (Eden et al., 2000; White & Locke, 2000). When the expectation was seen to be higher, the dominant person-leader was observed as employing a softer voice, a long and direct, yet warm gaze, direct speech, and a slight decrease in physical distance (tilting the body forward or approaching), which was regarded as an attempt to increase the sense of importance in the subordinate. The effect of this behavior was also seen as intending to produce greater and more adequate motivation for the quality and efficient execution of the corresponding task.

Based on the results of this study, it can be concluded that the nonverbal behavior and signs of facial expression of the dominant person-leader here are in line with the expectations based on the results of previous relevant research. Also, it can be concluded that the nonverbal behaviors of the dominant person-leader, as attributes of the leader, can influence the motivation and efficiency of subordinates.

Concluding Remarks

The presented study is a kind of operationalization of the point of view which served as the foundation and impetus of this chapter—that leadership is a complex interactive relationship based on, among other things, the social perception of the nonverbal behavior of actors directed at each other within the structure and dynamics of the group. For the purposes of this study, a special protocol was constructed and a design was devised which would include the actors in the processes of leadership: the leader and the members of the group. One dimension of the hierarchical relationship contained in the characteristics of domination was singled out; a set of nonverbal indicators was defined, which were treated as indicators of nonverbal behavior. The obtained results are interpretive, which indicates that the constructed protocol, with certain modifications and verifications, would be applicable in other studies with a similar intended subject of measurement. Also, based on the obtained results, it can be concluded that in examining nonverbal behavior in leadership, it is necessary that this process be monitored for a more extended period of time. This means monitoring in and across different situations through a series of activities in which multiple dynamic nonverbal signals are assessed. It is important to note that the monitoring of nonverbal behavior over a long period of time and in different situations allows for and combines the employment of the multiple approaches to studying leadership that we have elaborated upon. In this way, more complete insight can be gained into the importance of certain nonverbal indicators in other people, into the frequency of their presence and stability in the interpretation of domination, and into the effect of that experience on one's own behavior in close relationships, such as leadership. These factors also highlight that the applied protocol and research design implied, and imply in future relevant studies, the monitoring of nonverbal behavior in people who have functioned as a group for a longer period of time. This ensures that they know each other and through their joint work have certainly built cultural patterns and schemes in expressing, interpreting, and reacting to dominant forms of behavior. We are of the opinion that in addition to the basic and universal regularities and principles of nonverbal behavior in leadership, the specific factors of the established group structure and the dynamics and culture within each unique small group can also play a significant role.

The results of this and future similar research could serve as a scientific basis for building special skills of nonverbal communication, that is, the content of educational programs. The essential question is how to regard nonverbal communication as a skill.

Although it is extremely demanding, if not perhaps practically impossible, to single out and analyze only aspects of nonverbal behavior from the general processes of interaction in close relationships, such as leadership, which involve intense interactions, it is necessary for the purpose of scientific study. By highlighting nonverbal communication, isolating it in an almost unnatural way, as one of the skills that comprise the processes of leadership and management, we can present certain theoretical assumptions on how this subject may be possibly perceived and examined. Here, *social sensitivity* could be regarded as a key term, which raises the basic question: how can social sensitivity be understood and developed as a *skill* in at least two fundamentally relevant meanings of this word? The term *Skill* is, on the one hand, a characteristic that increases the probability of success in performing a task. Yet the term *skills* also refers to those personal characteristics that can develop to some extent under the assumption of possessing certain psychological dispositions. In our opinion, the general characteristic *social sensitivity* can become a skill in the context of the subject of *the leader*, in terms of the person's awareness of the importance of, and the corresponding ability to control, the manifestation of nonverbal signals. Yet social sensitivity as a skill implies the interpreting of, primarily at the level of a hypothesis rather than as a firm conclusion, other people's manifest verbal and nonverbal behavior in regard to their meaning and connection to the enduring characteristics of group members. This further necessitates the testing of such hypotheses through the processes of interaction between the leader and group members. Correspondingly, social sensitivity as a skill would further require the distinguishing of clear indicators of nonverbal behavior for assessing the characteristics of a particular person as a leader or of a particular person as a member of the group. From these indicators, schemes of interpretation of hierarchically different positions and roles in the group could be adopted and applied. In examining close relationships, such as leadership, this would inherently invoke the hierarchical dimension, which focuses on perceiving and interpreting certain aspects of nonverbal behavior that people find informative in explaining social situations based on the vertical difference of actors within the dynamics of a group.

References

Barnes, M. L., & Sternberg, R. J. (1989). Social intelligence and decoding of nonverbal cues. *Intelligence, 13*(3), 263–287.

Bass, B. M. (1990). *Bass and Stogdill's handbook of leadership*. Free Press.

Bass, B. M., & Bass, R. (2009). *The Bass handbook of leadership: Theory, research, and managerial applications*. Free Press.

Birdwhistell, R. L. (1968). Communication. *International Encyclopedia of the Social Sciences, 8*, 24–29.

Blake, R. R., & Mounton, J. S. (1964). *The managerial grid*. Gulf Publishing Company.

Blurton Jones, N. G. (1971). Criteria for use in describing facial expressions of children. *Human Biology, 43*(3), 365–413.

Brannigan, C. R., & Humphries, D. A. (1972). Human non-verbal behavior, a means of communication. In I. N. Blurton Jones (Ed.), *Ethological studies of child behavior* (pp. 37–64). Cambridge University Press.

Bryman, A. (1992). *Charisma and leadership in organizations*. Sage.

Burgoon, J. K., & Dunbar, N. E. (2006). Nonverbal expressions of dominance and power in human relationships. In V. Manusov & M. L. Patterson (Eds.), *The Sage handbook of nonverbal communication* (pp. 279–297). Sage Publications.

Camras, L. A. (1977). Facial expressions used by children in a conflict situation. *Child Development, 48*(4), 1431–1435. https://doi.org/10.2307/1128503

Cartwright, D., & Zander, A. (1960). *Group dynamics research and theory*. Row, Peterson.

Caruso, D. R., & Wolfe, C. J. (2004). Emotional intelligence and leadership development. In D. V. Day, S. J. Zaccaro, & S. M. Halpin (Eds.), *Leadership development for transforming organizations: Growing leaders for tomorrow* (pp. 237–266). Lawrence Erlbaum.

Chance, M. R. A. (1967). Attention structure as the basis of primate rank orders. *Man, 2*(4), 503–518.

Eden, D., Geller, D., Gewirtz, A., Gordon-Terner, R., Inbar, I., Liberman, M., Pass, Y., Salomon-Segev, I., & Shalit, M. (2000). Implanting Pygmalion Leadership Style through workshop training: Seven field experiments. *Leadership Quarterly, 11*, 171–210.

Ellsworth, P., & Ross, L. (1975). Intimacy in response to direct gaze. *Journal of Experimental Social Psychology, 11*(6), 592–613.

Ellyson, S. L., & Dovidio, J. F. (1985). *Power, dominance and nonverbal behavior* (Springer series in social psychology). Springer Nature Switzerland AG. ISBN 978-1-4612-5106-4.

Franceško, M. (2000). *Socijalno psihološki činioci stila rukovođenja u preduzeću*. Doktorska disertacija, Univerzitet u Novom Sadu.

Franceško, M. (2001). Psihološke dimenzije stila rukovođenja u preduzeću. *Strategijski menadžment*. Vol. 2. Ekonomski fakultet Subotica, pp. 98–104.

Franceško, M. (2003). *Kako unaprediti menadžment u preduzeću: Psihologija i menadžment*. Prometej.

Franceško, M., Kosanović, B., & Popović, J. (2009). Psihološka osnova suočavanja sa krizom: autoritarna struktura ličnosti i stil rukovođenja budućih menadžera (Psychological grounds for confronting the crisis: Authoritarian structure of personality and leadership style of future managers). In *Zbornik radova međunarodne konferencije Pojedinac, porodica i preduzeće u uslovima društveno-ekonomske krize: stanje i mogućnosti prevazilaženja (The Individual, the Family and the Company in the Light of Social and Economic Crisis)* (pp. 38–60). USEE Fakultet za pravne i poslovne studije. ISBN 978-86-7910-020-7.

Gifford, R. (1991). Mapping nonverbal behavior on the interpersonal circle. *Journal of Personality and Social Psychology, 61*, 398–412.

Grant, E. C. (1969). Human facial expression. *Man, 4*, 525–536.

Hall, J. A., Coats, E. J., & Smith LeBeau, L. (2005). Nonverbal behavior and the vertical dimension of social relations: A meta-analysis. *Psychological Bulletin, 131*(6), 898–924. https://doi.org/10.1037/0033-2909.131.6.898

Judge, T. A., Bonom, J. E., Ilies, R., & Gerhardt, M. W. (2002). Personality and leadership: A qualitative and quantitative review. *Journal of Applied Psychology, 87*, 765–780.

Katz, D., & Kahn, R. L. (1951). Human organization and worker motivation. In R. Tripp (Ed.), *Industrial productivity* (pp. 146–171). Industrial Relations Research Association.

Keating, C. F. (1985). Human dominance signals: The primate in us. In S. L. Ellyson & J. F. Dovidio (Eds.), *Power, dominance, and nonverbal behavior* (pp. 89–108). Springer-Verlag.

Keating, C. F., Mazur, A., & Segall, M. (1977). Facial gestures which influence the perception of status. *Sociometry, 40*, 374–378.

Kiesler, D. J., & Auerbach, S. M. (2003). Integrating measurement of control and affiliation in studies of physician-patient interaction: The interpersonal circumplex. *Social Science & Medicine, 57*(9), 1707–1722.

Kostić, A. (2008). *Govor bez reči.* [Speak without words]. University of Niš. Niš: Punta.

Kostić, A., Chadee, D., & Nedeljković, J. (2020). Reading faces: Ability to recognize true and false emotion. In R. J. Sternberg & A. Kostić (Eds.), *Social intelligence and nonverbal communication*. Palgrave Macmillan.

Larsen, K. S., Triplett, J. S., Brant, W. D., & Langenberg, D. (1979). Collaborator status, subject characteristics, and conformity in the Asch paradigm. *The Journal of Social Psychology, 108*(2), 259–263.

Lewin, K. (1951). *Field theory in social science*. Harper.

Likert, R. (1961). *New patterns of management*. McGraw-Hill.

Likert, R. (1967). *The human organization: Its management and value*. McGraw Hill.

Mann, R. D. (1959). A review of the relationships between personality and performance in small groups. *Psychological Bulletin, 56*(4), 241–270.

Mayer, J. D., Roberts, R. D., & Barsade, S. G. (2008). Human abilities: Emotional intelligence. *Annual Review of Psychology, 59*, 507–536. https://doi.org/10.1146/annurev.psych.59.103006.093646.

Mehrabian, A. (1972). *Nonverbal communication*. Aldine-Atherton.

Mintzberg, H. (1973). *The nature of managerial work*. Harper & Row.

Moskowitz, G. B. (1993). Individual differences in social categorization: The influence of personal need for structure on spontaneous trait inferences. *Journal of Personality and Social Psychology, 65*(1), 132–142.

Northouse, P. (2018). *Leadership: Theory and practice*. SAGA Publishing.

Pettinger, R. (1996). *Introduction to organizational behavior*. Macmillan Press Ltd.

Schmid Mast, M., & Hall, J. A. (2004). Who is the boss and who is not? Accuracy of judging status. *Journal of Nonverbal Behavior, 28*, 145–165.

Schmid Mast, M., & Hall, J. A. (2008). Expression and perception of dominance. In A. Kostić (Ed.), *Govor bez reči*. [Speech without words] (pp. 75–98). University of Niš. Niš: Punta.

Schmid Mast, M., & Cousin, G. (2013). Power, dominance, and persuasion. In J. Hall & M. Knapp (Eds.), *Nonverbal communication* (Handbooks of Communication Science) (pp. 613–635). Berlin/Boston: De Gruyter Mouton.

Stogdill, R. M. (1948). Personal factors associated with leadership: A survey of the literature. *Journal of Psychology, 25*, 35–71.

Stogdill, R. M. (1974). *Handbook of leadership – A survey of theory and research*. A Division of Macmillan Publishing, Inc.

Stogdill, R. M., & Coons, A. E. (Eds.). (1957). *Leader behaviors: Its description and measurement (Research monograph 88)*. Ohio State University, Bureau of Business Research.

Strongman, K. T., & Champness, B. G. (1968). Dominance hierarchies and conflict in eye contact. *Acta Psychologica, 28*, 376–386.

Tiedens, L. Z., & Jimenez, M. C. (2003). Assimilation for affiliation and contrast for control: Complementary self-construals. *Journal of Personality and Social Psychology, 85*(6), 1049–1061.

White, S. S., & Locke, E. A. (2000). Problems with the Pygmalion effect and some proposed solutions. *The Leadership Quarterly, 11*(3), 389–415.

Yukl, G. (1998). *Leadership in organizations*. Prentice Hall.

Yukl, G. (2006). *Leadership in organizations*. Pearson Educations.

Zaccaro, S. J., Kemp, C., & Bader, P. (2004). Leader traits and attributes. In J. Antonakis, A. T. Cianciolo, & R. J. Sternberg (Eds.), *The nature of leadership* (pp. 101–124). Sage Publications, Inc.

4

The Look of Love: Evolution and Nonverbal Signs and Signals of Attraction

Mark G. Frank, Anne Solbu, Zachary R. Glowacki, Zena Toh, and Madison Neurohr

Do you remember the first time you met someone and found yourself being attracted to them? What was it about them that made you feel that way? It could be their looks or certain personality traits that charmed us. Perhaps it was the kindness you saw in their eyes or their strong physique that made you feel safe. Or maybe it was how they moved, their fleeting smile or gestures that captivated. Whatever it was, scientists have been intrigued with first impressions and attraction, and whether attraction is something arbitrary, or a function of our upbringing, or based upon something deeper within our species.

In this chapter, we delve into the depths of time to speculate about how evolution may have shaped those appearance and behavioral signs

M. G. Frank (✉) • A. Solbu • Z. R. Glowacki • Z. Toh • M. Neurohr
University at Buffalo, State University of New York, Buffalo, NY, USA
e-mail: mfrank83@buffalo.edu; as255@buffalo.edu; zglowack@buffalo.edu; zenatoh@buffalo.edu; mneurohr@buffalo.edu

R. J. Sternberg, A. Kostić (eds.), *Nonverbal Communication in Close Relationships*,
https://doi.org/10.1007/978-3-030-94492-6_4

and signals that are perceived as more desirable—and hence more attractive—in human beings. We begin by examining the evolutionary process by which attractiveness matters, followed by describing those specific static and dynamic nonverbal features that are viewed as more attractive during initial encounters. We also outline nonverbal behaviors signaling and contributing to us falling for someone, and eventually experiencing trust and commitment, which evolved to facilitate further reproductive success (Diamond, 2003). We do note the vast majority of the theorizing we report has been done on or in relation to heterosexual relationships that have the potential for, or goal of, reproduction. This does not mean we discount any other romantic relationship of any consenting individual, but instead means the literature we describe may not capture the entire array of human romantic relationships.

Primitives of Attraction

Individuals from the same species compete for mates (Darwin, 1871). Darwin proposes that individuals with heritable traits that allowed them to adapt to their environments would be more likely to survive to the age of reproduction. Once at that age, they can vie for reproductive partners with the most desirable characteristics. Sexual selection can be classified as intraspecific and interspecific selection. Intraspecific selection involves competition between same-sex members for mating (most often male-male competition); interspecific selection involves selection of mate—often made by females (Brennan, 2010).

Although intraspecific selection was largely accepted, interspecific selection faced skepticism due to the lack of explanations for why females held preferences for certain sexual traits (Hosken & House, 2011). To address this, we note that it was Darwin who first argued that selection was not based on a beauty alone, but on abilities for females to distinguish between males. Furthermore, Fisher (1999) suggested there are cues that signaled healthier genes within males. Females who are more equipped to distinguish these cues would gain direct and indirect benefits from it. Direct benefits include material advantages such as protection and high-quality territory (Andersson & Simmons, 2006). Indirect benefits relate to the quality of offspring (Hosken & House, 2011). Females that attend to these cues would produce offspring who inherit these traits, thus leading to the evolution of specific sexual traits (Hosken & House, 2011). Those desirable features are considered to have high "reproductive fitness," meaning individuals high in those features are vied for within a group and are more likely to pass on their genes (Maynard-Smith, 1989).

Attraction is proposed to be paired with passion to produce sexual desire (Gonzaga et al., 2006). The attraction element is typically a rapid, nonconscious judgment that serves an adaptive function because those characteristics we find attractive are perceived to reflect healthier and stronger genes in that individual (Thornhill & Gangestad, 1999). In turn, those we find attractive have higher value as mates because being strong, free from disease, and able to have healthy children, were characteristics indicating fitness for reproduction. Individuals with higher reproductive fitness were seen as more desirable and better equipped to pass on their (our) genes to the next generation. Given that faces are the first thing we register when we look at another human being (Matsumoto et al., 2013), it is reasonable to suggest that *Homo sapiens* would be sensitive to (and attracted to) facial features of others. Those facial elements that indicate attractiveness would thus indicate higher mate value. This in turn helps comprehend why individuals seek to mate with attractive individuals (Little, 2014). Moreover, recent research has revealed that most of those aspects of a face we associate with attractiveness are also associated with health (Frank & Shaw, 2016; Re & Rule, 2016). Thus, at the proximal level, we may think we go about our lives being drawn to people because their face looks attractive to us; yet at a more distal level, we can argue that we instead go about our lives being drawn to people because their face signals health and good genes.

Nonverbal Static Features of the Face

The face is typically the first thing we see when engaging with a person, hence the phrase a "face-to-face" encounter. There are three types of nonverbal clues within a face that render information about the individual that will influence judgments of attractiveness (Ekman, 1978). Dynamic clues refer to facial expressions; these are facial movements done deliberately or involuntarily and reveal information about the emotional or cognitive state of the individual. Slow clues reflect the passage of time, such as facial maturity (Berry & McArthur, 1985), or the presence of wrinkles, sags, and other signs of aging. Static facial clues refer to simply appearance—when no movements are attempted.

There are numerous static qualities in a face that make an individual appear more or less attractive. Some features require context—for example, how attractive is someone's eyebrows? We argue that the attractiveness of those eyebrows likely depends upon a person's other facial features. Therefore, will not examine specific facial features, but instead report on more general static features that do not require as much context to evaluate their effect on attractiveness.

Those general qualities that make a face attractive are surprisingly similar across various cultures. Four types of static features are often discussed in the context of facial judgments of health and attractiveness: symmetry (e.g., Grammer & Thornhill, 1994; Penton-Voak et al., 2001; Rhodes et al., 2001); averageness (e.g., Rhodes et al., 2001); adiposity (e.g., Coetzee et al., 2009); and skin color/texture (e.g., Fink et al., 2001). Related to these are additional characteristics that are more gender dependent, such as sexual dimorphism (e.g., Perrett et al., 1998; Penton-Voak et al., 2001), and youth via adult baby faces (Berry & McArthur, 1985).

Symmetry

The more symmetrical a face, the more attractive it is perceived to be (e.g., Little et al., 2007). Symmetry has also been linked to physiological robustness (indicating higher genetic quality; Wade, 2010). Although many argue that a symmetrical face is preferred because it is easier to process visually, other work indicates only a symmetrical human female face was preferred to the asymmetrical version of that face—whereas no preference was shown for symmetrical macaque faces or art works (Little, 2014). Many studies have also shown symmetry to be strongly related to perceptions of increased health (Jones et al., 2004; Rhodes et al., 2001), whereas others have argued the association between actual health and symmetry is relatively weak (Kowner, 1996). More recent reviews have argued that despite the weak findings, trends indicate stronger immune system function with symmetrical faces (e.g., Re & Rule, 2016). Therefore, in an initial meeting, a person with a more symmetrical face will be seen as more attractive, and preferred over those with less symmetrical faces. Moreover, this symmetry has a mild relationship to that individual's various health markers.

Averageness

Averageness refers to the degree to which a face exhibits the mean variation of a sample of known human faces on features such as eye position, eye size, nose size, and so forth (e.g., Valentine et al., 2004). Research shows that more average faces are viewed as more attractive and healthier than more distinctive faces (e.g., Langlois & Roggman, 1990). Similar to symmetry, averageness is also associated (weakly) with actual health. For instance, one study showed that more distinctive faces of young adults—thus stronger deviation from an average face—was linked to poor childhood health in men and poor current health in women (Rhodes et al., 2001). It seemed that the most distinctive faces, compared to moderately distinctive or average faces, were the primary driver of this association to poor health (Zebrowitz & Rhodes, 2004). Some moderately distinctive faces are associated with attractiveness (e.g., adult female "babyfaces"; Berry & McArthur, 1985), but for other reasons that will be discussed later. Taken together, it appears that an average face is seen as more attractive, and is tied to health.

Facial Adiposity

Facial adiposity—the amount of fat under the surface of the skin on a face—affects perceptions of not only the weight of an individual (Coetzee et al., 2009), but also the attractiveness of that individual (Re & Rule,

2016). People with mid-range adiposity are seen as more attractive than those with too little or too much adiposity (see Re & Rule, 2016). Higher adiposity has been found to correlate with anxiety, stress, depression, and negative mood in women (Tinlin et al., 2012). Thus, for first impressions it seems symmetrical, average faces in terms of feature size and location, and average amounts of adiposity, are perceived as more attractive, and healthier, in both men and women.

Skin Color and Smoothness

The skin color is one of the most salient aspect of almost all human complexions (Re & Rule, 2016). Within the basic skin color, there are specific hues that can also reflect a person's health and attractiveness. Slightly redder skin is seen as healthier, as it reflects more oxygenation of the blood, which is a good sign of cardiovascular health (Armstrong & Welsman, 2001). A reddish skin hue also indicates better mate quality as it is related to both increased estrogen and testosterone (see Re & Rule, 2016). Research on nonhuman male primates shows males are particularly attracted to females displaying red (see Elliot & Niesta, 2008). For example, female baboons and chimpanzees will redden conspicuously when nearing ovulation, sending a clear sexual signal designed to attract males (Barelli et al., 2007). Therefore, a female face with more red hues in her face—either naturally or through blushing—is seen as more attractive (see Elliot & Niesta, 2008).

Relatedly, a slight yellow hue indicates a stronger immune system, as it suggests higher levels of beta carotene, an antioxidant that neutralizes free radicals that can harm a person's health (reviewed by Re & Rule, 2016).

Compared to darker skin, lighter skin allows for greater ultraviolet B ray penetration from sunlight. Ultraviolet B converts to vitamin D, which is important for mother and unborn child during pregnancy (Jablonski & Chaplin, 2000). As a result, this highlights a preference for lighter skin across cultures, including in darker skinned African cultures (Coetzee et al., 2012). However, paleness of the skin could indicate illness. Smoking hardens the capillaries and the connective tissue in the face, resulting in more skin wrinkles, making smokers to appear older and less attractive (Grady & Ernster, 1992). Taken together, skin that is smooth and one uniform color (versus blotched) and that displays subtle reds and yellows are seen as more attractive, younger, and healthier (e.g., Coetzee et al., 2012; Re & Rule, 2016).

Subtle color effects in the face continue this trend of symmetry, averageness, and adiposity whereby these colors not only accentuate attractiveness, but also reflect strong health. These are all important factors drawing an individual toward another, and suggest reproductive fitness can be a distal factor in driving our proximal judgments of attractiveness.

Color hues in the static face of individuals also introduce the topic of gender differences in the static facial qualities that represent reproductive fitness. For example, lighter skin is preferred by females (for themselves), or males are attracted to females in red (e.g., Elliot & Niesta, 2008). This is where reproductive fitness diverges for males and females. Although static features that indicate health apply to both sexes, additional features that suggest fertility will apply more strongly to females, whereas additional features that suggest dominance will apply more strongly to males (Frank & Shaw, 2016). The next set of static facial features will show this divergence.

Sexual Dimorphism

Sexual dimorphism refers to the appearance differences in a masculine versus a feminine face. Faces of males and females change at puberty (Farkas, 1987). An increase in testosterone levels in males enhances their jaw line and cheekbone; for females, estrogen inhibits the growth of those features, but an increase in lip size occurs (Rhodes, 2006). Although no single feature determines attraction (Armstrong, 2006), several facial features articulate the biological strength for reproductive success and therefore appear attractive. The good genes perspective predicts that humans prefer exaggerated sexual characteristics within the opposite sex as these signal fertility for women and dominance for males (i.e., sexual dimorphism; Penton-Voak et al., 2003; Scott et al., 2014). Thus, it is argued that a preference for masculinity in males and femininity in females guides our perceptions of attractiveness, particularly in an initial interaction.

Masculinity Masculinity in men's faces, such as a strong eyebrow ridge, a squared jaw, and high cheek bones, is associated with better health in puberty and adolescence (Rhodes et al., 2003). Although masculinity may be more attractive to women, ironically the higher testosterone typically handicaps a man through lower resistance to infection (see Muehlenbein & Bribiescas, 2005). This immunocompromise appears to break that pattern identified with other facial features, where attractive features reflect better health. However, scientists invoke the "Zahavi effect" (Zahavi, 1975) to address this apparent contradiction. The Zahavi effect argues that a factor that seems to reduce one's ability to survive—yet despite that handicap, the individual thrives—becomes evidence for overall genetic superiority. This is illustrated by the male peacock—those males with the most elaborate tails are seen as most desirable by female peahens even though the elaborate and heavy/oversized tail would drastically hinder the peacock's ability to escape predators. Therefore, if this male can survive with that sort of tail handicap, it must have otherwise excellent genes. High testosterone has other mixed positive and negative effects on behavior; it is associated with greater ability to fight and compete (Andersson, 1994) but also is associated with aggression and cheating on their romantic partner (e.g., Booth & Dabbs, 1993). Therefore, the relationship between masculinity and attractiveness in men's faces is less clear than the association between femininity and attractiveness in women's faces (e.g., DeBruine, 2014; also see below). Although some studies have documented a preference for more feminized male faces (Little et al., 2002), others suggested a preference for masculinized faces (DeBruine et al., 2006). Masculine features correlate with personality traits such as dominance (Perrett et al., 1998). Females tend to prefer more masculine male faces for short-term sexual relationships rather than long-term stable ones (Little & Jones, 2012). Moreover, women who live in rough dangerous neighborhoods, who fear crime, are more likely to choose more dominant-looking males than women living in nicer, safer neighborhoods (Penton-Voak et al., 2004; Ryder et al., 2016; Snyder et al., 2011).

Femininity Femininity in female faces is characterized by large eyes, full lips, a small and pointed chin, and high cheek bones. Johnston and Franklin (1993) noted when individuals created beautiful female faces, they generated more feminine traits by reducing chin size, creating fuller lips, and lowering the position of the eyes and nose in the facial areas. The hormone estrogen accounts for feminine facial features. Estrogen is linked to higher success in conceiving (Lipson & Ellison, 1996), and female faces are thus judged as more attractive (e.g., Jones, 2014). Feminine traits are further perceived as more nurturing, honest, and likeable (Paunonen et al., 1999).

Babyfaces One specific type of face, coined "babyface," combines these femininity features with perceived age features (Berry & McArthur, 1985). Babyface is a configuration of facial features in an adult face that more closely resemble the array of an infant's face than a mature adult's face. For example, infants have proportionally larger eyes, smaller noses, with eyes and brows positioned lower in the face. Human adults with babyface are perceived as kinder, warmer, more naïve, more approachable, easy going, and physically weaker—characteristics of the young—than mature-faced people (Gorn et al., 2008; Berry & McArthur, 1985; Masip et al., 2003; McArthur & Apatow, 1983, 1984). This difference in impression creates higher perceptions of attractiveness for those with babyfaces (Han et al., 2018). Scholars propose the reason we have these perceptions of people with a babyface is due to our evolutionary derived responses to infants. We perceive infants as weak and helpless and therefore in need of protection, whereas we ascribe more power and self- reliance to older members (Berry & McArthur, 1985). Evolutionary psychology goes further and suggests that women with these features are viewed as youthful, and youth in females is associated with fertility. Thus, a babyfaced female is seen as having higher reproductive fitness and hence is rated as more attractive (Zebrowitz & Franklin, 2014). In contrast, men with these babyface features would not be seen as more attractive, as maturity—not youth—is associated with dominance, and dominance has more reproductive fitness for men (reviewed in Frank & Shaw, 2016).

Summary of Static Facial Features

First impressions based upon someone's static features suggest those with symmetrical, average size and position of facial features, and average levels of adiposity, with smooth skin, with subtle red and yellow hues, will have advantages over others. This advantage is not based solely on their attractiveness, but those same features that cause them to look attractive also are weak to moderate reflections of their health. This in turn reflects of their good genes, which in turn suggests greater reproductive fitness. As a result, static features diverge into those tied to attractive perceptions of males, and those tied to the attractive perceptions of females. The proposed evolutionary significance of these attractive features remains reproductive fitness, but now fitness is proposed to be related to dominance for males, and fertility for females.

Nonverbal Static Features of the Body

When eyeing someone for the first time, we see not just their faces, but often their bodies. Research has shown that some of the same principles of reproductive fitness in static facial features also applies to static body features. Given that men are, on average, taller, have a higher proportion of muscle, and have heavier bones than women, we might expect these differences to parallel the sexual dimorphic notions of dominance and fertility found in male and female faces. This is what we find.

Height In males, size is associated with dominance. Men who are taller earn more money, and have higher authority status (Gawley et al., 2009). When evaluating resumes of two males that were identical except for their height, recruiters picked the taller man (Kurtz, 1969). Women prefer men taller than them (e.g., Swami et al., 2008), which might be why men often lie about height on online dating sites (Toma & Hancock, 2010). And if women are fearful in their environments—for whatever reason—their desire for more formidable (taller, more muscular, hence dominant) men increases (Ryder et al., 2016). Thus taller, larger men are usually seen as more attractive.

Body Shape In females, body mass index (BMI), or weight scaled for height, is associated with health and fertility. In Western populations, obese, and to a lesser extent overweight, female bodies are judged less attractive (e.g., Swami & Tovée, 2005) and less healthy than normal-weight bodies (e.g., Furnham et al., 2006). Likely, as a result, women may lie about their weight on online dating sites (Toma & Hancock, 2010). Preferences do change with culture and, in some non-Western (especially African) cultures, high-weight female bodies are considered attractive and fertile (e.g., Furnham et al., 2002). Both Western and non-Western observers judge underweight female bodies less attractive than normal-weight bodies (e.g., Furnham & Baguma, 1994).

However, it may be more than size alone, but the specific shape—as female body shape is associated with fertility. Women with a waist to hip ratio of 0.70 (e.g., see Singh, 2002) are judged to be more attractive to men in almost all cultures studied. This can be explained by the waist to hip ratio's relation to female fertility and that men are initially attracted to women who are more likely to be able to bear their offspring. Women with a waist to hip ratio higher than 0.85 are more likely to suffer from type II diabetes and heart disease, and are less likely to be fertile.

Interestingly, when we look at the conscious fashion choices of males and females, such as clothing, hair style, and so forth, they tend to enhance those features associated with dominance for males, and fertility for females. Clothing is the perfect vehicle to display a culture or social category (Morris, 1985) and can significantly influence perceptions of attractiveness. Studies show that women shown wearing red are rated significantly more attractive and sexually desirable by men than the exact same women shown with other colors (Elliot & Niesta, 2008). Clothing can connote dominance, and thus induce compliance, such that we are more likely to be persuaded by a man who wears a guard uniform (Bickman, 1974). These types of uniforms in men tend to slim the waist and exaggerate the shoulders. In contrast, women's fashions typically narrow the waist and exaggerate the hips and shoulders to produce a more hourglass shape, consistent with enhancing their waist to hip ratio.

Summary of Static Body Features

Taken together, it seems those features reflecting femininity in woman are seen as attractive, and associated with fertility. In contrast, those features reflecting masculinity in males are also seen as more attractive, but associated with dominance. These are the static features available on an initial encounter, and that are seen as attractive, and seem to denote reproductive fitness through health for both sexes; but diverge toward signs of fertility for females, and signs of dominance for males.

The Mere Exposure Factor

Regardless of these static features of faces or bodies, we know from research that the more exposed you are to someone, the more you tend to like them. Several experiments have shown that mere exposure to others can produce feelings of attraction (Moreland & Zajonc, 1982), even if little or no social interaction has taken place, such that people who are encountered more frequently will elicit greater feelings of attraction. Although the average attractiveness rating of typical faces and distinctive faces increased following exposure, there is no differential effect of exposure on typical and distinctive faces. Typical faces are significantly more attractive than distinctive faces (Peskin & Newell, 2004).

Moreover, repeated exposure to other people produces a belief that people are more similar to us in many ways (Moreland & Zajonc, 1982). Within interpersonal relationships, it can be seen that similarity is related to increased self-disclosure (Brockner & Swap, 1976). The more familiar a person is, the more one elicits greater feelings of attraction. We find others who are similar to us more attractive. Similarity also leads to likeability (Moreland & Zajonc, 1982). Furthermore, liking, exposure, and similarity, all jointly affect attraction (Brockner & Swap, 1976).

One evolutionary argument put forth is that males needed to be around to provide resources for the female after birth of a child; thus, females are more predisposed to reliable males who are more physically present (Buss, 1994). Thus, we would expect that this mere exposure effect would be stronger for females than for males, where their preference for faces would rise faster with exposure compared to males. In fact, research does show that females do prefer more familiar faces, compared to males, who prefer looking at novel faces (Little et al., 2014).

Nonverbal Dynamics of Attraction

When you meet someone, you take stock of their static features and consciously or unconsciously assess their attractiveness, which can proxy for their mate quality. At this point, expression intervenes—and these dynamic movements affect both judgments of attractiveness, as well as judgments of the other's interest in advancing the relationship in a direction of an actual romantic date. After all, people are not still photographs—they move. However, these characteristics tend to reflect the intention of someone initiating a relationship, rather than an expression of health, fertility, or dominance—sort of. We commonly call many of these behaviors 'flirting', as they express interest in the other. Although men and women do tend to show similar dynamic behaviors when flirting, when they do diverge it is again in the direction of receptive, demure, submissive style face and body behaviors by women, and more assertive, dominant style behaviors for men (Hall & Xing, 2015).

The Face

The Smile One element that stands out is that facial expressions can make people look more or less attractive. The smile is the foremost expression that makes people look more approachable, and hence attractive. In fact, a smile can raise the attractiveness rating of a face so as to more than compensate for an unattractive static face (Golle et al., 2014). Smiles are also one of the top signs that someone is in fact interested in another person as well (Muehlenhard et al., 1986; Wade et al., 2021). Darwin (1872/1998) suggested that the smile is the most distinct human facial expression, and its movement elements are designed to simply not look like negative facial expressions such as anger or fear (his principle of 'antithesis', or the opposite of those negative expressions). Research has shown that the smile, and its underlying emotion happiness, is the least likely confused with other more negative emotions such as anger, contempt, disgust, fear, and sadness (Ekman, 2003). Taken together, the smile serves to both make one look more attractive, as well as signal he or she is approachable.

The Blush When a woman becomes sexually aroused, there is an increase in blood flow to various parts of her body, the two most visible during a face to face encounter being her cheeks (particularly visible in Caucasian woman) and her lips. This produces a blush, and it is an involuntary action—meaning it is produced whether or not a woman wishes to show it. Women who show these signals are seen as more attractive (McKinney & Sprecher, 1991). We note that the application of cosmetics in women mimics these signs of sexual arousal, such that blush is applied to the cheeks, and red-hued lipstick applied to the lips, and this can make a non-aroused woman look more attractive. We do know nonhuman primates often signal sexual receptivity by conspicuously blushing—or reddening, typically in their backside—which very effectively attracts males (e.g., Barelli et al., 2007). Thus, it appears that human females suggesting sexual receptivity via arousal clues also attracts heterosexual males, who in turn rate them as more attractive.

The Eyes The eyes also can reflect an involuntary action that makes someone not only look more attractive, but also connotes interest in the other—and that action is the dilation of the eye's pupils (Hess, 1965). Identical photos of women, where only one image has the woman's pupils artificially dilated, shows routinely men and women rate the photo with the dilated image as more attractive (Hess, 1965; although there have been some failures to replicate; e.g., Hensley, 1990). Thus, one sign a person is interested in another—for both men and women—is their pupil dilation (Stass & Willis, 1967), although the dilation is harder to detect in those with dark brown eyes.

A second way in which eye behavior can signal attraction is in our gaze. In day-to-day life, we gaze and glance at others around us. Typically, we feel more comfortable with short acknowledgments of eye contact with strangers (known as "civil inattention"; Goffman, 1959). This means a quick glance feels better than an extended stare, or a complete avoidance of eye contact (Zuckerman et al., 1983).

When someone is interested, the length of the eye contact increases; both men and women agree (Muehlenhard et al., 1986; Wade et al., 2021). Eye contact triggers the release of oxytocin, and can be a powerful nonverbal cue that plays a vital role in relationships and falling in love (Aron et al., 1997). Moreover, looking deeply and comfortably into the eyes communicates a lot about the emotional desire a person has, and holding eye gaze for periods of time (e.g., four seconds) has shown to indicate signal signs of not just attraction but love (Aron et al., 1997).

The Body

The movements of the body, including its position compared to the body of the other, is an important source of information regarding behavioral intentions. These movements tend to represent instrumental actions (Frank & Svetieva, 2013)—instrumental toward making one's self more presentable, as well as instrumental in getting closer to the desired person.

Preening Gestures Making the individuals body more attractive is accomplished through preening gestures, which are gestures designed to organize and groom so as to make one appear more 'presentable' (Moore, 1985). This term was first used to describe birds, who during courtship rituals would use their beaks to smooth out their feathers (e.g., Richner & Wilson, 2019). Within humans, this is often displayed in females by flipping her hair, or running her fingers through their hair so as to organize it, adjusting her clothing, smoothing it out, and so forth. Males typically do not have as long a hair as females, so the hair flip does not show up in the literature, however other hair and clothing adjustments do (Moore, 1998). Preening gestures suggest one is preparing for closer contact with another person.

Postural Proximity If one is attracted to another, it seems reasonable that they will want to get physically closer to that other. Within the posture, we see individuals who are interested will incline, or lean in, toward each other, will stand closer together—to the edge of the 'intimate zone' (18 inches/45 cm; Hall, 1966) which is closer than normal casual conversations. They will also orient themselves so as to face each other directly, versus the normal oblique social angles people adopt when in casual conversation (Moore, 1985, 1998; Muehlenhard et al., 1986). These actions also have the effect of closing off other potentially distracting information from the two individuals. Within these behaviors, women may be more likely to show a head cant—a tilt slightly sideways and backward, that some ethologists suggest exposes the neck and hence displays submission, whereas a male will stiffen and stand more upright, hence making himself larger and hence more dominant (Morris, 1967).

Although proximity is a key factor for falling in love, it should not be forced (Braxton-Davis, 2010; Moore, 1998). This process should occur naturally, comfortably, and with ease, or else it might reflexively be rejected. Prior research supports postural expansiveness (similar to proximity) and relaxation to convey greater intimacy, affection, receptivity/trust, similarity/depth/equality, composure, and informality compared to a closed or tense posture (Vacharkulksemsuk et al., 2016). However, Burgoon (1991) concluded that relaxation cues to be associated primarily with status, thereby, a relaxed, open posture is only dominant when enacted by men. Close proximity is also more immediate, but dominant. When proximity is combined with postural openness, it creates a strong message of composure, similarity, and affection. Thus, these behaviors—typically implicated as involvement, affection, and dominance signals—carry significant meaning to similarity, receptivity/trust, informality, and composure (Burgoon, 1991).

Touch The ultimate 'distance closer' is to actually touch the individual. A touch can express affection via physical closeness. Intimate touch may include kissing, hugging, and holding hands amongst others and are signs of strong romantic interest. Research has shown touching to convey more composure, immediacy, receptivity/trust, affection, similarity/depth/equality, and informality, and in particular when it is reciprocal (Burgoon, 1991).

Human beings are wired to touch and be touched as this is the bedrock of how we bond, form relationships, and engage in prosocial behaviors (Williams, 2020). Both hugging and positive touch (e.g., hand on the shoulder) send signals to the brain to release oxytocin—a hormone involved in increasing positive, feel-good sensations of trust, emotional bonding, and social connection (Dunbar, 2010). It also facilitates the release of dopamine—a pleasurable feel-good hormone that promotes more enjoyable sensory experiences (Lieberman & Long, 2018). Similarly, hugs decrease fear and anxiety responses in the brain while positive human touch helps fight off infections (Zak, 2012). Further, hugs convey proximity and intimacy that help establish and maintain close relationships (Sekerdej et al., 2018). Additionally, positive touch enhances prosocial behavior; while influencing helping behavior. Thus, when two individuals are romantically interested, physical touch becomes enjoyable—producing several positive physiological responses, which does motivate a male to stay in closer proximity to a female and for a longer period of time, facilitating the establishment of pair-bonds (Frank, 1988; Gonzaga & Haselton, 2008; Zeifman & Hazan, 1997).

There again are implications for dominance. Early in a relationship, males tend to initiate touch, whereas in stable relationships females initiate (Guerrero & Andersen, 1991). Touching a lesser-known other—which is an intrusion upon their space—can be an expression of dominance (Matsumoto et al., 2016). Women tend to touch more indirectly, maybe with shoulder lean in to the male, or other forms of more 'incidental' contact. This also includes touches in socially acceptable safe zones of the body, such as the forearm or shoulder (Moore, 1985), but as the encounter progresses touches can move to more intimate zones, such as above the knee (Muehlenhard et al., 1986). However, touches that are not reciprocated, or rejected, are a clear sign that the rejector has no romantic interests in the other (Moore, 1998).

Dyadic Actions Instrumental actions convey closeness between two individuals in a potential romantic encounter, but there are also interactive dyadic actions that suggest a relationship is forming. A result of this mutual attention and positivity, the individuals move next toward coordinating their behaviors in the interaction; this state is referred to as being in rapport (Tickle-Degnen & Rosenthal, 1987, 1990). When individuals are in rapport, they disclose more information (Collins et al., 2002; Frank et al., 2006; Novotny et al., 2021), which research suggests is one of the strongest ways to build intimacy between individuals (Jenner & Myers, 2019). Moreover, rapport also involves the synchronization, or mirroring of each other's general body postures (Tickle-Degnen & Rosenthal, 1990); and this more likely occurs when the individual is enjoying the interaction; moreover, by actively mirroring another one can get them to like you more (Chartrand & Bargh, 1999). The nonverbal elements of rapport between two individuals becomes like a subtle, coordinated dance; which then becomes a feedback loop where the more comfortable they feel with each other, the more coordination; and the more coordination, the more comfortable they feel with each other.

Summary of Nonverbal Dynamics of the Face and Body

The static features of individual's faces and bodies suggest those features that we find attractive tend to reflect good genes, and reflect signs of fertility in females, and signs of dominance in males. In contrast, those dynamic features of individual's faces and bodies tend to reflect preparation for engagement, and intentions for intimacy. They are often involuntary displays of arousal, which make an individual look more attractive, as well as voluntary actions designed to get closer to, and obtain physical contact with, the desired other. These behaviors ultimately coordinate and synchronize as these individuals approach a state of rapport. Note that there is still a mild thread of sexual dimorphism in these behaviors, such that when female and male courtship behaviors diverge, they diverge along the lines of submissive, receptive type behaviors in females, and assertive, dominant type behaviors in males.

Nonverbal Dynamics of a Genuine Relationship

Once the two individuals have identified each other as attractive, and then taken steps to get closer, and have fallen into rapport and are now considered in a relationship, there are nonverbal signs and signals that this relationship is moving forward or deepening.

Attention

Paying attention to one another is clearly a sign that a relationship exists. Thus, eye gaze, and being physically close, and touching, all demonstrate attention. These signs serve to monitor whether one needs attention; and can be used—specifically touch and eye gaze—to command attention (Matsumoto et al., 2013). Attention also plays a crucial role in creating memories and allows us to avoid distractions so we can focus on and complete specific tasks (Myers et al., 2017). Attentiveness is a vital sign someone is deepening a romantic relationship. This involves an investment of a tremendous amount of time and resources into their partner—time and resources that cannot be given to other potential mates (Galperin & Haselton, 2010). This process is coined an 'honest signal'—because it is difficult to commit and 'fake' love—thus, the recipient can be assured that his or her partner is committed to the relationship (Galperin & Haselton, 2010). From an evolutionary perspective, women have higher levels of investment in offspring (e.g., pregnancy) and are more dependent on others to provide resources (e.g., food) as well as assistance in caring for the offspring. As a result, women are faced with higher pressure (e.g., getting pregnant) to find a man willing to 'commit' and devote his full attention to the romantic relationship. Therefore, there is usually a greater responsibility on men to show commitment (e.g., attention)—an honest signal that one is in love (Galperin & Haselton, 2010).

Trust

Trust is believed to be the single most important element for the development and maintenance of happy, well-functioning relationships. Attachment theory and theory of psychosocial development are built on the premise that higher levels of trust in relationships lay the psychological foundation for happier and better-functioning relationships in adulthood (Bowlby, 1969; Erikson, 1963). Further research suggests that processing trust signals evolved in humans, given the importance of accurately gauging the intentions of others. Trust entails certain beliefs and attitudes about how likely romantic partners are to be reliable, cooperative, or helpful in various life situations (Simpson, 2007). Therefore, those who send clear signals—nonverbal or otherwise—will be trusted more than those who send unclear, or subtle signals. Research supports this notion as participants who showed overt facial expressions of disgust when drinking a sour drink were rated more trustworthy than those who showed micromomentary facial expressions of disgust (Glowacki et al., 2021).

Trust is also depicted as the psychological state of one individual (e.g., truster) toward a partner (e.g., trustee) with whom the truster is codependent with the trustee's cooperation to attain positive outcomes and resources. The specific nonverbal behaviors that convey trust are best categorized as those that connote affiliation. Conversely, the specific nonverbal behaviors that suggest untrustworthiness connote avoidance. Some of the specific nonverbal signals of trust shown in a competitive economic game include smiles, leaning forward, laughing, and nodding; untrustworthiness signals included touching one's own face and hands, crossing one's arms, and leaning away (DeSteno et al., 2012).

Commitment

Some scholars contend that long-lasting love to include three major components: intimacy, passion, and commitment (Sternberg, 1986). These three components (e.g., intimacy, passion, and commitment) have been linked with relationship satisfaction and tend to vary as relationships evolve. Intimacy, passion, and commitment increase over time as couples begin to progress through their various relationship stages (e.g., dating, monogamy, engagement; Gao, 2001). However, Sternberg (1986) proposes that passion and intimacy decline within a relationship, yet commitment increases for partners that stay in love. Commitment has shown to be the strongest link with relationship satisfaction (Acker & Davis, 1992).

When people are committed, they reinforce their relationship with gaze, soft voices, and touch (Sim et al., 2019). In a longer-term commitment, these nonverbal signals are expressed often (Gottman, 1994), and are reciprocated, although in longer-term commitments women tend to initiate touch more than men (Guerrero & Andersen, 1991).

Conclusion

The journey from noticing, approaching, interacting, and then claiming a relationship with another involves nonverbal communication at each step of the process. Moreover, each of these nonverbal behaviors does not occur in some theoretical vacuum; they seem to be remnants of our evolutionary past. On a proximal level, it would seem we find someone attractive, approach them without rejection, seem to be 'in sync', and then find ourselves together in the mystery of love. This description is the fodder for novels. Yet on the distal level, it is instead proposed we find someone attractive because they look healthy, likely have good genes, and depending upon their sex are fertile or dominant. We then find attractive the fact that we sexually arouse the other, and we then move in closer physically, and then rhythmically coordinate our behavior, and then find ourselves pair-bonded and ready to reproduce. This description is the fodder for evolutionary social scientists.

In conclusion, we would argue that the romantic notions that seed our novels do in fact have deep evolutionary roots. At each step in the process, there are measurable static and nonverbal behaviors that suggest health, attraction, compatibility, and commitment. We hasten to add that anatomy, phylogeny, and nonverbal signs are not destiny. We are not passive prisoners of our biological drives, but are constantly learning, forming likes and dislikes, establishing and adhering to social norms for conduct that reduces conflict and advances toward equality for all. In relationships, so many other qualities intervene, including compatibility of personalities, morals, values, and other characteristics individual to each. Once these bonds become stronger, other evolutionary factors such as attention, trust, and commitment come in to play to serve needs of the individuals involved—be it child rearing, or longer-term romantic engagement, or both. However, even with these more abstract qualities, we believe nonverbal communication will always play a part in expressing these qualities to each of the romantic partners, as well as expressing the status of their relationship to any civilian or social scientist observing them in public.

References

Acker, M., & Davis, M. H. (1992). Intimacy, passion and commitment in adult romantic relationships: A test of the triangular theory of love. *Journal of Social and Personal Relationships, 9*(1), 21–50.

Andersson, M., & Simmons, L. W. (2006). Sexual selection and mate choice. *Trends in Ecology & Evolution, 21*(6), 296–302.

Andersson, M. B. (1994). *Sexual selection*. Princeton University Press.

Armstrong, J. (2006). *The secret power of beauty*. Penguin Global.

Armstrong, N., & Welsman, J. R. (2001). Peak oxygen uptake in relation to growth and maturation in 11–17 year old humans. *European Journal of Applied Physiology, 85*, 546–551.

Aron, A., Melinat, E., Aron, E. N., Vallone, R. D., & Bator, R. J. (1997). The experimental generation of interpersonal closeness: A procedure and some preliminary findings. *Personality and Social Psychology Bulletin, 23*(4), 363–377.

Barelli, C., Heistermann, M., Boesch, C., & Reichard, U. H. (2007). Sexual swellings in wild white-handed gibbon females (Hylobates lar) indicate the probability of ovulation. *Hormones and Behavior, 51*(2), 221–230.

Berry, D. S., & McArthur, L. Z. (1985). Some components and consequences of a babyface. *Journal of Personality and Social Psychology, 48*(2), 312–323.

Bickman, L. (1974). The social power of a uniform. *Journal of Applied Social Psychology, 4*, 47–61.

Booth, A., & Dabbs, J. M. (1993). Testosterone and men's marriages. *Social Forces, 72*, 463–477.

Bowlby, J. (1969). *Attachment and loss, volume 1 attachment*. Basic Books.

Braxton-Davis, P. (2010). The social psychology of love and attraction. *McNair Scholars Journal, 4*(1), 6–12.

Brennan, P. (2010). Sexual selection. *Nature Education Knowledge, 3*(10), 79.

Brockner, J., & Swap, W. C. (1976). Effects of repeated exposure and attitudinal similarity on self-disclosure and interpersonal attraction. *Journal of Personality and Social Psychology, 33*(5), 531.

Burgoon, J. K. (1991). Relational interpretations of touch, conversational distance, and posture. *Journal of Nonverbal Behavior, 15*, 233–259.

Buss, D. (1994). *The evolution of desire*. Basic Books.

Chartrand, T. L., & Bargh, J. A. (1999). The chameleon effect: The perception–behavior link and social interaction. *Journal of Personality and Social Psychology, 76*(6), 893–910. https://doi.org/10.1037/0022-3514.76.6.893

Coetzee, V., Faerber, S. J., Greeff, J. M., Lefevre, C. E., Re, D. E., & Perrett, D. I. (2012). African perceptions of female attractiveness. *PLoS One, 7*, e48116.

Coetzee, V., Perrett, D. I., & Stephen, I. D. (2009). Facial adiposity: A cue to health? *Perception, 38*, 1700–1711.

Collins, R., Lincoln, R., & Frank, M. G. (2002). The effect of rapport in forensic interviewing. *Psychiatry, Psychology, & Law, 9*, 69–78.

Darwin, C. (1871). *The descent of man: Selection in relation to sex*. John Murray.

Darwin, C. (1872/1998). *The expression of the emotions in man and animals*. (3rd Ed.) With *introduction, afterword, and commentary* by Paul Ekman. New York: Oxford University Press.

DeBruine, L. M. (2014). Women's preferences for male facial features. In V. A. Weekes-Shackelford & T. K. Shackelford (Eds.), *Evolutionary perspectives on human sexual psychology and behavior* (pp. 261–275). Springer.

DeBruine, L. M., Jones, B. C., Little, A. C., Boothroyd, L. G., Perrett, D. I., Penton-Voak, I. S., . . . Tiddeman, B. P. (2006). Correlated preferences for facial masculinity and ideal or actual partner's masculinity. Proceedings of the Royal Society B-Biological Sciences, 273, 1355–1360.

DeSteno, D., Breazeal, C., Frank, R. H., Pizarro, D., Baumann, J., Dickens, L., & Lee, J. J. (2012). Detecting trustworthiness of novel partners in economic exchange. *Psychological Science, 23*(12), 1549–1556.

Diamond, L. (2003). What does sexual orientation orient? A biobehavioral model distinguishing romantic love and sexual desire. *Psychological Review, 110*(1), 173–192. https://doi.org/10.1037//0033-295X.110.1.173

Dunbar, R. I. M. (2010). The social role of touch in humans and primates: Behavioural function and neurobiological mechanisms. *Neuroscience Biobehavioral Reviews, 34*, 260–268.

Ekman, P. (1978). Facial signs: Facts, fantasies, and possibilities. In T. Sebeok (Ed.), *Sight, sound, and sense* (pp. 124–156). Indiana University Press.

Ekman, P. (2003). *Emotions revealed: Recognizing faces and feelings to improve emotional life*. Times Books/Henry Holt & Co.

Elliot, A. J., & Niesta, D. (2008). Romantic red: Red enhances men's attraction to women. *Journal of Personality and Social Psychology, 95*, 1150–1164.

Erikson, E. H. (1963). *Youth: Change and challenge*. Basic books.

Farkas, L. G. (1987). Age-and sex-related changes in facial proportions. In L. G. Farkas & I. R. Munro (Eds.), *Anthropometric facial proportions in medicine* (pp. 29–56). Charles C Thomas Publisher Ltd.

Fink, B., Grammer, K., & Thornhill, R. (2001). Human (Homo sapiens) facial attractiveness in relation to skin texture and color. *Journal of Comparative Psychology, 115*, 92–99.

Fisher, H. E. (1999). *The first sex: The natural talents of women and how they are changing the world*. Random House.

Frank, M. G., & Shaw, A. Z. (2016). Evolution and nonverbal communication. In D. Matsumoto, H. C. Hwang, & M. G. Frank (Eds.), *Handbook of nonverbal communication* (pp. 45–76). American Psychological Association press.

Frank, M. G., & Svetieva, E. (2013). The role of nonverbal behavior in detecting and telling lies. In M. L. Knapp & J. A. Hall (Eds.), *Nonverbal communication* (pp. 471–511). Mouton de Gruyter.

Frank, M. G., Yarbrough, J. D., & Ekman, P. (2006). Improving interpersonal evaluations: Combining science and practical experience. In T. Williamson (Ed.), *Investigative interviewing: Rights, research, regulation* (pp. 229–255). Willan Publishing.

Frank, R. H. (1988). *Passions within reason: The strategic role of the emotions*. W. W. Norton.

Furnham, A., & Baguma, P. (1994). Cross-cultural differences in the evaluation of male and female body shapes. *International Journal of Eating Disorders, 15*(1), 81–89.

Furnham, A., Moutafi, J., & Baguma, P. (2002). A cross-cultural study on the role of weight and waist-to-hip ratio on female attractiveness. *Personality and Individual Differences, 32*(4), 729–745.

Furnham, A., Swami, V., & Shah, K. (2006). Body weight, waist-to-hip ratio and breast size correlates of ratings of attractiveness and health. *Personality and Individual Differences, 41*(3), 443–454.

Galperin, A., & Haselton, M. (2010). Predictors of how often and when people fall in love. *Evolutionary Psychology, 8*(1), 147470491000800102.

Gao, G. (2001). Intimacy, passion, and commitment in Chinese and US American romantic relationships. *International Journal of Intercultural Relations, 25*(3), 329–342.

Gawley, T., Perks, T., & Curtis, J. (2009). Height, gender, and authority status as work: Analyses or a national sample of Canadian workers. *Sex Roles, 60*, 208–222.

Glowacki, Z. R., Frank, M. G., & Neurohr, M. (2021). *Do we like Honest Signal Givers? An Evolutionary lens comparing different facial displays of disgust on various traits.* Paper to be presented at the Annual National Communication Association Conference, Seattle, November 18–21.

Goffman, E. (1959). *The presentation of self in everyday life*. Penguin.

Golle, J., Mast, F. W., & Lobmaier, J. S. (2014). Something to smile about: The interrelationships between attractiveness and emotional expression. *Cognition & Emotion, 28*(2), 298–310. https://doi.org/10.1080/02699931.2013.817383

Gonzaga, G. C., & Haselton, M. G. (2008). The evolution of love and long-term bonds. *Social Relationships: Cognitive, Affective, and Motivational Processes, 10*, 39.

Gonzaga, G. C., Turner, R. A., Keltner, D., Campos, B., & Altemus, M. (2006). Romantic love and sexual desire in close relationships. *Emotion, 6*(2), 163.

Gorn, G. J., Jiang, Y., & Johar, G. V. (2008). Babyfaces, trait inferences, and company evaluations in a public relations crisis. *Journal of Consumer Research, 35*(1), 36–49.

Gottman, J. M. (1994). *What predicts divorce? The relationship between marital processes and marital outcomes*. Hillsdale, NJ: Lawrence Erlbaum Associates, Inc.

Grady, D., & Ernster, V. (1992). Does cigarette smoking make you ugly and old? *American Journal of Epidemiology, 135*(8), 839–842.

Grammer, K., & Thornhill, R. (1994). Human (Homo sapiens) facial attractiveness and sexual selection: The role of symmetry and averageness. *Journal of Comparative Psychology, 108*, 233–242.

Guerrero, L. K., & Andersen, P. A. (1991). The waxing and waning of relational intimacy: Touch as a function of relational stage, gender, and touch avoidance. *Journal of Personal and Social Relationships, 8*, 147–165.

Hall, E. T. (1966). *The hidden dimension*. Doubleday.

Hall, J. A., & Xing, C. (2015). The verbal and nonverbal correlates of the five flirting styles. *Journal of Nonverbal Behavior, 39*(1), 41–68.

Han, S., Li, Y., Liu, S., Xu, Q., Tan, Q., & Zhang, L. (2018). Beauty is in the eye of the beholder: The halo effect and generalization effect in the facial attractiveness evaluation. *Acta Psychologica Sinica, 50*(4), 363–376.

Hensley, W. E. (1990). Pupillary dilation revisited: The constriction of a nonverbal cue. *Journal of Social Behavior and Personality, 5*, 97–104.

Hess, E. H. (1965). Attitude and pupil size. *Scientific American, 212*, 45–54.

Hosken, D. J., & House, C. M. (2011). Sexual selection. *Current Biology, 21*(2), 62–65. https://doi.org/10.1016/j.cub.2010.11.053

Jablonski, N. G., & Chaplin, G. (2000). The evolution of human skin coloration. *Journal of Human Evolution, 39*, 57–106.

Jenner, B. M., & Myers, K. C. (2019). Intimacy, rapport, and exceptional disclosure: A comparison of in-person and mediated interview contexts. *International Journal of Social Research Methodology, 22*(2), 165–177. https://doi.org/10.1080/13645579.2018.1512694

Johnston, V. S., & Franklin, M. (1993). Is beauty in the eye of the beholder? *Ethology and Sociobiology, 14*(3), 183–199. https://doi.org/10.1016/0162-3095(93)90005-3

Jones, B. C. (2014). Agreement and individual differences in men's preferences for women's facial characteristics. In V. A. Weekes-Shackelford & T. K. Shackelford (Eds.), *Evolutionary perspectives on human sexual psychology and behavior* (pp. 87–102). Springer.

Jones, B. C., Little, A. C., Burt, D. M., & Perrett, D. I. (2004). When facial attractiveness is only skin deep. *Perception, 33*, 569–576.

Kowner, R. (1996). Facial asymmetry and attractiveness judgement in developmental perspective. *Journal of Experimental Psychology: Human Perception and Performance, 22*(3), 662.

Kurtz, D. L. (1969). Physical appearance and stature: Important variables in sales recruiting. *The Personnel Journal, 48*, 981–983.

Langlois, J. H., & Roggman, L. A. (1990). Attractive faces are only average. *Psychological Science, 1*, 115–121.

Lieberman, D. Z., & Long, M. E. (2018). *The molecule of more: How a single chemical in your brain drives love, sex, and creativity – And will determine the fate of the human race*. BenBella Books, Inc.

Lipson, S. F., & Ellison, P. T. (1996). Comparison of salivary steroid profiles in naturally occurring conception and non-conception cycles. *Human Reproduction, 11*, 2090–2096.

Little, A. C. (2014). Domain specificity in human symmetry preferences: Symmetry is most pleasant when looking at human faces. *Symmetry, 6*, 222–233. https://doi.org/10.3390/sym6020222

Little, A. C., DeBruine, L. M., & Jones, B. C. (2014). Sex differences in attraction to familiar and unfamiliar opposite-sex faces: Men prefer novelty and women prefer familiarity. *Archives of Sexual Behavior, 43*(5), 973–981.

Little, A. C., & Jones, B. C. (2012). Variation in facial masculinity and symmetry preferences across the menstrual cycle is moderated by relationship context. *Psychoneuroendocrinology, 37*, 999–1008.

Little, A. C., Jones, B. C., Burt, D. M., & Perrett, D. I. (2007). Preferences for symmetry in faces change across the menstrual cycle. *Biological Psychology, 76*, 209–216.

Little, A. C., Penton-Voak, I. S., Burt, D. M., & Perrett, D. I. (2002). Evolution and individual differences in the perception of attractiveness.: How cyclic hormonal changes in self-perceived attractiveness influence female preferences for male faces. In G. Rhodes & L. A. Zebrowitz (Eds.), *Facial attractiveness* (pp. 59–90). Ablex.

Masip, J., Garrido, E., & Herrero, C. (2003). Facial appearance and judgments of credibility: The effects of facial babyishness and age on statement credibility. *Genetic Social and General Psychology Monographs, 129*(3), 269.

Matsumoto, D., Frank, M. G., & Hwang, H. C. (2013). *Nonverbal communication: Science and applications*. Sage.

Matsumoto, D., Hwang, H. C., & Frank, M. G. (2016). The body: Postures, gait, proxemics, and haptics. In D. Matsumoto, H. C. Hwang, & M. G. Frank (Eds.), *Handbook of nonverbal communication* (pp. 387–400). American Psychological Association press.

Maynard-Smith, J. (1989). *Evolutionary genetics*. Oxford University Press. ISBN 978-0-19-854215-5

McArthur, L. Z., & Apatow, K. (1983–84). Impressions of baby-faced adults. *Social Cognition, 2*(4), 315–342.

McKinney, K., & Sprecher, S. (1991). *Sexuality in close relationships*. Lawrence Erlbaum Associates Inc.

Moore, M. M. (1985). Nonverbal courtship patterns in women: Context and consequences. *Ethology and Sociobiology, 6*, 237–247.

Moore, M. M. (1998). Nonverbal courtship patterns in women: Rejection signaling – An empirical investigation. *Semiotica, 118*(3–4), 201–214.

Moreland, R. L., & Zajonc, R. B. (1982). Exposure effects in person perception: Familiarity, similarity, and attraction. *Journal of Experimental Social Psychology, 18*(5), 395–415.

Morris, D. (1967). *The naked ape*. Delta.

Morris, D. (1985). *Bodywatching: A field guide to the human species*. Outlet.

Muehlenbein, M. P., & Bribiescas, R. G. (2005). Testosterone-mediated immune functions and male life histories. *American Journal of Human Biology, 17*, 527–558.

Muehlenhard, C. L., Koralewski, M. A., Andrews, S. L., & Burdick, C. A. (1986). Verbal and nonverbal cues that convey interest in dating: Two studies. *Behavior Therapy, 17*(4), 404–419. https://doi.org/10.1016/S0005-7894(86)80071-5

Myers, N. E., Stokes, M. G., & Nobre, A. C. (2017). Prioritizing information during working memory: Beyond sustained internal attention. *Trends in Cognitive Sciences, 21*(6), 449–461.

Novotny, E., Frank, M. G., & Grizzard, M. (2021). A laboratory study comparing the effectiveness of verbal and nonverbal rapport-building techniques in interviews. *Communication Studies.* https://doi.org/10.1080/10510974.2021.1975141

Paunonen, S. V., Ewan, K., Earthy, J., Lefave, S., & Goldberg, H. (1999). Facial features as personality cues. *Journal of Personality, 67*(3), 555–583.

Penton-Voak, I. S., Jacobson, A., & Trivers, R. (2004). Populational differences in attractiveness judgements of male and female faces: Comparing British and Jamaican samples. *Evolution and Human Behavior, 25*, 355–370.

Penton-Voak, I. S., Jones, B. C., Little, A. C., et al. (2001). Symmetry, sexual dimorphism in facial proportions and male facial attractiveness. *Proceedings of the Royal Society of London B: Biological Sciences, 268*(1476), 1617–1623.

Penton-Voak, I. S., Little, A. C., Jones, B. C., Burt, D. M., Tiddeman, B. P., & Perrett, D. I. (2003). Female condition influences preferences for sexual dimorphism in faces of male humans (Homo sapiens). *Journal of Comparative Psychology, 117*, 264–271.

Perrett, D. I., Lee, K. J., Penton-Voak, I., et al. (1998). Effects of sexual dimorphism on facial attractiveness. *Nature, 394*(6696), 884–887.

Peskin, M., & Newell, F. N. (2004). Familiarity breeds attraction: Effects of exposure on the attractiveness of typical and distinctive faces. *Perception, 33*(2), 147–157. https://doi.org/10.1068/p5028

Re, D. E., & Rule, N. O. (2016). Appearance and physiognomy. In D. Matsumoto, H. C. Hwang, & M. G. Frank (Eds.), *Handbook of nonverbal communication* (pp. 221–256). American Psychological Association press.

Rhodes, G. (2006). The evolutionary psychology of facial beauty. *Annual Review of Psychology, 57*, 199–226. https://doi.org/10.1146/annurev.psych.57.102904.190208

Rhodes, G., Chan, J., Zebrowitz, L. A., & Simmons, L. W. (2003). Does sexual dimorphism in human faces signal health? *Proceedings of the Royal Society of London Series B-Biological Sciences, 270*, S93–S95.

Rhodes, G., Yoshikawa, S., Clark, A., Lee, K., McKay, R., & Akamatsu, S. (2001). Attractiveness of facial averageness and symmetry in non-Western populations: In search of biologically based standards of beauty. *Perception, 30*, 611–625.

Richner, H., & Wilson, K. (2019). Reproductive behavior and parasites. In J. C. Choe (Ed.), *Encyclopedia of Animal Behavior* (2nd ed., pp. 718–726). Elsevier.

Ryder, H., Maltby, J., Rai, L., Jones, P., & Flowe, H. D. (2016). Women's fear of crime and preference for formidable mates: How specific are the underlying psychological mechanisms? *Evolution and Human Behavior, 37*(4), 293–302.

Scott, I. M., Clark, A. P., Josephson, S. C., Boyette, A. H., Cuthill, I. C., Fried, R. L., … Honey, P. L. (2014). Human preferences for sexually dimorphic faces may be evolutionarily novel. *Proceedings of the National Academy of Sciences, 111*(40), 14388–14393. https://doi.org/10.1073/pnas.1409643111

Sekerdej, M., Simão, C., Waldzus, S., & Brito, R. (2018). Keeping in touch with context: Non-verbal behavior as a manifestation of communality and dominance. *Journal of Nonverbal Behavior, 42*(3), 311–326.

Sim, S., Shin, J. E., & Sohn, Y. W. (2019). Effects of non-verbal priming on attachment-style activation. *Frontiers in Psychology, 10*, 684.

Simpson, J. A. (2007). Psychological foundations of trust. *Current Directions in Psychological Science, 16*(5), 264–268.

Singh, D. (2002). Female mate value at a glance: Relationship of waist-to-hip ratio to health, fecundity, and attractiveness. *Neurodndocrinoloy Letters, 23*, 81–91.

Snyder, J. K., Fessler, D. M., Tiokhin, L., Frederick, D. A., Lee, S. W., & Navarrete, C. D. (2011). Trade-offs in a dangerous world: Women's fear of crime predicts preferences for aggressive and formidable mates. *Evolution and Human Behavior, 32*(2), 127–137.

Stass, J. W., & Willis, F. N. (1967). Eye contact, pupil dilation, and personal preference. *Psychonomic Science, 7*(10), 375–376.

Sternberg, R. J. (1986). A triangular theory of love. *Psychological Review, 93*(2), 119.

Swami, V., Furnham, A., Balakumar, N., Williams, C., Canaway, K., & Stanistreet, D. (2008). Factors influencing preferences for height: A replication and extension. *Personality and Individual Differences, 45*(5), 395–400.

Swami, V., & Tovée, M. J. (2005). Female physical attractiveness in Britain and Malaysia: A cross-cultural study. *Body Image, 2*(2), 115–128.

Thornhill, R., & Gangestad, S. W. (1999). Facial attractiveness. *Trends in Cognitive Sciences, 3*, 452–460.

Tickle-Degnen, L., & Rosenthal, R. (1987). Group rapport and nonverbal behavior. *Review of Personality and Social Psychology, 9*, 113–136.

Tickle-Degnen, L., & Rosenthal, R. (1990). The nature of rapport and its nonverbal correlates. *Psychological Inquiry, 1*(4), 285–293. https://doi.org/10.1207/s15327965pli0104_1

Tinlin, R. M., Watkins, C. D., Welling, L. L. M., DeBruine, L. M., Al-Dujaili, E. A. S., & Jones, B. C. (2012). Perceived facial adiposity conveys information about women's health. *British Journal of Psychology, 104*, 235–248.

Toma, C. L., & Hancock, J. T. (2010). Looks and lies: The role of physical attractiveness in online dating self-presentation and deception. *Communication Research, 37*(3), 335–351.

Vacharkulksemsuk, T., Reit, E., Khambatta, P., Eastwick, P. W., Finkel, E. J., & Carney, D. R. (2016). Dominant, open nonverbal displays are attractive at zero-acquaintance. *Proceedings of the National Academy of Sciences, 113*(15), 4009–4014.

Valentine, T., Darling, S., & Donnelly, M. (2004). Why are average faces attractive? The effect of view and averageness on the attractiveness of female faces. *Psychonomic Bulletin & Review, 11*, 482–487.

Wade, T. J. (2010). The relationships between symmetry and attractiveness and mating relevant decisions and behavior: A review. *Symmetry, 2*, 1081–1098.

Wade, T. J., Fisher, M. L., & Clark, E. (2021). I saw him first: Competitive nonverbal flirting among women, the tactics used and their perceived effectiveness. *Personality and Individual Differences, 179*. https://doi.org/10.1016/j.paid.2021.110898

Williams, G. C. (2020). *Sex and evolution*. (MPB-8), Vol. 8. Princeton University Press.

Zahavi, A. (1975). Mate selection—A selection for a handicap. *Journal of Theoretical Biology, 53*, 205–214.

Zak, P. J. (2012). *The moral molecule: The source of love and prosperity*. Random House.

Zebrowitz, L. A., & Franklin, R. G. (2014). The attractiveness halo effect and the babyface stereotype in older and younger adults: Similarities, own-age accentuation, and older adult positivity effects. *Experimental Aging Research, 40*(3), 375–393. https://doi.org/10.1080/0361073x.2014.897151

Zebrowitz, L. A., & Rhodes, G. (2004). Sensitivity to "bad genes" and the anomalous face overgeneralization effect: Cue validity, cue utilization, and accuracy in judging intelligence and health. *Journal of Nonverbal Behavior, 28*(3), 167–185.

Zeifman, D., & Hazan, C. (1997). A process model of adult attachment formation. In S. Duck (Ed.), *Handbook of personal relationships: Theory, research and interventions* (pp. 179–195). Wiley.

Zuckerman, M., Miserandino, M., & Bernieri, F. (1983). Civil inattention exists – In elevators. *Personality and Social Psychology Bulletin, 9*, 578–586.

5

Love Signals and the Reproductive Force

David B. Givens and John White

Introduction

On behalf of establishing close relationships, human love signals are nonverbal signs of sexual attraction, courtship, attachment, and love (Givens, 2005; Givens & White, 2021). Myriad signs, signals, and cues of attraction are in service to what the authors call the "reproductive force," proposed as a fundamental force of nature. The reproductive force remains a potent motivator in humans today, in their overall demeanor, facial expressions, gestures, goals, clothing, automobiles, music, media, art, religion, hairdos, shoes, prom dresses, and diverse additional nonverbal signs, signals, and cues. In considering the representation of this myriad

D. B. Givens (✉)
Center for Nonverbal Studies, School of Leadership Studies, Gonzaga University, Spokane, WA, USA
e-mail: givens@gonzaga.edu

J. White
Dublin City University, Dublin, Ireland
e-mail: john.white@dcu.ie

R. J. Sternberg, A. Kostić (eds.), *Nonverbal Communication in Close Relationships*,
https://doi.org/10.1007/978-3-030-94492-6_5

of human signals, the authors have divided the chapter into three key areas:

1. Some Psychology Behind Love Signals and the Reproductive Force
2. Human Nonverbal Actions and Reproductive Forces
3. Self-presentation, Nonverbal Love Signals, and the Reproductive Force

Some Psychology Behind the Reproductive Force

Evolution: Selfishly Reinforced

The reproductive force appeared some 3.7 billion years ago with RNA and later, DNA, in the origin of life on Earth. RNA and DNA molecules encode information (via codons) about how to reproduce themselves. Selfishly enforced, guided, and shaped by primordial messaging molecules, self-replication became the prime directive—the summum bonum or "greatest good"—of life and living, pursued for its own sake and solely on its own behalf.

Intimacy

Intimacy is an important component of the reproductive force and manifests itself in a multitude of nonverbal behaviors, many of which are spontaneous. For example, it has been identified within the following realms: immediacy (touch), the actual physical or spiritual presence of the other, chronemics and in particular an awareness of time, the removal of boundaries between individuals, smooth interaction norms (e.g., polite turn taking), composure (e.g., few vocal pauses), expressiveness (e.g., facial animation such as surprise), and altercentrism (attention to the partner in question) (Burgoon & Newton, 1991).

Passion

There are many theories about what passion looks like. For example, some argue that it is a way of feeling, thinking, and acting toward another (Hatfield, 1988; Hatfield & Sprecher, 1986). Others emphasize the importance of erotic love, with passion being a central factor in sexual courtship between partners, typically taking the form of reciprocated sexual teasing behaviors which lead to sexual excitement and encounters (Douglas & Atwell, 1988). Douglas and Atwell (1988) emphasize sexual courtship in their conception of passion. These theorists argue that erotic love is the result of repeated sexually teasing behaviors that are accepted, confirmed, and reciprocated by the other, and that therefore lead to mutually peaked sexual excitation. Others locate discourse on sexual passion within the realm of psychology, where sexual experiences and excitement form one part of the psychological basis of passion. In addition to a psychological need for sexual experiences, this basis also emphasizes other motivators associated with passion such as contributions to self-esteem and the need for dominance (Sternberg, 1986).

Human Nonverbal Actions and Reproductive Forces

Courtship

Nonverbal Negotiation

Courtship is a process of sending and receiving messages to seek someone's favor or love. A significant measure of nonverbal communication is in service to courtship, which itself serves the reproductive force. From gestures (e.g., shoulder-shrugs) to footwear (high heels) to clothing (puffy sleeves, cowl necks, and the above-mentioned prom dress), nonverbal signs may transmit information about attractiveness, sexuality, and love. Such matters need not be explicitly stated in words.

From Reptiles to Humans

In all cultures, human beings attain the closeness of sexual intimacy through courtship, a usually slow negotiation based on exchanges of words and nonverbal cues. Vertebrates from reptiles to human beings reproduce through mating, via internal fertilization of the female's body. Givens (1978, 2005) has proposed that human courtship may advance in a series of five communicative phases:

1. Attention,
2. Recognition,
3. Conversation,
4. Touching, and
5. Lovemaking.

The English word "court" traces to the ancient Indo-European root, gher-, "to grasp, enclose."

Facial Expressions

Play Face

Research by Dimberg (2000) shows that people respond unconsciously and spontaneously to 'emotional facial stimuli' and that such responses involve the same facial muscles as those perceived in the 'emotional facial stimuli'. Moreover, these responses, while not necessarily visible to the naked eye, affect one's voluntary facial actions.

Makeup

To cover blemishes and wrinkles—to highlight the infantile schema, men and especially women have used facial cosmetics for millennia. "'Lead has been eroding European women's skin for at least 3,000 years,' claims a team of archaeologists who recently discovered 50 grams of toxic face powder in a 3000-year-old tomb in a Mycenean cemetery in Greece" (Anonymous, 1994, 1655). Its composition " . . . —80% calcium carbonate and 20% lead sulfate hydrate—is similar to that of preparations used as cosmetics throughout history" (Anonymous, 1994, 1655).

> Finely ground green malachite, a particular favorite [in Ancient Egypt] from 4000 B.C. on, consists of oxide of copper—lethal both to bacteria and fly eggs. The exaggerated eye makeup that we associate with Queen Cleopatra in Hollywood spectaculars was originally of this nature. (Barber, 1994, 201)

Gaze

Gaze and Romance

Gaze is an indicator of liking another human being, as Argyle (1988, 162) observes, "people look more at those they like." We gaze more at romantic partners, friends, and people we like than people we dislike (Guerrero et al., 2007; Kleinke, 1986). Typically, increased gaze is associated with friendliness and affiliation, while averted gaze is associated with dislike and hostility (Burgoon et al., 1984). In conveying empathy and warmth, direct and continuous gaze is important (McAdams et al., 1984).

Gaze and Sexual Interest

Extended gaze has been connected with sexual interest (Thayer & Schiff, 1977). Absence of gaze has been identified as signaling inattentiveness with mutual gaze signaling openness and attraction (Kleinke, 1986). Givens (1983) observes that gaze is one of the key cues in communicating attraction. In this regard, there are some gender differences. It has been found that women receive more gaze than men. Interestingly, females show a preference for males who gaze at them a lot, while males prefer a lower degree of gaze (Kleinke et al., 1973).

Laughter and Mating

Laughter can form an important piece of the dyadic interplay between couples, with romantic attraction and interpersonal closeness being one of the dividends (Treger et al., 2013). Indeed, in developing romantic feelings and associated moods of 'closeness', shared laughter between a couple has been shown to be an important factor (Kurtz & Algoe, 2015).

Laughter may be a signal of 'sexual solicitation' during encounters between sexes (Freud, 1912; Duncan & Fiske, 1977). In such encounters, laughter may be accompanied by other nonverbal signals such as body orientation and posture. With regard to these 'additional signals' there are some interesting gender differences. It seems males communicate interest in females during laughter with fewer nonverbal 'body' signals such as body orientation and posture. On the other hand, laughter signals by females may be accompanied by more body orientation signals and self-presentation signals, some of which may be described as submission signals.

Vocal Intonation and Mating

The sound of the human voice may "serve as an important multidimensional fitness indicator" (Hughes et al., 2010, 295) and so it is no surprise that humans alter their voices when in romantic relationships or when attracted to a possible mate. Indeed, the human has been known to alter their voice in order to entice a potential mate (Anolli & Ciceri, 2002; Snyder et al., 1977). Such alteration is focused on making the voice more 'pleasant', with lowering of the voice being one of the common practices (Hughes et al., 2010). In romantic relationships, the term 'babytalk' has been used to describe voice modulation which involves the human using a higher vocal register (Bombar & Littig, 1996).

Interestingly, there are some conflicting theories on voice modulation within romantic and sexual relationships. In some cases, voice pitch may be lowered within contexts where private and personal information is being shared, while in contexts of elation and excitement, it may be heightened. It seems that voice modulation convergence is key here, with one partner 'mirroring' the voice tone of the other as they converge emotionally (Floyd & Ray, 2003).

Kissing

The Sensation of Kissing

The most sensitive area of our face is the perioral area (which includes the lips and nose). Kissing sensations travel through the trigeminal nerve (cranial V), which carries impulses received from the lips. Reflecting its importance, trigeminal is served by three sensory nuclei, extending from the upper spinal cord through the brain stem to the amphibian brain. Pleasurable light-touch sensations travel from the principal and spinal nuclei through evolutionary-old pathways to the thalamus, then to areas of the mammalian brain (including the cingulate gyrus, prefrontal cortex, and basal forebrain), as well as to primary sensory areas of the parietal cortex. When kissing, humans move their heads together, with mirror neurons also playing a role. Within this synchronized movement of heads, humans participate [via mirror neurons] "in an aspect of the other's experience" (Stern, 2007, 38).

Kissing and the Assessment of a Potential Mate

When engaged in the act of kissing, it is argued that the human collects a multitude of information. For example, the act of kissing may serve the purpose of assessing the partner as a potential genetic match based on pheromonal information and an assessment of the actual health and genetic fitness of the partner (Wedekind et al., 1995; Durham et al., 1993; Thornhill & Gangestad, 1999). Additionally, gustatory chemical information gleaned from the act of kissing may also be processed in the assessment of the partner as a potential mate (Durham et al., 1993). Kissing has also been shown to increase autonomic arousal, and in so doing, may lead to sexual intercourse (Byers & Heinlein, 1989).

Kissing and Signs of Love

Mouth to mouth kissing is common in 90% of the world's cultures (Kirshenbaum, 2011) and even in cultures where it is not practiced, close facial contact in forms such as nose rubbing is practiced. As an experience, "mouth-to-mouth contact with the lips" is a worldwide sign of love (Morris, 1994, 155). Kissing also serves to communicate feelings of attachment and satisfaction with a relationship (Floyd et al., 2009).

Kissing and Head Movement

As Givens (1983) notes, the act of kissing resembles a 'docking spacecraft' where the faces roll several degrees right or left, in synchrony, so the noses will clear. Some studies show that individuals turn their heads proportionally more to the right when kissing (e.g. Güntürkün, 2003). However, more recent research by Sedgewick et al. (2019), suggests that such head turns are context specific. For example, they found no head turning bias among types of kisses which could be described as non-romantic kisses.

Kissing and Gender

Across the genders, there is evidence that certain types of kissing can be interpreted differently by men and women. Women are inclined to place greater overall value on romantic kissing in contrast to men (Hughes et al., 2007). With a male partner, women may interpret kissing as an act of playfulness or a sign of warmth/love, in comparison to men, who are more inclined to see such behaviors as indicative of sexual desire (Pisano et al., 1986).

Kissing in the Animal World

The act of kissing is not unique to humans. Givens (1983) notes that the kiss originates from a mammal-wide sucking reflex. Many mammals 'kiss' before mating as a way of stimulating a partner's maternal instincts.

Dolphins nibble, cats give playful bites, dogs lick faces or nuzzle flanks, and chimps press lips in their courtship (Givens, 1983).

Shoulder Shrug

Socio emotional stimuli for shrug-display cues involve the forebrain's amygdala (LeDoux, 1996) and basal ganglia (MacLean, 1990). Submissive feelings find expression in coordinated muscle contractions designed to bend, flex, and rotate parts of the axial and appendicular skeleton, to "shrink" the body and show a harmless "lower" profile. Individually or in combination, signs from the shoulder-shrug display (e.g., head-tilt-side, shoulder-shrug, and pigeon-toes) may suggest feelings of resignation, powerlessness, and submission. In courtship and rapport, the cues show harmlessness and friendly intent, thus inviting physical approach and affiliation.

Touch and Love Signals

The Importance of Touch as a Signal of Love

Touch is one of the earliest and most basic forms of stimulation in human experiences, beginning in the womb. It has primal origins and as Sachs (1988, 28) observes: "Touch, in short, is the core of sentience, the foundation for communication with the world around us and probably the single sense that is as old as life itself." As such, its value in terms of love signals is most important, with one of the key reasons being its presence and meaning from early life. There is much evidence to support this. For example, the importance of touch for the physical and biological well-being of infants and their later development in social and psychological spheres is well recognized (Richmond et al., 2000). Indeed, a study by Adler and Towne in 1996 found that despite being well cared for in terms of bodily needs, institutionalized babies had slower rates of thriving and had higher mortality rates than the norm. They attributed the inability of these babies to thrive as a product of not being lifted, fondled, or cuddled as frequently as babies in non-institutional settings. Research by Gerhart (2004) and Perry (2002) discovered that in the first year and a half of life, toddlers who received inadequate tactile stimulation had underdeveloped brain pathways used for the processing of social and emotional information. In short, touch in the very early stages of human life lays important foundations for later emotional development and relationships.

Biology of Touch and Love

Touch is an important component of intimate relationships (Jakubiak & Feeney, 2016, 2019; Heslin & Boss, 1980; Dunbar, 2010). In this regard, touch is significant because it can release oxytocin and endorphins (Uvnäs-Moberg et al., 2015) and dopamine (Keltner, 2009). Such physiological reactions are important in the sphere of love and signals of love. Take for instance, the situation where a wife holds her husband's hand. FMRI scans show that in situations where a wife is undergoing a stressful procedure, holding her husband's hand during the procedure produces less threatening neural activity by comparison to wives who held the hand of a stranger or didn't have any hand to hold.

Gender and Touch Signals of Love

There are some intriguing findings in relation to how the sexes view touch. Evidence suggests that there is no difference in the frequency with which men touch women and women touch men (Hall & Veccia, 1990). However, there is a difference in how such touching is enacted and read. Sexual desire plays a role in the reading of touch. For example, sitting on a partner's lap or kissing may be read as playful by women, but for men such behaviors may be viewed as an indication of sexual desire (Pisano et al., 1986).

Women's reading of intimate touch is grounded in relational commitment and the intimacy of the relationship (Johnson & Edwards, 1991). It seems men rate intimate touch differently with less of a grounding in the relational commitment context of the touch. Indeed, it has been found that men will rate intimate touch as 'pleasant' when either initiated by a stranger or close friend (Heslin et al., 1983).

Touch Signals of Love: Stage and Type of Relationship

There is some evidence to suggest that the stage of a romantic relationship also has an impact on how touches and love signals are read. In the early stages of romantic relationships, it is more probable that men will initiate touch; however, in marriages, it is more probable that women will initiate touching (Willis & Dodds, 1998). In this regard, the work of Hanzal et al. (2008) provides intriguing insights on relationship status and reading love signals. Hanzal et al. (2008) found that married women perceive touch as an indicator of warmth and love to a greater degree than unmarried women. The opposite was true for men! Unmarried men perceive touch as an indicator of warmth and love more than married men.

Types of Touch and Love Signals

Burgoon et al. (2016) describe a number of touches, which fall into the category of love signals. For example, they describe 'affectionate touches', which function primarily to convey affection and have general friendship, and warmth as their basis, "without necessarily conveying sexual attraction" (Burgoon et al., 2016, 154). An example of such a touch would be hugging. Another touch they describe which falls into the category of a love signals is the 'comforting touch'. These touches provide comfort and social assurance to a distressed other. An example of such a touch would be a pat on the back. A third touch which they describe is the 'sexual touch'. This touch is often concentrated in "more vulnerable areas of the body" (Burgoon et al., 2016, 156) such as the genitals, mouth, or thigh. It can involve numerous kinds of touches which may occur together. For example, French kissing and the touching of private body parts.

In terms of specific actions which have been identified as a sole indicator of love, interlocking fingers has gained attention. For example, studies by Hertenstein et al. (2006) found that interlocked fingers were identified by subjects as an indicator of love.

Dance

Mithen (2005) argues that dance may have origins in a rudimentary form as far back in history as 1.8 million years ago, when the bipedal anatomy of the human allowed for gestural communication and body language. Indeed, a somewhat misguided perception exists that human dance is primarily driven by seductive/mating motives. The main reason for such perceptions lies in comparisons with the animal world. For example, Birdwhistell (1970) used the phrase 'courtship dance' to describe the movements of wild turkeys and American teenagers. Similarly, Darwin argued that dance is primarily concerned with courtship and mating. However, more modern discourse identifies its value as an "external system of autoregulation that aids in the maintenance of psychobiological and mental health" (Christensen et al., 2017, 9). As such, pleasure and sexual success are "correlates of the deeper psychobiological effects that drove the evolution of dance because they made it intrinsically rewarding" (Christensen et al., 2017, 9).

In considering the connections between dance and sex, the perceptions of the observer are important. These perceptions of the sexuality of the dance depend on the form of the dance, its context, the historical period in question, culture, and the actual situation (Hanna, 1983). Hanna (2010, 213) makes the point that 'sexualized' dancing may "imaginatively stylize" actual sexual practices where a form of identity of the dancer is portrayed which can include attraction, flirtatiousness, friendliness, exhibitionism, eroticism, and love-making. For example, the dance might involve disrobing, where the dance may be a "showcase, audition or advertisement to be a sexual partner." Indeed, as Frith and McRobbie (1990, 338) observe: "the dance floor is the most public setting for musical as well as sexual expression."

In terms of gender, some research points specifically to the inferences women can make from male dancing. It has been shown that women can make inferences about male strength and biochemical states based on their dance moves (and their grip strength), with other research indicating that women prefer male dancers with more masculine traits (Fink et al., 2007; Santos et al., 2005).

Self-Presentation, Nonverbal Love Signals, and the Reproductive Force

Attractiveness

Evolution and the Halo Effect

The human develops a sense of the importance of physical appearance early in life. For example, infants react positively to beautiful faces and look away from faces that are ugly. In preschool, children are able to identify the better-looking children (Berscheid & Walster, 1974). Indeed, there are some who argue that the value of attractiveness has an evolutionary and biological basis with the human being very conscious of the need to attract a mate (Buss, 1994). This beauty bias, which is sometimes called the halo effect, begins in childhood. The inference being that beauty connotes goodness (Larose & Standing, 1998). Perceptions of beauty may also involve other factors such as personality and self-care.

Personality and Self-Care

A study by Mehrabian and Blum in 1997, examined photographs of young adults and had them rated in terms of physical attractiveness by both males and females. Among other factors self-care and pleasantness were identified as factors related to attractiveness. In terms of self-care, factors such as a shapely figure, good grooming, and well-fitting clothes were identified. With regard to pleasantness, personality characteristics inferred from the photographs related to 'pleasantness' and associated personal traits such as friendliness and happiness and babyish features. Interestingly, ethnicity was also a factor in this study. Assertiveness may also play a role with younger adults. Reis et al. (1990) found that attractive male students are more assertive and interact more with women. On the other hand, attractive female students are less assertive.

Cultures and Judgments of Attractiveness

While there are cultural differences in how humans define markers of attractiveness, there is significant research to show that there are a number of physical attributes within and across cultures which are remarkably similar. For example, Cunningham et al. (1995) examined how people across different races judged the attractiveness of Caucasian, Asian, Hispanic, and Black women. Their work points to the fact that "beauty is not in the eye of the beholder." Rather, many signals of attractiveness are judged consistently both within a culture and across cultures (Floyd, 2006). This is particularly true for judgments of the face. There may be some differences across cultures in terms of judgments of the body. In parts of the world which are prone to famine or disease, fleshiness can be an indicator of health, whereas in others slender physiques are an indicator of access to high protein and low-fat foods (Anderson et al., 1992).

Factors Related to 'Body Attractiveness'

In considering factors that influence judgments of the attractiveness of the physical human form, the following key criteria emerge:

(a) Waist-to-Hip Ratio. While there may be some cultural variations, across the globe, there is very considerable agreement that men prefer women with waist-to-hip ratios of about 0.70. The hour-glass figure. This ratio suggests health and fertility. For men, the waist to hip ratio is 0.9. With men, this can be represented in the shape of a 'V'.
(b) The Golden Ratio or Phi: Phi is the ratio of 1:1.618. Pythagoras, the Greek mathematician and philosopher, made a case for an association between human beauty and Phi. Indeed, Pythagoras claimed that this ratio extended beyond human beauty to beauty in nature. For the perfectly beautiful body, the distance from your belly button to the bottom of your feet would be 1.618 times the distance from the top of your head to your belly button. Likewise, the distance from the top of your head to your elbow would be 1.618 times the

distance from your elbow to the end of your middle finger. Beautiful faces are also marked by Phi. For instance, in especially beautiful faces, the mouth is 1.618 times as wide as the nose.

Facial Beauty

Nonverbal Perception

Qualities or features of the human face that may excite aesthetic admiration, attraction, desire, and love.

Usage

Though facial beauty is "in the eye of the beholder," some qualities, features, and proportions—such as those of the infantile schema—may be universally esteemed.

Eyes and Cheekbones

Based on a study of Japanese and U.S. observer judgments of female attractiveness, high cheekbones, a thin lower jaw, large eyes, a shorter distance between the mouth and chin, and between the nose and mouth, are usually preferred qualities in women's faces (Perrett et al., 1994).

Jaws

The size (a. normal, b. vertically excessive ["too long"], or c. vertically deficient ["too short"]) and placement (a. normal, b. prognathic [protruding], or c. retrusion) of the upper and/or lower jaws may affect perceptions of facial beauty. Cross-culturally, bimaxillary prognathism (protruding upper and lower jaws) is less attractive than either normal or bimaxillary retrusion. Vertical deficiency is more attractive than vertical excess; and normal jaw occlusion is more attractive than either retrograde or protruded lower jaws (Kiyak N.D.).

Love at First Sight

A research team led by Knut Kampe of the Institute of Cognitive Neuroscience at University College, London, determined that eye contact with a pretty face—one judged to be attractive by the viewer on variables such as radiance, empathy, cheerfulness, motherliness, and conventional beauty—activates the ventral striatum, a pleasure center of the brain.

Koinophilia

This is the tendency to perceive faces which have average features as being attractive (Jones & Hill, 1993).

Facial Neoteny and Sexual Maturity

The degree to which a face displays sexual maturity and baby-like features (facial neoteny) has a bearing on perceptions of attractiveness (Berry & McArthur, 1985; Cunningham, 1986). Facial neoteny for a woman would include attributes such as fuller lips, wider eyes, small chins and shorter distances between the eyes and nose, and larger distances between the eyes and hairline (Johnston & Franklin, 1993). For men, facial neoteny can be signaled by large eyes (Cunningham et al., 1990). Indeed, Cunningham et al. note that men who possess "the neotenous features of large eyes, the mature features of prominent cheekbones and a large chin, the expressive feature of a big smile, and high-status clothing were seen as more attractive than other men" (Cunningham et al., 1990, 61). Within the sphere of sexual maturity for women high cheekbones are viewed as attractive. For men, sexual maturity is signaled by a strong jawline, a large chin, combined with the less mature features of large eyes and a wide smile (Cunningham et al., 1990). In a study utilizing Asian, Hispanic, and White judges, the most attractive female faces had larger, wider-set eyes, smaller noses, narrower facial breadths, smaller chins, higher eyebrows, larger lower lips, larger smiles, more dilated pupils, and well-groomed, fuller hair (Cunningham et al., 1995).

Symmetry

Another preferred beauty trait involves facial symmetry between the right and left sides. In a review of symmetry in mate selection, researchers found that animals from scorpion flies to zebra finches showed a preference for symmetrical patterns and shapes (perhaps because asymmetry may be a sign of weakness or disease; Watson & Thornhill, 1994). College-student ratings of young adult faces reveal that vertical and horizontal symmetry are attractive features, at least in photographs. In another study based on the subjective ratings of judges: "The more symmetric twin of a pair was consistently rated as more attractive, and the magnitude of the difference between twins in perceived attractiveness was directly related to the magnitude of the difference in symmetry" (Mealey et al., 1999, 151). In short, the more symmetrical a face is, the more it will be judged as attractive (Shackelford & Larsen, 1997).

Prom Dresses

"I am here"

In service to the reproductive force, clothing cues encoded in American prom dresses evolved in the early twentieth century to broadcast information about physical presence ("I am here"), gender ("I am female"), and reproductive fitness ("I am fertile") for purposes of courtship (see below, Courtship). Worldwide, the reproductive force is similarly celebrated in diverse coming-of-age ceremonies as teenagers reach reproductive age. Japanese women may don kimonos, young women from Ghana wear colorful beads and body paint, and Tamil women from Sri Lanka display with heavy makeup, eye-catching jewelry, and saris.

Wedding Dresses

Nonverbally, bridal gowns are designed to feature feminine signs and draw attention to wearers in marriage ceremonies. A nuptial dress is an expressive garment, often of ample fabric, whose color may be of emotional, social, or symbolic significance, promising—quite apart from words—fertility and romantic closeness.

Messaging Features

Like prom dresses, wedding gowns are designed to highlight the physical contrasts between female and male bodies. For example, a gown may suggestively reveal a woman's gracile neck, curvilinear shoulders, and thinner waist, arms, and wrists. Sleeveless gowns bare the shoulders, while puffy sleeves echo diffident signs of the shoulder-shrug display (see below, Gestures). Excessive fabric may encode surreal messages of "floating" and a "larger-than-life" presence (see below, Clothing).

Red, White, and Plaid

In China, Japan, and other Eastern countries, wedding dresses may be bright red to attract attention and symbolize good luck. In Canada, Ireland, and the U.S., wedding gowns may be white to suggest purity and wealth. White was widely emulated in the West after England's Queen Victoria wore white at her wedding in 1840. Native American brides of California's Yurok tribe wore plaid designs of white (symbolizing east), blue (south), yellow or orange (west), and black (north) to suggest an emotional connection to Earth. Apart from spoken or written words, such color cues announced physical presence directly ("I am here") and the promise of emotional closeness ("I love you") for all to see.

Clothing

Cloth Signs

In courtship, attractive clothing is just that, attractive to the senses of vision, hearing, touch, and smell. After its invention ca. 9000 years ago: "Cloth would soon become an essential part of society, as clothing and as adornment expressing self-awareness and communicating variations in social rank" (Wilford, 1993, C1). Nonverbally, as well, clothing plays a role in each of courting's five expressive stages. Both females and males look firstly at clothes in same-sex encounters. However, females look at clothes first when they meet a man, but when a male meets a female, he looks at clothes thirdly, with figure and face apparently taking precedence over glances at her clothes (Knapp & Hall, 2006). There is evidence to suggest that while dressing provocatively can enhance one's chances of attracting a sexual partner, such dress may in fact be counterproductive in attracting a long-term partner (Hill et al., 1987).

Wearable Cues

Body adornment is the act of decorating the human frame to accent its grace, strength, beauty, and presence, and to mask its less-attractive features and traits. Visually distinctive patterns of bodily dress, piercing, scarification, insignia, and tattoos may be worn to express personal, social, ethnic, military, and national identity—and often to attract the attention of a colleague, partner, or prospective mate.

Bracelets

Wrist-wear is a telling case in point. "Bracelets have nearly always been worn by females and it has been suggested that the custom originated as a way of exaggerating the gender signal of the slender feminine arm, the fine bracelets emphasizing the thinness of the arm diameter inside them" (Morris, 1985, 144).

Anatomy

Before pants, skirts, or shoes, there was the unadorned primate body itself: eyes, teeth, skin, hair, and nails along with shapes formed of muscle, fat, and bone. With the advent of clothing the body's nonverbal vocabulary grew as shoulders "widened," ankles "thinned," and feet stood up on tiptoes in high heels. As optical illusions, stripes, colors, buttons, and bows accented or concealed natural body signs and drew attention to favored—while diverting eyes from less favorable—body parts.

Flounce & Weave

Unwoven skirts and shawls made of flounces of tufted wool or flax were worn by the Sumerians 5000 years ago. More recently, the invention of the flying shuttle (1733), the spinning jenny (1764), and the nineteenth century power-loom made cotton fabrics available in greater quantities as consumer goods. Mass produced clothing debuted in 1851 with the invention of the sewing machine and increased in production with the use of synthetic fibers (e.g., Orlon in 1952). As the adornment media became subject to greater control, the diversity and number of nonverbal clothing cues burgeoned. To the very visual primate brain, fashion statements are "real," because, neurologically, "seeing is believing."

Hairdos

Gender Signs

Hairdos encode the style, color, shape, and sheen of the cylindrical, filamentous projections covering one's scalp. They include any of the visual, tactile, and olfactory signs emanating from human head hair. Hair is of key value in matters of identity, attractiveness, and courtship.

Biology

We spend a great deal of time noticing, monitoring, and commenting on each other's hair or its absence. This is because, in mammals generally, clean hair is a sign of high status, good health, and careful grooming. The biological equivalent of scales, feathers, and fur, hair not only keeps our head warm and dry, but protects the braincase from sunshine. Hair once provided camouflage, as well, to help ancestors blend into the natural landscape. Hairstyles help us blend into the social scene today.

Media

In the 1950s, magazine and TV images of Elvis Presley popularized the rebellious ducktail, in which hair sweeps back to meet in an upturned point at the rear of the head, and the bangs ascend in a topknot, not unlike the tuft of a displaying male bird.

In the 1960s, antiestablishment bushy hair for men was popularized by magazine and TV images of the Beatles, a British pop group whose members wore hair noticeably longer than male peers of the day. In the 1970s, very long straight hair for women was popularized by magazine and TV images of American folksinger, Joan Baez, whose dark tresses contrasted with shorter, chemical-permanent styles of the time. In the 1980s, pop singer Madonna's TV-pictured soft-tousled blond hair popularized the sexy, Marilyn Monroe look of the 1950s. In the 1990s, TV ads of Chicago Bulls basketball player, Michael Jordan popularized the shaved-head look introduced by actor Yul Brynner in the 1956 movie, The King and I.

Art: Faces and Bodies

Aesthetic Signage

Art signals include auditory, tactile, taste, vestibular, and visual signs designed to affect the human sense of beauty. They include arrangements, combinations, contrasts, rhythms, and sequences of signs designed as an emotional language bespeaking elegance, grace, intensity, refinement, romance, and truth. From the beginning of human prehistory, artistic expression has been in service to attractiveness, courtship, and the reproductive force.

Artistic Emotion

Before neuroscience—and solely through his artistic eyes—sculptor Auguste Rodin knew that an important link between muscle movement and emotion existed in the human nervous system. Indeed, Rodin expressed emotion artistically through the mobility of the muscles. Artists frequently address or allude to the reproductive force in their work, as in Sandro Botticelli's The Birth of Venus (ca. 1485), Leonardo da Vinci's Mona Lisa (ca. 1503–06), and Marcel Duchamp's Nude Descending a Staircase, No. 2 (1912).

Sfumato

Da Vinci suggests a smile on Mona Lisa's face. Originating from the primate "play face," the human smile invites closeness and suggests harmless intent ("I am friendly"). That her beckoning smile seems both alive and elusive, according to Harvard visual physiologist, Margaret Livingstone, is due to the way our brain's visual system perceives it. Viewed directly, neurons for sharp vision see less of a smile than when viewed indirectly by peripheral-vision neurons (as when we focus on her eyes) which are more responsive to blurry details. Da Vinci intentionally blurred Mona Lisa's lips through the Italian sfumato ("smoky") brush-stroke technique. When we look directly at her lips, after having looked at her eyes, the smile seems to disappear.

* * *

Shoes

Uniqueness v. Uniformity

Along with sandals, boots, and slippers, shoes are consumer products designed to protect and decorate human feet. Footwear includes highly expressive articles of clothing designed to convey information about age, gender, status, personality, and sexual orientation, and personality.

Worldwide, shoes are among the most expressive of our nonverbal cues. This reflects the foot's primate evolution as a grasping organ and neurological "smart part," and the curious fact that our foot's sensory mapping on the brain's parietal lobe abuts that of the genital organs—feet are similarly sensitive, ticklish, and sexy.

Feminine footwear may show personality and uniqueness—as if to say, "I'm someone special"—while masculine footwear is part of a uniform to mark membership in a group (to say, "I'm on the management team" or "I'm a cowboy."

Archaeology

Humans have been decorating their sandals and shoes at least since the beginning of the Neolithic ca. 10,000 years ago. According to archaeologists who found them in homes, tombs, and burials, the earliest sandals came in hundreds of designs. Thus style in footwear was important from the very beginning, much as it is today.

Motor Vehicles

Multiply Adapted

Few consumer products have adapted as expressively to the reproductive force as automobiles. Through a process of product selection beginning with the Model A Ford, cars have become ever more attractive, "sexy," and expressive of one's gender identity. Gleaming exteriors echo mammalian cleanliness and good grooming, as curvilinear design features combine to reflect an automotive avatar of owner identity, personality, and mood. Nonverbally, of notable mention here is the automotive grille.

Vehicular Grille

A grille is a nose- or mouth-shaped grating of metal or vinyl, used as a decoration at the front end of an automobile, truck, or bus. Its configuration is the vehicle's "face," unwittingly designed to show attitude. Modern grilles express personality by mimicking features of the human face, notably of the lips, nose, and teeth. Windshields and headlights may participate as illusory "eyes." Grilles suggest a variety of facial mood signs—from the friendly smile to the angry tense-mouth expression—as they beckon for deference, demeanor, and respect on the road.

Evolution

Originally in the Ford family, for example, the 1903 Model A (1st edition) had neither a grille nor a vertical front end, but from 1908–1927, the Model T had a vertical front with a framed radiator as a proto-grille. In 1928, the (2nd edition) Model A had a shapely, contoured radiator that suggested a vertically ascending nose.

In the 1940s, grille design shifted from noses to mouths. A case in point is Mercury's aggressive, tooth-showing grille of 1946, which resembled an angry bulldog poised to bite. In 1966, the Mercury Cougar's front end featured a bumper that curled up on the outer extremities, and an insouciant grille resembling the aggressive silent-bared teeth face of monkeys and apes (Van Hooff, 1967). Links between biting, chewing, showing fangs, anger, and fear have been found in the anterior hypothalamus "in a region of converging nerve fibres involved in angry and defensive behaviour" (MacLean, 1973, 16). Like faces, grilles are decoded in the anterior inferotemporal cortex, while their familiarity registers in the superior temporal polysensory area (Young & Yamane, 1992, 1327). The emotional impact of grilles registers in the amygdala.

Vroom-Vroom

Vehicles may also serve the reproductive force through auditory means. Nonverbal vrooming sounds, for example, may be used by young men to attract attention to themselves in service to courtship. A vroom is a loud roaring noise emitted by a motor vehicle as it accelerates or as a driver pumps the gas. A popular recorded version of vrooming by The Shangri-Las singing group became a number-one U.S. hit in 1964. "Leader of the Pack" featured rhythmically repeated motorcycle-engine revving sounds to accent the song's instrumentation and words.

Emotional Valence

That we perceive a vrooming noise as being either pleasant or unpleasant is due, in part, to the evolutionary nature of sound. Since the auditory sensation evolved from the tactile sense, it may connote a sense of physical touch, which to humans is an intimately personal sensation.

Vrooming Semantics

The essential meaning of vrooming is "I am here; notice me!" Like its more pleasant biological cousin, birdsong, noisy revving may simultaneously attract potential mates and challenge rivals. The deep growling, guttural sound of vrooming may be sensed as a hostile or angry message by the brain's amygdala. Its loudness elicits a looming response that makes the vehicle—and the driver—seem "larger." The sound's sudden onset may trigger the auditory startle reflex. As in each of the nonverbal venues addressed in this chapter, motor vehicle bids for attention appeal for closeness quite apart from words.

Conclusion

The manner in which the human produces love signals which have a reproductive undertone invades many aspects of our nonverbal communication in both a nuanced and multifaceted way. For example, it may well be in the delicate touch of a hand or the loud roar of an automobile. What is fascinating about these signals is their prevalence across the ways we typically communicate nonverbally. For example, reproductive messages can be communicated by tone of voice, facial expression (e.g., play face), gesture, body movement, gaze, clothing, and even dance moves.

Before we delved into this variety of messaging styles, we thought it was important to devote the first section of the chapter to a consideration of some of the psychology behind 'reproductive love signals' and to give specific attention to two in particular: passion and intimacy. Obviously, both are interconnected, and both produce nonverbal behaviors in acts of reciprocated sexual teasing which then may lead to sexual excitement and encounters. Such behaviors can include touch, physical presence, and vocal intonation to mention but a few. Later sections of our chapter delve into these signals in more detail.

In considering the variety of signals which have nonverbal reproductive value, it is evident that there are many scenarios of human communication which provide fertile ground for their expression. How long one gazes at another, the nature of shared laughter, the manner in which a couple dance, the tone of their voice, their facial expressions, use of touch, manner in which they kiss, types of facial expressions, and even time spent together create the tapestry for courtship which may result in reproduction.

These forms of interaction often have backdrops which too play a role. First to consider is the actual attractiveness of the possible mate. Evolutionary pre-programming often has on influence on nonverbal perceptions of attraction and suitability of a mate. For example, facial symmetry, Pythagoras's Golden Ratio, facial neoteny, koinophilia, chemical feedback from kissing, and even tone of voice feed into evolutionary algorithms which calculate optimum mate suitability.

Of course, human intelligence and deliberate efforts to present oneself as 'the optimum mate' are also very much at play. Whether it be the loud roar of an automobile, the alluring movements of a dance, the careful application of make-up, the suggestive style of clothing, healthy and well coiffured hair, or even the beauty of a shoe, the human is very capable at sending nonverbal messages which proclaim availability and suitability.

In considering the host of nonverbal messages we send to spark reproductive interest, there are some cultural similarities, gender similarities, and indeed historical similarities which are worth noting. Across all cultures, human beings attain the closeness of sexual intimacy through courtship, a usually slow negotiation based on exchanges of words and nonverbal cues. It seems that perceptions of human attractiveness are also largely similar across cultures (e.g., perceptions of symmetry). And finally, across the ages, and in line with our evolutionary programming, evidence from history suggests that many key nonverbal messages related to reproduction have remained largely unchanged. Perceptions of beauty, the wearing of make-up, artistic presentation of human virility, type of clothing being worn, and ceremonial dancing to mention but a few, date back thousands of years. It would seem these nonverbal forces for reproduction prevail to this very day and indeed thanks to social media have an even wider platform.

References

Adler, R., & Towne, N. (1996). *Looking out, looking in* (8th ed.). Harcourt Brace.
Anderson, J. L., Crawford, C. B., Nadeau, J., & Lindberg, T. (1992). Was the Duchess of Windsor right? A cross-cultural review of the socioecology of ideals of female body shape. *Ethology and Sociobiology, 13*, 197–227.
Anolli, L., & Ciceri, R. (2002). Analysis of the vocal profiles of male seduction: From exhibition to self-disclosure. *Journal of General Psychology, 129*, 149–169.
Anonymous. (1994). Making Up the Ancients. *Science*, September 16, (265), 1655.
Argyle, M. (1988). *Bodily communication* (2nd ed.). Methuen.
Barber, E. W. (1994). *Women's work: The first 20,000 years*. W. W. Norton.
Berry, D. S., & McArthur, L. Z. (1985). Some components and consequences of a babyface. *Journal of Personality and Social Psychology, 48*, 312–323.
Berscheid, E., & Walster, E. (1974). Physical attractiveness. In L. Berkowitz (Ed.), *Advances in experimental social psychology* (Vol. 7, pp. 158–215). Academic Press.
Birdwhistell, R. (1970). *Kinesics and context*. University of Pennsylvania.
Bombar, M. L., & Littig, L. W., Jr. (1996). Babytalk as a communication of intimate attachment: An initial study in adult romances and friendships. *Personal Relationships, 3*, 137–158.
Burgoon, J. K., Buller, D. B., Hale, J. L., & deTruck, M. (1984). Relational messages associated with nonverbal behaviours. *Human Communication Research, 10*, 351–378.
Burgoon, J. K., & Newton, D. A. (1991). Applying a social meaning model to relational message interpretations of conversational involvement: Comparing observer and participant perspectives. *Southern Communication Journal, 56*, 96–113.
Burgoon, J., Guerrrero, L., & Floyd, K. (2016). *Nonverbal communication*. Routledge.
Buss, D. M. (1994). *The evolution of desire: Strategies of mate selection*. Basic Books.

Byers, S., & Heinlein, L. (1989). Predicting initiations and refusals of sexual activities in married and cohabiting heterosexual couples. *Journal of Sex Research, 26*, 210–231.

Christensen, J., Cela-Conde, C. J., & Antoni, G. A. (2017). Not all about sex: Neural and biobehavioral functions of human dance. *Annals New York Academy of Science*, 8–32. New York Academy of Sciences.

Cunningham, M. R. (1986). Measuring the physical in physical attractiveness: Quasi-experiments on the sociobiology of female facial beauty. *Journal of Personality and Social Psychology, 50*, 925–935.

Cunningham, M. R., Barbee, A. R., & Pike, C. L. (1990). What do women want? Facialmetric assessment of multiple motives in the perception of male facial physical attractiveness. *Journal of Personality and Social Psychology, 59*, 61–72.

Cunningham, M. R., Roberts, A. R., Barbee, A. P., Druen, P. B., & Wu, C. H. (1995). "Their ideas of beauty are, on the whole, the same as ours": Consistency and variability in the cross-cultural perception of female physical attractiveness. *Journal of Personality and Social Psychology, 68*(2), 261–279.

Dimberg, U., Thunberg, M., & Elmehed, K. (2000). Unconscious facial reactions to emotional facial expressions. *Psychological Science, 11*, 86–89.

Douglas, J. D., & Atwell, F. C. (1988). *Love, intimacy, and sex*. Sage.

Dunbar, R. I. M. (2010). The social role of touch in humans and primates: Behavioural function and neurobiological mechanisms. *Neuroscience and Biobehavioral Reviews, 34*(2), 260–268.

Duncan, S., & Fiske, D. W. (1977). *Face to face interaction: Research methods and theory*. Erlbaum.

Durham, T. M., Malloy, T., & Hodges, E. D. (1993). Halitosis: Knowing when "bad breath" signals systemic disease. *Geriatrics, 48*, 55–59.

Fink, B., Seydel, H., Manning, J., et al. (2007). A preliminary investigation of the associations between digit ratio and women's perception of men's dance. *Journal of Personality and Individual Differences, 42*, 381–390.

Floyd, K. (2006). An evolutionary approach to understanding nonverbal communication. In V. Manusov & M. L. Patterson (Eds.), *The Sage handbook of nonverbal communication* (pp. 481–500). Sage.

Floyd, K., & Ray, G. B. (2003). Human affection exchange: IV, Vocalic predictors of perceived affection in initial interactions. *Western Journal of Communication, 67*, 56–73.

Floyd, K., Boren, J., Hannawa, A., Hesse, C., McEwan, B., & Veksler, A. (2009). Kissing in marital and cohabiting relationships: Effects on blood lipids, stress, and relationship satisfaction. *Western Journal of Communication, 73*, 113–133.

Freud, S. (1912). *Der Witz und seine Beziehung zum Unbewußten*. Denticke.
Frith, S., & McRobbie, A. (1990). Rock and sexuality. In S. Frith & A. Goodwin (Eds.), *On record: Rock, pop, and the written word*. Pantheon.
Gerhart, S. (2004). *Why love matters: How affection shapes a baby's brain*. Brunner-Routledge.
Givens, D. B. (1978). The nonverbal basis of attraction: Flirtation, courtship, and seduction. *Psychiatry, 41*, 346–359.
Givens, D. B. (1983). *Love signals*. Crown.
Givens, D. B. (2005). *Love signals: A practical field guide to the body language of courtship*. St. Martin's Press.
Givens, D. B., & White, J. (2021). *The Routledge dictionary of nonverbal communication*. Routledge.
Guerrero, L. K., Andersen, P. A., & Afifi, W. A. (2007). *Close encounters: Communication in relationships* (2nd ed.). Sage.
Güntürkün, O. (2003). Human behaviour: Adult persistence of head-turning asymmetry. *Nature, 421*, 711.
Hall, J. A., & Veccia, E. M. (1990). More "touching" observations: New insights on men, women, and interpersonal touch. *Journal of Personality and Social Psychology, 59*, 1155–1162.
Hanna, J. L. (1983). *The performer-audience connection: Emotion to metaphor in dance society*. University of Texas Press.
Hanna, J. L. (2010). Dance and sexuality: Many moves. *The Journal of Sex Research, 47*(2/3), 212–241.
Hanzal, A., Segrin, C., & Dorros, S. M. (2008). The role of marital status and age on men's and women's reactions to touch from a relational partner. *Journal of Nonverbal Behaviour, 32*, 21–35.
Hatfield, E. (1988). Passionate and companionate love. In R. J. Sternberg & M. L. Barnes (Eds.), *The psychology of love* (pp. 191–217). CT Yale University Press.
Hatfield, E., & Sprecher, S. (1986). Measuring passionate love in intimate relationships. *Journal of Adolescence, 9*, 383–410.
Hertenstein, M. J., Keltner, D., App, B., Bulleit, B. A., & Jaskolka, A. R. (2006). Touch communicates distinct emotions. *Emotion, 2006*(3), 528–533.
Heslin, R., & Boss, D. (1980). Nonverbal intimacy in airport arrival and departure. *Personality & Social Psychology Bulletin, 6*, 248–252.
Heslin, R., Nguyen, T. D., & Nguyen, M. L. (1983). Meaning of touch: The case of touch from a stranger or same sex person. *Journal of Nonverbal Behavior, 7*, 147–157.

Hill, E. M., Nocks, E. S., & Gardner, L. (1987). Physical attractiveness: Manipulation by physique and status displays. *Ethology and Sociobiology, 8*, 143–154.

Hughes, S. M., Harrison, M. A., & Gallup, G. G. J. (2007). Sex differences in romantic kissing among college students: An evolutionary perspective. *Evolutionary Psychology, 5*, 612–631.

Hughes, S. M., Farley, S. D., & Rhodes, B. C. (2010). Vocal and physiological changes in response to the physical attractiveness of conversational partners. *Journal of Nonverbal Behavior, 34*, 155–167.

Jakubiak, B. K., & Feeney, B. C. (2016). Keep in touch: The effects of imagined touch support on stress and exploration. *Journal of Experimental Social Psychology, 65*, 59–67.

Jakubiak, B. K., & Feeney, B. C. (2019). Interpersonal touch as a resource to facilitate positive personal and relational outcomes during stress discussions. *Journal of Social and Personal Relationships, 36*(9), 2918–2936.

Johnson, K. L., & Edwards, R. (1991). The effects of gender and type of romantic touch on perceptions of relational commitment. *Journal of Nonverbal Behavior, 15*, 43–55.

Johnston, V. S., & Franklin, M. (1993). Is beauty in the eye of the beholder? *Journal of Ethology and Sociobiology, 14*(3), 183–199.

Jones, D., & Hill, K. (1993). Criteria of facial attractiveness in five populations. *Human Nature, 4*, 271–296.

Keltner, D. (2009). *Born to be good: The science of a meaningful life*. W W Norton & Co.

Kirshenbaum, S. (2011). *The science of kissing: What our lips are telling us*. Grand Central Publishing.

Kleinke, C. L. (1986). Gaze and eye contact: A research review. *Psychological Bulletin, 100*, 78–100.

Kleinke, C. L., Bustos, A. A., Meeker, F. B., & Staneski, R. A. (1973). Effects of self-attributed and other-attributed gaze on interpersonal evaluations between males and females. *Journal of Experimental Social Psychology, 9*(2), 154–163.

Knapp, M., & Hall, J. (2006). *Nonverbal communication in human interaction* (6th ed.). Thompson Learning.

Kurtz, L. E., & Algoe, S. B. (2015). Putting laughter in context: Shared laughter as behavioral indicator of relationship well-being. *Personal Relationships, 22*(4), 573–590.

Larose, H., & Standing, L. G. (1998). Does the halo effect occur in the elderly? *Social Behavior and Personality: An International Journal, 26*(2), 147–150.

LeDoux, J. (1996). *The emotional brain: The mysterious underpinnings of emotional life*. Simon & Schuster.
MacLean, P. D. (1973). *A triune concept of the brain and behaviour*. University of Toronto Press.
MacLean, P. D. (1990). *The triune brain in evolution*. Plenum Press.
McAdams, D. P., Jackson, R. J., & Kirshnit, C. (1984). Looking, laughing, and smiling in dyads as a function of intimacy motivation and reciprocity. *Journal of Personality, 52*, 261–273.
Mealey, L., Bridgstock, R., & Townsend, G. C. (1999). Symmetry and perceived facial attractiveness: A monozygotic co-twin comparison. *Journal of Personality and Social Psychology, 76*, 151–158.
Mehrabian, A., & Blum, J. (1997). Physical appearance, attraction and the mediating role of emotions. *Current Psychology: Developmental, Learning, Personality, Social, 16*, 20–42.
Mithen, S. (2005). *The singing Neanderthals: The origins of music, language, mind and body*. Weidenfeld and Nicolson.
Morris, D. (1985). *Bodywatching*. Crown Publishing.
Morris, D. (1994). *Bodytalk: The meaning of human gestures*. Crown Publishers.
Perrett, D. I., May, K. A., & Yoshikawa, S. (1994). Facial shape and judgments of female attractiveness. *Nature, 368*, 239–242.
Perry, B. D. (2002). Childhood experience and the expression of genetic potential: What childhood neglect tells us about nature and nurture. *Brain and Mind, 3*, 79–100.
Pisano, M. D., Wall, S. M., & Foster, A. (1986). Perceptions of nonreciprocal touch in romantic relationships. *Journal of Nonverbal Behavior, 10*, 29–40.
Reis, H. T., Wilson, I. M., Monestere, C., Bernstein, S., Clark, K., Seidl, E., & Radoane, K. (1990). What is smiling is beautiful and good. *European Journal of Social Psychology, 20*, 259–267.
Richmond, V. P., McCroskey, J. C., & Payne, S. K. (2000). *Nonverbal behavior in interpersonal relations* (5th ed.). Prentice-Hall.
Sachs, F. (1988). *The intimate sense. Sciences, 28*(1), 28–34.
Santos, P. S., Schinemann, J. A., Gabardo, J., et al. (2005). New evidence that the MHC influences odor perception in humans: A study with 58 Southern Brazilian students. *Journal of Hormones and Behaviour, 47*, 384–388.
Sedgewick, J. R., Holtslander, A., & Elias, L. J. (2019). Kissing right? Absence of rightward directional turning bias during first kiss encounters among strangers. *Journal of Nonverbal Behaviour, 43*, 271–282.

Shackelford, T. K., & Larsen, R. J. (1997). Facial asymmetry as indicator of psychological, emotional, and physiological distress. *Journal of Personality and Social Psychology, 72*, 456–466.

Snyder, M., Tanke, E. D., & Berscheid, E. (1977). Social perception and interpersonal behavior: On the self-fulfilling nature of social stereotypes. *Journal of Personality and Social Psychology, 35*, 656–666.

Stern, D. N. (2007). Chapter 2: "Applying Developmental and Neuroscience Findings on Other-centered Participation to the Process of Change in Psychotherapy". In S. Braten (Ed.), *On being moved: From mirror neurons to empathy* (pp. 35–47). John Benjamins.

Sternberg, R. J. (1986). A triangular theory of love. *Psychological Review, 93*, 119–135.

Thayer, S., & Schiff, W. (1977). Gazing patterns and attribution of sexual involvement. *Journal of Social Psychology, 101*(2), 235–246.

Thornhill, R., & Gangestad, S. W. (1999). The scent of symmetry: A human sex pheromone that signals fitness? *Evolution and Human Behavior, 20*, 175–201.

Treger, S., Sprecher, S., & Erber, R. (2013). Laughing and liking: Exploring the interpersonal effects of humor use in initial social interactions. *European Journal of Social Psychology, 43*(6), 532–543.

Uvnäs-Moberg, K., Handlin, L., & Petersson, M. (2015). Self-soothing behaviors with particular reference to oxytocin release induced by non-noxious sensory stimulation. *Frontiers in Psychology, 5*, 1529.

Van Hooff, J. (1967). The facial displays of the catarrhine monkeys and apes. In D. Morris (Ed.), *Primate ethology* (pp. 7–68). Aldine.

Watson, P. W., & Thornhill, R. (1994). Fluctuating asymmetry and sexual selection. *Trends in Ecology and Evolution, 9*, 21–25.

Wedekind, C., Seebeck, T., Bettens, F., & Paepke, A. J. (1995). MHC dependent mate preferences in humans. *Proceedings of the Royal Society B: Biological Sciences, 260*, 245–249.

Wilford, J. N. (1993). Site in Turkey yields oldest cloth ever found. In *New York Times* (July 13, "Science Times"), pp. C1, C8.

Willis, F. N., & Dodds, R. A. (1998). Age, relationship, and touch initiation. *Journal of Social Psychology, 138*, 115–123.

Young, M. P., & Yamane, S. (1992). Sparse population coding of faces in the inferotemporal cortex. *Science, 256*, 1327–1331.

6

The Verbal and Nonverbal Communication of Romantic Interest

Terrence G. Horgan, Judith A. Hall, and Melissa J. Grey

The human need to develop romantic relationships is usually very strong. But the path to fulfilling that need can be fraught with obstacles. You might have to approach someone you do not know well or at all. You need to open yourself up to possible rejection, disappointment, or harm. You may read your interest in someone incorrectly or embarrassingly misinterpret their interest in you. All this likely explains why cues of submissiveness and affiliation undergird human courtship,[1] as they signal safety/

[1] "Courtship" is an antiquated term that is often associated with the process leading up to reproduction in various species or social processes that serve as the prologue to marriage. Romantic relation-

T. G. Horgan (✉)
Department of Psychology, University of Michigan, Flint, MI, USA
e-mail: thorgan@umich.edu

J. A. Hall
Northeastern University, Boston, MA, USA
e-mail: j.hall@northeastern.edu

M. J. Grey
Monroe County Community College, Monroe, MI, USA

R. J. Sternberg, A. Kostić (eds.), *Nonverbal Communication in Close Relationships*,
https://doi.org/10.1007/978-3-030-94492-6_6

protection (e.g., I do not want to harm you/be harmed by you) along with a desire for connection (Givens, 1978).

Yet we all know how clichés about finding a partner unfold. Boy sees girl. Thump goes his heart, and away go his feet. The girl smiles coyly at the approaching boy before she distances herself from him. The boy pursues the girl and then bumbles his way to her heart with compliments ("You're so pretty"), humor, disarming smiles, and covetous gazes. A romantic relationship soon follows, as do their offspring.

Well, at least this is how the popular-media-driven schema about romance unwinds in our head. In reality, human courtship is not well understood at all and is likely *quite different from* what we see on TV shows or *even learn from researchers.*

In the sea of human courtship, the early spyglass and compass represent the technical and theoretical tools researchers have used to explore how individuals signal their interest in another person. Most of the action is likely below the water's surface, in places where researchers cannot see or are not permitted to look for ethical reasons (e.g., homes and bedrooms). Prevailing assumptions impact which islands of human courtship researchers travel to and train their spyglasses on; for example, *straight* ahead to sexually charged nightclubs frequented by predominantly cisgender, heterosexual individuals looking to possibly meet, flirt, and hook up with someone.

In the present day, researchers still cannot—and for good reason—peer into individuals' homes or bedrooms. Yet researchers can spot currents of human courtship activity, whether that is via online dating sites or from people who are now openly displaying their interest in same-sex partners, and attempt to study these and other phenomena in order to broaden everyone's understanding of human experiences of courtship.

The goals of this chapter are to introduce and review previously overlooked aspects of human courtship, namely the *communication of romantic interest* within the context of heterosexual and other types of relationships (e.g., same-gender ones). To this end, we define romantic interest, propose a new model of human courtship that distinguishes

---

ship development is a more fitting phrase. However, for the sake of readability, we have used courtship in various parts of this chapter.

romantic interest from flirtation, and then show why this distinction is needed. Afterward, we describe where and how flirtation and romantic interest are expressed verbally and especially nonverbally in heterosexual relationships. We then argue that conventional or prevailing research perspectives and theoretical models, such as evolutionary psychology, limit and distort our understanding of human courtship because they tend to be heteronormative, that is, derived from and focused on heterosexual relationships, which are taken to be the only normal type of romantic relationships in nature. We close our chapter by acknowledging that research on courtship processes has thus far focused on cisgender, heterosexual people, with little to no attention to the many individuals who vary on the multiple dimensions of gender identity and sexual orientation. We challenge the applicability of existing models of human courtship to these less-studied groups. We hope that this is seen as a call for researchers to explore new research questions that capture a broader range of human experiences in this domain.

The Communication of Romantic Interest

Numerous theorists have suggested that men and women court each other in a sequential fashion (Birdwhistell, 1970; Eibl-Eibesfeldt, 1970; Givens, 1978; Perper, 1985). For example, flirtation, which is often considered the initial phase of the human courtship process, involves a series of steps: men and women notice each other, approach each other or not, talk to and evaluate each other, and perhaps touch and synchronize their behavior with each other (e.g., Cunningham & Barbee, 2008). Although this process allows for individual differences in flirting style (Hall & Xing, 2015), commonly utilized verbal and nonverbal cues have been well-documented during this phase (Moore, 2010; Hall & Gunnery, 2013). If flirtation is successful, men and women may enter into a relationship characterized by intimacy and affection, and this phase is also associated with specific verbal and nonverbal cues (Andersen et al., 2006; Guerrero & Wiedmaier, 2013).

Unfortunately, existing models of the initial phases of human courtship do not address sufficiently the transition from flirting to being in a romantic relationship. We propose that they communicate a romantic interest at some point during this transition. We are not the first to allude to this transition. Knapp's (1978) relationship-development model includes a pre-relationship step ("intensifying") in which sexual (flirting) and romantic interests are expressed, but not a specific transitional point. We define the communication of romantic interest in a very specific way; namely as that point when one or both parties indicate a desire to enter into a relationship characterized by commitment to each other along with psychological/emotional intimacy and possible sexual contact. The diagram below depicts our

No relationship>. <Flirtation>. <Communication of Romantic Interest>. < New Intimate Relationship>

proposed model of the initial phases of human courtship.

We treat flirtation as the expression of sexual interest, and, in our model, it precedes the communication of romantic interest. Two points are important to make about our model. First, it captures tendencies, as opposed to a static, invariant progression of events. For example, we understand that some individuals may have never flirted with each other before beginning a romantic relationship; they communicated a romantic interest in each other right away, or they were already close friends when they developed a romantic interest and the 'flirting' phase was bypassed. Second, it is biased toward those cultures where individuals have greater autonomy in choosing their romantic partners. In other cultures, if families select who their adult children date or marry, but the individuals involved must consent to that arrangement, then we might expect that romantic interest would be expressed before the two start showing a sexual interest in each other.

Dots between each phase represent breaks in the sequence; that is, the individuals do not progress to the next phase. Consider the following examples: A woman flirts with a man, which is marked by a forward arrow, but she never communicates a romantic interest in him; a woman communicates her romantic interest in another woman, but the second woman does not reciprocate in kind; or romantic interest is expressed and reciprocated, but a new romantic relationship never gets started (e.g., one person has to leave for school or the service). Backward arrows signify movement to an earlier stage in the sequence. For example, coworkers signal a romantic interest in each other, but then one of them decides that an office romance is not possible, so they return to only flirting with each other or being just friends.

Why is this revised model needed? In our opinion, the literature on courtship does not distinguish the expression of sexual interest from the expression of romantic interest adequately. Let's take a look at flirtation to illustrate this point. Some scholars define flirtation as the expression of only sexual interest or only romantic interest, or they treat these two terms as interchangeable (Brak-Lamy, 2015; Guerrero & Wiedmaier, 2013; Hall & Xing, 2015; Moore, 2010; Remland, 2009).

Based on your life experiences, you might be perplexed as to why scholars confuse these two terms. You probably remember times when you were sexually attracted to someone and decided to flirt (or even hook up) with them (see Fielder & Carey, 2010). Afterward, or even while flirting, you may have realized that the person was already in a monogamous relationship, that they were not attracted to you or that they were not the right person for you, among other "deal-breakers." Describing this phase as one marked by the expression of sexual interest makes sense.

Sometimes, if flirtation was successful, you and the other person might have started hanging out more or even dating. The sexual interest phase may have cooled, leading both of you to become "just friends." Or the sexual interest phase may have led to sexual contact, even though neither you nor the other person wanted to be in a serious relationship (e.g., "friends with benefits"). However, there were likely times when one or both of you decided to become a "couple." We argue that this represents a transition marked by the expression of romantic interest. Last, we recognize that some couples might have a romantic interest but not a sexual interest in each other (as in a sexless but loving marriage).

Why Is This Distinction Between Flirtation and Romantic Interest Needed?

The nature of people's intentions unites the numerous reasons for distinguishing flirtation from romantic interest. Flirtation is marked by uncertainty and ambiguity regarding people's true desires and intentions (Guerrero & Wiedmaier, 2013), and it usually does *not* lead to dating or an intimate relationship (Back et al., 2011; Brak-Lamy, 2015). The communication of romantic interest, on the other hand, represents that point in which at least one person signals a desire to take a relationship with someone else further. Whether people tend to be successful at this point is not known.

Moreover, people's flirting behavior does not appear to be strongly linked to their actual interest in or desire to date someone (Back et al., 2011; Grammer et al., 2000; Houser et al., 2008). This may be because flirting serves many *non-relationship purposes*, such as seeking to have only sex or fun or enhancing one's own perceived sexual worth (Brak-Lamy, 2015; Henningsen, 2004). The purpose of expressing romantic interest, on the other hand, is to try to *build a relationship*, even if the desire to have sex with that person or up one's own perceived sexual worth is in the motivational mix.

Next, we provide evidence that suggests people can distinguish between the expression of sexual interest and romantic interest. This evidence comes from a sample of nearly 700 college students whom we recruited from universities in different parts of the USA before the 2020 COVID-19 pandemic. All of the included students reported being cisgender and heterosexual, that they had experienced a heterosexual relationship that progressed into a romantic phase, and that for the most recent such relationship they could remember who initiated the idea of progressing in this way. Students were given a detailed explanation of what we meant by "romantic interest," so that we could be sure they were not thinking about just flirting or about a relationship that became deeper in a platonic, but not romantic, way.

The Expression of Sexual Interest Versus Romantic Interest: Who Does It First and Where in Heterosexual Relationships?

Given the uncertainties associated with finding a partner, it might be comforting to know that some nonverbal courtship displays, such as "moon-walking" (a gliding backwards dance movement) and "twerking" (a dance move that involves buttocks-shaking), have a long, tried-and-true evolutionary history. But, alas, unless you are a male red-capped

Manakin (a bird) sitting on a perch or a male Black Widow spider crawling on a web, these particular displays may not help you.

For human relationships, three factors must be taken into consideration when we think about who signals romantic interest first, where they signal that interest, and the cues they use to do so: gender differences in behavior; long-standing, firmly entrenched gender stereotypes; and a rapidly evolving landscape of social communication technologies and social/gender norms. These factors, either in isolation or conjunction, likely cloud many people's thinking. Regarding new technologies, "sliding into someone's DMs" (sending a private message to another person via social media), "caking" (e.g., talking to someone on the phone for a long time), "swiping right" (a way to indicate one's interest in another person as a potential friend, hook-up, or dating partner on the website Tinder), and setting "thirst traps" (posting a sexy picture of oneself on social media in order to get others' attention) are commonly understood terms associated with modern-day courtship. Although these terms apply aptly to the new world of social media, they likely obscure the deeper relationship-building purposes of the behaviors they describe.

With respect to the communication of romantic interest, the "Who does it first?" question seems like a no-brainer, given what we "know" about men and women. Some have argued that men's sex drive tends to be stronger than women's (Baumeister et al., 2001). If true, one would think that men "should" try to initiate the sexual-interest phase of courtship via flirtation more than women. And because women tend to be more interested in relationships than men (Cross & Madson, 1997), they "should" be more likely than men to try to deepen a relationship. So, logically, because romantic interest is not strictly about sexual desire, women should be first to communicate it; after all, the goal is to get the other person to enter into a close, intimate relationship.

However, logic, documented gender differences, and stereotypes *do not* map nicely onto the human courtship sequence among heterosexuals. For instance, women are more likely than men to flirt *first* in many different settings (Grammer et al., 1998; McCormick & Jones, 1989; Moore, 2010). Men do, however, engage in more sexual and nonsexual touching while flirting than do women, and, among young heterosexual dating couples, men initiate sexual contact via nonverbal cues more often than do women (Ballard et al., 2003; Brak-Lamy, 2015; McCormick & Jones, 1989; Moore, 2010). (It is important to note that it is not known if, in 2022, men use sexual and nonsexual touch more than women do while flirting, given our society's growing awareness of the importance of consensual touch in all social contexts. However, it also is important to note that, even if people are more aware of the importance of consensual touching, sexual harassment and aggression are likely to continue if gender scripts are such that men feel they have the right to touch women non-sexually and sexually in a range of settings, such as school, work, a night club, a dorm room, etc.) Yet men are also more likely than women to show a number of relationship-building behaviors first, including asking for the other person's number or a first date, and disclosing their feelings of love (Ackerman et al., 2011; Brak-Lamy, 2015; Clark et al., 1999; DeWeerth & Kalma, 1995; Harrison & Shortall, 2011).

What about the communication of romantic interest? Our findings showed that, when only one person was signaling romantic interest, men were more than twice as likely as women to report being the first one to do so. Mutual signaling was commonly reported by men (especially) and women. Of importance, the least reported event was women reporting that they signaled romantic interest first. Thus, it appears that men tend to be more active in initially trying to take a relationship from nonromantic to romantic.

In terms of the communication of romantic interest, the "where" question is more challenging to answer because of the history of courtship research. To date, flirting has been examined in a variety of specialized physical and cyber settings, such as a laboratory (Grammer et al., 1998), nightclub (Brak-Lamy, 2015; Renninger et al., 2004), speed-dating venue (Back et al., 2011), and web-based dating sites (Albright & Simmens, 2014; Whitty, 2009).

These specialized "settings" are problematic to understanding where romantic interest might be expressed for two main reasons. First, whether men and women are in a lab, nightclub, or speed-dating venue, they might interact *only once* with each other. And even if flirting does occur that one time, a romantic relationship usually does not follow (Back et al., 2011; Brak-Lamy, 2015). The opportunities to develop the desire to take a relationship from flirting to one marked by an emotional commitment seem limited, too, although we are sure it does occur occasionally (love at first sight).

We maintain that the expression of romantic interest is more likely to occur in everyday physical settings, such as one's school or home/apartment. Men and women become attracted to each other in these settings because they are near each other *often* (proximity), see each other *often* (mere exposure), and have *more opportunities* to learn whether they are similar to each other (similarity) (e.g., see Hays, 1985; Reis et al., 2011; Whitbeck & Hoyt, 1994).

The second reason why the settings typically studied for flirting do not give good insight into romantic progression is that web-based dating sites and social media do not allow men and women to use their full repertoire of nonverbal cues to express a romantic interest. For instance, men and women cannot physically touch each other when interacting on a dating site or via various social media platforms, such as Facebook.

We contend that face-to-face interactions in everyday settings are important to the communication of romantic interest, given the importance of *nonverbal cues*, such as physical closeness (e.g., sitting next to someone), actual touching, and mutual gazing, to the communication of felt intimacy (e.g., Andersen, 1998; Andersen et al., 2006; Prager, 2000; Guerrero & Wiedmaier, 2013). Touching is one example of a nonverbal cue linked to desired or mutually felt intimacy, given that more of it is observed throughout the initial phases of courtship, from flirting, dating, and initiating sexual contact to the early stages of actual romantic relationships (Andersen et al., 2006; Baxter & Bullis, 1986; Burgoon, 1991; Docan-Morgan et al., 2013; Jesser, 1978; Guerrero & Wiedmaier, 2013; Marston et al., 1998; Tolhuizen, 1989; Willis & Briggs, 1992). Indeed, Docan-Morgan et al. noted that frequency of touch was used to signal a change in a relationship from nonromantic (less touching) to romantic (more touching). However, this study was conducted in 2013; it is unknown if touch is used as frequently in 2022 to signal this change. This may be the case because it may be more unclear in today's world, which rightly stresses the importance of consensual touching between individuals, that this is a situation in which one person has permission to touch another person.

We found that men and women were over eight times more likely to communicate their romantic interest in each other in their school environment, and six times more likely in their school setting, than on a dating site. In fact, a dating site or a bar/night club was seldom selected as a place where romantic interest was expressed. A social event, such as a party, was selected more frequently than social media, presumably because men's and women's use of nonverbal cues is less restricted in the former setting (two people can sit next to each other). Interestingly, romantic interest was not expressed at a person's work setting—surely an everyday physical environment for many men and women—more frequently than via social media. This points to the possibility that, in today's world, social media might be a safer outlet for the expression of romantic interest than one's place of employment, given people's growing awareness of sexual harassment (e.g., inappropriate touching) in the workplace (see Karami et al., 2019).

Now that we have shown that, in terms of who does it first and where, romantic interest is different from what is known about flirtation, we turn to similarities and differences in the cues that men and women use to express flirtation versus romantic interest.

The Expression of Sexual and Romantic Interest: What Cues Are Used?

In our study, students were given a checklist of over 50 nonverbal and verbal behaviors that the initiator of romantic interest might use to take a relationship from nonromantic to romantic. These were drawn from common sense as well as past research and reviews on cues that are often used to express intimacy. Some of these cues we deemed to be quite direct indicators of romantic intention, such as looking at the person for a long time, touching them sexually or on the head/hair, kissing them, saying they were interested in sex or a deeper relationship with them, complimenting their body or appearance, or asking to spend more time together. But, because communicating a romantic interest in someone entails some risks, we included other items that we considered indirect and more ambiguous in nature, such as laughing or giggling, smiling a lot, looking and then quickly looking away, teasing playfully, expressing concern and support, and asking about interests, goals, and values.

Some cues were used much more than others. The top nonverbal cues involved smiling, looking, setting a smaller physical distance, acting nervous, and hugging/kissing, and the top verbal cues were asking to spend more time, complimenting in various ways, telling stories or jokes, saying they liked the person, and asking questions about interests, goals, and values. Some cues on our list were rarely used, such as whispering in the person's ear and sending a sexy text message. Students could check as many cues as they remembered, and as you might expect, most people checked several—to be more exact, about five (out of 29) nonverbal cues and about seven (out of 25) verbal cues. Some named many and others just a small number.

Of special interest, in light of the past research on flirting, is whether men and women differed in how they conveyed their romantic interest.[2] The answer is different for nonverbal versus verbal cues. For nonverbal cues, there was not a notable difference between the genders. This is quite interesting because, although women tend to use more nonverbal cues and subtler nonverbal cues than men during the flirtation stage (Moore, 1985, 2010), there was no evidence of this during the communication of romantic interest. But for verbal cues, men impressively outnumbered women in terms of how often they said they used words, both direct and indirect. For indirect verbal cues, men who initiated reported more than women who initiated that they complimented the other's intelligence/knowledge, complimented the other's clothes/shoes, told stories/jokes, and invited the other to an event. For direct verbal cues, men reported that they told the other that they liked them and complimented the other's body/appearance more than women reported about themselves when initiating. Along the same lines, men reported using, in total, more verbal cues than women reported using.

[2] Although we are not describing it here, we also asked everyone what their partner did, if the partner was the initiator. Those results corroborated the reports by people who did the initiating themselves, to a remarkable extent.

Thus, it seems that at this (successful) transition point in a heterosexual relationship, the man takes on a more direct and assertive role, verbally speaking. This is quite different from the flirting situation and suggests the intriguing possibility that the pattern we observed is a tacit way of upholding traditional gender-stereotypical scripts about the balance of power in heterosexual romantic relationships, at least in their formative stages. To paraphrase, our results may represent a tacit agreement that the man is more in charge of *this transition* and the woman is okay with not rocking the boat. What happens to the balance of power later in the relationship remains, of course, to be navigated. Other nonverbal cue research suggests that, in terms of interpersonal touching, the balance of power may actually reverse in more developed relationships. Findings show that in younger or less attached heterosexual couples, touching the other person with the hand is more often done by the man, whereas this asymmetry evens out and can even reverse in older or more established couples (Knapp et al., 2021; Willis & Briggs, 1992). Results such as these remind us that there is no single model of relationship behaviors that applies across the board.

Similarly, our research reported here, as well as that of many others, is limited because it was restricted to those individuals who described themselves as cisgender and heterosexual. In the remaining sections, we point out that this limits our understanding of how flirtation and romantic interest are expressed in other types of relationships, such as same-gender ones. We note that certain barriers to this understanding may need to be removed by LGBTQIA+ [lesbian, gay, bisexual, transgender, queer, intersex (individuals with differences in sex development), asexual (individuals who are not sexually attracted to others), and other gender-diverse individuals] perspectives on human courtship because they are not moored to the same evolutionary-based and heteronormative assumptions, which we discuss shortly.

How Do We Navigate Through Uncharted Areas of Romantic Relationship Development?

Our current understanding of how people flirt and signal their romantic interest is quite limited. This is due to the fact that current theoretical models and programs of research, especially evolutionary psychology (we describe this model below), do not fully capture the full range of people's experiences in this domain. The following examples help to make this point.

At a party, Ginger sees Bob for the first time. She finds Bob easy on her eyes, and a sexual interest in him soon wells up. Bob sees her, finds her attractive, and soon develops a sexual interest in her. What might happen next?

As we stated earlier, women are more likely to initiate the courtship process than men. Indeed, women tend to be the selectors because they display nonverbal cues that signal their readiness to be approached by a specific man (Moore, 2010). Therefore, it is more likely that Ginger will be the first one to flirt.

What might she do? In order to be successful in getting Bob to approach her, she is likely to use multiple nonverbal cues (Moore, 1985). So, in full view of him, she might use bodily presentation, self-grooming, gazing and smiling, and showing a pleasant facial expression (DeWeerth & Kalma, 1995; Grammer, 1990; McCormick & Jones, 1989; McQuillen et al., 2014; Moore, 1985, 2010; Walsh & Hewitt, 1985). She also might use a room-encompassing look, then a short, darting look followed by a fixed gaze at Bob (Knapp et al., 2021). If she is successful, Bob may pick up the courtship ball and run with it.

Now let's change the scenario. Karen and Amy meet at this party and they become sexually attracted to each other. What happens next? If women tend to be the selectors during heterosexual courtship, who might signal first? If women use more nonverbal cues and subtler nonverbal cues during the flirtation stage around men, what cues might they use around another woman?

Let's also consider another scenario. Mark is at the party with Jim. The two have been sexually interested in each other for a long time and have flirted often. Mark wants to communicate a romantic interest in Jim, so that they can become a couple. Where might Mark communicate this interest, and what nonverbal and verbal cues might he use?

If you cannot answer these questions about Karen and Amy and Mark and Jim, you are not alone. There are many reasons for this, of which we will mention two. First, with few identifiable exceptions (Klinkenberg & Rose, 1994), the research community has neglected the study of the nonverbal cues that LGBTQIA+ individuals use to flirt or communicate their romantic interest.

Second, trying to understand all types of romantic relationships by comparing and contrasting them with what is "known" about cisgender, heterosexual individuals' relationships from an evolutionary perspective is problematic. From this perspective, the behaviors, tactics, and cues that we see from heterosexual men and women in today's world were passed down to them from their ancestors. These behaviors, tactics, and cues survived across a long span of time because they presumably allowed men and women to survive and reproduce successfully. But the model of a female and a male with complementary, active and passive, roles coming together to form a romantic relationship through a linear sequence of increasing intimacy does not apply universally. Although it is possible researchers would find more similarities with heterosexual conventions (e.g., Klinkenberg & Rose, 1994; Peplau & Fingerhut, 2007), there are reasons to expect including LGBTQIA+ experiences could lead to deeper or new understandings of romantic relationships and improve the generalizability of the literature's findings (Vencill & Israel, 2018).

There Are Heteronormative Smudges on Our Lens

As ships in waters around the world pass each other, there is a universal flag code for communication, especially when radio communications are disrupted or one ship is in distress. In this *International Code of Signals,* a rectangular blue and yellow flag means a communication is requested, for example. This global system is an impressive human feat of uniform communication or conformity. However, if the eyes on the boat are not looking for other kinds of communication from fellow ships, it would be possible to miss important signals. Similarly, if we do not know what to look for in the spyglass, other indicators of our subject in the waters or on the horizon could be missed or obscured.

It is unclear whether or how the mainstream romantic-relationship-development literature can account for and illuminate LGBTQIA+ experiences. Evolutionary psychology-based predictions about romantic relationship development stem from Trivers' (1972) parental investment theory, which asserts that men and women have different relationship behaviors because of the different demands parenting requires of them. For example, females make fewer eggs than males make sperm, and Trivers believes females need to devote more time and resources to parenting than males do. With respect to our human ancestors, females not only carried the pregnancy, they also were especially needed to feed their offspring for years after birth (nursing). That is a lot of "investment." It is possible males could leave after impregnation, which reflects a lower "investment."

Trivers' (1972) ideas were based, in part, on Bateman's (1948) studies of fruit flies. Bateman's flies followed a familiar pattern: males were more promiscuous, and females were more selective; males were more active and females more passive. Sexual selection was used to link the flies' behavior to their gonads, or ovaries and testes, and that explanation was extended to humans as well. For example, after females initiate flirting, males are more direct or active (e.g., touching her face) because they have more to gain and less to lose from a sexual encounter than the female who acts more indirectly or passively (e.g., looking away and laughing). This explanation, which relies on fixed traits (e.g., men are promiscuous; women, picky), has since been identified as a sexist Victorian idea (Tang-Martínez, 2016). Bateman's conclusions also are contended for several reasons, including that they were not well-supported by the data and alternative explanations may be stronger (Tang-Martínez).

New findings have begun to further erode the already shaky theoretical framework of romantic relationship development offered by evolutionary psychologists. For instance, the fixed-trait explanation has been challenged by research showing variation in mate or partner preferences when the context also varies (Eastwick et al., 2011; Zentner & Mitura, 2012), which is consistent with an alternative perspective in which flexibility in mating behavior is seen as adaptive (Gowaty, 2018; Hrdy & Williams, 1983). There also is some evidence that heterosexuals' dating preferences and romantic-relationship-development behaviors may not align with so-called fixed gender differences. For example, heterosexual men and women might desire similar levels of care and support from their partners (e.g., a rose left on their pillow; their birthday being remembered, etc.) (Perrin et al., 2011).

The research literature on sexual and romantic interest also may reflect heteronormativity, which is a pattern of beliefs and practices that make heterosexuality seem like the only natural or normal disposition (Kim et al., 2007; Rich, 1980; Warner, 1991). This perspective reinforces the assumption that individuals must be cisgender men or women who can only be heterosexual in sexual orientation and that different-gender romantic relationships are the only natural form.

As a consequence of heteronormativity, the following behaviors may seem "right" or "normal" to some researchers[3] and some in the general public, too. Women are attracted to "masculine" men and men to "feminine" females (e.g., Basow, 1992), leading both to present themselves in a manner perceived desirable to the other gender. Because men's romantic feelings are more tied to women's appearance (e.g., youth and beauty are nonverbal cues to her fertility) than vice versa (e.g., Feingold, 1992; Pines, 2001), women might try to enhance their appearance and feminine appeal to men (Brak-Lamy, 2015), and men might be more likely to compliment a women's appearance than vice versa (Hall & Xing, 2015). Women, on the other hand, "should" value men's intelligence and status/dominance (Feingold, 1992; Prokosch et al., 2009) because those are cues to his future ability to protect and provide the needed resources to the care of offspring. Therefore, it would only make sense that men should have greater success in attracting women when they are displaying dominance-related cues, such as taking up more space, exhibiting an

[3]We are not, of course, accusing any of the researchers listed in this section of having this perspective.

open-body position, and engaging in the nonsexual touching of other men (Grammer, 1990; Renninger et al., 2004).

There are ramifications of heteronormativity for trying to understand the diversity of romantic relationship behaviors and dynamics. As noted by Knapp et al. (2021), nonverbal communication researchers do not have a program of research devoted to understanding the nonverbal cues that cisgender women or men use (or do not use) when romantically pursuing someone of their own gender, let alone a program of research that includes individuals who are transgender or gender nonbinary. Furthermore, treating only certain enactments of heterosexuality as natural denies or casts as deviant all other experiences of gender and sexual orientation (Rich, 1980).

A Different Lens for Romantic Relationship Development

Examining the influence of social power and context has been a powerful tool in LGBTQIA+ research (e.g., Herek & McLemore, 2013; Meyer, 2013). Humphry's (1970) study of men's sexual encounters is a historical example of signaling sexual interest in social context. The men in Humphrey's "Tearoom Trade" study met each other in public places to engage in secret sex with a code of nonverbal behavior. The men's sequences of positioning, making eye contact, and timing their movements into bathroom stalls, for example, were all done in silence. Their nonverbal behaviors were generated (at least in part) in response to societal stigma and discrimination that made open same-gender relationships difficult and dangerous. An LGBTQIA+ spyglass needs to be able to consider such external factors, including factors hidden by assumptions of heteronormativity.

If we were attending the party with Ginger and Bob, we could likely identify their heterosexual flirtation as signs they were interested in each other. Her gazing at him, laughing and smiling wide, and fixing her hair are recognizable ways women flirt with men. Interpersonal scripts describe sequences of behaviors we experience as belonging to certain roles and intentions. Like in a play or film, scripts dictate specific and detailed behaviors, but they are not influenced by a playwright. Instead, they often come from a broader cultural script (Eaton & Rose, 2011; Simon & Gagnon, 1986). As an example, a woman might be more likely to dress in a way that appears feminine and use her appearance to attract a boyfriend because of cultural messages that this is effective or natural. There is plenty of evidence that culture plays a significant role in these behaviors. Some of the same "courtship strategies" heterosexual men and women use to develop romantic relationships are related to how much media they consume and how much they endorse sexism (Hall & Canterberry, 2011; Lippman et al., 2014; Seabrook et al., 2016; Ward & Cox, 2021; Zurbriggen & Morgan, 2006).

Many LGBTQIA+ individuals develop romantic relationships without models, guides, and scripts that relate to their experiences (e.g., Greene et al., 2015). Without a cultural script, LGBTQIA+ individuals can make it up as they go along (Brown, 1989). Creativity is often part of LGBTQIA+ individuals' ways of coping, cultural traditions, and character strengths. For example, ways of connecting with other LGBTQIA+ people, self-reflection, and identity development processes can be outgrowths of "coming out" or of reconciling one's experiences with irrelevant and even hostile social contexts (Riggle et al., 2011; Rostosky et al., 2010; Vaughan & Rodriguez, 2014). In a study of bisexual women's appearance, some participants described "dressing it down" or wearing more masculine dress when they were partnered with men to avoid being stereotyped as heterosexual and to increase the chances of being read accurately as bisexual. In relationships with women, they tended to dress in ways that are often seen as more feminine for the same reasons (Daly et al., 2018). These dynamic and fluid social norms might be a reason not to expect a static list of behaviors to emerge from LGBTQIA+ romantic relationship beginnings.

LGBTQIA+ experiences reveal new possible waters to explore. LGBTQIA+ romantic relationship development may be characterized as fluid and nonlinear (e.g., Sullivan et al., 2018), with egalitarian dynamics (e.g., Peplau & Fingerhut, 2007), by communicative and collaborative consent (Bauer, 2020), and with context and community-specific practices (e.g., Klinkenberg & Rose, 1994). Rather than focus on the fit of mainstream models to LGBTQIA+ individuals, the research field could benefit from engaging those with relevant lived experience to collaborate within interpreting and generating data on romantic relationship development.

Conclusion

Human hearts will continue to thump for others. But who those others are and how they navigate the tricky courtship process, if at all, are not well understood.

We proposed that a transitional phase may occur after the flirtation stage and prior to the start of a new romantic relationship. We described this romantic interest stage as a time in which one or both parties communicate a desire to enter into a relationship that is characterized by commitment, psychological/emotional intimacy, and possible sexual contact. Based on our research on cisgender, heterosexual participants, we discussed where romantic interest tends to be communicated and the verbal and nonverbal cues that men and women use to express it. We provided evidence that this stage is different from what is known about heterosexual flirtation in terms of which gender signals it first; specifically, even though women tend to flirt first, when only one person was signaling romantic interest, men were more than twice as likely as women to report being the first one to do so. We also noted some interesting differences in the number and types of nonverbal cues that women use (relative to men) during the communication of romantic interest. Unlike the flirtation stage, there was no evidence that women use more or subtler nonverbal cues than men during the communication of romantic interest. Instead, we found strong evidence that a gender difference in romantic interest expression lay in men's much greater use of verbal statements: words that indicated their hopes and intentions.

Many unknowns remain, including understanding what cues were used when one person initiates the transition to romantic involvement but is rebuffed by their heterosexual counterpart. Perhaps in unsuccessful attempts, men tried it using a more nonverbal approach, which was perceived as violating or presumptuous by the woman and led to rejection.

Maybe in some such cases, the man learned his lesson and they talked it out and managed a successful transition at a later date, whereas in others they went their separate ways. These are speculations that deserve research attention because these are important moments in many people's lives.

Our hope is that, by revising traditional courtship models that do not separate flirtation from the expression of romantic interest (as we defined it), researchers will pursue new lines of research about how humans use verbal and nonverbal cues to communicate their desire to take a relationship from nonromantic to romantic.

However, we are mindful that our understanding of flirtation and the communication of romantic interest is almost entirely limited to observations of, or self-reports by, people who are cisgender and heterosexual. At the theoretical level, models and research agendas dealing with how romantic relationships develop are heavily influenced by evolutionary-based and heteronormative assumptions. As a consequence, how individuals in same-gender relationships, for example, flirt or express romantic interest may be ignored, interpreted incorrectly, or treated as abnormal.

Finally, we fully recognize that, with our belief that romantic interest is a unique phase in the human courtship sequence, we have turned the compass needle and spyglass only slightly. We encourage researchers to continue this turning process by including the experiences of those in the LGBTQIA+ communities, so that the true scope of verbal and nonverbal cues used during romantic relationship development can be brought into better focus. Those best equipped to explore these experiences might be researchers who are also members of the LGBTQIA+ communities or individuals whose scientific approach is not anchored to evolutionary or heteronormative assumptions about human romantic relationships.

References

Ackerman, J. M., Griskevicius, V., & Li, N. P. (2011). Let's get serious: Communicating commitment in romantic relationships. *Journal of Personality and Social Psychology, 100*(6), 1079–1094. https://doi.org/10.1037/a0022412

Albright, J. M., & Simmens, E. (2014). Flirting, cheating, dating and mating in a virtual world. In M. Grimshaw (Ed.), *Oxford handbook of virtuality* (pp. 284–303). Oxford University Press. https://doi.org/10.1093/oxfordhb/9780199826162.013.034

Andersen, P. A. (1998). The cognitive valence theory of intimate communication. In M. T. Palmer & G. A. Barnett (Eds.), *Progress in communication sciences: Mutual influence in interpersonal communication theory and research in cognition, affect, and behavior* (pp. 39–72). Ablex. https://doi.org/10.4135/9781412976152.n14

Andersen, P., Guerrero, L., & Jones, S. (2006). Nonverbal behavior in intimate interactions and intimate relationships. In V. Manusov, & M. L. Patterson The SAGE handbook of nonverbal communication (pp. 259–278). SAGE Publications, Inc., https://dx.doi.org/10.4135/9781412976152.n14

Back, M. D., Penke, L., Schmukle, S. C., Sachse, K., Borkenau, P., & Asendorpf, J. B. (2011). Why mate choices are not as reciprocal as we assume: The role of personality, flirting, and physical attractiveness. *European Journal of Psychology, 25*(2), 120–132. https://doi.org/10.1002/per.806

Ballard, M. E., Green, S., & Granger, C. (2003). Affiliation, flirting, and fun: Mock aggressive behavior in college students. *The Psychological Record, 53*(1), 33–49.

Basow, S. A. (1992). *Gender: Stereotypes and roles* (3rd ed.). Thomson Brooks/Cole Publishing Company.

Bateman, A. (1948). Intra-sexual selection in Drosophila. *Heredity, 2*, 349–368. https://doi.org/10.1038/hdy.1948.21

Bauer, R. (2020). Queering consent: Negotiating critical consent in les-bi-trans-queer BDSM contexts. *Sexualities*, 1–17. https://doi.org/10.1177/1363460720973902

Baumeister, R. F., Catanese, K. R., & Vohs, K. D. (2001). Is there a gender difference in strength of sex drive? Theroetical views, conceptual distinctions, and a review of relevant evidence. *Personality and Social Psychology Review, 5*(3), 242–273.

Baxter, L. A., & Bullis, C. (1986). Turning points in developing romantic relationships. *Human Communication Research, 12*(4), 469–493. https://doi.org/10.1111/j.1468-2958.1986.tb00088.x

Birdwhistell, R. L. (1970). *Kinesics and context: Essays on body motion and communication.* University of Pennsylvania Press.

Brak-Lamy, G. (2015). Heterosexual seduction in the urban night contexts: Behaviors and meanings. *Journal of Sex Research, 52*(6), 690–699. https://doi.org/10.1080/00224499.2013.856835

Brown, L. S. (1989). New voices, new visions: Toward a lesbian/gay paradigm for psychology. *Psychology of Women Quarterly, 13*(4), 445–458. https://doi.org/10.1111/j.1471-6402.1989.tb01013.x

Burgoon, J. K. (1991). Relational message interpretations of touch, conversational distance, and posture. *Journal of Nonverbal Behavior, 15*(4), 233–259. https://doi.org/10.1007/BF00986924

Clark, C., Shaver, P., & Abrahams, M. (1999). Strategic behaviors in romantic relationship initiation. *Personality and Social Psychology Bulletin, 25*(6), 707–720. https://doi.org/10.1177/0146167299025006006

Cross, S. E., & Madson, L. (1997). Models of the self: Self-construals and gender. *Psychological Bulletin, 122*(1), 5–37. https://doi.org/10.1037/0033-2909.122.1.5

Cunningham, M. R., & Barbee, A. P. (2008). Prelude to a kiss: Nonverbal flirting, opening gambits, and other communication dynamics in the initiation of romantic relationships. In S. Sprecher, A. Wenzel, & J. Harvey (Eds.), *Handbook of relationship initiation* (pp. 97–120). Psychology Press.

Daly, S. J., King, N., & Yeadon-Lee, T. (2018). 'Femme it Up or Dress it Down': Appearance and bisexual women in monogamous relationships. *Journal of Bisexuality*, 1–21. https://doi.org/10.1080/15299716.2018.1485071

DeWeerth, C., & Kalma, A. (1995). Gender differences in awareness of courtship initiation tactics. *Sex Roles, 32*(11–12), 717–734. https://doi.org/10.1007/BF01560186

Docan-Morgan, T., Manusov, V., & Harvey, J. (2013). When a small thing means so much: Nonverbal cues as turning points in relationships. *Interpersona, 7*(1), 110–124. https://doi.org/10.5964/ijpr.v7i1.119

Eastwick, P. W., Finkel, E. J., & Eagly, A. H. (2011). When and why do ideal partner preferences affect the process of initiating and maintaining romantic relationships? *Journal of Personality and Social Psychology, 101*(5), 1012–1032. https://doi.org/10.1037/a0024062

Eaton, A. A., & Rose, S. (2011). Has dating become more egalitarian? A 35 year review using sex roles. *Sex Roles: A Journal of Research, 64*(11–12), 843–862. https://doi.org/10.1007/s11199-011-9957-9

Eibl-Eibesfeldt, I. (1970). *Ethology: The biology of behavior*. Holt, Rinehart, & Winston.

Feingold, A. (1992). Good-looking people are not what we think. *Psychological Bulletin, 111*(2), 304–341. https://doi.org/10.1037/0033-2909.111.2.304

Fielder, R. L., & Carey, M. P. (2010). Predictors and consequences of sexual "hookups" among college students: A short-term prospective study. *Archives*

of Sexual Behavior, 39(5), 1105–1119. https://doi.org/10.1007/s10508-008-9448-4
Givens, D. B. (1978). The nonverbal basis of attraction: Flirtation, courtship, and seduction. *Psychiatry: Journal for the Study of Interpersonal Processes, 41*(4), 346–359. https://doi.org/10.1080/00332747.1978.11023994
Gowaty, P. A. (2018). On being and becoming female and male: A sex-neutral evolutionary perspective. In N. K. Dess, J. Marecek, & L. C. Bell (Eds.), *Gender, sex, and sexualities: Psychological perspectives* (pp. 77–102). Oxford University Press.
Grammer, K. (1990). Strangers meet: Laughter and nonverbal signs of interest in opposite-sex encounters. *Journal of Nonverbal Behavior, 14*(4), 209–236. https://doi.org/10.1007/BF00989317
Grammer, K., Kruck, K. B., & Magnusson, M. S. (1998). The courtship dance: Patterns of nonverbal synchronization in opposite-sex encounters. *Journal of Nonverbal Behavior, 22*(1), 3–29. https://doi.org/10.1023/A:1022986608835
Grammer, K., Kruck, K. B., Juette, A., & Fink, B. (2000). Non-verbal behavior as courtship signals: The role of control and choice in selecting partners. *Evolution and Human Behavior, 21*(6), 371–390. https://doi.org/10.1016/S1090-5138(00)00053-2
Greene, G. J., Fisher, K. A., Kuper, L., Andrews, R., & Mustanski, B. (2015). "Is this normal? Is this not normal? There's no set example": Sexual health intervention preferences of LGBT youth in romantic relationships. *Sexuality Research and Social Policy, 12*(1), 1–14.
Guerrero, L. K., & Wiedmaier, B. (2013). Nonverbal intimacy: Affectionate communication, positive involvement behavior, and flirtation. In J. A. Hall & M. L. Knapp (Eds.), *Handbooks of communication science. Nonverbal communication* (pp. 577–612). De Gruyter Mouton. https://doi.org/10.1515/9783110238150.577
Hall, J. A., & Canterberry, M. (2011). Sexism and assertive courtship strategies. *Sex Roles: A Journal of Research, 65*(11–12), 840–853. https://doi.org/10.1007/s11199-011-0045-y
Hall, J. A., & Gunnery, S. D. (2013). Gender differences in nonverbal communication. In J. A. Hall & M. L. Knapp (Eds.), *Handbooks of communication science. Nonverbal communication* (pp. 639–669). De Gruyter Mouton. https://doi.org/10.1515/9783110238150.639
Hall, J. A., & Xing, C. (2015). The verbal and nonverbal correlates of the five flirting styles. *Journal of Nonverbal Behavior, 39*(1), 41–68. https://doi.org/10.1007/s10919-014-0199-8

Harrison, M. A., & Shortall, J. C. (2011). Women and men in love: Who really feels it and says it first? *Journal of Social Psychology, 151*(6), 727–736. https://doi.org/10.1080/00224545.2010.522626

Hays, R. B. (1985). A longitudinal study of friendship development. *Journal of Personality and Social Psychology, 48*(4), 909–924. https://doi.org/10.1037/0022-3514.48.4.909

Henningsen, D. D. (2004). Flirting with meaning: An examination of miscommunication in flirting interactions. *Sex Roles, 50*(7–8), 481–489. https://doi.org/10.1023/B:SERS.0000023068.49352.4b

Herek, G. M., & McLemore, K. A. (2013). Sexual prejudice. *Annual Review of Psychology, 64*, 309–333. https://doi.org/10.1146/annurev-psych-113011-143826

Houser, M. L., Horan, S. M., & Furler, L. A. (2008). Dating in the fast lane: How communication predicts speed-dating success. *Journal of Social and Personal Relationships, 25*(5), 749–768. https://doi.org/10.1177/0265407508093787

Hrdy, S. B., & Williams, G. C. (1983). Behavioral biology and the double standard. In S. K. Wasser (Ed.), *Social behavior of female vertebrates* (pp. 3–17). Academic Press.

Humphry, L. (1970). *Tearoom Trade: Impersonal sex in public places*. Duckworth.

Jesser, C. J. (1978). Male responses to direct verbal sexual initiatives of females. *Journal of Sex Research, 14*(2), 118–128. https://doi.org/10.1080/00224497809551000

Karami, A., Swan, S. C., White, C. N., & Ford, K. (2019). Hidden in plain sight for too long: Using text mining techniques to shine a light on workplace sexism and sexual harassment. *Psychology of Violence*. https://doi.org/10.1037/vio0000239

Kim, J. L., Sorsoli, C. L., Collins, K., Zylbergold, B. A., Schooler, D., & Tolman, D. L. (2007). From sex to sexuality: Exposing the heterosexual script on primetime network television. *Journal of Sex Research, 44*(2), 145–157. https://doi.org/10.1080/00224490701263660

Klinkenberg, D., & Rose, S. (1994). Dating scripts of gay men and lesbians. *Journal of Homosexuality, 26*(4), 23–35. https://doi.org/10.1300/J082v26n04_02

Knapp, M. L. (1978). *Social intercourse: From greeting to goodbye*. Needham Heights, MA, USA: Allyn & Bacon.

Knapp, M. L., Hall, J. A., & Horgan, T. G. (2021). *Nonverbal communication in human interaction* (9th ed.). Kendall Hunt.

Lippman, J. R., Ward, L. M., & Seabrook, R. C. (2014). Isn't it romantic? Differential associations between romantic screen media genres and romantic beliefs. *Psychology of Popular Media Culture, 3*(3), 128–140. https://doi.org/10.1037/ppm0000034

Marston, P. J., Hecht, M. L., Manke, M. L., McDaniel, S., & Reeder, H. (1998). The subjective experience of intimacy, passion, and commitment in heterosexual loving relationships. *Personal Relationships, 5*(1), 15–30. https://doi.org/10.1111/j.14756811.1998.tb00157.x

McCormick, N. B., & Jones, A. J. (1989). Gender differences in nonverbal flirtation. *Journal of Sex Education and Therapy, 15*(4), 271–282. https://doi.org/10.1515/9783110238150.639

McQuillen, J. S., McQuillen, M. Z., & Garza, R. D. (2014). Hispanic women's use of nonverbal flirting cues. *International Journal of Humanities and Social Sciences, 4*(10), 25–30.

Meyer, I. H. (2013). Prejudice, social stress, and mental health in lesbian, gay, and bisexual populations: Conceptual issues and research evidence. *Psychology of Sexual Orientation and Gender Diversity, 1*(S), 3–26. https://doi.org/10.1037/2329-0382.1.S.3

Moore, M. M. (1985). Nonverbal courtship patterns in women: Context and consequences. *Ethology and Sociobiology, 6*(4), 237–247. https://doi.org/10.1016/1062-3095(85)90016-0

Moore, M. M. (2010). Human nonverbal courtship behavior: A brief historical review. *Journal of Sex Research, 47*(2), 171–180. https://doi.org/10.1080/00224490903402520

Peplau, L. A., & Fingerhut, A. W. (2007). The close relationships of lesbian and gay men. *Annual Review of Psychology, 58*, 405–424. https://doi.org/10.1146/annurev.psych.58.110405.085701

Perper, T. (1985). *Sex signals: The biology of love*. ISI Press.

Perrin, P. B., Heesacker, M., Tiegs, T. J., Swan, L. K., Lawrence, A. W., Jr., Smith, M. B., Carrillo, R. J., Cawood, R. L., & Mejia-Millan, C. M. (2011). Aligning Mars and Venus: The social construction and instability of gender differences in romantic relationships. *Sex Roles: A Journal of Research, 64*(9–10), 613–628. https://doi.org/10.1007/s11199-010-9804-4

Pines, A. M. (2001). The role of gender and culture in romantic attraction. *European Psychologist, 6*(2), 96–102. https://doi.org/10.1027/1016-9040.6.2.96

Prager, K. J. (2000). Intimacy in personal relationships. In C. Hendrick & S. S. Hendrick (Eds.), *Close relationships: A sourcebook* (pp. 229–242). Sage.

Prokosch, M. D., Scheib, J., Coss, R. G., & Blozis, S. (2009). Intelligence and mate choice: Intelligent men are always appealing. *Evolution and Human Behavior, 30*(1), 11–20. https://doi.org/10.1016/j.evolhumbehav.2008.07.004

Reis, H. T., Maniaci, M. R., Caprariello, P. A., Eastwick, P. W., & Finkel, E. J. (2011). Familiarity does indeed promote attraction in live interaction. *Journal of Personality and Social Psychology, 101*(3), 557–570. https://doi.org/10.1037/a0022885

Remland, M. S. (2009). *Nonverbal communication in everyday life* (2nd ed.). Pearson Learning Solutions.

Renninger, L. A., Wade, T. J., & Grammer, K. (2004). Getting that female glance: Patterns and consequences of male nonverbal behavior in courtship contexts. *Evolution and Human Behavior, 25*(6), 416–431. https://doi.org/10.1080/00224490903402520

Rich, A. (1980). Compulsory heterosexuality and lesbian existence. *Signs, 5*(4), 631–660.

Riggle, E. D. B., Rostosky, S. S., McCants, L. E., & Pascale-Hague, D. (2011). The positive aspects of a transgender self-identification. *Psychology & Sexuality, 2*(2), 147–158. https://doi.org/10.1080/19419899.2010.534490

Rostosky, S. S., Riggle, E. D. B., Pascale-Hague, D., & McCants, L. E. (2010). The positive aspects of a bisexual self-identification. *Psychology & Sexuality, 1*(2), 131–144. https://doi.org/10.1080/19419899.2010.484595

Seabrook, R. C., Ward, L. M., Reed, L., Manago, A., Giaccardi, S., & Lippman, J. R. (2016). Our scripted sexuality: The development and validation of a measure of the heterosexual script and its relation to television consumption. *Emerging Adulthood, 4*(5), 338–355. https://doi.org/10.1177/2167696815623686

Simon, W., & Gagnon, J. H. (1986). Sexual scripts: Permanence and change. *Archives of Sexual Behavior, 15*(2), 97–120. https://doi.org/10.1007/BF01542219

Sullivan, S. P., Pingel, E. S., Stephenson, R., & Bauermeister, J. A. (2018). "It was supposed to be a onetime thing": Experiences of romantic and sexual relationship typologies among young gay, bisexual, and other men who have sex with men. *Archives of Sexual Behavior, 47*(4), 1221–1230. https://doi.org/10.1007/s10508-017-1058-6

Tang-Martínez, Z. (2016). Rethinking Bateman's principles: Challenging persistent myths of sexually reluctant females and promiscuous males. *Journal of Sex Research, 53*(4–5), 532–559. https://doi.org/10.1080/00224499.2016.1150938

Tolhuizen, J. H. (1989). Communication strategies for intensifying dating relationships: Identification, use and structure. *Journal of Social and Personal Relationships, 6*(4), 413–434. https://doi.org/10.1177/0265407589064002

Trivers, R. L. (1972). Parental investment and sexual selection. In B. Campbell (Ed.), *Sexual selection and the descent of man, 1871–1971* (pp. 136–179). Aldine.

Vaughan, M. D., & Rodriguez, E. M. (2014). LGBT strengths: Incorporating positive psychology into theory, research, training, and practice. *Psychology of Sexual Orientation and Gender Diversity, 1*(4), 325–334. https://doi.org/10.1037/sgd0000053

Vencill, J. A., & Israel, T. (2018). Shining a light into the darkness: Bisexuality and relationships. *Sexual and Relationship Therapy, 33*(1–2), 1–5. https://doi.org/10.1080/14681994.2018.1416826

Walsh, D. G., & Hewitt, J. (1985). Giving men the come-on: Effect of eye contact and smiling in a bar environment. *Perceptual and Motor Skills, 61*(3, Pt 1), 873–874.

Ward, L. M., & Cox, V. (2021). Is that a real woman? Reality TV viewing and black viewers' beliefs about femininity. *Psychology of Popular Media.*

Warner, M. (1991). Introduction: Fear of a queer plane. *Social Text, 29*, 3–17. https://doi.org/10.1037/ppm0000291

Whitbeck, L. B., & Hoyt, D. R. (1994). Social prestige and assertive mating: A comparison of students from 1956 and 1988. *Journal of Social and Personal Relationships, 11*(1), 137–145. https://doi.org/10.1177/0265407594111008

Whitty, M. T. (2009). Revealing the 'real' me, searching for the 'actual' you: Presentations of self on an internet dating site. *Computers in Human Behavior, 24*(4), 1707–1723.

Willis, F. N., & Briggs, L. F. (1992). Relationship and touch in public settings. *Journal of Nonverbal Behavior, 16*(1), 55–63. https://doi.org/10.1007/BF00986879

Zentner, M., & Mitura, K. (2012). Stepping out of the caveman's shadow: Nations' gender gap predicts degree of sex differentiation in mate preferences. *Psychological Science, 23*(10), 1176–1185.

Zurbriggen, E. L., & Morgan, E. M. (2006). Who wants to marry a millionaire? Reality dating television programs, attitudes toward sex, and sexual behaviors. *Sex Roles: A Journal of Research, 54*(1–2), 1–17. https://doi.org/10.1007/s11199-005-8865-2

7

Misunderstood Non-verbal Cues in Close Relationships: Contributions of Research over Opinions

Amy S. Ebesu Hubbard

The possibility of reading another's body language is sometimes too alluring to avoid. Promises of being able to "see" a relational partner's true intentions, having insight into whether he or she is cheating on you, knowing who is the boss in the relationship, recognizing his or her actual commitment level, or detecting their romantic and sexual interest are quite tantalising. Unfortunately, there is a difference between what patterns of non-verbal communicative behaviour might reveal about close relationships in general and the non-verbal behaviour exhibited by a specific individual in a close relationship. Research might shed light on the former but cannot make predictions about the latter. This does not stop talk shows from bringing on guests to "read" people or news organizations from presenting experts who can dissect a politician, person of

I have no conflicts of interest to disclose.

A. S. Ebesu Hubbard (✉)
Department of Communicology, University of Hawai'i at Mānoa,
Honolulu, HI, USA
e-mail: aebesu@hawaii.edu

R. J. Sternberg, A. Kostić (eds.), *Nonverbal Communication in Close Relationships*,
https://doi.org/10.1007/978-3-030-94492-6_7

interest, or celebrity's conduct. Magazine writers offer tips and quizzes about the telltale behaviours of a host of traits pertaining to those on the dating scene or in loving relationships for entertainment purposes ostensibly, while readers might assume they are immutable facts. Romantic comedies and dramatic films depict close relationships that writers have imagined and created, perhaps inspired by their own personal experiences, but viewers may see these relationships, and the concomitant behaviours and non-verbal communication wisdom shared by the characters in the films, as reality for most people. The challenge continues to be how to tell the difference.

Knowledge about how scholars conduct studies and analyse non-verbal communication can aid in helping people to differentiate lay opinion and anecdote from scientific research findings. Additionally, the juxtaposition of examples of lay advice and public conceptualizations, generalizations, and biases with what we know from research conducted on non-verbal behaviour in the realm of relationships can further illuminate what is misunderstood and understood about non-verbal communication in close relationships.

Distinguishing Lay from Scientific

During our daily interactions, we encounter people making claims about the meaning and significance of ours and others' behaviours. These assertions may come from well-intentioned strangers, friends, family members, and co-workers dissecting the attributes of your loved one's behaviour on social media or from experts a news organization recruited to comment on an instance of intimate partner violence by a sports figure or the supposed rejection of a politician by a spouse who refuses to hold hands in public, to name a few. Judgements of the accuracy may be based on a feeling, intuition, the reasonableness of the claim, or consistency among a panel of analysts. There is a danger here that people might mistake these sorts of analyses as facts about non-verbal communication and how they operate in close relationships.

To avoid this pitfall, familiarity with how non-verbal communication and close relationships are examined in scientific research is useful.

Scholars who study non-verbal behaviour use systematic methods that are orderly, planned, and documented to allow others to see how the study was conducted and to be able to replicate the study in the future. This may take two general forms: a grounded approach and a hypothesis-testing approach (Hecht & Guerrero, 2008). In the grounded approach, scholars pose research questions about an aspect of non-verbal communication and then the non-verbal behaviour is studied, observed, described, and organized in an attempt to answer the posed research questions. In the hypothesis-testing approach, scholars are attempting to rule out that chance explains a particular pattern of behaviour. They often do this by making predictions about non-verbal behaviour and then determine whether there is evidence to support the predictions. They collect data and estimate the probability that a certain outcome occurred. If this exceeds a predetermined benchmark, then the researchers conclude that there is evidence, within a reasonable degree of certainty that the outcome observed does not exist by chance alone.

Armed with this fundamental knowledge, it is possible to recognize when something does not meet the rigour of a scientific investigation. First, a basic tenet of the scientific method is that it involves a priori questions or predictions. Researchers ask questions or make educated guesses ahead of seeing any data. They do not want to be influenced by knowing a result. Thus, when you hear someone explaining a person's behaviour after the fact, there is reason to be suspicious that the claims that person is making to discuss another's behaviour is conjecture. It is very easy to state factors that caused an outcome, when you already know the outcome. The factors used to explain a known result may be coincidental or may be overstated. If a mom pleads in a press conference for the safe return of her kidnapped child and is later discovered to have killed her own child, then it is easy for a so-called expert, post hoc, to say these specific non-verbal behaviours the mother exhibited showed that she was lying. The validity of the expert's assertions is debatable because we are already aware of the outcome: the mother was known to have lied when the expert provided an analysis.

When an outcome is known and there are no predetermined questions to focus observation or predictions to test, bias is introduced which can color our perceptions. For example, Levine, Asada, and Park (2006) demonstrated that when people were told that the person they would be watching in a video clip was deceptive, the viewers thought the person they watched exhibited less eye contact, than when people were not given any information on whether the person in the video clip was deceptive. Participants watched the exact same video clips but saw two different degrees of eye contact, depending on whether they thought deception occurred or when they did not have that prime.

Second, scientific research on non-verbal communication and close relationships examines a group of people, many couples, or several instances, and not a solo individual, a single couple, or a sole instance. Scientific claims are about what is likely to happen overall, and not in a specific case. An individual person can report a contradictory experience. An undergraduate student who hears a professor discuss a research finding might dispute the results by saying that it does not apply to their situation. This is correct. The research finding might not apply, but this does not make the research finding necessarily incorrect. It highlights a misunderstanding when the student assumes a research result should apply to all cases, including their particular situation. Rather, a research finding is making a generalization about most people (who are like those who were studied and in the manner they were studied), not about a given instance. Individual cases vary. Scientists recognize this and are upfront that their claims are not about a specific individual. Thus, inherently, if someone is making a claim about your non-verbal behaviour in particular, this again is speculation about the non-verbal behaviour. Consider, for example, Van Raalte, Floyd, and Mongeau's (2021) finding that married couples who spent more time cuddling over four weeks showed improvements in their relationship satisfaction than married couples who spent more time together during meals or who did not change their behaviour. These researchers are not claiming that if you and your spouse engage in more physically affectionate touching, you both will be happier in your marriage. They are stating that, on the whole, married couples who engaged in more cuddling reported more relationship happiness than couples who did not. On the whole versus a single instance is the difference here.

Third, another aspect of scientific research to be attentive to when hearing claims about non-verbal communication in close relationships is probability. Probability is always involved. There is a chance that scientists could be wrong. Scientists do not rely on a single study, but look across many studies to draw tentative conclusions about non-verbal behaviour in close relationships. Scientists do not talk in absolutes, but they point to what the evidence indicates or supports in general while acknowledging that there is room for error. Science is an accumulation of knowledge that progresses over time. And, corrections, modifications, and refinements are an integral and fundamental part of the scientific process.

When studying non-verbal communication in close relationships, there are a multitude of researcher-driven decisions that make findings from a single research study tentative. Researchers make choices about how they will collect data, whether it is through self-reports, observer assessments, or physiological measurements. When observers are used, researchers also decide on whether the observers will be trained or untrained, whether they will be strangers who do not know the people they are observing or known others such as relational partners, friends, and family members. Researchers make decisions about where, when, how often, and how long they will collect the data. They decide on the measurement scheme they will use, the unit of analysis they will examine, and what type of data they will include.

As White and Sargent (2005) pointed out, there are advantages and disadvantages associated with the decisions researchers make when conducting a study of non-verbal behaviour. When people are observed in an experiment, they are aware they are being studied. This may change, intensify, or de-intensify their behaviour. Experimental studies introduce controls to be able to isolate the variables of interest, and there may be questions about the ecological validity of the study. Sometimes researchers visually record non-verbal behaviours, but the camera will only capture what is in its viewfinder and not the rest of the surrounding context. When scholars ask people to report on their behaviours, those people may not be fully aware of what they do and when they do it, or they may be biased toward recalling certain types of behaviours. When observers' assessments differ from the actual participants in a study, scientists will need to reconcile those impressions. When researchers connect people to equipment that will record physiological measurements, the unusualness of the situation may inhibit or impede some behaviours the participants might normally exhibit or introduce new behaviours.

Even when a naturalistic observation is conducted, there are trade-offs. When researchers try to observe people's behaviour without interfering and affecting the people they are observing, this means they have access to only certain types of non-verbal behaviours and may not be able to view others (Hertenstein et al., 2006). They may more readily see public and socially sanctioned behaviours and not those within the home or bedroom. For example, naturalistic observations of touch among adults have not captured aggressive or socially inappropriate touches in their descriptions (e.g., Heslin & Alper, 1983; Jones & Yarbrough, 1985). However, we do know that these forms of touch do occur from self-reports of violence experienced in relationships (Christopher & Lloyd, 2001) and from observations of young children at playgrounds who may be less constrained by societal standards (Guerrero & Ebesu, 1993). Reports of naturalistic observations of adults do not reveal these sorts of behaviours.

Examination of close relationships necessitates additional researcher decisions. Scientists must define the close relationship they will study, which will inevitably include some and exclude others. For instance, close relationships might be defined by a feeling experienced or behaviours enacted by one or both partners. They may be determined by the length of time the couple has been together at a certain relationship stage or the overall length of time they have known each other. Close relational partners who participate in research studies often report high levels of satisfaction in their relationships, even when not recruited with that characteristic. This is understandable, especially if the study is labour-intensive, if a couple needs to come to a study location multiple times, or if the research will span a longer period of time. People in less happy and less stable relationships may choose not to participate in research to avoid having their relationship scrutinized, and they may be prone to dropping out of longitudinal studies. There may also be differences in how they view and interpret the non-verbal behaviours of their relational partners. Indeed, Noller (1992, 2005) demonstrated, using a standard content methodology, that people in distressed marriages made more errors when decoding the non-verbal behaviours of their spouses and made more negative judgements about the intentions of their spouses than those in non-distressed marriages.

All of these researcher decisions have consequences for how scholars frame the claims they make regarding non-verbal communication in close relationships. Researchers, when reporting their results, are careful to match how the study was conducted when relaying the findings. For example, consider one non-verbal communication area about relationships that often interests the public: men's supposed preoccupation with women's physical appearance. You might hear lay people talking about sex differences between men and women that are associated with physical attractiveness research. Typically, a version of the findings that is repeated is that men care about good looks, but women care about good earning potential of romantic partners (and not their looks). The research, however, does not support this claim and the imprecision in paraphrasing what was actually found in studies of this nature sets up an either/or fallacy. The actual research findings do not demonstrate that a person either sees physical attractiveness as important or sees income potential as important. This is a false choice. Instead, when sex differences and characteristics of mates were found in studies (and there is controversy on that aspect in the research literature, see Eastwick, Luchies, Finkel, & Hunt, 2014; Eastwick, Neff, Finkel, Luchies, & Hunt, 2014; Meltzer et al., 2014), the comparison between men and women is on ratings or rankings of various attributes. Indeed, when asked to rank order traits or rate preferences for a mate, men will place being physically attractive higher than women, and women will place good income potential higher than men (Buss & Barnes, 1986). When asked to indicate the importance of each attribute in a mate or an ideal partner, men tended to score physical attractiveness as higher in importance than women; and women tended to score good earning potential higher in importance than men (Buss, 1989; Eastwick & Finkel, 2008). However, this does not mean that women judge physical attractiveness as unimportant when selecting a mate. Both men and women place importance on the physical attractiveness of others, but men just do so to a greater extent than women.

Additionally, when scholars conduct research, they are also attentive to past work in the area to situate their study in the body of knowledge accumulated and to know the current thinking on the subject matter. When findings become discussed in the public sphere, however, sometimes the research of a scholar that has since been refined as a matter of scientific progress is missed and then is reified. Non-verbal communication's impact is one that is oft-repeated but is a mistaken claim (Burgoon, 1994; Burgoon et al., 2010; Lapakko, 1997). The faulty assertion is that non-verbal communication accounts for 93% of a message's meaning while verbal communication accounts for only 7%. Sometimes, people will further apportion the 93% figure into meaning stemming from 55% facial non-verbal cues and 38% vocal non-verbal cues. These claims are based on Mehrabian and colleagues' initial work in the 1960s (Mehrabian & Ferris, 1967; Mehrabian & Wiener, 1967). Subsequent research, however, and commentary on these numbers, even by Mehrabian himself (as cited in Lapakko, 1997), have disputed reliance on those figures for several reasons. For example, Mehrabian's research was focused on the communication of attitudes and feelings and not on all communicative messages. The manner in which the research was conducted did not allow language or the verbal component to vary to be able to affect message meaning substantially. Further, the verbal, facial, and vocal cues were never actually compared in a single study. Mehrabian and Ferris (1967) proposed that such a study could be conducted in the future when discussing their research.

All this points to the idea that scientific study of non-verbal communication in close relationships is not infallible. There are choices that are being made that can affect the certainty with which scholars might make claims about non-verbal communication in close relationships. Researchers, however, readily acknowledge this and note there is a margin of error in any finding and that it is an accumulation of knowledge and a preponderance of evidence that gives more credence to claims that are being made. This recognition that there is a probability that the researchers could be wrong and that there are limitations to theirs and every study are hallmarks of scientific thinking. When someone speaks as if something is factual without any recourse, plug your ears and run the other way.

Some Non-verbal Misunderstandings

Now let us consider a few specific examples of non-verbal behaviours that can be misused or misjudged, leading to misunderstandings when thinking about communication in close relationships or when thinking about those who desire to have close relationships. This might happen when seeking to reconcile assumptions about longer eye gaze during initial romantic encounters, the role of non-verbal behaviors in the sexual consent process, observers' judgements versus people's self-reports of close relationship status and dynamics, and cross-cultural differences in non-verbal behaviours in close relationships.

The Advice to Make Eye Contact on a First Date

People may wax poetically about gazing into their lover's eyes. People may ruminate about the lingering gazes of mutual attraction and sexual tension when a relationship was new. The romantically inclined might feel the charge of excitement and intrigue at the prospect of a potential connection when meeting someone's interested gaze from across a room. Films and dating reality shows might intensify the focus on the eyes by featuring close-ups of peoples' faces as they exchange looks with a suitor. The assumption undergirding these examples is the positive messages thought to be conveyed with sustained eye contact. When this type of eye contact is not present, people may be anxious about it. For example, Spalding, Zimmerman, Fruhauf, Banning, and Pepin (2010) examined the relationship advice in the question-and-answer columns of five top-selling magazines targeted at men. One particular question they pointed to was related to a man who was perplexed by women who avoided eye contact with him when he thought they were interested in him. He wondered if the lack of eye contact signalled other issues such as timidness or conceitedness. Findings from research on non-verbal communication during courtship and the initiation of relationships as well as research on the functions of nonverbal communication provides some insights into these dynamics and generally tempers the notion that more eye contact is necessarily better eye contact.

Non-verbal communication research does demonstrate that longer gazes can enhance attraction, signal more intimacy, and reflect liking of another compared to shorter gazes or averted gazes (Burgoon & Le Poire, 1999; Palmer & Simmons, 1995). Kleinke, Staneski, and Berger (1975) also showed that a lack of gaze was viewed as inattentiveness to another person. However, there are important exceptions to the more-eye-contact-is-good and the less-eye-contact-is-bad mindset. In the case of courtship and flirting, research indicates that eye contact may be fleeting, intermittent, and sustained (Moore, 2010). Kleinke (1986) concluded after reviewing research on gaze that moderate amounts of eye contact were preferred over extensive gazing or no gazing at another person when assessing people's liking of another. Burgoon et al. (2010) noted that when heavy gazing is combined with negative facial expressions, intimidation and aggression are likely interpretations of that non-verbal cue combination and not affection.

Additionally, scholars have consistently demonstrated that the eyes can serve multiple functions in communication (Burgoon et al., 2010; Patterson 1991). These include not only expressing affection and intimacy, but also managing interaction and conversations, exerting influence and control, forming impressions, and aiding in accomplishing various goals. As such, eye contact can be misunderstood. Assuming longer gaze, mutual or otherwise, is desirable can be problematic in some situations.

For example, prolonged eye contact might hamper conversational effectiveness. Research has demonstrated that eye contact serves an important role in turn-taking and regulating conversations. Burgoon et al.'s (2010) discussion of the research on eye behaviour during conversations indicates a complex but routinized set of behaviours that are synchronized precisely. Eye contact, be it one-sided gazing, mutual looks, and gaze aversion, aids in the smooth coordination of signalling who has the conversational floor and who is listening and engaged. Knapp, Hart, Friedrich, and Shulman (1973) found that the most frequently used non-verbal behaviour to end conversations was breaks in eye contact. Sustained eye contact can disrupt the process by which we manage conversations and this can make interactions feel awkward and clunky. This may be particularly problematic for romantically interested but newly acquainted others out on their first date. Ebesu Hubbard, Aune, and Lee's (2018) research indicated that smooth, relaxed, and coordinated interactions were particularly important for having satisfying conversations during initial interactions. Additionally, other research has shown that being behaviourally in sync can increase feelings of intimacy, closeness, and sexual desire (Sharon-David et al., 2019). Thus, on the whole, too much eye contact may be counterproductive to having a successful first date, but eye contact that is appropriate and in sync with other non-verbal cues and the rest of the conversation can increase liking (Maxwell et al., 1985).

The Policy to Communicate "Yes" if You Are Interested in Sex

In the effort to reduce or successfully prosecute instances of sexual violence, particularly sexual coercion and rape, legislation, university policies, and educational interventions have been adopted in support of affirmative consent (Beres, 2020; Novack, 2017). Affirmative consent generally stipulates that agreement to engage in sexual acts between people must be given prior to the act, voluntarily, consciously, continuously, and clearly (Little, 2005). Affirmative consent explanations are often accompanied with the dictum, "yes means yes". One challenging aspect to this standard is the role of non-verbal communication in the process and whether non-verbal behaviour sans verbal behaviour can be clear, and if it can be, then by whose judgement and whose judgement will determine the non-verbal behaviour's meaning.

Reviews of research on the role of non-verbal communication in sexual encounters indicate that there are important considerations that may be overlooked or underappreciated in affirmative consent decrees (Pugh & Becker, 2018). For example, Hickman and Muehlenhard (1999) found that both men and women most frequently reported indicating agreement to engage in sexual activity with no response or not resisting the activity. Hall (1998) noted that ongoing consent was rarely given for all individual sexual behaviours, and when permission was asked, it was often at the onset of sexual activity and before sexual intercourse and was given non-verbally. Hall also found that when verbal and non-verbal cues in response to someone initiating sexual activity co-occurred, this tended to be for more intimate activities such as intercourse and oral sex.

Vannier and O'Sullivan (2011) examined diaries they asked young adults in committed heterosexual relationships to keep and discovered that initiations of sexual activity were primarily non-verbal in nature as well and partners generally responded in reciprocal fashion. Participants described non-verbal invitations being met with non-verbal responses, and verbal invitations being met with verbal responses. Vannier and O'Sullivan also reported that the majority of the non-verbal initiation strategies and responses shared by the young adults in their study were indirect behaviours, such as smiling, hugging, and kissing a partner. Vannier and O'Sullivan concluded that in committed heterosexual young adult relationships, actions matter more than words during the seeking and responding to sexual invitations. Beres, Herold, and Maitland (2004) reported similar results for same-sex relationships when initiating and responding to invitations for sex. Responses to asking for and giving consent to engage in sexual activity were communicated primarily through non-verbal means rather than verbal, and this was especially true for men when they responded to other men who desired sex with them.

Bedera (2021) reported on interviews with college men about their sexual encounters in long-term and short-term relationships. Bedera concluded that the men appeared to endorse the notion embodied in affirmative consent policies but described indicators of consent during their actual sexual encounters that were primarily physical and non-verbal in nature. Bedera reported that nearly 40% of the cues the men reported relying upon as an indicator of consent were ambiguous and non-sexual in nature. The two most common among them were moaning and engaging in eye contract. King, Fallon, Reynolds, Williamson, Barber, and Giovinazzo (2020) similarly found that about a third of college men rated several non-verbal cues (e.g., dancing closely with grinding and kissing with tongues), some of which that did not involve intimate touching and could occur in non-sexual friendships (e.g., not moving away), as indicating some degree of sexual consent. King, et al. also reported that when combinations of non-verbal cues were present, both college men and women saw this as indicating sexual consent when compared to single non-verbal cues.

Another way the communication of consent was examined is through their portrayal in films. These films may reflect, reinforce, or influence the sexual behaviour of viewers. If films teach its audience about sexual consent, they appear to be teaching audiences to do so non-verbally. Jozkowski, Marcantonio, Rhoads, Canan, Hunt, and Willis (2019) conducted a content analysis of mainstream films released in 2013. They focused specifically on how sexual consent and refusals were depicted. Unsurprisingly, they found that characters in these films showed sexual consent most often non-verbally and implicitly. They also discovered that there were two common consent patterns displayed by characters: implicit non-verbal behaviours followed by explicit non-verbal behaviours or implicit verbal behaviours followed by implicit non-verbal behaviours. These researchers also reported that refusals to engage in sexual activity were typically portrayed as non-verbal or as an explicit verbal behaviour. Jozkowski et al. further examined relationship status and found that sexual activity in established relationships were most frequently depicted without a consenting process but skipped to showing established relational partners already engaged in sexual behaviour as compared to other relationship types (e.g., novel relationships).

Thus, public policies requiring and encouraging the communication of clear agreement to engage in sex must account for the fact that sexual consent is regularly conveyed non-verbally and implicitly and consent in established relationships may be different than newly formed ones. Moreover, the non-verbal behaviours relied upon for consent may not mean "yes" to sex by all parties.

Distinguishing Observers from Relational Partners' Reports on Haptic Behaviour

Sometimes what is seen is not what is actually occurring in relationships. For example, in public settings, if you see a pair of people from different sexes sitting together and touching each other, you might think that they are romantically involved. Paparazzi make a living by photographing celebrities in potentially compromising situations when they hold hands, kiss, or hug someone who is not their primary romantic partner. Research on haptics or touch in public settings demonstrates that sometimes observations of behaviour can be misleading. For example, Afifi and Johnson (1999, 2005) coded the behaviour of different-sex friendships and heterosexual daters in college bars. They found that some forms of touching behaviour were exhibited by both friends and daters. They reported that these touches were observed with relatively equal frequency between friends and daters and they did not differentiate the type of relationship. Those types of touches, sometimes intimate in nature, included fully embracing each other, leaning one's head on the other, patting or rubbing the other's shoulders or legs, and holding each other's hands. Observations of non-verbal behaviour to determine what is happening in a close relationship and the reliance on single cues increase the need to verify judgements.

In another instance, when people are asked to observe people holding hands or review photographs of people holding hands, researchers commonly found that those in the upper hand or lead hand position were the men in the romantic relationship and implied or conferred the status of being the more dominant person (Chapell et al., 1998, 1999; Pettijohn II et al., 2013). However, when relational partners are doing the hand holding themselves and dominance in the relationship is determined through actions other than the hand holding or through relational partners' self-reports, the lead hand dominance connection washes away and it appears that height is the better predictor of who has the lead hand in couples (Che et al., 2013; Ebesu Hubbard et al., 2018).

These studies point to misunderstandings that can happen when we observe non-verbal behaviour from a distance and examine individual cues in relative isolation. Close relationships are not always what they appear to be non-verbally.

Non-verbal Cultural Blinders

Cultures can vary along several dimensions. Burgoon et al. (2010) identified five cultural dimensions that are tied to non-verbal communication: individualist/collectivist cultures, high-/low-power distance cultures, feminine/masculine cultures, immediate/non-immediate cultures, and high-/low-context cultures. The latter two of these seem particularly relevant to non-verbal communication in close relationships. People from immediate cultures are more non-verbally immediate in that they engage in more physical touch, stand closer to each other, make more eye contact, face each other more directly, and speak louder than people from non-immediate cultures (Andersen, Hecht, Hoobler, & Smallwood, 2002). Someone in a high-context culture privileges the physical context, environment, and non-verbal cues. They also rely on people's judgements and interpretations for understanding meaning. Someone in a low-context culture privileges the verbal messages themselves and values clear and explicit language (Hall, 1981).

Misunderstandings can happen when people's cultural differences clash in a close relationship. For example, Tili and Barker (2015) conducted semi-structured interviews of couples in intercultural marriages in which one partner was Caucasian American and one partner was Asian. Their analysis of the interviews revealed that a common theme that influenced marital couples' communication with each other was reflected in high-context and low-context cultural differences. Caucasian American spouses showed low-context culture preferences in that they wanted their Asian spouses to more directly communicate with them and say what was on their minds. Asian spouses exhibited high-context culture preferences in that they wanted their Caucasian American spouses to be able to see their meaning through their non-verbal behaviours and contextual cues without needing to directly verbalize their specific thought or feeling.

Research has provided evidence that cultures share both similarities and dissimilarities in their communicative behaviours and this pattern holds true for nonverbal cues in close relationships. For instance, Sorokowska et al. (2021) conducted a sweeping study on haptic behaviour across 45 countries. They specifically examined interpersonal affective touch (e.g., kissing and hugging) in close relationships (i.e., intimate partner, female friend, male friend, and own child). People from China reported the lowest frequency of affective touch over the past week with an intimate partner, as well as with their own child. South Koreans had the lowest reported frequency of affective touch with a female friend. People from Poland had the lowest reported frequency of affective touch with a male friend. Karandashev, Zarubko, Artemeva, Neto, Surmanidze, and Feybesse (2016) compared cues associated with romantic physical attraction for four European countries. They found that the non-verbal cues associated with romantic attraction reported by people from Portugal, Georgia, Russia, and France shared similarities, especially for facial animation and pleasantness, but there were also some differences. For example, Portuguese, Georgian, and Russian men's romantic physical attraction to women was increased by women's expressive face and speaking. Georgian men also included women's smiles and laughter, and their facial structure as factors which increased their romantic physical attraction to women. For Russian men, they included women's smiling and laughter and their lips as increasing their romantic physical attraction, while singing was a factor that decreased their romantic physical attraction. For women from Portugal, the factors that increased their romantic physical attraction to men were men's eyes and body, and their romantic physical attraction was decreased by men's dress. For women from Georgia, it was an expressive face and speaking, smiles and laughter, and good skin which increased their romantic physical attraction to men. For women from Russia, romantic physical attraction was increased by men's expressive face and speaking, smiling and laughter, their body, and their dancing. For people from France, the only factor of those studied that significantly contributed to increasing their romantic physical attraction was body, and this finding only pertained to men's attraction to women.

Cultural differences can change how we interpret non-verbal behaviours in relationships. These differences can challenge our notions of what is important and how we judge our partner's behaviours.

Conclusion

Understanding how research on non-verbal communication in close relationships is conducted and attention to the match or mis-match between what claims are made and whether there is scientific evidence that tested those claims are worthy efforts. These endeavours can help to reduce misunderstanding, misinterpretations, and overreaching proclamations about the role of non-verbal behaviour in our relationships with others.

References

Afifi, W. A., & Johnson, M. L. (1999). The use and interpretation of tie-signs in a public setting: Relationship and sex differences. *Journal of Social and Personal Relationships, 16*(1), 9–38. https://doi.org/10.1177/0265407599161002

Afifi, W. A., & Johnson, M. L. (2005). The nature and function of tie-signs. In V. Manusov (Ed.), *The sourcebook of nonverbal measures: Going beyond words* (pp. 189–198). Lawrence Erlbaum Associates.

Andersen, P. A., Hecht, M. L., Hoobler, G. D., & Smallwood, M. (2002). Nonverbal communication across culture. In W. B. Gudykunst & B. Mody (Eds.), *Handbook of international and intercultural communication* (pp. 89–106). Sage.

Bedera, N. (2021). Moaning and eye contact: Men's use of ambiguous signals in attributions of consent to their partners. *Violence Against Women, 27*(15–16), 3093–3113. https://doi.org/10.1177/1077801221992870

Beres, M. (2020). Perspectives of rape-prevention educators on the role of consent in sexual violence prevention. *Sex Education, 20*(2), 227–238. https://doi.org/10.1080/14681811.2019.1621744

Beres, M. A., Herold, E., & Maitland, S. B. (2004). Sexual consent behaviors in same-sex relationships. *Archives of Sexual Behavior, 33*(5), 475–486. https://doi.org/10.1023/B:ASEB.0000037428.41757.10

Burgoon, J. K. (1994). Nonverbal signals. In M. L. Knapp & G. R. Miller (Eds.), *Handbook of interpersonal communication* (2nd ed., pp. 229–285). Sage.

Burgoon, J. K., & Le Poire, B. A. (1999). Nonverbal cues and interpersonal judgments: Participant and observer perceptions of intimacy, dominance, composure, and formality. *Communication Monographs, 66*(2), 105–124. https://doi.org/10.1080/03637759909376467

Burgoon, J. K., Guerrero, L. K., & Floyd, K. (2010). *Nonverbal communication.* Allyn & Bacon.

Buss, D. (1989). Sex differences in human mate preferences: Evolutionary hypotheses tested in 37 cultures. *Behavioral and Brain Sciences, 12*(1), 1–14. https://doi.org/10.1017/S0140525X00023992

Buss, D. M., & Barnes, M. (1986). Preferences in human mate selection. *Journal of Personality and Social Psychology, 50*(3), 559–570. https://doi.org/10.1037/0022-3514.50.3.559

Chapell, M., Basso, E., DeCola, A., Hossack, J., Keebler, J., Marm, J., Reed, B., Webster, E., & Yoggev, D. (1998). Men and women holding hands: Whose hand is uppermost? *Perceptual and Motor Skills, 87*(1), 127–130. https://doi.org/10.2466/pms.1998.87.1.127

Chapell, M., Beltran, W., Santanello, M., Takahashi, M., Bantom, S. R., Donovan, J. S., Hernandez, S. C., Oculato, T. M., & Ray, N. M. (1999). Men and women holding hands II: Whose hand is uppermost? *Perceptual and Motor Skills, 89*(6), 537–549. https://doi.org/10.2466/pms.1999.89.2.537

Che, A., Siemens, I., Fejtek, M., & Wassersug, R. (2013). Who takes the lead hand? Correlates of handholding position in lesbian couples. *Journal of Homosexuality, 60*(11), 1625–1634. https://doi.org/10.1080/00918369.2013.824344

Christopher, F. S., & Lloyd, S. A. (2001). Physical and sexual aggression in relationships. In C. Hendrick & S. S. Hendrick (Eds.), *Close relationships* (pp. 331–343). Sage.

Eastwick, P. W., & Finkel, E. J. (2008). Sex differences in mate preferences revisited: Do people know what they initially desire in a romantic partner? *Journal of Personality and Social Psychology, 94*(2), 245–264. https://doi.org/10.1037/0022-3514.94.2.245

Eastwick, P. W., Luchies, L. B., Finkel, E. J., & Hunt, L. L. (2014). The predictive validity of ideal partner preferences: A review and meta-analysis. *Psychological Bulletin, 140*(3), 623–665. https://doi.org/10.1037/a0032432

Eastwick, P. W., Neff, L. A., Finkel, E. J., Luchies, L. B., & Hunt, L. L. (2014). Is a meta-analysis a foundation, or just another brick? Comment on Meltzer, McNulty, Jackson, and Karney (2014). *Journal of Personality and Social Psychology, 106*(3), 429–434. https://doi.org/10.1037/a0034767

Ebesu Hubbard, A. S., Aune, K. S., & Lee, H. E. (2018). Communication qualities, quantity, and satisfaction in newly developing relationships. *Journal of Speech, Media and Communication Research, 17*(4), 41–70.

Ebesu Hubbard, A. S., DelGreco, M., Hashi, E. C., Wharton, M. C. K., Aune, A., Quick, J., & Collins, H. (2018, February 16–19). *Couples holding hands in public: Does the person with the upper hand have the upper hand in the relationship?* [Paper presentation]. Western States Communication Association Annual Meeting, Santa Clara, CA., United States.

Guerrero, L. K., & Ebesu, A. S. (1993, May 27–31). *While at play: An observational analysis of children's touch during interpersonal interaction* [Paper presentation]. International Communication Association 43rd Annual Meeting, Washington, DC, United States.

Hall, E. T. (1981). *Beyond culture.* Anchor/Doubleday.

Hall, D. S. (1998). Consent for sexual behavior in a college student population. *Electronic Journal of Human Sexuality, 1.* Retrieved November 1, 2021, from http://www.ejhs.org/volume1/consent1.htm

Hecht, M. L., & Guerrero, L. K. (2008). Perspectives on nonverbal research methods. In L. K. Guerrero, J. A. DeVito, & M. L. Hecht (Eds.), *The nonverbal communication reader: Classic and contemporary readings* (3rd ed., pp. 24–41). Waveland Press.

Hertenstein, M. J., Verkamp, J. M., Kerestes, A. M., & Holmes, R. M. (2006). The communicative functions of touch in humans, nonhuman primates, and rats: A review and synthesis of the empirical research. *Genetic, Social, and General Psychology Monographs, 132*(1), 5–94. https://doi.org/10.3200/MONO.132.1.5-94

Heslin, R., & Alper, R. (1983). Touch: A bonding gesture. In J. M. Wiemann & R. P. Harrison (Eds.), *Nonverbal interaction* (pp. 47–75). Sage.

Hickman, S. E., & Muehlenhard, C. L. (1999). "By the semi-mystical appearance of a condom": How young women and men communicate sexual consent in heterosexual situations. *The Journal of Sex Research, 36*(3), 258–272. https://doi.org/10.1080/00224499909551996

Jones, S. E., & Yarbrough, A. E. (1985). A naturalistic study of meanings of touch. *Communication Monographs, 52*, 19–56. https://doi.org/10.1080/03637758509376094

Jozkowski, K. N., Marcantonio, T. L., Rhoads, K. E., Canan, S., Hunt, M. E., & Willis, M. (2019). A content analysis of sexual consent and refusal communication in mainstream films. *The Journal of Sex Research, 56*(6), 754–765. https://doi.org/10.1080/00224499.2019.1595503

Karandashev, V., Zarubko, E., Artemeva, V., Neto, F., Surmanidze, L., & Feybesse, C. (2016). Sensory values in romantic attraction in four Europeans countries: Gender and cross-cultural comparison. *Cross-Cultural Research, 50*(5), 478–504. https://doi.org/10.1177/1069397116674446

King, B. M., Fallon, M. R., Reynolds, E. P., Williamson, K. L., Barber, A., & Giovinazzo, A. R. (2020). College students' perceptions of concurrent/successive nonverbal behaviors as sexual consent. *Journal of Interpersonal Violence*. Advance online publication. https://doi.org/10.1177/0886260520905544

Kleinke, C. L. (1986). Gaze and eye contact: A research review. *Psychological Bulletin, 100*(1), 78–100. https://doi.org/10.1037/0033-2909.100.1.78

Kleinke, C. L., Staneski, R. A., & Berger, D. E. (1975). Evaluation of an interviewer as a function of interviewer gaze, reinforcement of subject gaze, and interviewer attractiveness. *Journal of Personality and Social Psychology, 31*(1), 115–122. https://doi.org/10.1037/h0076244

Knapp, M. L., Hart, R. P., Friedrich, G. W., & Shulman, G. M. (1973). The rhetoric of goodbye: Verbal and nonverbal correlates of human leave-taking. *Speech Monographs, 40*(3), 182–198. https://doi.org/10.1080/03637757309375796

Lapakko, D. (1997). Three cheers for language: A closer examination of a widely cited study of nonverbal communication. *Communication Education, 46*, 63–67. https://doi.org/10.1080/03634529709379073

Levine, T., Asada, K. J., & Park, H. (2006). The lying chicken and the gaze avoidant egg: Eye contact, deception, and causal order. *Southern Communication Journal, 71*(4), 401–411. https://doi.org/10.1080/10417940601000576

Little, N. J. (2005). From no means no to only yes means yes: The rational results of an affirmative consent standard in rape law. *Vanderbilt Law Review, 58*, 1322–1364.

Maxwell, G. M., Cook, M. W., & Burr, R. (1985). The encoding and decoding of liking from behavioral cues in both auditory and visual channels. *Journal of Nonverbal Behavior, 9*(4), 239–263. https://doi.org/10.1007/BF00986883

Mehrabian, A., & Ferris, S. R. (1967). Inference of attitudes from nonverbal communication in two channels. *Journal of Consulting Psychology, 31*(3), 248–252. https://doi.org/10.1037/h0024648

Mehrabian, A., & Wiener, M. (1967). Decoding of inconsistent communications. *Journal of Personality and Social Psychology, 6*(1), 109–114. https://doi.org/10.1037/h0024532

Meltzer, A. L., McNulty, J. K., Jackson, G. L., & Karney, B. R. (2014). Men still value physical attractiveness in a long-term mate more than women: Rejoinder to Eastwick, Neff, Finkel, Luchies, and Hunt (2014). *Journal of Personality & Social Psychology, 106*(3), 435–440. https://doi.org/10.1037/a0035342

Moore, M. M. (2010). Human nonverbal courtship behavior-a brief historical review. *The Journal of Sex Research, 47*(2–3), 171–180. https://doi.org/10.1080/00224490903402520

Noller, P. (1992). Nonverbal communication in marriage. In R. S. Feldman (Ed.), *Applications of nonverbal behavioral theories and research* (pp. 31–60). Psychology Press. https://doi.org/10.4324/9781315807140

Noller, P. (2005). Standard content methodology: Controlling the verbal channel. In V. Manusov (Ed.), *The sourcebook of nonverbal measures: Going beyond words* (pp. 417–430). Lawrence Erlbaum Associates.

Novack, S. (2017). Sex ed in higher ed: Should we say yes to "affirmative consent?". *Studies in Gender and Sexuality, 18*(4), 302–312. https://doi.org/10.1080/15240657.2017.1383074

Palmer, M. T., & Simmons, K. B. (1995). Communicating intentions through nonverbal behaviors conscious and nonconscious encoding of liking. *Human Communication Research, 22*(1), 128–160. https://doi.org/10.1111/j.1468-2958.1995.tb00364.x

Patterson, M. L. (1991). A functional approach to nonverbal exchange. In R. S. Feldman & B. Rimé (Eds.), *Fundamentals of nonverbal behavior* (pp. 458–495). Cambridge University Press.

Pettijohn, T. F., II, Ahmed, S. F., Dunlap, A. V., & Dickey, L. N. (2013). Who's got the upper hand? Hand holding behaviors among romantic couples and families. *Current Psychology, 32*(3), 217–220. https://doi.org/10.1007/s12144-013-9175-4

Pugh, B., & Becker, P. (2018). Exploring definitions and prevalence of verbal sexual coercion and its relationship to consent to unwanted sex: Implications for affirmative consent standards on college campuses. *Behavioral Sciences, 8*(8), 1–28. https://doi.org/10.3390/bs8080069

Sharon-David, H., Mizrahi, M., Rinott, M., Golland, Y., & Birnbaum, G. E. (2019). Being on the same wavelength: Behavioral synchrony between partners and its influence on the experience of intimacy. *Journal of Social & Personal Relationships, 36*(10), 2983–3008. https://doi.org/10.1177/0265407518809478

Sorokowska, A., Saluja, S., Sorokowski, P., Frąckowiak, T., Karwowski, M., Aavik, T., Akello, G., Alm, C., Amjad, N., Anjum, A., Asao, K., Atama, C. S., Atamtürk Duyar, D., Ayebare, R., Batres, C., Bendixen, M., Bensafia, A., Bizumic, B., Boussena, M., … Croy, I. (2021). Affective interpersonal touch in close relationships: A cross-cultural perspective. *Personality and Social Psychology Bulletin*. Advance online publication. https://doi.org/10.1177/0146167220988373

Spalding, R., Zimmerman, T. S., Fruhauf, C. A., Banning, J. H., & Pepin, J. (2010). Relationship advice in top-selling men's magazines: A qualitative document analysis. *Journal of Feminist Family Therapy, 22*(3), 203–224. https://doi.org/10.1080/08952833.2010.503795

Tili, T. R., & Barker, G. G. (2015). Communication in intercultural marriages: Managing cultural differences and conflicts. *The Southern Communication Journal, 80*(3), 189–210. https://doi.org/10.1080/1041794X.2015.1023826

Van Raalte, L. J., Floyd, K., & Mongeau, P. A. (2021). The effects of cuddling on relational quality for married couples: A longitudinal investigation. *Western Journal of Communication, 85*(1), 61–82. https://doi.org/10.1080/10570314.2019.1667021

Vannier, S. A., & O'Sullivan, L. F. (2011). Communicating interest in sex: Verbal and nonverbal initiation of sexual activity in young adults' romantic dating relationships. *Archives of Sexual Behavior, 40*(5), 961–969. https://doi.org/10.1007/s10508-010-9663-7

White, C. H., & Sargent, J. (2005). Researcher choices and practices in the study of nonverbal communication. In V. Manusov (Ed.), *The sourcebook of nonverbal measures: Going beyond words* (pp. 3–21). Lawrence Erlbaum Associates.

8

What Words Don't Tell Us: Non-verbal Communication and Turmoil in Romantic Relationships

Diana K. Ivy and Shane A. Gleason

We only touch on rare occasions when we have sex. What happened to good old affection?

There's a lot of distance now. I guess we're just giving each other space.

We're a well-oiled machine when running the household, but sometimes I wish she'd look at me like she used to.

I don't know what's wrong; he's just so...quiet.

D. K. Ivy (✉)
Department of Communication & Media, Texas A&M University-Corpus Christi, Corpus Christi, TX, USA
e-mail: diana.ivy@tamucc.edu

S. A. Gleason
Department of Social Studies, Texas A&M University-Corpus Christi, Corpus Christi, TX, USA
e-mail: shane.gleason@tamucc.edu

R. J. Sternberg, A. Kostić (eds.), *Nonverbal Communication in Close Relationships*,
https://doi.org/10.1007/978-3-030-94492-6_8

What do these statements have in common? Each alludes to non-verbal communication (i.e., messages sent without words or that accompany words) that may reveal turmoil in a romantic relationship. Sometimes romantic partners are barely aware that their relationship is problematic or headed for trouble; no more or less conflict may occur than partners consider normal. Feelings and thoughts may be just under the surface, more as instincts or concerns emerging on one's radar, rather than fully thought-out, realized problems. Partners may just get a vibe or a sense that something isn't quite right, but it's not yet the time to convert the vibe into a full-fledged conversation topic. In other situations, trouble or distress is obvious, but unspoken, not dealt with nor confronted, perhaps because partners are in denial, conflict avoidant, distracted, or unwilling to work on the relationship. In yet other relationships, the turmoil is quite real, as conflict threatens the relationship's continuation. Across a range of what can be considered turmoil in a relationship, non-verbal cues are affected and revealing, if one pays attention or knows what to look for.

Given research that suggests that approximately 93% of human emotion is communicated non-verbally, with only 7% communicated verbally, a focus on non-verbal cues in relationships experiencing turmoil is appropriate (Argyle, 1988; Kunecke et al., 2017; Mehrabian, 1972, 1981; Planalp, 2008). Thus, the purpose of this chapter is, first, to explore four sets of non-verbal cues associated with romantic relationships in turmoil. Then we overview relational turbulence, primarily via the work of communication scholars Denise Haunani Solomon and Leanne Knobloch, with an emphasis on the lack of non-verbal dyadic synchrony during times of turbulence.

Non-verbal Communication and Romantic Relationships in Turmoil

Several decades of research identifies key non-verbal cues that emerge in romantic relationships experiencing turmoil, those characterized by high degrees of conflict or periods of decline. To be clear, in this chapter we do not examine relationships that necessarily fail; many relationships are resilient, as partners determine how to weather the trouble, perhaps seeking counselling to help heal wounds, reconcile differences, and rekindle connections. Our interest is in non-verbal communication associated with the turmoil many couples experience, regardless of whether the relationship succeeds or fails. While many nonverbal cues exist that affect the health of romantic relationships, for our purposes, we will concentrate on the following four codes of non-verbal communication: (1) touch/affection; (2) proxemics (i.e., use of space and territory); (3) oculesics (i.e., eye gaze); and (4) vocalics (i.e., paralanguage, tone of voice).

Touch and Affection in Romantic Relationships

Touch is a key non-verbal cue in any relationship, but it is arguably *the* most important form of non-verbal communication in a romantic relationship. Touch and affection are primary ways we express our emotions (Durbin et al., 2021; Floyd & Hesse, 2017; Hesse & Mikkelson, 2017; Luerssen et al., 2017; Smith et al., 2011). Emotional expression is critical to the development of successful romantic relationships and the satisfaction levels of partners (Keltner et al., 2019; Sauter, 2017; Trask et al., 2020). Physical affection alters our hormones, affects our immune systems, assists in pain management, impacts sleep quality, and helps reduce the stress we register in our bodies (Eisenberger et al., 2011; Floyd, 2016, 2019; Floyd et al., 2010, 2018; Floyd & Riforgiate, 2008; Holt-Lunstad, 2018).

One potential source of difficulty for romantic couples pertains to touch ethic, people's beliefs about and preferences for touch, typically developed in early years through experiences with family members (Ivy & Wahl, 2019). Romantic partners who have divergent beliefs about the appropriateness of certain forms of touch may need to negotiate so that both persons' views are respected. For example, if one partner feels that affection in public (i.e., tie signs; Morris, 1977) communicates closeness and signals to others the status of a relationship, but the other partner believes public displays of affection are inappropriate, even embarrassing, conflict may ensue. Part of the touch ethic involves preferences. If one partner likes to sleep completely wrapped up in the other partner's body, but that partner prefers to "go to separate corners" for sleep, such a contrast may become a source of strain.

Oxford scholar Peter Collett (2004) is an expert and scholar of non-verbal communication. While an experimental psychologist at Oxford, Collett served as a commentator on the British original version of the television show *Big Brother*. In the UK show, houseguests were videotaped in their day-to-day interactions; then hosts and experts analysed what occurred in each episode. Collett has written and lectured on non-verbal cues between royal spouses, starting with Queen Elizabeth's marriage to Prince Phillip, extending to Prince Charles and Diana's relationship, then contrasting non-verbal cues in their wedding ceremony with those evidenced in Prince Charles' wedding to Camilla Parker Bowles. Public touch was virtually nonexistent between Elizabeth and Phillip—primarily a sign of the times, in that royals were seldom seen exhibiting any form of physical contact. In their example, the lack of touch was not likely an indicator of turmoil in the relationship, but more a matter of protocol and the role of a royal. In the case of Charles and Diana, awkward and infrequent touch likely revealed relational turmoil right from the start. News accounts documented Charles' uncomfortable attempts at affection (and Diana's squeamish reactions) when prompted by reporters and well-wishers to show how they felt about each other. They exchanged a brief kiss on the balcony after their wedding, prompted by the crowd below yelling for them to kiss.

Collett (2018) has continued his analysis, writing frequently for the UK's *The Guardian* newspaper, comparing non-verbal cues between Prince William and wife Kate Middleton and Prince Harry and wife Meghan Markle. Reinforcing other research on affection in romantic relationships, touch between younger spouses is much more evident, even for royals. The younger royals seem more comfortable with public touch than their elders, with William often seen steering Kate in a direction or including her in an interaction by placing his hand on the small of her back. Harry and Meghan use more intimate proxemics than other royal couples, frequently seen sitting closely together with legs or arms touching, and often holding hands at events and during interviews.

Over several decades, scholar Antonia Abbey produced a body of research documenting sex differences in perceptions of touch (Abbey,

1982, 1987, 1991; Abbey et al., 2005). While some findings pertain to non-verbal cues in courtship and relationship initiation, other results suggest that a gap between intention and interpretation exists in ongoing romantic relationships as well. Consistent research findings have implications for heterosexual romantic couples, in that male participants in studies often misinterpreted the meaning behind women's touches. In these studies, many men interpreted women's touches as more intimate and sexual than the women intended. A woman may intend to only convey friendship, interest, and attraction through touch, but a male recipient of her touch may infer love, intimacy, and even sexual arousal. Such a gap between intention and interpretation can be a challenge in a romantic relationship, possibly leading one person to feel misunderstood and the other to feel "teased."

Scholars also examine touch in terms of quantity and quality. Partners in long-term relationships, including marriages, tend to touch each other less frequently and less intimately than people establishing relationships or repairing ones that have experienced upheaval or a loss of intimacy (Debrot et al., 2017; Guerrero & Andersen, 1991, 1994; Jakubiak & Feeney, 2017; Spott et al., 2010). Turmoil in a romantic relationship is often revealed through diminished or altered non-verbal cues, such as reduced touch either in frequency or quality, being ignored, decreased direct eye contact, increased physical distance, and a general lack of animation or energy in the voice (Patterson et al., 2012). A couple in turmoil may exhibit more or less affection than usual in the form of touch, depending on whether the relationship is in decline and characterized by frequent conflict or in a process of renewal, emerging out of turmoil.

Proxemics in Romantic Relationships

Proxemics pertains to the way distance and space non-verbally communicate messages (Ivy & Wahl, 2019). Research bears out what likely many of us have witnessed and experienced in our daily lives: Intimate partners tend to maintain closer physical distances than people in other kinds of relationships, like those among friends, coworkers, and family members (Andersen et al., 2006; Fagundes & Schindler, 2012; Okken et al., 2012;

Sluzki, 2016; Szpak et al., 2016). However, partners in troubled romantic relationships often use physical distance as a parallel to psychological distance felt toward their partner (Guerrero & Floyd, 2006). According to the National Sleep Foundation (Miller, 2020), 25% of American married couples sleep in separate beds; 10% sleep in separate rooms. While decisions for separate sleeping arrangements aren't always related to a desire for physical distance, separate beds and rooms may reveal turmoil in a relationship.

Most people decrease affectionate touch and increase physical distance during periods of conflict (Allsop et al., 2021; Beebe et al., 2022; Guerrero, 2013). During conflict episodes, some partners choose to leave the scene, which may be an effective tactic to let "cooler heads prevail," although postponing or avoiding conflict by leaving the scene sometimes reduces intimacy and trust, leading to more conflict (Samp, 2016). As compared to the process of relational escalation, when relationships build and physical closeness is a key non-verbal cue, during relational de-escalation physical distance increases (Knapp et al., 2013). It is interesting that the term for major distancing between partners is "separation," which can mean partners take a break, see each other infrequently, and perhaps sever living arrangements. Whether these separations are temporary or permanent, they typically involve a significant decrease of physical proximity between partners.

One form of conflict pattern studied for decades by communication and psychology scholars is demand-withdrawal, common among married couples (Beebe et al., 2022; Burrell et al., 2014; Schrodt et al., 2014). In this pattern, one person makes a demand and the other responds by refusing to concede to (or even acknowledge) the demand, avoiding a conflict, and sometimes just walking away, increasing physical distance from the partner (Eldridge et al., 2017; Holley et al., 2018; Li & Johnson, 2018; Pickover et al., 2017). For example, one spouse might say to the other, "Why won't you talk about what's wrong in this marriage? I always have to bring things up, so this time, YOU have to talk to me about our problems." The other spouse typically ignores or disagrees with the accusation and withdraws from the conflict, often physically. As previously stated, walking away and cooling off in response to conflict can be an effective strategy. However, couples whose conflict episodes frequently involve a demand-withdrawal pattern typically report lower levels of satisfaction with their partners and their relationship in general (Papp et al., 2009; Spencer et al., 2017).

Research on gay and lesbian couple conflict has produced mixed results. In some studies, gay and lesbian partners were more conflict avoidant than heterosexual couples, opting for a withdrawing, distancing tactic rather than actively engaging in conflict (Dominique & Mollen, 2009; Li & Samp, 2021). However, other studies found few differences across couple types in terms of frequency of conflicts, topics of disagreement, and use of the demand-withdraw pattern (Baucom et al., 2010; Holley et al., 2010; Kurdek, 2004; Ogolsky & Gray, 2016; Whitton et al., 2018).

Eye Gaze in Romantic Relationships

Mutual eye gaze (i.e., eye contact) is a critical form of non-verbal communication between people in all types of relationships, particularly romantic partners (Bernecker et al., 2019; Docan-Morgan et al., 2013; Lawson, 2015; Mason et al., 2005; Petrican et al., 2011; Tang & Schmeichel, 2015). Eye contact conveys attention, interest, attraction, even respect. We've long known of the key role the eyes play in conveying emotions—a central feature in successful romantic relationships (Campbell et al., 2017; Flykt et al., 2021; Lea et al., 2018; Widman et al., 2018).

Guerrero, Jones, and Burgoon (2000) conducted an experimental study of romantic partners across four conditions of intimacy. After an initial conversation (video recorded in a research lab), one partner in each dyad left the lab and became a confederate in the study. Each confederate was asked to manipulate verbal and non-verbal communication, including levels of eye contact, to indicate an increase or decrease in intimacy for subsequent taped conversations with their partners. Behavioural changes exhibited by partners in confederate roles impacted how their unsuspecting partners behaved, as those partners mirrored the changing language and non-verbal cues. Romantic partners are often motivated to adapt to each other's non-verbal communication, as such adaptation indicates intimacy, closeness, understanding, and mutual respect. However, non-verbal cues that convey decreasing intimacy or distress in a relationship are also "catching," showing that non-verbal cues conveyed by one's partner have a powerful effect on one's own behaviour.

In the United States, where eye contact is highly valued, people who avoid eye gaze or exhibit low levels of eye contact tend to be viewed as suspicious, untrustworthy, and deceptive (Knapp et al., 2015; Levine & Knapp, 2018; Novotny et al., 2018). This tendency applies across all sorts of connections, from people casually passing each other on the street to intimate partners. Such negative perceptions can be devastating to romantic relational partners. Changes in eye gaze patterns between partners can signal trouble and reveal a decline in relationship satisfaction (Hessels et al., 2017; Kleinke, 1986).

Vocalics in Romantic Relationships

Vocal non-verbal cues can be revealing, given that they are so centrally connected to our physiology. For example, hormones play a significant role in voice production; hormonal changes help us discern if we're speaking on the phone to a child or an elderly person (Banai, 2017; Davidson, 2016; Wells, 2004). Our voices are hard to control when we're nervous or in heightened emotional states; the voice can shake or sound gravelly because of dry tissues in the vocal mechanism. Heightened emotions may cause us to speed up our rate of speech, as well as exhibit more speech errors, disfluencies, and awkward pausing (Frank et al., 2013; Juslin et al., 2018; Karpf, 2006).

Romantic partners experiencing turmoil may not be aware that their vocalics reveal their emotions or their declining satisfaction with the relationship. For some people, levels of volume, pitch variation, and speaking rate increase as emotions reveal turmoil. For others, pitches flatten, speaking rates slow, and volume levels decrease (Feinberg et al., 2006; Hartmann & Mast, 2017; Kuhn et al., 2017). Energy can drain out of the voice, such that articulation is affected, causing mumbling or slurred speech. Typical animation in the voice can diminish because of turmoil, such that a partner may feel like the other person "just doesn't *sound* interested anymore." In contrast, in times of high conflict, voices may reveal turmoil through raised pitches, increased volume levels, faster speaking rates, and more frequent and intrusive interruptions (Aldeis & Afifi, 2015; Ebesu Hubbard et al., 2013; Gnisci et al., 2012; Guerrero et al., 2000).

The absence of vocalics can also indicate turmoil, sometimes called the "silent treatment" (Acheson, 2008; Baker, 1955; Bruneau, 1973; Wright & Roloff, 2009). In their book about non-verbal cues in close relationships, Guerrero and Floyd (2006) describe silence as "intimidating and threatening," especially when used as a response to conflict (p. 158). Romantic partners can be in throes of battle, then one partner stops talking *and* listening; in such a scenario, silence can be a power play or a stall tactic. While silence may also be a calming technique for oneself or one's partner and a means of promoting peace, it can heighten resentment and frustration, leading to more serious problems in the relationship (Cheng & Tardy, 2010; Knapp et al., 2013).

Laura Pritchitt (2016), a writer for *The New York Times*, published an account of how her marriage ended after two decades. She described how she spun the story to neighbors, saying that some marriages just "run their course"; some end in a civil way, quietly, without yelling and drama. But she also offered this perspective:

> I smile at neighbors and wave as they get into their cars. I do not speak about the sting of all of this. I don't tell them how I recently sank to my knees and laughed in half-sorrow, half-relief, only because of this: My marriage had long ago turned into the cliché of roommate-ness, and that it could suffer such a change without any emotional upheaval was revealing. In fact, the silence said it all. The words I don't say to my neighbors, the words that get held on my tongue, are: I wish you had heard a good fight. I wish our voices had been loud enough to carry across the valley. He and I may have free speech, but we aren't so good at frank speech.

Relational Turbulence and Non-verbal Cues

Communication scholars Denise Haunani Solomon and Leanne Knobloch (2001) proposed the relational turbulence model (RTM) as a means of better understanding turmoil in romantic relationships that had achieved moderate levels of intimacy. They operationalized moderate intimacy as evidenced in the shift from a casual dating relationship to something more serious, a more "emotionally attached, mutually recognized, and interdependent relationship" (p. 805). This research launched a significant body of work, as scholars found relational turbulence an important construct to help better understand the role of communication in romantic relationships. Solomon et al.'s (2016) initial focus was on relationships evolving from casual dating to a deeper, more intimate, stage. However, over time, the model "shifted from an emphasis on intimacy … to a focus on relational uncertainty and interference from a partner as phenomena that increase during relationship transitions" (Solomon et al. 2016, pp. 507–508). Relational uncertainty is ambiguity about the nature of involvement in a relationship, while interdependence is how much influence one partner allows from the other. Solomon et al. (2016) revised view of turbulence focused on relationship transitions, defined as "periods of discontinuity between times of relative stability, during which individuals adapt to changing roles, identities, and circumstances" (p. 510).

Transitions that can create turbulence and affect the life and trajectory of romantic relationships include how couples manage parenthood (Theiss et al., 2013), in-law relationships (Mikucki-Enyart & Caughlin, 2018), infertility (Steuber & Solomon, 2008, 2011), military deployment and reintegration (Knobloch et al., 2015; Knobloch & Theiss, 2011), becoming empty nesters (Nagy & Theiss, 2013), cancer diagnoses (Weber & Solomon, 2008), and most recently, the COVID-19 pandemic (Goodboy et al., 2021). A variety of relational experiences have been clarified through the lens of the relational turbulence model, including the impact of hurtful messages (McLaren et al., 2011, 2012; McLaren & Solomon, 2014; Priem & Solomon, 2011; Theiss et al., 2009), negative emotional expression (Knobloch et al., 2007), and relational irritations (Theiss & Solomon, 2006).

Most of the research on turbulence has focused on verbal communication; however, one process inherent in turbulence is dyadic synchrony, which includes both verbal and non-verbal elements. Here, we briefly explore dyadic synchrony in general, then focus on key non-verbal cues emergent as romantic partners in turbulence evidence a decline in synchrony.

Dyadic Synchrony

Harrist and Waugh (2002) define dyadic synchrony as "an observable pattern of dyadic interaction that is mutually regulated, reciprocal, and harmonious" (p. 557). More succinctly, it is "the degree of coordination between individuals engaged in interaction" (Solomon et al. 2016, p. 520). Other researchers call it interactive synchrony, meaning the coordination of speech and body movement between at least two people (Alda, 2018; Baimel et al., 2018; Brambilla et al., 2016; Lozza et al., 2018; Schmidt et al., 2012). It's not unusual for relational partners in turmoil or distress to be described as being "out of synch" or "not having a rhythm." Partners may vary their schedules, such that they rarely see each other in the home environment or much of anywhere else. They may prefer to spend time with colleagues or friends rather than their partner, or they may no longer do tasks or activities with each other that they used to enjoy.

Verbal communication associated with synchrony includes coherence around a conversation topic, meaning offering comments that follow someone's thread, rather than going on a tangent or shifting to a topic one would rather talk about. For example, a couple in synch might communicate at a social gathering, where one partner raises the topic of a recent sporting contest. Rather than shifting away from sports to a different topic, the romantic partner in synch amplifies details, provides supplemental information, or adds her or his perspective on the sporting event. Voicing agreement with a partner's expressed view also conveys synchrony. Another behaviour is word choice, meaning when partners echo the language of each other's comments (Bernieri & Rosenthal, 1991; Knobloch, 2008; Knobloch & Solomon, 2003). Using our earlier example, if one partner describes the sporting event as "amazing," the other will use that descriptor in subsequent comments, reinforcing the first partner's word choice. It sounds like a tiny thing, this inspection of word choice among romantic partners, but if one partner shifts the topic or responds with "that game was completely boring," such a verbalization could be a sign of turmoil, especially when made in public. Verbal and nonverbal cues indicating synchrony (or the lack of it) often emerge to reveal a relationship.

Other research frames verbal synchrony as language style matching (Cannava & Bodie, 2017; Gleason & Ivy, 2021; Gonzalez et al., 2010; Ireland et al., 2011; Ireland & Henderson, 2014; Meinecke & Kauffeld, 2019; Pennebaker et al., 2003; Richardson et al., 2019). Scholars from various disciplines have termed the behaviour linguistic coordination (Fusaroli et al., 2012); interactive alignment (Fusaroli & Tylén, 2016; Pickering & Garrod, 2004, 2013); and the echo effect (Kulesza et al., 2014). Nelson et al. (2017) describe the phenomenon as autonomic attunement, which goes beyond an assessment of communication style to effects on interactants' physiological functioning and mental/physical health. Couples in or out of synch can affect each other's breathing, heart rates, cortisol levels, moods, and a host of other physical and mental manifestations.

Of particular interest to our investigation of dyadic synchrony among romantic partners is research that emphasizes non-verbal communication (Feniger-Schaal et al., 2021; Lakin et al., 2003; Van Bommel et al., 2021). Dyadic or interactive synchrony has been termed "nonverbal adaptation" (Bodie et al., 2016, p. 3), "the chameleon effect" (Chartrand & Bargh, 1999, p. 893), "social rhythm" (Knapp et al., 2013, p. 222), and "postural echo" ("Do You Know?", 2006, p. 40). However, we prefer the term mimicry, which Guégen (2011) defines as "the imitation of postures, facial expressions, mannerisms, and other verbal and nonverbal behaviors" (p. 725). Some scholars contend such imitation or mirroring is intentional; others believe it is organic, something that develops over time between interactants (Bernhold & Giles, 2020; Manusov, 1992). College students on the job market are often advised to mimic the nonverbal cues of potential employers in job interviews, to convey a sense of solidarity and "fit" for a position or within an organization. Salespersons are often trained in "people watching," so that they can work to mimic clients and customers, creating a stronger likelihood of being persuasive or making a sale. (If not handled subtly, such mimicry can backfire.) Wait staff at restaurants are often trained to lean down or squat by diners' tables, in an effort to put themselves more on the level of customers, a technique that research shows can actually result in enhanced customer–employee rapport, as well as increased food sales and tips (Lin & Lin, 2017; Rush, 2006).

Vocal mimicry, sometimes termed vocal accommodation (Bernhold & Giles, 2020), is the subject of much research. A good deal of this research focuses on parent–child mimicry, with studies of how mothers and infants, as well as grandparents and grandchildren, use their voices to adjust to each other and encourage language acquisition (Bernhold & Giles, 2017; Roe & Drivas, 1997). However, research also examines vocal mimicry among romantic partners (Floyd, 2019). Mimicked vocal cues can reveal coordination among romantic partners, whereas vocal cues that aren't in synch can reveal relational turbulence. It's important to use the word *can* here, in that partners may evidence coordinated vocal patterns that have developed over time, simply through the process of becoming used to each other. The coordination may be more habit than a sign of a healthy relationship. Likewise, sometimes couples may seem or sound out of synch for various reasons, not necessarily a signal of turmoil, distress, or turbulence in the relationship. It can be the result of a simple misunderstanding, minor argument, or irritation on the part of one or both partners. If the lack of mimicry persists or a wider range of non-verbal cues are in evidence, then a judgement of relational turmoil or turbulence may be justified.

Studies have linked vocal mimicry to partner affiliation, affection, and positive views of communication quality (Chartrand & Dalton, 2009; Floyd & Ray, 2003). Lee et al. (2010) found that when marital partners discussed problems in their turbulent marriage, they synchronized the energy and pitch of their voices. Couples who believed such discussions were positive and beneficial to the relationship mirrored higher vocal pitches in conversation; in contrast, couples who viewed the discussions negatively used lower vocal energy and pitches. Farley et al. (2013) studied whether third-party observers could determine through vocal cues if study participants were talking to a dating partner or a same-sex friend over the phone. The results showed high accuracy among observers, as men consistently increased pitches when saying "How are you?" to dating partners and decreased pitches with a male friend. In contrast, women decreased pitches when using the same phrase with a male dating partner and increased pitches with a female friend. While romantic relational partners more often attend to obvious non-verbal signals like distance, lack of touch, and diminished eye contact, subtle vocalic cues may be the most revealing about the status and quality of a romantic relationship.

Conclusion

Communication scholarship helps us better understand how relationships of various types are initiated, maintained, deepened, and sometimes terminated. A central part of relationship maintenance is the management of turmoil between partners. The purpose of this chapter was, first, to explore four sets of non-verbal cues associated with romantic relationships in turmoil. Specific emphasis was given to touch/affection, proxemics, eye behaviour, and vocalic cues communicated by romantic relational partners. Changes in expected patterns and non-verbal cues such as decreased frequency and quality of touch, increased physical distance and time spent apart versus together, avoiding making eye contact with one's partner, and vocal changes (greater or lesser volume, speaking rates, and pitch variation) reveal much more about a relationship than what partners say to each other.

Next we overviewed relational turbulence, defined in Solomon and Knobloch's research as periods of uncertainty and flux in partner interdependence during significant relationship transitions. Of the most interest to our inquiry was non-verbal dyadic synchrony lacking among relational partners experiencing turbulence. While most of the research on turbulence focuses on verbal communication, we contend that nonverbal cues are more revealing. Research reviewed in this chapter suggests that upwards of 93% of what human beings feel is communicated nonverbally, leaving a paltry 7% communicated verbally. Thus, an emphasis on non-verbal cues in romantic relationships is warranted and appropriate, given what words don't tell us.

References

Abbey, A. (1982). Sex differences in attributions for friendly behavior: Do males misperceive females' friendliness? *Journal of Personality and Social Psychology, 42*, 830–838.

Abbey, A. (1987). Misperception of friendly behavior as sexual intent: A survey of naturally occurring incidents. *Psychology of Women Quarterly, 11*, 173–194.

Abbey, A. (1991). Misperception as an antecedent of acquaintance rape: A consequence of ambiguity in communication between men and women. In

A. Parrot & L. Bechhofer (Eds.), *Acquaintance rape: The hidden crime* (pp. 96–111). Wiley.

Abbey, A., Zawacki, T., & Buck, P. O. (2005). The effects of past sexual assault perpetration and alcohol consumption on reactions to women's mixed signals. *Journal of Social and Clinical Psychology, 25*, 129–157.

Acheson, K. (2008). Silence as gesture: Rethinking the nature of communicative silence. *Communication Theory, 18*, 535–555.

Alda, A. (2018). *If I understood you, would I have this look on my face? My adventures in the art and science of relating and communicating*. Random House.

Aldeis, D., & Afifi, T. D. (2015). Putative secrets and conflict in romantic relationships over time. *Communication Monographs, 82*, 224–251.

Allsop, D. B., Leavitt, C. E., Saxey, M. T., Timmons, J. E., & Carroll, J. S. (2021). Applying the developmental model of marital competence to sexual satisfaction: Associations between conflict resolution quality, forgiveness, attachment, and sexual satisfaction. *Journal of Social and Personal Relationships, 38*(4), 1216–1237. https://doi.org/10.1177/0265407520984853

Andersen, P. A., Guerrero, L. K., & Jones, S. M. (2006). Nonverbal behavior in intimate interactions and intimate relationships. In V. Manusov & M. L. Patterson (Eds.), *The SAGE handbook of nonverbal communication* (pp. 259–277). Sage.

Argyle, M. (1988). *Bodily communication*. Methuen.

Baimel, A., Birch, S. A. J., & Norenzayan, A. (2018). Coordinating bodies and minds: Behavioral synchrony fosters mentalizing. *Journal of Experimental Social Psychology, 74*, 281–290.

Baker, S. J. (1955). The theory of silence. *Journal of General Psychology, 53*, 145–167.

Banai, J. P. (2017). Voice in different phases of menstrual cycle among naturally cycling women and users of hormonal contraceptives. *PLoS One, 12*, e0183462.

Baucom, B. R., McFarland, P. T., & Christensen, A. (2010). Gender, topic, and time in observed demand-withdraw interaction in cross- and same-sex couples. *Journal of Family Psychology, 24*, 233–242. https://doi.org/10.1037/a0019717

Beebe, S. A., Beebe, S. J., & Ivy, D. K. (2022). *Communication: Principles for a lifetime* (8th ed.). Pearson.

Beebe, S. A., Beebe, S. J., & Redmond, M. V. (2022). *Interpersonal communication: Relating to others* (9th ed.). Pearson.

Bernecker, K., Ghassemi, M., & Brandstatter, V. (2019). Approach and avoidance relationship goals and couples' nonverbal communication during conflict. *European Journal of Social Psychology, 49*(3), 622–636. https://doi.org/10.1002/ejsp.2379

Bernhold, Q. S., & Giles, H. (2017). Grandparent-grandchild communication: A review of theoretically informed research. *Journal of Intergenerational Relationships, 15*, 368–388. https://doi.org/10.1080/15350770.2017.1368348

Bernhold, Q. S., & Giles, H. (2020). Vocal accommodation and mimicry. *Journal of Nonverbal Behavior, 44*(1), 41–62. https://doi.org/10.1007/s10919-019-00317-y

Bernieri, F. J., & Rosenthal, R. (1991). Interpersonal coordination: Behavior matching and interactional synchrony. In R. S. Feldman & B. Rimé (Eds.), *Fundamentals of nonverbal behavior* (pp. 401–432). Cambridge University Press.

Bodie, G. D., Cannava, K. E., Vickery, A. J., & Jones, S. M. (2016). Patterns of nonverbal adaptation in supportive interactions. *Communication Studies, 67*, 3–19.

Brambilla, M., Sacchi, S., Menegatti, M., & Moscatelli, S. (2016). Honesty and dishonesty don't move together: Trait content information influences behavioral synchrony. *Journal of Nonverbal Behavior, 40*(3), 171–186.

Bruneau, T. (1973). Communicative silences: Forms and functions. *Journal of Communication, 23*, 17–46.

Burrell, N. A., Kartch, F. F., Allen, M., & Hill, C. B. (2014). A meta-analysis of demand/withdraw interaction patterns. In N. A. Burrell, M. Allen, B. M. Gayle, & R. W. Preiss (Eds.), *Managing interpersonal conflict: Advances through meta-analysis* (pp. 297–312). Routledge.

Campbell, A., Murray, J. E., Atkindon, L., & Ruffman, T. (2017). Face age and eye gaze influence older adults' emotion recognition. *Journal of Gerontology, 72*, 633–636.

Cannava, K. E., & Bodie, G. D. (2017). Language use and supportive conversations between strangers and friends. *Journal of Social and Personal Relationships, 34*, 467–485.

Chartrand, T. L., & Bargh, J. A. (1999). The chameleon effect: The perception-behavior link and social interaction. *Journal of Personality and Social Psychology, 76*, 893–910.

Chartrand, T. L., & Dalton, A. N. (2009). Mimicry: Its ubiquity, importance, and function. In E. Morsella, J. A. Bargh, & P. M. Gollwitzer (Eds.), *Oxford handbook of human action* (pp. 458–483). Oxford University Press.

Cheng, C.-C., & Tardy, C. (2010). A cross-cultural study of silence in marital conflict. *China Media Report Overseas, 6*, 95–105.

Collett, P. (2004). *The book of tells*. Bantam.

Collett, P. (2018, May 16). *What can we learn from the body language of the royals?* Available https://news.sky.com/video/what-can-we-learn-from-body-language-of-the-royals-11374745, retrieved May 17, 2018.

Davidson, J. (2016, October 3–6). Where the top notes go: Why do voices deepen and thin over time? *New York*, pp. 113–118.

Debrot, A., Meuwly, N., Muise, A., Impett, E. A., & Schoebi, D. (2017). More than just sex: Affection mediates the association between sexual activity and well-being. *Personality and Social Psychology Bulletin, 43*, 287–299.

Do you know? (2006, June). *Martha Stewart Living*, 40.

Docan-Morgan, T., Manusov, V., & Harvey, J. (2013). When a small thing means so much: Nonverbal cues as turning points in relationships. *Interpersona: An International Journal on Personal Relationships, 7*(1), 110–124. https://doi.org/10.5964/ijpr.v7i1.119

Dominique, R., & Mollen, D. (2009). Attachment and conflict communication in adult romantic relationships. *Journal of Social and Personal Relationships, 26*(5), 678–696.

Durbin, K. B., Debrot, A., Karremans, J., & van der Wal, R. (2021). Can we use smart-phones to increase physical affection, intimacy, and security in couples? Preliminary support from an attachment perspective. *Journal of Social and Personal Relationships, 38*(3), 1035–1045. https://doi.org/10.1177/0265407520970278

Ebesu Hubbard, A. S., Hendrickson, B., Fehrenbach, K. S., & Sur, J. (2013). Effects of timing and sincerity of apology on satisfaction and changes in negative feelings during conflicts. *Western Journal of Communication, 77*, 305–322.

Eisenberger, N. I., Master, S. L., Inagaki, T. K., Taylor, S. E., Shirinyan, D., Lieberman, M. D., & Naliboff, B. D. (2011). Attachment figures activate a safety signal-related neural region and reduce pain experience. *PNAS: Proceedings of the National Academy of Sciences of the United States of America, 108*(28), 11721–11726. https://doi.org/10.1073/pnas.1108239108

Eldridge, K., Cencirulo, J., & Edwards, E. (2017). Demand-withdraw patterns of communication in couple relationships. In J. Fitzgerald (Ed.), *Foundations for couples' therapy: Research for the real world* (pp. 112–122). Routledge.

Fagundes, C. P., & Schindler, I. (2012). Making of romantic attachment bonds: Longitudinal trajectories and implications for relationship stability. *Personal Relationships, 19*, 723–742.

Farley, S. D., Hughes, S. M., & LaFayette, J. N. (2013). People will know we are in love: Evidence of differences between vocal samples directed toward lovers and friends. *Journal of Nonverbal Behavior, 37*, 123–138. https://doi.org/10.1007/s10919-013-0151-3

Feinberg, D. R., Jones, B. C., Law Smith, M. J., Moore, F. R., DeBrunie, L. M., Cornwall, R. E., et al. (2006). Menstrual cycle, trait estrogen level, and masculinity preferences in the human voice. *Hormones and Behavior, 46*, 215–222.

Feniger-Schaal, R., Schonherr, D., Altmann, U., & Strauss, B. (2021). Movement synchrony in the mirror game. *Journal of Nonverbal Behavior, 45*(1), 107–126. https://doi.org/10.1007/s10919-020-00341-3

Floyd, K. (2016). Affection deprivation is associated with physical pain and poor sleep quality. *Western Journal of Communication, 67*, 379–398.

Floyd, K. (2019). *Affectionate communication in close relationships*. Cambridge University Press.

Floyd, K., & Hesse, C. (2017). Affection deprivation is conceptually and empirically distinct from loneliness. *Western Journal of Communication, 81*, 446–465.

Floyd, K., Pauley, P. M., & Hesse, C. (2010). State and trait affectionate communication buffer adults' stress reactions. *Communication Monographs, 77*, 618–636.

Floyd, K., Pauley, P. M., Hesse, C., Eden, J., Veksler, A. E., & Woo, N. T. (2018). Supportive communication is associated with markers of immunocompetence. *Southern Journal of Communication*. https://doi.org/10.1080/1041794X.2018.1488270

Floyd, K., & Ray, G. B. (2003). Human affection exchange: IV. Vocalic predictors of perceived affection in initial interactions. *Western Journal of Communication, 67*, 56–73. https://doi.org/10.1080/10570310309374758

Floyd, K., & Riforgiate, S. (2008). Affectionate communication received from spouses predicts stress hormone levels in healthy adults. *Communication Monographs, 75*, 351–368.

Flykt, A., Horlin, T., Linder, F., Wennstig, A.-K., Sayeler, G., Hess, U., & Banziger, T. (2021). Exploring emotion recognition and the understanding of others' unspoken thoughts and feelings when narrating self-experienced emotional events. *Journal of Nonverbal Behavior, 45*, 67–81.

Frank, M. G., Maroulis, A., & Griffin, D. J. (2013). The voice. In D. Matsumoto, M. G. Frank, & H. S. Hwang (Eds.), *Nonverbal communication: Science and application* (pp. 53–74). Sage.

Fusaroli, R., Bahrami, B., Olsen, K., Roepstorff, A., Rees, G., Frith, C., & Tylén, K. (2012). Coming to terms: Quantifying the benefits of linguistic coordination. *Psychological Science, 23*, 931–939.

Fusaroli, R., & Tylén, K. (2016). Investigating conversational dynamics: Interactive alignment, interpersonal synergy, and collective task performance. *Cognitive Science, 40*, 145–171.
Gleason, S. A., & Ivy, D. K. (2021). As she was saying: The role of gender and narratives in oral argument amicus success. *Justice System Journal*. https://doi.org/10.1080/0098261X.2020.189631
Gnisci, A., Sergi, I., DeLuca, E., & Errico, V. (2012). Does frequency of interruptions amplify the effect of various types of interruptions? Experimental evidence. *Journal of Nonverbal Behavior, 36*, 39–57.
Gonzalez, A. L., Hancock, J. T., & Pennebaker, J. W. (2010). Language style matching as a predictor of social dynamics in small groups. *Communication Research, 37*(1), 3–19.
Goodboy, A. K., Dillow, M. R., Knoster, K. C., & Howard, H. A. (2021). Relational turbulence from the COVID-19 pandemic: Within-subjects mediation by romantic partner interdependence. *Journal of Social and Personal Relationships, 38*(6), 1800–1818. https://doi.org/10.1177/02654075211000135
Guégen, N. (2011). The mimicker is a mirror of myself: Impact of mimicking on self-consciousness and social anxiety. *Social Behavior and Personality, 39*, 725–728.
Guerrero, L. K. (2013). Emotion and communication in conflict interaction. In J. G. Oetzel & S. Ting-Toomey (Eds.), *The SAGE handbook of conflict communication: Integrating theory, research, and practice* (pp. 105–131). Sage.
Guerrero, L. K., & Andersen, P. A. (1991). The waxing and waning of relational intimacy: Touch as a function of relational stage, gender, and touch avoidance. *Journal of Social and Personal Relationships, 8*, 147–165.
Guerrero, L. K., & Andersen, P. A. (1994). Patterns of matching and initiation: Touch behavior and touch avoidance across romantic relationship stages. *Journal of Nonverbal Behavior, 18*, 137–153.
Guerrero, L. K., & Floyd, K. (2006). *Nonverbal communication in close relationships*. Erlbaum.
Guerrero, L. K., Jones, S. M., & Burgoon, J. K. (2000). Responses to nonverbal intimacy change in romantic dyads: Effects of behavioral valence and degree of behavioral change on nonverbal and verbal reactions. *Communication Monographs, 67*(4), 325–346. https://doi.org/10.1080/03637750009376515
Harrist, A. W., & Waugh, R. M. (2002). Dyadic synchrony: It's structure and function in children's development. *Developmental Review, 22*(45), 555–592. https://doi.org/10.1016/S0273-2297(02)00500-2

Hartmann, M., & Mast, F. W. (2017). Loudness counts: Interactions between loudness, number magnitude, and space. *Quarterly Journal of Experimental Psychology, 70*, 1305–1322.

Hesse, C., & Mikkelson, A. C. (2017). Affection deprivation in romantic relationships. *Communication Quarterly, 65*, 20–38.

Hessels, R. S., Cornelissen, T. H. W., Hooge, I. T. C., & Kemner, C. (2017). Gaze behavior to faces during dyadic interaction. *Canadian Journal of Experimental Psychology, 71*(3), 226–242.

Holley, S. R., Haase, C. M., Chui, I., & Bloch, L. (2018). Depression, emotion regulation, and the demand/withdraw pattern during intimate relationship conflict. *Journal of Social and Personal Relationships, 35*(3), 408–430.

Holley, S. R., Sturm, V. E., & Levenson, R. W. (2010). Exploring the basis for gender differences in the demand-withdraw pattern. *Journal of Homosexuality, 57*, 666–684. https://doi.org/10.1080/00918361003712145

Holt-Lunstad, J. (2018). Relationships and physical health. In A. L. Vangelisti & D. Perlman (Eds.), *The Cambridge handbook of personal relationships* (2nd ed., pp. 449–463). Cambridge University Press.

Ireland, M. E., & Henderson, M. D. (2014). Language style matching, engagement, and impasse in negotiations. *Negotiation and Conflict Management Research, 7*(1), 1–16.

Ireland, M. E., Slatcher, R. B., Eastwick, P. W., Scissors, L. E., Finkel, E. J., & Pennebaker, J. W. (2011). Language style matching predicts relationship initiation and stability. *Psychological Science, 22*(1), 39–44.

Ivy, D. K., & Wahl, S. T. (2019). *Nonverbal communication for a lifetime* (3rd ed.). Kendall Hunt.

Jakubiak, B. K., & Feeney, B. C. (2017). Affectionate touch to promote relational, psychological, and physical well-being in adulthood: A theoretical model and review of the research. *Personality and Social Psychology Review, 21*, 228–252.

Juslin, P. N., Laukka, P., & Banziger, T. (2018). The mirror to our soul? Comparisons of spontaneous and posed vocal expression of emotion. *Journal of Nonverbal Behavior, 42*(1), 1–40. https://doi.org/10.1007/s10919-017-0268-x

Karpf, A. (2006). *The human voice: How this extraordinary instrument reveals essential clues about who we are*. Bloomsbury.

Keltner, D., Sauter, D., Tracy, J., & Cowen, A. (2019). Emotional expression: Advances in basic emotion theory. *Journal of Nonverbal Behavior, 43*, 133–160.

Kleinke, C. L. (1986). Gaze and eye contact—A research review. *Psychology Bulletin, 100*(1), 78–100.
Knapp, M. L., Hall, J. A., & Horgan, T. G. (2013). *Nonverbal communication in human interaction* (8th ed.). Wadsworth/Cengage Learning.
Knapp, M. L., McGlone, M. S., Griffin, D. L., & Earnest, W. (2015). *Lying and deception in human interaction* (2nd ed.). Kendall Hunt.
Knapp, M. L., Vangelisti, A. L., & Caughlin, J. (2013). *Interpersonal communication and human relationships* (7th ed.). Pearson.
Knobloch, L. K. (2008). Extending the emotion-in-relationships model to conversation. *Communication Research, 35*, 822–848. https://doi.org/10.1177/0093650208324273
Knobloch, L. K., Miller, L. E., & Carpenter, K. E. (2007). Using the relational turbulence model to understand negative emotion within courtship. *Personal Relationships, 14*, 91–112. https://doi.org/10.1111/j.1475-6811.2006.00143.x
Knobloch, L. K., & Solomon, D. H. (2003). Manifestations of relationship conceptualizations in conversation. *Human Communication Research, 29*, 482–515. https://doi.org/10.1111/j.1468-2958.2003.tb00853.x
Knobloch, L. K., & Theiss, J. A. (2011). Depressive symptoms and mechanisms of relational turbulence as predictors of relationship satisfaction among returning service members. *Journal of Family Psychology, 25*, 470–478. https://doi.org/10.1037/a0024063
Knobloch, L. K., Theiss, J. A., & Wehrman, E. C. (2015). Communication of military couples during deployment: Topic avoidance and relational uncertainty. In E. Sahlstein & L. M. Webb (Eds.), *A communicative perspective on the military: Interactions, messages, and discourses* (pp. 39–58). Peter Lang.
Kuhn, L. K., Wydell, T., Lavan, N., McGettigan, C., & Garrido, L. (2017). Similar representations of emotions across faces and voices. *Emotion, 17*, 912–937.
Kulesza, W., Dolinski, D., Huisman, A., & Majewski, R. (2014). The echo effect: The power of verbal mimicry to influence prosocial behavior. *Journal of Language and Social Psychology, 33*, 183–201.
Kunecke, J., Wilhelm, O., & Sommer, W. (2017). Emotion recognition in nonverbal face-to-face communication. *Journal of Nonverbal Behavior, 41*, 221–238.
Kurdek, L. A. (2004). Are gay and lesbian cohabiting couples really different from heterosexual married couples? *Journal of Marriage and Family, 66*, 880–900. https://doi.org/10.1111/j.0022-2445.2004.00060.x

Lakin, J. L., Jefferis, V. W., Cheng, C. M., & Chartrand, T. L. (2003). The chameleon effect as social glue: Evidence for the evolutionary significance of nonconscious mimicry. *Journal of Nonverbal Behavior, 27*, 145–161.

Lawson, R. (2015). I just love the attention: Implicit preference for direct eye contact. *Visual Cognition, 23*, 450–488.

Lea, R. G., Qualter, P., Davis, S. K., Perez-Gonzalez, J.-C., & Bangree, M. (2018). Trait emotional intelligence and attentional bias for positive emotion: An eye tracking study. *Personality and Individual Differences, 128*, 88–93.

Lee, C.-C., Black, M., Katsamanis, A., Lammert, A., Baucom, B., Christensen, A., & Narayanan, S. (2010). Quantification of prosodic entrainment in affective spontaneous spoken interactions in married couples. In K. Hirose, S. Nakamura, & T. Kobayashi (Eds.), *Proceedings of the 11th annual conference of the international speech communication association* (pp. 793–796). Makahuri. http://www.interspeech2010.org/index.html

Levine, T. R., & Knapp, M. L. (2018). Lying and deception in close relationships. In A. L. Vangelisti & D. Perlman (Eds.), *The Cambridge handbook of personal relationships* (2nd ed., pp. 329–340). Cambridge University Press.

Li, P.-F., & Johnson, L. N. (2018). Couples' depression and relationship satisfaction: Examining the moderating effects of demand/withdraw communication patterns. *Journal of Family Therapy, 40*(S1), S63–S85. https://doi.org/10.1111/1467-6427.12124

Li, Y., & Samp, J. A. (2021). The impact of the COVID-19 pandemic on same-sex couples' conflict avoidance, relational quality, and mental health. *Journal of Social and Personal Relationships, 38*(6), 1819–1843. https://doi.org/10.1177/02654075211006199

Lin, C.-Y., & Lin, J.-S. C. (2017). The influence of service employees' nonverbal communication on customer-employee rapport in the service encounter. *Journal of Service Management, 28*(1), 107–132.

Lozza, N., Spoerri, C., Ehlert, U., Kesselring, M., Hubmann, P., Tschacher, W., & La Marca, R. (2018). Nonverbal synchrony and complementarity in unacquainted same sex dyads: A comparison in a competitive context. *Journal of Nonverbal Behavior, 42*(3), 179–197.

Luerssen, A., Jhita, G. J., & Ayduk, O. (2017). Putting yourself on the line: Self-esteem and expressing affection in romantic relationships. *Personality and Social Psychology Bulletin, 43*, 940–956.

Manusov, V. (1992). Mimicry or synchrony: The effects of intentionality attributions for nonverbal mirroring behavior. *Communication Quarterly, 40*, 69–83. https://doi.org/10.1080/01463379209369821

Mason, M. F., Tatkow, E. P., & Macrae, C. N. (2005). The look of love: Gaze shifts and person perception. *Psychological Science, 16*(3), 236–239. https://doi.org/10.1111/j.0956-7976.2005.00809.x

McLaren, R. M., & Solomon, D. H. (2014). Victim and perpetrator accounts of hurtful communication: An actor-partner interdependence model. *Human Communication Research, 40*, 291–308. https://doi.org/10.1111/hcre.12031

McLaren, R. M., Solomon, D. H., & Priem, J. S. (2011). Explaining variation in contemporaneous responses to hurt in premarital romantic relationships: A relational turbulence model perspective. *Communication Research, 38*, 543–564. https://doi.org/10.1177/0093650210377896

McLaren, R. M., Solomon, D. H., & Priem, J. S. (2012). The effect of relationship characteristics and relational communication on experiences of hurtful messages from romantic partners. *Journal of Communication, 62*, 950–971. https://doi.org/10.1111/j.1460-2466.2012.01678.x

Mehrabian, A. (1972). *Nonverbal communication*. Atherton.

Mehrabian, A. (1981). *Silent messages* (2nd ed.). Wadsworth.

Meinecke, A. L., & Kauffeld, S. (2019). Engaging the hearts and minds of followers: Leader empathy and language style matching during appraisal interviews. *Journal of Business and Psychology, 34*(4), 485–501.

Mikucki-Enyart, S. L., & Caughlin, J. P. (2018). Integrating the relational turbulence model and a multiple goals approach to understand topic avoidance during the transition to extended family. *Communication Research, 45*(3), 267–296. https://doi.org/10.1177/0093650215595075

Miller, R. W. (2020, February 9). *Why so many married couples are sleeping in separate beds*. Available www.usatoday, retrieved June 15, 2021.

Morris, D. (1977). *Man watching: A field guide to human behavior*. Abrams.

Nagy, M. E., & Theiss, J. A. (2013). Applying the relational turbulence model to the empty-nest transition: Sources of relationship change, relational uncertainty, and interference from partners. *Journal of Family Communication, 13*, 280–300. https://doi.org/10.1080/15267431.2013.823430

Nelson, B. W., Laurent, S. M., Bernstein, R., & Laurent, H. K. (2017). Perspective-taking influences autonomic attunement between partners during discussion of conflict. *Journal of Social and Personal Relationships, 34*(2), 139–165. https://doi.org/10.1177/0265407515626595

Novotny, E., Carr, Z., Frank, M. G., Dietrich, S. B., Shaddock, T., Cardwell, M., & Decker, A. (2018). How people really suspect and discover lies. *Journal of Nonverbal Behavior, 42*, 41–52.

Ogolsky, B., & Gray, C. (2016). Conflict, negative emotion, and reports of partners' relationship maintenance in same-sex couples. *Journal of Family Psychology, 30*, 171–180. https://doi.org/10.1037/fam0000148

Okken, V., van Rompay, T., & Pruyn, A. (2012). Exploring space in the consultation room: Environmental influences during patient-physician interaction. *Journal of Health Communication, 17*, 397–412.

Papp, L. M., Kouros, C. D., & Cummings, E. M. (2009). Demand-withdrawal patterns in marital conflict in the home. *Personal Relationships, 16*, 285–300.

Patterson, J., Gardner, B. C., Burr, B. K., Hubler, D. S., & Roberts, M. K. (2012). Nonverbal behavioral indicators of negative affect in couple interaction. *Contemporary Family Therapy, 34*, 11–28.

Pennebaker, J. W., Mehl, M. R., & Niederhoffer, K. G. (2003). Psychological aspects of natural language use: Our words, our selves. *Annual Review of Psychology, 54*, 547–577.

Petrican, R., Burris, C. T., Bielak, T., Schimmack, U., & Moscovitch, M. (2011). For my eyes only: Gaze control, enmeshment, and relationship quality. *Journal of Personality and Social Psychology, 100*(6), 1111–1123. https://doi.org/10.1037/a0021714

Pickering, M. J., & Garrod, S. (2004). Toward a mechanistic psychology of dialogue. *Behavioral and Brain Sciences, 27*, 169–190.

Pickering, M. J., & Garrod, S. (2013). An integrated theory of language production and comprehension. *Behavioral and Brain Sciences, 36*, 329–347.

Pickover, A. M., Lipinksi, A. H., Dodson, T. S., Tran, H. N., Woodward, M. J., & Beck, J. G. (2017). Demand/withdraw communication in the context of intimate partner violence: Implications for psychological outcomes. *Journal of Anxiety Disorders, 52*(1), 95–102. https://doi.org/10.1016/j.janxdis.2017.07.002

Planalp, S. (2008). Varieties of emotional cues in everyday life. In L. K. Guerrero & M. L. Hecht (Eds.), *The nonverbal communication reader: Classic and contemporary readings* (pp. 397–401). Waveland.

Priem, J. S., & Solomon, D. H. (2011). Relational uncertainty and cortisol responses to hurtful and supportive messages from a dating partner. *Personal Relationships, 18*, 198–223. https://doi.org/10.1111/j.1475-6811.2011.01353.x

Pritchitt, L. (2016, May 20). *No sound, no fury, no marriage*. Available www.nytimes.com, retrieved May 16, 2021.

Richardson, B. H., McCulloch, K. C., Taylor, P. J., & Wall, H. J. (2019). The cooperation link: Power and context moderate verbal mimicry. *Journal of Experimental Psychology: Applied, 25*, 62–76.

Roe, K. V., & Drivas, A. (1997). Reciprocity in mother-infant vocal interactions: Relationship to the quantity of mothers' vocal stimulation. *American Journal of Orthopsychiatry, 67*, 645–649. https://doi.org/10.1037/h0080262
Rush, C. (2006). *The mere mortal's guide to fine dining*. Broadway Books.
Samp, J. A. (Ed.). (2016). *Communicating interpersonal conflict in close relationships*. Routledge.
Sauter, D. A. (2017). The nonverbal communication of positive emotions: An emotion family approach. *Emotion Review, 9*(3), 222–234. https://doi.org/10.1177/1754073916667236
Schmidt, R. C., Morr, S., Fitzpatrick, P., & Richardson, M. J. (2012). Measuring the dynamics of interactional synchrony. *Journal of Nonverbal Behavior, 36*, 263–279.
Schrodt, P., Witt, P. L., & Shimkowski, J. R. (2014). A meta-analytical review of the demand/withdraw pattern of interaction and its associations with individual, relational, and communicative outcomes. *Communication Monographs, 81*, 28–58.
Sluzki, C. E. (2016). Proxemics in couple interactions: Rekindling an old optic. *Family Process, 55*, 7–15.
Smith, J. C. S., Vogel, D. L., Madon, S., & Edwards, S. R. (2011). The power of touch: Nonverbal communication within married dyads. *The Counseling Psychologist, 39*(5), 764–787. https://doi.org/10.1177/0011000010385849
Solomon, D. H., & Knobloch, L. K. (2001). Relationship uncertainty, partner interference, and intimacy within dating relationships. *Journal of Social and Personal Relationships, 18*, 804–820. https://doi.org/10.1177/0265407501186004
Solomon, D. H., Knobloch, L. K., Theiss, J. A., & McLaren, R. M. (2016). Relational turbulence theory: Explaining variation in subjective experiences and communication within romantic relationships. *Human Communication Research, 42*, 507–532.
Spencer, T. A., Lambertsen, A., Hubler, D. S., & Burr, B. K. (2017). Assessing the mediating effect of relationship dynamics between perceptions of problematic media use and relationship satisfaction. *Contemporary Family Therapy, 39*(2), 80–86. https://doi.org/10.1007/s10591-017-9407-0
Spott, J., Pyle, C., & Punyanunt-Carter, N. M. (2010). Positive and negative nonverbal behaviors in relationships: A study of relationship satisfaction and longevity. *Human Communication, 13*, 29–41.
Steuber, K. R., & Solomon, D. H. (2008). Relational uncertainty, partner interference, and infertility: A qualitative study of discourse within online forums.

Journal of Social and Personal Relationships, 25, 831–855. https://doi.org/10.1177/0265407508096698

Steuber, K. R., & Solomon, D. H. (2011). Factors that predict married partners' disclosures about infertility to social network members. *Journal of Applied Communication Research, 39*, 250–270. https://doi.org/10.1080/00909882.2011.585401

Szpak, A., Nicholls, M. E. R., Thomas, N. A., Laham, S. M., & Loetsher, T. (2016). "No man is an island": Effects of interpersonal proximity on spatial attention. *Cognitive Neuroscience, 7*, 45–54.

Tang, D., & Schmeichel, B. J. (2015). Look me in the eye: Manipulated eye gaze affects dominance mindsets. *Journal of Nonverbal Behavior, 39*, 181–194.

Theiss, J. A., Estlein, R., & Weber, K. M. (2013). A longitudinal assessment of relationship characteristics that predict new parents' relationship satisfaction. *Personal Relationships, 20*, 216–235. https://doi.org/10.1111/j.1475-6811.2012.01406.x

Theiss, J. A., Knobloch, L. K., Checton, M. G., & Magsamen-Conrad, K. (2009). Relationship characteristics associated with the experience of hurt in romantic relationships: A test of the relational turbulence model. *Human Communication Research, 35*, 588–615. https://doi.org/10.1111/j.1468-2958.2009.01364.x

Theiss, J. A., & Solomon, D. H. (2006). A relational turbulence model of communication about irritations in romantic relationships. *Communication Research, 33*, 391–418. https://doi.org/10.1177/0093650206291482

Trask, S. L., Horstman, H. K., & Hesse, C. (2020). Deceptive affection across relational contexts: A group comparison of romantic relationships, cross-sex friendships, and friends with benefits relationships. *Communication Research, 47*(4), 623–643.

Van Bommel, T., Merritt, S., Shaffer, E., & Ruscher, J. B. (2021). Behavioral mimicry and interaction expectations influence affect in interracial interactions. *Journal of Nonverbal Behavior, 45*(2), 207–239. https://doi.org/10.1007/s10919-020-00353-z

Weber, K. M., & Solomon, D. H. (2008). Locating relationship and communication issues among stressors associated with breast cancer. *Health Communication, 23*, 548–559.

Wells, L. K. (2004). *The articulate voice: An introduction to voice and diction* (4th ed.). Allyn & Bacon.

Whitton, S. W., James-Kangal, N., Rhoades, G. K., & Markman, H. J. (2018). Understanding couple conflict. In A. L. Vangelisti & D. Perlman (Eds.), *The*

Cambridge handbook of personal relationships (2nd ed., pp. 297–310). Cambridge University Press.

Widman, A., Schroger, E., & Wetzel, N. (2018). Emotion lies in the eye of the listener: Emotional arousal to novel sounds is reflected in the sympathetic contribution to the pupil dilation response and the P3. *Biological Psychology, 133*, 10–17.

Wright, C. N., & Roloff, M. E. (2009). Relational commitment and the silent treatment. *Communication Research Reports, 29*(1), 12–21.

9

Negative Emotions, Facial Clues, and Close Relationships: Facing the End?

Aleksandra Kostić, Marija Pejičić, and Derek Chadee

Love

Does the word *love*, despite its frequent use, signify the same or different terms in the conceptual system of every individual? Both laypeople and scientists seem to be confronted with this question, so relying on the non-verbal signals is the strategy explicitly or implicitly chosen by many people when they want to conclude whether they are loved. Besides this, each of us establishes different forms of relations and experiences different kinds of love. This refers to different categories of interpersonal relationships, such as parental love, love by a partner or a friend, and to those

A. Kostić (✉) • M. Pejičić
Faculty of Philosophy, Department of Psychology, University of Niš, Niš, Serbia
e-mail: marija.pejicic@filfak.ni.ac.rs

D. Chadee
ANSA McAl Psychological Research Centre, The University of the West Indies, St. Augustine, Trinidad
e-mail: derek.chadee@sta.uwi.edu

R. J. Sternberg, A. Kostić (eds.), *Nonverbal Communication in Close Relationships*,
https://doi.org/10.1007/978-3-030-94492-6_9

within which this complex emotion can have different forms. Some people are more capable of a more subtle differentiation of these categories than other people. Experts are probably equally puzzled by this question, as are some laypersons. Several theories are offered to understand partnership love.

Baumeister and Bushman (2011) refer to the classification of *passionate* and *companionate* love. Passionate love involves the existence of an exquisite desire and longing for one's partner, the feeling of excitement with the very encounter with him/her and the need for physical closeness, including intercourse. There is no similar excitement in companionate love or affectionate love, and the partner is more viewed as a soulmate. Companionate love is associated with loyalty, dedication, mutual understanding, and caring. They conclude that the latter kind of love is the building block for a successful long-term marriage.

These two types of love are vital for relationship development. As passion decreases in a relationship, there is the potential for a gradual transfer from a romantic into a companionate love (e.g. Acker & Davis, 1992; Hatfield et al., 2008; Tucker & Aron, 1993). Such an idea also has its theoretical support. According to the triangular theory of love by Robert Sternberg (1986), love consists of three components: *intimacy, passion*, and *decision/commitment.* Intimacy "refers to feelings of closeness, connectedness, and bondedness in loving relationships" (p. 119). "The passion component refers to the drives that lead to romance, physical attraction, sexual consummation, and related phenomena in loving relationships" (p. 119). "The decision/commitment component refers to, in the short term, the decision that one loves someone else, and in the long term, the commitment to maintain that love" (p. 119). Depending on the fact which of these components is prevalent, Sternberg (1986) distinguishes eight types of love: nonlove, liking, infatuated love, empty love, romantic love, companionate love, fatuous love, and consummate love. *Nonlove* refers to a series of relations that do not include either of the above-mentioned components. *Liking* implies a relationship that contains only the first component, intimacy. Therefore, it is viewed as a friendship filled with closeness and warmth. *Infatuated love* includes the experience of passionate excitement, with the lack of intimacy and decision/commitment. *Empty love* is a type of relationship that has commitment but does not have passion and intimacy, which usually characterises the final or near-final stage of a long-term relationship. An individual has decided to love another individual, and he/she is dedicated to that relationship but feels neither closeness nor passion towards him/her. *Romantic love* implies the presence of intimacy and passion—an individual feels passionate excitement, as with infatuation, but also feels an intense emotional attachment to the partner, which does not exist with infatuation. Companionate love is characterised by deep friendship, which is present in long-lasting relationships with significantly reduced passion. *Fatuous love* represents a relationship in which commitment is developed based on the experienced passion, but it usually has a short lifespan due to the lack of intimacy. In *Consummate or complete love,* there is a combination of passion, intimacy, and commitment. An individual feels passionate toward a partner, to whom he/she has a strong emotional attachment. The individual is dedicated to that relationship.

These three components differ, depending on the degree of stability within the relationship. Intimacy and decision/commitment are under voluntary control to a higher degree (especially decision/commitment) and have greater stability over time than the passion component. However, for an individual to have control over the first two components, he/she has to be aware of them, which is something people are not able to do. Although they feel warmth and concern for the partner's welfare and happiness, it is important to understand and recognise these components. The author emphasises the complexity of this phenomenon. Love should be observed with its specific quality. Love obtains its significance in people's implicit theories.

In an attempt to define partnership love, Hazan and Shaver (1987) utilised John Bowlby's (1969) attachment theory. They represented love as a combination of three control systems of behaviour: *attachment, caregiving, and sexual behavioural system.* While describing these systems, Bowlby (1969) states that each of them, although they appear automatic, also possesses cognitive-behavioural mechanisms, which enable monitoring and correcting the primary strategy, directed towards the achievement of the set goal, while adjusting to the environmental requirements, that is, the context. The goal of the first system is the feeling of protection and safety, the second system is focused on the reduction of suffering and the encouragement of growth of another individual by experiencing his/

her state, while the third one refers to the fulfilment of the partner's sexual desires. If an activation of primary strategies does not fulfil the goal, there is an activation of the secondary ones: hyperactivation and deactivation. According to Hazan and Shaver (1987), stable partner relationships are characterised by an optimum functionality of all three systems, while their dysfunctionality leads to conflicts, dissatisfaction, and instability of the relationship. Hyperactivation of the first system is reflected in overemphasising the unavailability of the attachment figure, that is, the partner's excessive dependence and attempts to control and attract attention (Shaver & Mikulincer, 2002). On the other hand, deactivation implies alienation, focusing, and relying on oneself to avoid rejection by the attachment figure. The hyperactivation of caregiving system is manifested through an individual's assertive attempts to give attention and support; the hypersensitivity is in observing the signals of other people's needs, while neglecting one's own needs, which leads to a higher level of stress in both partners. On the contrary, deactivation implies lack of empathy, insensitivity to the needs, and distancing oneself from the partner when he/she needs attention. With the hyperactivation of the third control system, an individual overemphasises the significance of sexual intercourse for the relationship, insists on it, and becomes overly sensitive to each signal he/she receives from a partner, which may indicate either presence or the lack of sexual interest. All that increases anxiety and creates tension in the relationship. In deactivation, an individual rejects his/her sexual needs, distances from the partner when he/she shows interest in sex, and inhibits sexual excitement.

Need to Belong

An inborn tendency to belong and be intimate represents one of the most fundamental human needs that shape emotions, cognition, and behaviour. This tendency to belong motivates us to search for a soulmate. We establish a close and stable relationship as we discover the desired elements of similarity in a particular individual. The achieved closeness satisfies the need for belonging and, at the same time, encourages the awakening of positive feelings. The image of oneself then becomes overwhelmed by a sudden increase in self-respect and self-confidence with the increased sense of accomplishment and achievement. Although most people feel confident, uncertainty within the relations may worry them.

Despite the beginning enthusiasm and hope that the achieved closeness will remain stable over time, many people are worried over the relationship's future. In trying to free themselves from the uncomfortable threat, people sometimes resort to the idealised projection of perfect, unchangeable, and "unique" closeness. The harmonious functioning of the partnership dyad indeed rests on an intrinsic tendency of both members to be happy, which does not exclude an occasional possibility of experiencing negative emotions, which should be handled carefully and with understanding. Over time, however, partners notice that the companionship is exposed to different changes, especially when it comes to emotional dynamics and the functioning of the dyad. Some of these mutually synchronised changes can empower and increase partnership closeness, while, on the contrary, emotionally desynchronised changes usually cause an unstable, vulnerable, and weak connection.

For decades, those who have studied the nature and functions of emotions have emphasised their important role in all kinds of relationships, from those related to business, friends, and family to intimate relationships in which emotions have an immense significance (Ekman, 2003, xiii). According to Tomkins (1962), emotions are the generators that motivate us and contribute to the quality of our lives. There is a tendency to multiply positive emotional experiences and decrease the negative ones. We are sometimes unable to achieve this despite great effort, especially in important relationships.

Emotions are essential because they have the power to create outcomes of our relations, connect us with others, make us more distant, or completely separate us from them, and influence positive and negative characteristics of our relations, and their future. Living in harmony with emotions implies a serious knowledge of the phenomenology of emotions. Persons who understand the nature of emotions, their antecedents and functions, and recognise emotions and their changes within themselves and others and learn to regulate and control them, can easily manage their relations and outcomes.

Paul Ekman's fifty-year dedication to the systematic research of emotions has provided powerful support to the development of this area and has encouraged many scientists to dedicate themselves to the studies of emotions. The theoretical hypotheses and empirical discoveries by Paul Ekman have enriched the scientific knowledge on the nature and functions of emotions (Ekman & Cordaro, 2011), which is why his work has become an inevitable guide in understanding important phenomena of emotional experience, primarily in the field of expressing primary emotions (Ekman & Keltner, 2014). Ekman's approach has also become our platform for analysing facial communication of emotions within the interactions of close individuals (Ekman, 2016).

Toward Emotions

Although it is generally known that emotions have an undoubted significance in our life, thus making it sometimes better, fuller, and more meaningful, and occasionally completely different, we should pay attention to Ekman's observation, which he has revealed in the introduction of his book "Emotions Revealed" (2003, xiv): "It still amazes me that up until very recently we – both scientists and laymen – knew so little about emotion, given its importance in our lives. But it is in the nature of emotion itself that we would not fully know how emotions influence us and how to recognize their signs in ourselves and others."

This remark by Ekman most certainly refers to some earlier periods during which there was a visible disharmony between the importance of emotions in life and the incomplete understanding of their nature and the power they have over us. Why are emotions so difficult to understand and sometimes impossible to know? Ekman believes that the nature of emotion is "responsible" for this state, that is, the *promptness* it awakens. A rapid appearance of emotions often does not make us aware of why we feel and act in a certain way. Due to the promptness of that appearance, we also lose control over situations and events that incite emotions, or behaviours they cause.

Although emotions can be excellent allies in most situations, providing us with a lot of energy, we sometimes understand that our emotional reactions may be inappropriate for some social situations. The emotional response itself can be inappropriate when it comes to the category of the experienced emotion, its excessive intensity or expression. If we were "oriented" more toward internal emotional states and if we carefully analysed the types of events that incited certain emotions in most situations, we would be more aware of *when* we become emotionally excited and *how* we behave in that case. This could help establish certain control and implement changes that make easier not only our life but also life with others. Ekman believes that anyone who thinks about the benefits of regulating one's emotional behaviour can invest some effort into learning to be constructive and ready to bring changes into everything that makes us emotionally inadequate but allows certain corrections. Many of us are sometimes ashamed of our negative and inappropriate emotional reactions, which have disrupted important interpersonal relations. These inappropriate reactions can leave feelings of guilt and regret, which is the first step toward our willingness to change something (Ekman, 2003, xiv, p. 17).

Verbal Versus Non-verbal

Verbal communication occupies an important place in all kinds of social interactions, regardless of the participants, their relations and goals, and their mutual influences and changes (Havelka, 2012). When used adequately, which primarily implies using a shared code, language can provide a good flow, quality, and a successful outcome of an interaction. In such conditions, conversation partners exchange clear and precisely articulated verbal messages which are based on the optimum number of relevant information spoken at the right moment. An ideal outcome and the basic quality of such verbal communication is the rich exchange of spoken messages composed in a way that is both understood and accepted by the participants.

However, the presence of specific differences can disrupt the willingness of conversation partners to continue the conversation and connect among themselves adequately. Differences that make verbal communication more difficult can emerge due to educational, generational, individual, socio-cultural, and contextual factors. These factors are sometimes difficult to overcome (Havelka, 2012).

Communication with others does not only imply relying on the spoken words, although their speaking capacities are what makes people different than other species. Besides language, conversation partners also use numerous non-verbal signals combined with speech. The non-verbal elements of behaviour are crucial to interaction (Argyle, 2017). A diverse and intriguing collection of non-verbal signals, often sent without an individual's conscious and voluntary intention, becomes a form of behaviour that the conversation participant trusts. Rot (2010) believes that spontaneity and involuntariness of non-verbal behaviour support the hypothesis on the validity and reliability of these signals. Unlike that, spoken phrases can be planned in advance, carefully constructed, and often completely inconsistent with reality, but therefore in accordance with the current interests of the conversation partners.

Sometimes, the interaction participants are not either brave enough or willing to talk about their delicate inner states. Instead, they rather choose a non-verbal context, utilising lack of specificity and unstable connections between signs and meanings, to only *hint* at inner states, without any verbal articulation.

In some situations, however, relatively non-specific and uncertain meanings of non-verbal signals can provide protection from unpleasant exposure. However, non-verbal expressions can be the source of miscommunication. This is only one of the reasons that makes this kind of interactive situation very complex. Added to the complexity of non-verbal communication is the spectrum of a number of different non-verbal signals (e.g., facial expression, physical contact, glance, gestures, body position, tone of voice), as well as the many messages that are transferred by these signals, including messages about emotions, interpersonal attitudes, and individuals' honesty. Participants, therefore, carefully monitor the course of interaction and react at the right moment to the sent non-verbal signals by adequately connecting them with appropriate meanings while responding in the given relation and broader social context.

The dyad interaction between close individuals is performed through both verbal and non-verbal, while the communication channels can act either individually or together. In this chapter, our interests are focused on the exchange of non-verbal, or more precisely, facial messages in partner relations, which is why it is now necessary to reflect on the communication tools of the face.

Closer to Face and Its Signals

Even within the communication from which we do not expect significant gains and do not give special significance, our view is focused on the face of the conversation partner. The face can be the source of useful information about the person with whom we communicate. The degree of closeness and attachment increases or decreases interest in facial expressions. The analysis of facial communication of close individuals reflects a frequent exchange of non-verbal signals and an effort to notice, differentiate, and successfully decode them. Frequent and direct face-to-face communication provides an opportunity to distinguish visible facial expressions, which are treated as the indicators of the quality of the relationship. High interest in the partner's face rests on the belief that facial expressions are tightly connected to an individual's inner states, expectations, motives, and particularly, emotions. Although we can count on the direct connection between the inner state and its external manifestation in many situations, there are circumstances in which that connection is lost. Every facial behaviour, which is a product of intentional manipulation of signals, and not the expression of an actual experience, compromises the above-mentioned connection and questions the reliability of the source of information.

The face is a multi-signal system that often produces numerous facial configurations that are similar in appearance but that can have completely different meanings (Ekman, 1993). The one who observes the face has a double assignment—to deal with similarities and differences in the appearance of facial behaviours, and then discover and differentiate the messages sent by those behaviours. Due to the complexity of facial behaviours, the promptness of appearance, and the tendency to combine both, at some point, interpretation of facial signals can be challenging. Despite that, the opportunity to obtain information sent by the face needs an investment of effort. The additional difficulty in understanding facial behaviour is the simultaneous use of both verbal and non-verbal channels of communication. Conversation partners usually pay more attention to speech content and less to non-verbal behaviour, while some of the messages that come from the face can disappear after being easily missed (Ekman et al., 1982; Buck, 1988; Kostić, 2014; Kostić & Chadee, 2015).

Although facial signals research has been undertaken on the transfer of different messages, including information on gender, age, the state of physical and mental health, (Harper et al., 1978; Knapp et al., 2014), the most frequently researched facial expressions are those connected to emotions (Ekman & Friesen, 1971, 1982; Frijda & Mesquita, 1994; Kostić, 1995; Kostić et al., 2020). As a complex stimulus, the face relies on different types of facial signals—static, slow, artificial, and rapid (Ekman & Friesen, 2003). *Static* facial signals point to identity and particularity; *slow* signals indicate its maturing and ageing; *artificial* signals show aesthetic and health-related interventions; and *rapid* signals convey internal experiences. A "calm" face does not show any movement and depicts personal characteristics but attracts attention. In contrast, a "face in motion" completely fascinates us with its ability to express the most delicate and sensitive states. Our fascination with the nature and functions of dynamic facial signals, the changes they produce on the face, as well as the meanings they convey, led us to consider especially fast signs. Additionally, the dual nature of messages (informative and communicative) warned of the caution and careful distinction of reliable spontaneous expressions directly related to inner states from those that were not (Ekman, 1997; Kostić et al., 2020).

The category of dynamic, *rapid* facial signals contains several sub-categories—facial expressions of emotions, facial emblems, facial manipulators, illustrators, and regulators, and each of the stated sub-categories plays a separate role within social interactions. In this way, facial expressions are used for sending messages on emotions and interpersonal attitudes, while the use of regulators starts, manages, and shapes the interaction, and illustrators provide greater vividness and interest in the conversation. In situations in which speech is not possible, instead of words one can use facial emblems that transfer meanings understood by the conversational partner. There is one more sub-category of rapid facial signals (i.e., facial manipulators), which speak of discomfort, trepidation, anxiety, and expectations of those who interact (Ekman & Friesen, 1969, 2003).

Rapid facial signals occur due to short-term changes in the neuromuscular activity of the face with a duration, at times, of a split second. Depending on the strength of the contraction of facial muscles, the changes of the face are noticeable. When muscle contractions are weak, changes are slight, difficult to notice, and require careful observation or recognition through touch. Instantaneous facial movements, which are the result of the change in the facial muscle tone (facial expression), signal different emotions of an individual. Although they can also be the source of information about interpersonal attitudes, including emotions (Kostić, 2014; Ekman, 1982; Kostić et al., 2020). Facial expressions of experienced emotions are correctly treated as involuntary facial configurations which primarily have an informative function (Ekman & Keltner, 2014). However, there is also a communicative-interactive function of facial emotional expressions that facilitates the dynamic of social encounters (Ekman, 1982; Kostić, 2014; Ekman et al., 1982). The origin of facial expressions has always been the subject of debates and disagreement among scientists. Nativists have claimed that it is inborn, that is, universal facial behaviour, and relativists that it is acquired and culture-specific. There is, however, solid empirical proof (Ekman, 1973, 1997, 1999; Ekman & Scherer, 1984) that the expression of seven primary emotions has a phylogenetic basis and shows through universal facial expressions (Ekman, 1992a). This means that independently of all differences (including gender, age, education, social stratum, social class, nationality or cultural affiliation), individuals who feel happiness, sadness, fear, surprise, anger, disgust, or contempt show these feelings with the same specific facial expressions. According to Izard (1990), public situations with a prescribed regulation and control of emotional behaviour could be an exception.

Emotional Bonds

At the end of the 1970s, scientists showed a significant interest in researching different aspects of emotional communication of close individuals, utterly crucial for the lives of partners who usually share the same space and face an array of wonderful and challenging moments in their relationships. Levinger (1980) investigated in close relationships possible changes during short or long intervals of union and identified several stages, from initial attraction to relationship-building, its decline and end.

Starting from the point of view of his practice dedicated to marital problems, Gottman (1979) revealed a positive connection between the non-verbal competence of a partner and marital satisfaction, thus identifying different styles of communication that depend on satisfaction or dissatisfaction with the marital relationship. Gottman has emphasised that it is necessary to work on the improvement of communication skills, that is, on non-verbal sensitivity of marital partners. The results of Gottman and Porterfield's research (1981) also pointed out that long-term partners develop personal systems of meaning on which they base their interpretations of the partner's behaviour and which are often completely different from the interpretations of professional observers.

Considering the significance of emotional exchanges within a partnership dyad, we will consider potential ways of responding to changes in the experience of closeness or changes in the quality of the existing status of attachment. Baumeister and Leary (1995, p. 497) write about the "belongingness hypothesis", according to which "human beings have a pervasive drive to form and maintain at least a minimum quantity of lasting, positive, and significant interpersonal relationships". They believe that every change in the status of belonging to another person, regardless of whether it is real or possible, has positive and negative emotional implications for closeness, with the former increasing and the latter reducing closeness. In the same article, the authors mentioned above note that it is justified to expect that, in stable circumstances, a strong attachment to another individual and their feeling of acceptance and inclusion will produce positive and very intense feelings. On the contrary, a long-term dissatisfied or only partially satisfied need for belonging will be the source of different negative emotions. Also, noticing rejection and significant changes in the level of closeness, will lead to the same negative emotional effect. We conclude that the awakening of many strong emotions can be positively and negatively connected to belonging.

The attachment to another individual encourages numerous *positive* feelings (happiness, satisfaction, joy, enjoyment, bliss, thankfulness, compassion) whose occurrence speaks of the relationship's continuous stability and success. Baumeister and Leary (1995, p. 508) concluded that stable close relations are an essential or even necessary precondition for the occurrence of the feeling of happiness, while the lack of close attachment is a potential source of the awakening of negative feelings (sadness, depression, jealousy, loneliness, guilt, fear). Other authors also emphasise the significance of belongingness and loneliness in influencing psychological health (e.g., Mellor et al., 2008; Townsend & McWhirter, 2005). For example, Mellor et al. (2008) have found that the discrepancy between the need to belong and satisfaction with personal relationships is associated with loneliness, which has confirmed Baumeister and Leary's "belongingness hypothesis". McAdams and Bryant (1987) believe that individuals who have established intimacy in social relationships also enjoy happiness more intensely and the subjective feeling of bliss.

What jeopardises most the quality or the survival of a close relationship are *negative* emotions. What happens when partners feel the decrease in closeness or experience a more frequent exchange of negative emotions and even overt hostility? Do they manage to correctly recognise facial signs or, at least, hints of negative emotions and emotional distance from their partner? There are situations in which the partners deny feeling negative emotions and reduced partner closeness. Then they may try to hide their negative feelings or show them as more positive than they are, lying and saying that everything is fine. Hiding or falsifying emotions leads their partner on the path of wrong judgements. A careful observation of emotional exchange and noticing potential deviations from the usual expressive style in showing emotions should be a necessary precondition for judging the relationship.

What Makes Stable Relationships Different from Unstable Ones?

Gottman and DeClaire (2001) give special significance to the emotional connection involving exchanging emotional messages and sending and receiving signals that demonstrate an understanding and caring about the partner's feelings. They speak about "bids". "A bid can be a question, a gesture, a look, a touch – any single expression that says, 'I want to feel connected to you.' A response to a bid is just that – a positive or negative answer to somebody's request for emotional connection" (p. 4). These authors have concluded that husbands do not respond to 19% of these signals from their wives within a stable relationship. On the contrary, husbands headed for divorce are not responsive in 82% of the cases. When it comes to women, in a stable relationship unresponsiveness is 14%, and in an unstable one, 50%. Similar differences are also noticed when we monitor the frequency of establishing connections during short time intervals (100 vs. 65 during a 10-minute interval). Emotional needs that an individual wants to satisfy through close relations are the need for inclusion, the need for experiencing an achieved control over one's life, and the need to be liked by others. Every relation develops through exchanging these emotional messages, that is, their acknowledgement when they occur and a positive response to them (*turning toward*). A timely and positive response to them will lead to further dependence on a relationship, which will be filled with a richer exchange of bids regarding intensity and frequency. This does not mean that one partner responds to every bid of the other partner. In such a relationship, there are many opportunities for establishing connections. On the contrary, a negative response through sarcastic comments and other forms of hostility (*turning against*) and neglecting and ignoring (*turning away*) will make a relationship *empty* and unstable. The research by Gottman and DeClaire (2001) has even shown that this second form of interaction jeopardises the relationship's survival more quickly than the first one. Survival is significantly jeopardised by a relationship in which one partner continually turns towards the other's bids while the other partner constantly turns away or against. In such interactions, the former partner most often gives up relatively quickly, decreasing further bids.

In every relationship, certain disagreements shape the characteristics of partner communication and exchange, depending on the stability or instability of their relations. Gottman and DeClaire (2001) noticed that establishing an emotional connection by responding to emotional needs, emitted through bids, during everyday interaction, equips partners with good feelings, which also enables them to understand each other better when there is an argument. When this happens, negative emotions also occur in stable and happy relationships. However, partners still stay connected and engaged with each other. This connection is manifested through greater expressions of humour, affection, interest, mutual respect, and the absence of negative feelings, such as contempt. On the contrary, the other two forms of interaction, in which there are negative reactions to the expression of emotional needs of a partner (*turning against*) or they are completely absent (*turning away*), are, in fact, not resistant to negative emotions. Their arguments are accompanied by hostility and defensiveness.

Gottman and DeClaire (2001) believe that sending and recognising bids are skills that partners can master. Some patterns of behaviour established in partnership relations can have their roots in insensitive parental responses to child's signals. These authors give the example of a wife who did not send signals to her husband that her emotional needs have not been satisfied. She occasionally reacted angrily when overwhelmed with frustration. She should have learned how to send a bid for connection, while her partner should have realised that her anger could have been that bid. Ascribing true meaning to her reactions would have made the husband more willing to help her develop the skill of signalling her own needs. Not only can anger, but sometimes sadness and fear, can signal a need for connection.

Bids can be verbal and non-verbal. Some of the non-verbal bids are *affectionate touching* (e.g., a handshake, a kiss, a hug), *facial signals* (e.g., smile or rolling one's eyes), *playful touching* (e.g., tickling, dancing, a gentle bump), *affiliating gestures* (e.g., opening a door or pointing to a shared interest), *vocalising* (e.g., laughing, grunting, sighing in a way that invites interaction or interest) (Gottman & DeClaire, 2001, p. 31). Responses to these bids can be manifested similarly.

Positive reactions to bids can be different: *nearly passive responses, low-energy responses, attentive responses,* or *high-energy responses,* but the recipient always gets a clear message—that they have been heard by a partner, that the partner is interested in them, and that a partner is by their side and wants to help them.

When an individual turns away from connecting bids, this is often done by focusing on a certain activity which he/she has performed until then (*preoccupied responses*), by completely ignoring the bid, by being silent or focusing on irrelevant details from the bid (*disregarding responses*), or by speaking about something which is not related to the topic introduced through the partner's bid (*interrupting responses*). Often, an individual fails to respond to bids not because he/she may not care about the partner or not recognise the bids. However, an individual who has sent a signal and has been deprived of an adequate reaction feels lonely, isolated, and rejected. Upset, he/she becomes increasingly sensitive to the signals of rejection, and, therefore, prone to a wrong interpretation of the partner's behaviour, thus confirming his/her own assumptions, which, in addition, influences negatively his/her self-confidence and self-respect. The individual feels defeated, which could result in further biddings and efforts in the relationship. Turning away from bids of connection may lead to disrupted relationships with the manifesting of anger and contempt, and defensive behaviours and the dynamics towards the breakdown of the relationship.

The third possible reaction to the partner's bids is turning against him/her. It consists of a very heterogeneous group of forms, but the outcome is the same, the establishment of the connection is refused. One of the forms is reacting with the facial expression of contempt (*contemptuous responses*), which leads to a superior stance in relation to the partner, thus hurting him/her by expressing disrespect and establishing distance. *Belligerent responses* are also one of the patterns that cause the situation of turning against bids. It refers to the behaviours used to wrongfully attack a partner, provoking him/her to confrontation or argument regardless of the content of communication. The third way in which an individual can turn away from the bid for connection is similar to the aforementioned, although it is less hostile (*contradictory responses*). *Domineering responses* are those in which an individual responds to the given bid by trying to establish control over his/her partner, thus taking a more dominant position with the intention to incite retreat and subordination of the partner. The fifth form refers to *critical responses*, in which the partner's signals are responded to by manipulative criticism, that is, by the one which refers to his/her personality instead of specific behaviour. *Defensive responses* are those in which a partner distances himself/herself from the responsibility for the bidder's words by taking the position of an innocent victim, even when the sent message does not contain the signs of an attack. Although Gottman and DeClaire (2001) believe that partners who respond to the signals in this manner do not intend to hurt another individual, but that such reactions are often the consequence of certain factors which are outside the partnership relation, the bidder is hurt and rejected, even more than the period when he/she experienced turning away. Facing these reactions can produce fear and lead to the avoidance of conflicts in the future. Such relationships, in which one of the partners suppresses his or her feelings to maintain peace, can last relatively long and be stable but not happy.

Contempt

Gottman's work on "fixing and strengthening" marital, friendly, and business relationships has convinced him that words cannot express everything that an individual feels. In his view, it is necessary to sharpen the skill of noticing, differentiating, and decoding different groups of non-verbal signals, including signals that occur on the face (Gottman & DeClaire, 2001).

When a relationship is considered particularly important, the face of a close individual is experienced as a precious source of sometimes pleasant and sometimes unpleasant information. Thanks to their multi-signal ability, faces "speak" to us about experienced, suppressed, or simulated emotions. Some facial clues signal support, affection, and approval, while others indicate reluctance, hostility, resentment, rejection. Frequently used, these signs can indicate successful or unsuccessful, stable or unstable partnerships. It is evident that besides the signs of love and respect which make us happy the most, facial expressions can also confirm disrupted closeness, worn-out connection, fading love, loss of trust, and disrespect. Gottman (1994) believes that frequent negative interaction in which partners are exposed to constant criticism, hostile attitudes, and facial expressions of contempt, produces a defensive reaction, and also undermines and imbalances communication, thus awakening the partner's anxiety that the relationship is close to an end.

Starting from the fundamental human need for belonging and the most suitable models of partnership communication, consideration is now given to the disruptions of interaction with close individuals. The "verbalisation" of facial communication of negative emotions and its appearance and timely observation can signify the quality, course, and fate of partnership relations. The facial *expression of contempt* is one of the most "verbal announcers" of a marital crisis, discordant and undermined communion, and disruptive partnership relationship. Coan and Gottman (2007) state that contempt is a complex and multi-meaningful emotion used for expressing deep disrespect, aversion, and superior power over one's partner. An individual who expresses this emotion has the *intention* to hurt and humiliate his/her partner, showing that he/she sees an irreparably incompetent, stupid, unfit, and inferior person in the partner. However, this situation becomes more significant when it is constantly repeated. It is difficult for partners to abandon the interaction in which they are used to frequent exchanges of contempt and sneer signals. The response to this situation is most often a defensive response, sending a message of guiltlessness (Gottman, 1994).

Margolin, John, and Gleberman (1988) have found that in conflict situations, during confrontations, women are equally as men prone to express contempt and anger toward their violent husbands. Kernsmith (2005) believes that a frequent expression of contempt during an argument is positively connected to higher willingness of both partners to react violently, which is also confirmed by research results presented by Sommer, Iyican, and Babcock (2019). However, an individual who is angry at his/her partner can react violently but that will not initiate a similar violent reaction in the other individual, as concluded by Sommer, Iyican, and Babcock. According to the findings of Coan and Gottman (2007), the expression of contempt is usually followed by sarcasm, sneering, and eye-rolling.

In his attempt to point out how important it is to focus on a more serious study of contempt, not only as an expression of superiority, but also as a feeling that "speaks" about the characteristics of the marital communication, especially in conflict situations, Ekman (2003, p. 181) directs us toward very interesting findings presented by Gottman and Levenson (1999, 2004). In particular, their long-term studies of many marital interactions revealed that women whose husbands had expressed contempt were overwhelmed with dissatisfaction. They thought more often that their problems were difficult, serious, and nearly unsolvable, which probably worsened their health during the following four years. This was not the case when husbands expressed only disgust or anger. Gottman and Silver (1994) stated that frequent expression of contempt and expressed hostility represent forms of permanent psychological abuse, an indicator of gravitation towards divorce or a relationship break-up.

If a facial expression of contempt is able to destroy a partnership relation, and even anticipate its ending, this would have to be rooted in a long-term negative view of the individual with whom one lives. The partner who this emotion is directed against and who recognises it experiences it as an attack on his/her own personality and self-esteem. It turns out that *contempt* is a destructive emotion because it increases and expands the existing conflict, thus introducing unpleasant forms of arguments and, perhaps, a similar response, instead of calming the situation or reconciliation. If the facial expression of contempt is directed against you many times during frequent arguments with your partner, you have received information, including rejection.

Social exclusion (rejection) produces negative emotions, which authors describe as *social pain* (Driscoll et al., 2017; MacDonald & Leary, 2005). MacDonald and Leary (2005) have defined this phenomenon as "a specific emotional reaction to the perception that one is being excluded from desired relationships or being devalued by desired relationship partners or groups" (p. 202). The results of seven experiments whose subjects were informed that the other participants had allegedly socially rejected them exhibited a lower level of prosocial (helping) behaviour (Twenge et al., 2007). The rejection caused their emotional response intended to protect them from the unpleasantness experienced, and those emotions temporarily reduced their capacities for compassion and understanding others and the need to help them.

Let us go back to the situation of partnership interaction in which someone from this dyad observes the partner's face and realises that he/she has been rejected. He/she emotionally responds to the information about the rejection and loses the capacity to listen, understand, and be tolerant and compassionate (Ekman, 2010), and to return the communication to a "safer" level. Can we forget instantly a message of contempt sent by our partner?

Analysing the nature, expression, and function of contempt, but believing that this emotion has not been explored enough, Ekman (2003, p. 182) pointed out that the awakening of someone's contempt is caused by individuals and their behaviour. The antecedents of contempt are never unpleasant smells, tastes, or touches, as is the case with the causes of disgust. In most cases, the expression of contempt is exclusively associated with the experience of one's own superiority over another person. Referring to Miller's observation, Ekman states (2003, p. 181) that the subordinates can feel and express contempt towards their superiors, as it happens in some interactions between women and men, adolescents and adults, and employee and their bosses. By expressing contempt, the subordinate wants to show that they are not worthless and inferior and do not deserve this kind of message. For those who experience it, contempt is not a negative emotion, and it can even produce a pleasant experience. The primary function of contempt is not an adaptation, but a clear manifestation of power, status, and belief in one's value compared to the much or slightly less valuable characteristics and capacities of others. There are those who nurture a contemptuous interpersonal attitude towards their environment, enjoying their own superiority and haughty behaviour, and sometimes unsupported high self-esteem while trying to maintain their imaginary status of being and incomparable individuals. It is interesting that the social environment sometimes views these persons with admiration and respect, considering only their interpersonal style of treating others.

Although the intensity of contempt can vary, as with any other emotion, it does not reach the highest intensity of disgust even to its full extent. With contempt, it is very hard to identify some internal sensations (Ekman, 2003), unlike specific sensations associated with disgust (in one's throat, for example) or anger (increased blood pressure and pulse).

Ekman (2003) drew attention to the existence of specific unilateral facial changes during the experience of contempt: raising one's chin, and then stretching and lifting one corner of the lips (see Photos 9.1 and 9.2). With increased intensity of this emotion, the changes in the face become more strongly expressed and, therefore, more visible. During a powerful

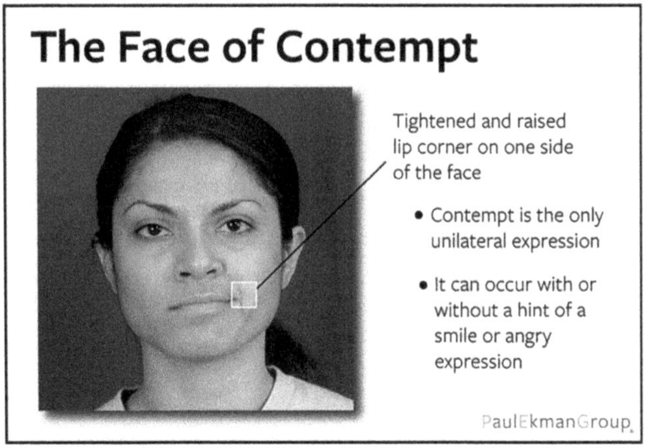

The Face of Contempt
Tightened and raised lip corner on one side of the face
• Contempt is the only unilateral expression
• It can occur with or without a hint of a smile or angry expression
PaulEkmanGroup

Photo 9.1 Facial expression of contempt (What is Contempt? – Paul Ekman Group. https://www.paulekman.com). (This photo has the permission of Paul Ekman (personal communication, September, 14, 2021))

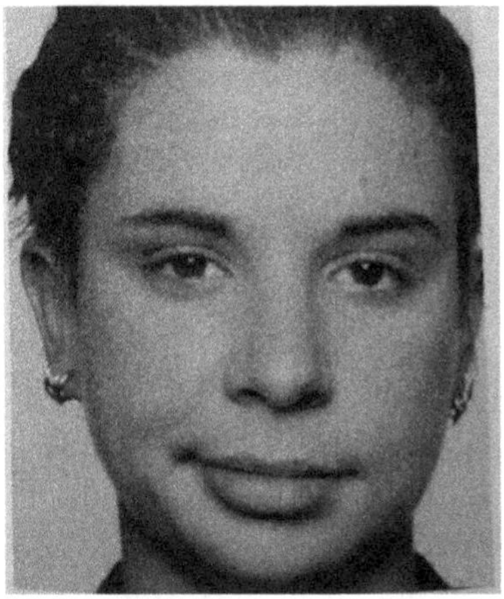

Photo 9.2 Facial expression of contempt (Ekman, *Emotions Revealed*, 2003, photo H, p. 185). (This photo has the permission of Paul Ekman (personal communication, September, 14, 2021))

expression of contempt accompanied with the elevation of one lip corner, there is a slight gap between the lips on that side. Empirical findings from cross-cultural studies, including isolated cultures, show that contempt has been the last emotion to join the list of six basic universal emotions (Ekman & Friesen, 1986; Ekman, 1994, 2003; Ekman & Heider, 1988). We are now convinced that despite earlier disputes (Russell, 1991), the facial expression of contempt represents a universal specific configuration, highly recognisable in different cultures (75%). Similar results have also been obtained by Matsumoto (1992).

Contempt Smile

According to Ekman, a smile is one of the most frequently used facial expressions (Ekman, 1992b, pp. 151, 153; Ekman & Friesen, 1982; Ekman et al., 1981), that is, an expression experienced by observers as simple and easily recognisable, although they are often difficult to interpret. A smile occurs due to the contraction of one facial muscle (zygomatic major), which pulls the corners of the lips towards the cheekbones. However, numerous kinds of smiles (18 smiles), which are different in their appearance and meaning, indicate the complexity of interpretation. Some of them are felt smile, false smile, fear smile, contempt smile, compliance smile, miserable smile, Chaplin smile, dampened smile, flirtatious smile, embarrassment smile, coordination smile, and listener response smile. A smile is also a convenient way to mask an emotion we would like to hide because it is not appropriate to show it at a given moment. A smile is relatively easy to perform and does not require a particular skill. It is a simple stretch of one's lips.

From the array of the aforementioned smiles, we will single out a *contemptuous smile* (see Photo 9.3). This smile is sometimes incorrectly interpreted as an expression of positive feelings. In a contemptuous smile, the contractions of facial muscles tighten the corners of the lips, thus making them bevelled upwards, similar to the smile expressing positive feelings. It is this similarity that creates confusion and deceives the observer. Another similarity between a contemptuous and a genuine smile is the dimple which sometimes also occurs during an expression of positive

Photo 9.3 Contemptuous smile (Ekman, *Telling Lies*, 1992b, p. 152). (This photo has the permission of Paul Ekman (personal communication, September, 14, 2021))

feelings, with protrusions in lip corners and around them. According to Ekman, the most significant difference between a contemptuous smile and a smile expressing pleasure or joy is the tightness of lip corners which can never be noticed with a truly experienced smile. Ekman (1992b, p. 153) notes that there is also a unilateral variant of a contemptuous smile, which contains visible changes in the lifting and tightening of a lip corner on one side of the face.

The Recognition of the Facial Expression of Contempt

Successful identification of any emotion implies knowing specific characteristics of its facial expression and relevant signals of the emotions with which it is usually combined (Ekman, 1984). Facial signs of mixed emotions that a partner experiences at the same time as contempt can represent a problem in an accurate interpretation of the whole facial configuration. Let us repeat that identifying an emotion becomes even more complicated due to the quickness with which it appears on the face and disappears. Suppose facial expressions last longer or shorter than that. In that case, it is a sign that these are not experienced but simulated emotions, which requires the ability to make a difference between honest and fake behaviours.

The next problem in the successful decoding of the facial expression of any emotion, including contempt, is the intensity of visible changes on the face. A stronger intensity of an emotion produces more visible changes, and its identification is easier. However, if contempt has recently been awakened and is being developed, its intensity is not strong enough, and the changes are subtle and hard to recognise (Ekman, 1984). Knowing the partner's style of expression contributes to the success in interpreting facial behaviour.

Due to their personal style of expression and what the situation demands, people control their facial expression of an emotion, which makes successful decoding of expressions harder. In marital arguments, for example, in their desire to protect themselves, their status or a relationship, partners tend to conceal or falsify negative emotions, including emotions of contempt, disgust, anger, and they deny having even experienced them at the given moment. The most important task of the other partner is to recognise the signs of both honest and dishonest facial behaviours.

Despite significant differences in the facial appearance and antecedents of contempt and disgust, it is not easy to successfully differentiate between these two emotions (Ekman & Friesen, 2003). For instance, if a partner experiences a combination of both emotions, signals of both contempt and disgust will appear on the face. This combination can make the differentiation between them more difficult, especially if there are signs of anger or some other emotions. The problem of distinguishing between contempt and disgust can occur due to apparently similar facial changes in the lower part of the face. When the rise of the upper lip, which is characteristic of the expression of disgust, does not have the same strength on both sides of the face, which makes the expression of disgust asymmetrical, the observer can think that it is a sign of contempt, although it is not. However, the typical facial configuration for contempt implies tightness and slight lifting of the corner of the upper lip exclusively on one side of the face. When contempt and disgust are mixed and represent one whole, changes can be seen in the wrinkled root of the nose, which is characteristic of disgust. If the emotion of anger is "added" to this configuration, which is not rare, the observer notices visible changes in the appearance of the upper and lower parts of the face. Eyebrows would be lowered and closer to each other, the upper eyelid elevated, while lips would be pressed together (Ekman, 2003, p. 185). Despite a different social function, these three mutually experienced and facially expressed emotions (i.e., contempt, disgust, and anger) are connected by their negative evaluation. Rozin (1999) justifiably called them the "triad of hostility". Compared with anger and disgust, contempt is a colder, less intense, but longer-lasting emotion (Miller, 1997).

How Does Facial Contempt Affect the Individual Against Whom It Is Directed?

Knowledge of nature and functions of contempt as well as the successful recognition of emotions with which it is combined, do not contribute to the understanding of effects which this cold emotion incites in the individual against whom it is directed. In their article "The Psychology of Self-Defense: Self-Affirmation Theory", Sherman and Cohen (2006) analysed possible reactions of an individual who feels socially excluded from a group or a friendly or romantic relationship. Someone's rejection or exclusion from an important relationship represents a threat to that individual's integrity. The individual experiences reduced adequacy, problematic and difficult adaptation to the given situation, which decreases his/her self-discipline and ability to make judgements. This situation leads most people to defensive behaviour (Twenge et al., 2003; Baumeister et al., 2005).

Sherman and Cohen (2006) conclude that defensive behaviour whose goal is to protect and strengthen the individual's integrity directly is often "responsible" for an unreal and distorted image of the given situation. The person loses his/her capacity to be constructive. Defensive behaviour protects the integrity of an individual but quite often inhibits adaptation by limiting and sometimes preventing the inflow of new experiences and information. Suppose an essential part of identity is jeopardised. In that case, an individual will hardly adapt to the fact that he/she is rejected and will comply with his/her unfavourable position in a previously romantic dyad of close individuals. This powerful defensive reaction protects the individual's integrity but can jeopardise and disrupt his/her relationships with others.

However, Sherman and Cohen (2006) believe that there are better and more constructive ways to protect jeopardised integrity and strengthen or regain one's self-respect. An individual who chooses better ways of responding tends to find alternative possibilities for self-change. New fields of self-affirmation (see theory of self-affirmation, Steele, 1988) help an individual overcome different kinds of biased defensive responding (i.e., rejection of threatening information, denial, avoidance of a threat in any manner) and deal with threatening knowledge and events without relying on defensive strategies.

Certain people can carefully evaluate the quality of a partnership relationship and the level of the feeling of closeness. They can talk with their partner to resolve problems or identify alternatives. Then, they may probably, as one alternative, step out bravely from the relationship and leave for new experiences. Therefore, if contempt on the partner's face sends a message: "You are not worthy of me!", that message could be utterly reciprocated.

Positive Side of Negative Emotions

Negative emotions are useful in the perpetuation and sustenance of relationships. The role of emotions and their expression via facial and other non-verbal cues are functional in human interaction and quite often used to send a message that a partner may feel uncomfortable in expressing verbally. Negative emotions in interpersonal relationships send the message that the relationship is not going in the right directions. Additionally, the partner may attempt to provide signals of dissatisfaction within a relationship, not only as a sign of termination but as a message of wanting changes to some aspects of a relationship. The misinterpretation, ignoring, taking for granted, reactance or resentful responses to negative emotions may shift the relationship into a downward spiral. Negative emotions such as anger, sadness, distress, and fear can, therefore, be positive in a relationship by motivating one toward the resolution of a problem and directing attention to the source of the issue (see Maslow, 1955; Plutchik, 2003; Frijda et al., 1989). These emotions are normally identifiable via facial expressions. Baker, McNulty, and Overall (2014, p. 102) note that from an evolutionary psychological perspective emotions focus our attention to the origin of the problem. They put it in this way:

> Experiencing negative emotions in the face of a problem can benefit individuals by helping them to recognize and understand, and thus be more likely to address and resolve, that problem (Frijda, 1986; Levenson, 1999; Tooby & Cosmides, 2008). Although the amount and severity of problems can vary across relationships, nearly all people acknowledge experiencing problems that have negatively affected their relationship at some point. (e.g., McGonagle et al., 1992)

In fact, some researchers have argued that the non-expression of negative affect states can be equally detrimental to a relationship. Yoo, Clark, Lemay, Salovey, and Monin (2011) note that anger, for example, as unpleasant as it is, allows the partner to express needs, vulnerabilities, unjust treatments, block goals, and frustrations.

Moving a relationship from one of a possible negative outcome towards a positive direction requires intervention and an understanding of the dynamics that may have led, in the first place, to the emergence of negative emotions. Equity theory (Adams, 1965; Polk, 2022) provides some insights into relationships and affect states. Equity theory is a social exchange theory and as all social exchange theories articulate, the rewards, costs, investments and profits are crucial for the healthy relational development. Distributive justice, both parties feeling equitable fairness after evaluating their input-output ratios, is essential to a harmonious relationship. But quite often in the wide range of interacting situations in relationships, one partner may over-benefit and the other under-benefit in one situation than another. Not all situations are equally reward weighted and, therefore, over-benefitting can derive accumulated rewards at the expense of the other partner who would be experiencing under-benefitting. As the rule of distributive justice is continually violated, and feelings of unfairness and inequity emerge, the non-verbal expressions of contemptuousness, anger, sadness, distress, frustration, guilt are not uncommon between partners. As inequity persists, negative affect states impact the emotions, moods, cognition, and behaviors associated in the relationship. Negative facial cues may signal to the deeper circumstances that lie within the inequities in a relationship.

Equity sensitivity determines the degree of emotional reactions towards inequity. Huseman, Hatfield, and Miles (1987) identify three equity sensitivities. These are benevolents, equity sensitives, and entitleds. Benevolents are less reactive to violations of the role of distributive justice and are more accommodating to under-benefitting. Entitleds feel a need to over-benefit while equity sensitives are motivated to equitable distribution and distributive justice in a relationship. Therefore, not everyone will respond similarly in the face of inequity. Expressions of facial anger, contempt, fear, or sadness may be a signal that a partner's well-being is being neglected (Sell et al., 2009). Within the context of equity theory, this expression is an attempt to re-establish a fair distributive justice. Sensitivity towards the negative emotional expression and positively responding in the context of the equity framework would push the relationship in a direction towards fairness with the potential of addressing the source of the negative facial reaction.

There are relational harmony strategies that partners can consider in response to relational strain. After assessing and determining cause of relational problems, a partner may adopt a number of strategies intended to strengthen the relationships including rebuilding trust, forgiveness, apologies, developing compassion. Forgiveness in relationships is one way of resetting and redirecting the affect state and increasing positive facial expressions. McCullough (2000, pp. 44–45) notes:

> When an offended relationship partner reports that he or she has not forgiven a close relationship partner for a hurtful action, the offended partner's perception of the offense is posited to stimulate relationship-destructive. … Conversely, when an offended relationship partner indicates that he or she has forgiven, his or her perception of the offense and offender no longer create motivation to avoid the offender and seek revenge.

Such changes in conceptualisation of partners and interaction dynamics would change the facial messages towards a positive direction. Worthington's (2021) five steps to forgiveness creating positive emotions and facial expressions are relevant. He refers to these five steps as the REACH process to achieving emotional forgiveness and they are:

R=Recall the Hurt
E=Empathise (Sympathise, feel Compassion for, Love) the Transgressor
A=give an Altruistic Gift of Forgiveness
C=Commit to the Emotional Forgiveness One Experienced
H=Hold on to Forgiveness When Doubts Arise

Additionally, apologies, empathy and perspective taking (see Davis, 1983; Batson, 1991; McCullough, 2000) are concomitants to forgiveness and allow interacting partners to be able to forego with an understanding and respect for each other. Ma et al. (2019) discuss the significance of trust within a relation and the efficacy of apology in the rebuilding of relational trust (see also Schniter & Sheremeta, 2014). The authors hypothesise about the negative emotions associated with trustworthiness, apologies and trusting behaviour arguing that apologies would be less effective in relational rebuilding when partners experience intense and prolonged negative emotions. Transgressor's negative emotions and trustworthiness were partial mediators in the rebuilding of trust. Rumination diminishes the propensity towards rebuilding of positive interpersonal interaction. There is a negative relationship between rumination and forgiveness. The more we ruminate about a negative relational issue the less forgiving we become, and suppression of these negative affect and cognition may contribute to avoidance and revenge (McCullough, 2000). Ruminating and suppression are quite often reflected non-verbally.

Negative emotions and the associate facial expressions, in fact may be exceedingly useful to a relationship. As Baker, McNulty and Overall (2014, p. 106) point out, "Negative emotions may benefit relationships by (1) leading to a better understanding by the partner, (2) eliciting support from the partner, and (3) regulating the partner's behaviour".

Our attachment, love, emotions, facial expressions, and many other factors create a complex psychological social exchange interactive structure. The fuel of negative emotions and the complexity of relational problems and the concomitant facial expressions can ignite and inflame the emergence of negative relationships. But negative emotions and facial feedbacks are not all negative. They can positively guide us away from facing the end.

References

Acker, M., & Davis, M. H. (1992). Intimacy, passion and commitment in adult romantic relationships: A test of the triangular theory of love. *Journal of Social and Personality Relationships, 9*, 21–50.

Adams, J. S. (1965). Inequity in social exchange. In L. Berkowitz (Ed.), *Advances in experimental social psychology* (Vol. 2, pp. 267–299). Academic Press.

Argyle, M. (2017). *Bodily communication* (2nd ed.). Taylor & Francis Group.

Baker, L. T., McNulty, J. K., & Overall, N. C. (2014). When negative emotions benefit relationships. In W. G. Parrott (Ed.), *The positive side of negative emotions* (pp. 101–125). Guilford Press.

Batson, C. D. (1991). *The Altruistic Question*. Hillsdale,N.J.: Erlbaum.

Baumeister, R. F., & Bushman, B. J. (2011). *Social psychology and human nature* (2nd ed.). Cengage.

Baumeister, R. F., & Leary, M. (1995). The need to belong: Desire for interpersonal attachments as a fundamental human motivation. *Psychological Bulletin, 117*(3), 497–529.

Baumeister, R. F., DeWall, N. C., Ciarocco, N. J., & Twenge, J. M. (2005). Social exclusion impairs self-regulation. *Journal of Personality and Social Psychology, 88*(4), 589–604.

Bowlby, J. (1969). *Attachment. Attachment and loss: Vol. 1. Loss*. Basic Books.

Buck, R. (1988). The perception of facial expression: Individual regulation and social coordination. In T. R. Alley (Ed.), *Social and applied aspects of perceiving faces* (pp. 141–165). Erlbaum.

Coan, J., & Gottman, M. J. (2007). The Specific Affect Coding System (SPAFF). In *Handbook of emotion elicitation and assessment*, Chapter: 16. Oxford University Press.

Davis, M. H. (1983). Measuring individual differences in empathy: Evidence for a multidimensional approach. *Journal of Personality and Social Psychology, 44*(1), 113–126. https://doi.org/10.1037/0022-3514.44.1.113.

Driscoll, R. L., Barclay, P., & Fenske, M. J. (2017). To be spurned no more: The affective and behavioral consequences of social and nonsocial rejection. *Psychonomic Bulletin & Review, 24*, 566–573.

Ekman, P. (1973). Cross-cultural studies of facial expression. In P. Ekman (Ed.), *Darwin and facial expression*. Academic Press.

Ekman, P. (1982). Methods for measuring facial action. In K. R. Scherer & P. Ekman (Eds.), *Handbook of methods in nonverbal behavior research* (pp. 45–90). Cambridge: Cambridge University Press.

Ekman, P. (1984). Expression and the nature of emotion. In K. S. Scherer & P. Ekman (Eds.), *Approaches to emotion* (pp. 319–343). Erlbaum.

Ekman, P., & Heider, K. G. (1988). The Universality of a Contempt Expression: A Replication. *Motivation and Emotion, 12*(3), 303–308.

Ekman, P. (1992a). An argument for basic emotions. *Cognition and Emotion, 6*, 169–200.

Ekman, P. (1992b). *Telling lies: Clues to deceit in the marketplace, politics and marriage*. Norton & Company.

Ekman, P. (1993). Facial expression and emotion. *American Psychologist, 48*, 384–392.

Ekman, P. (1994). Strong evidence for universals in facial expression: A reply to Russell's mistaken critique. *Psychological Bulletin, 115*(2), 268–287.

Ekman, P. (1997). Should We Call it Expression or Communication?. *Innovations in Social Science Research, 10*, 333–344.

Ekman, P. (1999). Basic emotions. In T. Dalgleish & M. J. Power (Eds.), *Handbook of cognition and emotion* (pp. 45–60). Wiley.

Ekman, P. (2003). *Emotion revealed: Recognizing faces and feelings to improve communication and emotional life*. Times Books/Henry Holt and Co.

Ekman, P. (2010). Darwin's compassionate view of human nature. *JAMA, 303*(6), 557–558.

Ekman, P. (2016). What scientists who study emotion agree about. *Perspectives on Psychological Science, 11*(1), 31–34.

Ekman, P., & Cordaro, D. (2011). What is meant by calling emotions basic. *Emotion Review, 3*(4), 364–370.

Ekman, P., & Friesen, W. V. (1969). The repertoire of nonverbal behavior: Categories, origins, usage, and coding. *Semiotica, 1*, 49–98.

Ekman, P., & Friesen, W. V. (1971). Constants across cultures in the face and emotion. *Journal of Personality and Social Psychology, 17*, 124–129.

Ekman, P., & Friesen, W. V. (1982). Felt, false, and miserable smiles. *Journal of Nonverbal Behavior, 6*(4), 238–252.

Ekman, P., & Friesen, W. V. (1986). A new pan-cultural facial expression of emotion. *Motivation and Emotion, 10*(2), 159–168.
Ekman, P., & Friesen, W. V. (2003). *Unmasking the face: A guide to recognizing emotions from facial clues*. Malor Books.
Ekman, P., & Keltner, D. (2014). Darwin's claim of universals in facial expressions. Not challenged. *Huffington Post.*
Ekman, P., & Scherer, K. R. (1984). Questions about emotion: An introduction. In K. Scherer & P. Ekman (Eds.), *Approaches to emotion* (pp. 1–8). Lawrence Erlbaum.
Ekman, P., Hager, J. C., & Friesen, W. V. (1981). The Symmetry of emotional and deliberate facial actions. *Psychophysiology, 18*(2), 101–106.
Ekman, P., Friesen, W. V., & Ellsworth, P. (1982). What are the relative contributions of facial behavior and contextual information to the judgment of emotion? In P. Ekman (Ed.), *Emotion in the human face* (pp. 111–127). CambridgeUniversity Press.
Frijda, N. H. (1986). *The emotions*. Cambridge University Press.
Frijda, N. H., & Mesquita, B. (1994). The social roles and functions of emotions. In S. Kitayama & H. R. Markus (Eds.), *Emotion and culture: Empirical studies of mutual influence* (pp. 51–87). American Psychological Association.
Frijda, N. H., Kuipers, P., & ter Schure, E. (1989). Relations among emotion, appraisal, and emotional action readiness. *Journal of Personality and Social Psychology, 57*, 212–228.
Gottman, J. M. (1979). *Marital interaction: Experimental investigations*. Academic Press.
Gottman, J. M. (1994). *What predicts divorce? The relationship between marital processes and marital outcomes*. Lawrence Erlbaum Associates, Inc.
Gottman, M. J., & DeClaire, J. (2001). *The relationship cure: A five-step guide for building better connections with family, friends, and lovers* (1st ed.). Crown.
Gottman, J. M., & Levenson, R. W. (1999). How stable is marital interaction over time? *Family Process, 38*, 159–165.
Gottman, J. M., & Levenson, R. W. (2004). Rebound from marital conflict and divorce prediction. *Family Process, 38*(3), 287–292.
Gottman, J. M., & Porterfield, A. L. (1981). Communicative competence in the nonverbal behavior of married couples. *Journal of Marriage and Family, 43*(4), 817–824.
Gottman, J. M., & Silver, N. (1994). *Why marriages succeed or fail: What you can learn from the breakthrough research to make your marriage last*. Simon & Schuster.

Harper, R. G., Wiens, A. N., & Matarazzo, J. D. (1978). *Nonverbal communication: The state of the art*. Wiley.

Hatfield, E., Pillemer, J. T., O'Brien, M. U., & Le, Y. L. (2008). The endurance of love: Passionate and companionate love in newlywed and long-term marriages. *Interpersona, 2*(1), 35–64.

Havelka, N. (2012). *Socijalna percepcija* [Social perception]. Zavod za udžbenike.

Hazan, C., & Shaver, P. (1987). Romantic love conceptualized as an attachment process. *Journal of Personality and Social Psychology, 52*(3), 511–524.

Huseman, R. C., Hatfield, J. D., & Miles, E. W. (1987). A New Perspective on Equity Theory: The Equity Sensitivity Construct. *The Academy of Management Review, 12*(2) , 222–234.

Izard, C. E. (1990). Facial expressions and the regulation of emotions. *Journal of Personality and Social Psychology, 58*, 487–498.

Kernsmith, P. (2005). Exerting power or striking back: A gendered comparison of motivations for domestic violence perpetration. *Violence and Victims, 20*(2), 173–185.

Knapp, M. L., Hall, J. A., & Horgan, T. G. (2014). *Nonverbal communication in human interaction*. Wadsworth Cengage Learning.

Kostić, A. (1995). Opažanje primarnih emocija na osnovu spontanih facijalnih ekspresija [Perceiving primary emotions from spontaneous facial expression]. *Psihologija, XXVIII*(1–2), 101–108.

Kostić, A. (2014). *Govor lica – značenja facijalnih ponašanja* [Facetalk – Meanings of facial behaviors] (3rd ed.). Filozofski fakultet Univerziteta u Nišu & SCERO Print.

Kostić, A., & Chadee, D. (2015). Emotional recognition, fear, and nonverbal behavior. In A. Kostić & D. Chadee (Eds.), *The social psychology of nonverbal communication* (pp. 134–150). Palgrave Macmillan, ISBN 978-1-137-34585-1, Printed by CPI Group (UK) Ltd.

Kostić, A., Chadee, D., & Nedeljković, J. (2020). Reading faces: Ability to recognise true and false emotion. In R. J. Sternberg & A. Kostić (Eds.), *Social intelligence and nonverbal communication* (pp. 255–281). Palgrave Macmillan, Springer Nature Switzerland AG.

Levenson, R. W. (1999). The intrapersonal functions of emotion. *Cognition and Emotion, 13*, 481–504.

Levinger, G. (1980). Toward the analysis of close relationships. *Journal of Experimental Social Psychology, 16*(6), 510–544.

Ma, F., Wylie, B. E., Luo, X., He, Z., Jiang, R., Zhang, Y., Xu, F., & Evans, A. D. (2019). Apologies repair trust via perceived trustworthiness and negative emotions. *Frontiers in Psychology, 3*(10), 758. https://doi.org/10.3389/fpsyg.2019.00758.

Macdonald, G., & Leary, M. R. (2005). Why does social exclusion hurt? The relationship between social and physical pain. *Psychological Bulletin, 131*(2), 202–223.

Margolin, G., John, R. S., & Gleberman, L. (1988). Affective responses to conflictual discussions in violent and nonviolent couples. *Journal of Consulting and Clinical Psychology, 56*(1), 24–33.

Maslow, A. (1955). Deficiency motivation and growth motivation. In M. R. Jones (Ed.), *Nebraska symposium on motivation* (pp. 1–30). University of Nebraska Press.

Matsumoto, D. (1992). American-Japanese cultural differences in the recognition of universal facial expressions. *Journal of Cross-Cultural Psychology, 23*(1), 72–84.

McAdams, D. P., & Bryant, F. B. (1987). Intimacy motivation and subjective mental health in a nationwide sample. *Journal of Personality, 55*(3), 395–413.

McCullough, M. (2000). Forgiveness as human strength: Theory, measurement and links to well-being. *Journal of Social and Clinical Psychology, 19*(3), 43–55.

McGonagle, K. A., Kessler, R. C., & Schilling, E. A. (1992). The frequency and determinants of marital disagreements in a community sample. *Journal of Social and Personal Relationships, 9*, 507–524.

Mellor, D., Stokes, M., Firth, L., Hayashi, Y., & Cummins, R. (2008). Need for belonging, relationship satisfaction, loneliness, and life satisfaction. *Personality and Individual Differences, 45*(3), 213–218.

Miller, W. I. (1997). *The anatomy of disgust*. Harvard University Press. See page 97.

Plutchik, R. (2003). *Emotions and life: Perspectives from psychology, biology, and evolution*. American Psychological Association.

Polk, D. (2022). Evaluating fairness: Critical assessment of equity theory. In D. Chadee (Ed.), *Theories in social psychology*. N.Y. Wiley-Blackwell.

Rot, N. (2010). *Znakovi i značenja, verbalna i neverbalna komunikacija*. Zavod za udžbenike.

Rozin, P., Haidt, J., & McCauley, C. R. (1999). Disgust: The body and soul emotion. In T. Dalgleish & M. J. Power (Eds.), *Handbook of cognition and emotion* (pp. 429–445). Wiley. See page 435.

Russell, J. A. (1991). Culture and the categorization of emotions. *Psychological Bulletin, 110*(3), 426–450. https://doi.org/10.1037/0033-2909.110.3.426.

Schniter, E., & Sheremeta, R. M. (2014). Predictable and predictive emotions: Explaining cheap signals and trust re-extension. *Frontiers in Behavioral Neuroscience, 8*, 401. https://doi.org/10.3389/fnbeh.2014.00401

Sell, A., Tooby, J., & Cosmides, L. (2009). Formidability and the logic of human anger. *Proceedings of the National Academy of Sciences, 106*, 15073–15078.
Shaver, P. R., & Mikulincer, M. (2002). Attachment-related psychodynamics. *Attachment and Human Development, 4*(2), 133–161.
Sherman, D. K., & Cohen, G. L. (2006). The psychology of self-defense: Self-affirmation theory. In *Advances in experimental social psychology* (Vol. 38).
Sommer, J., Iyican, S., & Babcock, J. (2019). The relation between contempt, anger, and intimate partner violence: A dyadic approach. *Journal of Interpersonal Violence, 34*(15), 3059–3079.
Steele, C. M. (1988). The psychology of self-affirmation: Sustaining the integrity of the self. In L. Berkowitz (Ed.), *Advances in experimental social psychology* (Social psychological studies of the self: Perspectives and programs) (Vol. 21, pp. 261–302). Academic Press.
Sternberg, R. J. (1986). A triangular theory of love. *Psychological Review, 93*, 119–135.
Tomkins, S. S. (1962). Affect, imagery, consciousness. In *The positive affects* (Vol. 1). Springer.
Tooby, J., & Cosmides, L. (2008). The evolutionary psychology of the emotions and their relationship to internal regulatory variables. In M. Lewis, J. M. Haviland-Jones, & L. F. Barrett (Eds.), *Handbook of emotions* (3rd ed., pp. 114–137). Guilford Press.
Townsend, K. C., & McWhirter, B. T. (2005). Connectedness: A review of the literature with implications for counseling, assessment, and research. *Journal of Counseling & Development, 83*(2), 191–201.
Tucker, P., & Aron, A. (1993). Passionate love and marital satisfaction at key transition points in the family life cycle. *Journal of Social and Clinical Psychology, 12*(2), 135–147.
Twenge, J. M., Campbell, K., & Foster, C. A. (2003). Parenthood and marital satisfaction: A meta-analytic review. *Journal of Marriage and Family, 65*(3), 574–583.
Twenge, J. M., Baumeister, R. F., DeWall, C. N., Ciarocco, N. J., & Bartels, J. M. (2007). Social exclusion decreases prosocial behavior. *Journal of Personality and Social Psychology, 92*(1), 56–66.
Yoo, S. H., Clark, M. S., Lemay, E. P., Jr., Salovey, P., & Monin, J. K. (2011). Responding to partners' expression of anger: The role of communal motivation. *Personality and Social Psychology Bulletin, 37*, 229–241. https://doi.org/10.1177/0146167210394205

10

Love in the Time of COVID-19: What We Can Learn About Non-verbal Behaviour from Living with a Pandemic

Valerie Manusov

The onset of social restrictions that arose alongside the COVID-19 pandemic in 2020–21 immediately implicated the various roles that non-verbal communication plays in our lives. Physical distancing, mask-wearing (which covers many of the facial cues we use and makes some vocal cues more difficult), social isolation, and less in-person contact were all part of the worldwide shifts that accompanied regulations for limiting the spread of the virus. Indeed, these behaviours became our "new normal," at least for a time. In so doing, however, the disruptions to what had been the norm illuminated several important features of non-verbal behaviour, particularly as they work within relationships. This chapter reviews some of these shifts, and the reactions to them, to show how the changes reveal important characteristics of non-verbal behaviour, some primary meanings non-verbal cues communicate, and the consequentiality of non-verbal cues in our relational lives. Perhaps more than anything, however, non-verbal cue use in the time of COVID-19

V. Manusov (✉)
Department of Communication, University of Washington, Seattle, WA, USA
e-mail: manusov@uw.edu

R. J. Sternberg, A. Kostić (eds.), *Nonverbal Communication in Close Relationships*,
https://doi.org/10.1007/978-3-030-94492-6_10

has helped us see how adaptable non-verbal cues are and how central a place they hold in our communication of connection—and love—for others.

I make two assumptions in providing this chapter and making these assertions. The first assumption is that communication of love and/or connection is a part of many of the interactions that we have. Whereas we may consider those messages to be tied to close relationships primarily, they are also a part of many other forms of engagement. In particular, certain professions (e.g., healthcare and hospitality), in some cultures at least, rely upon creating at least temporary personal connection to others, and these moments are accomplished in part through non-verbal means. Moreover, even brief interactions with strangers provide an opportunity to connect with others. As such, this chapter includes nonverbal cues within a range of interactional contexts where the feelings people have for one another and their mutual humanity are essential.

The second assumption is that non-verbal cues may be understood as occurring as part of a larger communication code (Philipsen, 1992). That is, communicators relate to one another within a system of behaviours, rules, meanings, and values that guide the ways in which they interact and help provide the range of meanings that are accepted for behaviours used within that system (Burgoon et al., 2021). I argue that making sense of the many shifts in non-verbal communication during the time of COVID-19 is aided by seeing our behaviour as embedded in these larger communication codes, in large part because the codes define what is normative and what counts as a deviation from such normalcy. The rules and meanings for the use of non-verbal cues also often reflect the underlying values of the culture in which the code is based (e.g., the importance of certain relationships). The pandemic provided an opportunity to see those norms and values in relief, in large part because there were many communicative behaviours that we could not use as we once did, and new accepted patterns and interpretations emerged.

This chapter uses existing research on non-verbal communication, the limited published academic work focusing on non-verbal communication during COVID-19 that is housed primarily in the health disciplines, and several popular articles written about non-verbal communication in the pandemic to showcase several features of non-verbal communicating that have been revealed during this time, particularly as they tie to our relationships with others. These features are: (1) the importance of non-verbal cues in sending relational messages; (2) the ability for the same messages to be communicated in different ways (or what is known as *equifinality*); (3) the rule-governed nature of communicating non-verbally; (4) the particular relevance of haptics (i.e., touch as communicative); (5) the changeable nature of the communication code in which non-verbal cues are centred; and (6) the imperative of empathy and compassion.

The Importance of Non-verbal Cues in Sending Relational Messages

A primary way in which people enact their relationships with others relies on non-verbal cues. Burgoon (Burgoon et al., 1984; Burgoon & Hale, 1984) referred to the means by which we reflect our existing or desired relationships as *relational messages*. Within these messages are those that show our degree of intimacy with others, and a central way of expressing that intimacy or closeness is to be physically near others. That is, we tend to have less physical distance from those with whom we feel close, and this behaviour can both reflect our closeness to another and make us feel relationally closer to them, at least when the behaviour is welcomed (Docan-Morgan et al., 2013; Guerrero, 2016). The larger communication code helps to delineate what these proxemics (or space) norms are and includes other "appropriate" behaviours to use to send relational messages of intimacy and closeness.

COVID-19 changed the opportunity to enact our feelings for many of our loved ones in these normative ways, however, by urging us to stay six feet away from them and avoid contact, thereby taking away two primary means (close proximity and touch) by which we show others that we have a close relationship. Friends who saw one another could no longer greet each other with a hug, and people could not be with many of their family members or sit close to them when they were able to interact. This new pattern of engagement was instantly termed "social distancing," though some suggested we instead use the term "physical distancing" to keep us from equating our behaviour (being physically apart) with our feelings for others (being emotionally apart). Popular articles were written to emphasize this point, including one (geisinger.org) that referenced psychologist Shahida Fareed who stated that, "[w]hile 'social distancing' is still widely used, it may be sending the wrong message and contributing to social isolation. Rather than sounding like you have to socially separate from your family and friends, 'physical distancing' simplifies the concept with the emphasis on keeping 6 feet away from others" (pars. 4 & 5).

This concern with social isolation was real, as many people, particularly those who lived alone, suffered from a sense of loneliness and other deleterious mental states. Indeed, practitioners saw social isolation as its own epidemic even prior to the beginning of the COVID-19 lockdowns (e.g., Chu et al., 2020; Vrach & Tomar, 2020). As such, some groups, such as the World Health Organization, tried to help people realize that being physically separate from others was not the same as losing their close relationship with them (Aziz, 2020). Fareed, for one, urged people to use technology as a means of interaction to help assuage the sense of disconnection that can come when we can't be near others.

Specifically, video "visits" were promoted for patients (e.g., Lindsay et al., 2021) and for older people more generally (Hajek & König, 2021), particularly with intergenerational family members (Chatterjee & Yatnatti, 2020), in large part because video allows for non-verbal cues to be a part of the interactions. Burgoyne and Cohn (2020) argued further that teletherapy (i.e., therapy via technology), if done well, can allow for enhanced relational development through closer attention to clients' non-verbal behaviour, by humanizing the therapist with environmental cues, as well as providing access for more people as compared to in-person therapy. Overall, however, people tend to prefer the opportunity to interact face-to-face, largely because of the immediacy of the non-verbal cues that can be accessed there (van der lee & Schellekens, 2020).

When vaccines became available and COVID-19 restrictions began to ease, many people wanted to get back to hugging their loved ones with whom they had not been living. The urge to hug suggests just how strongly we equate physical closeness with our feelings of intimacy and with expressing and enacting that closeness (i.e., sending relational messages). Part of this process is physiological: Hugging and other forms of wanted touch can make us feel better physically because of their effect on our physiology (Floyd et al., 2007; Floyd, Mikkelson, et al., 2007). But part is also social: We want to express our connection with others because doing so is valued within many codes, and touch is a primary way that we do so.

When people cannot touch one another as they would like to, they may experience tactile deprivation (Floyd, 2014b). According to a *Toronto Star* article (2020),

> [h]ug withdrawal is so real for Edie Weinstein, 61, who's been offering hugs to strangers since 2014 with her "Hug Mobsters," that one night she dreamed people discovered a way to hug each other back to back. "I don't know when it's going to be safe to go out and hug deprived people out there, but whenever it happens watch out, because there's a lot of people who need hugs," said Weinstein, a therapist and licensed social worker. (par. 2)

Other behaviours important to relational messages of intimacy or closeness were also modified during the pandemic. Specifically, masks covered our mouths, a site where we often show others what and how we feel, including our happiness to see another person. But along with staying farther away, we could not use the physical movements of our mouths to "make up" for the lack of physical closeness as a relational message to another person. Such relational messages are a part of our interactions with others with whom we have close relationships; but they are also relevant to other contexts, such as healthcare, where "covering a significant proportion of the face, masks could pose a substantial psychological barrier to the development of therapeutic relationships" (Marler & Ditton, 2020, p. 206). Because of the nature of non-verbal communication, however, people found other ways to show and/or develop their connection to and feelings for others.

Equifinality

Specifically, without close distances, touch, and mouth-based facial expressions, people adapted other means to show their sustained feelings of closeness and/or build psychological connection. They used "air hugs," for example, and they relied more on vocal cues (especially when people use their "mask voice," Yuko, 2020, reflecting the tendency to exaggerate our non-verbal cues when we are concerned that they be decoded accurately; Manusov, 1991) to, among other things, reflect their emotions overall and their feelings for others. A patient receiving a cancer diagnosis also reported "reading the eyes" of the practitioner as a suitable substitute for decoding other reflections of concern (cited in André, 2020).

Indeed, people's eye behaviour has become an even more central site of positive emotional expression during the pandemic. One specific behavioural substitute for showing happiness elsewhere on the face is something called "smizing" or "smiling with your eyes," a term created for models and popularized by Tyra Banks that references using one's eyes to show positivity when the rest of the face needs to remain immobile. A 2020 article by Jen Murphy in the *Wall Street Journal* advocated for adapting greeting/connection to customers by teaching workers to change their behaviour. Murphy noted that,

> [i]n normal times, humans can get by with what psychologist David Matsumoto calls a social smile, or when the lip corners turn up but the rest of the face stays put. "This is the smile that greases the wheels of society and keeps us connected," said Dr. Matsumoto, director of Humintell LLC, a San Francisco-based research and training company that specializes in the science of reading…nonverbal behavior. … The smize [on the other hand] is actually the upper half of the Duchenne Smile, the facial expression that relays genuine happiness. …It isn't as simple as smiling extra hard. Studies show the muscles around the eye respond only to true emotion. (par. 9)

The ability to substitute some cues for others to send the same messages reveals that non-verbal cues have *equifinality* (i.e., the same messages can be communicated in different ways; Burgoon et al., 2021; Patterson, 2003), and equifinality is a common part of our communication. We know, for example, that there are many different ways to show affection and love (Floyd, 2019; Marston et al., 1987; Sternberg & Sternberg, 2006), and people can substitute one form when another means is not wanted, available, or recognized. But in addition to the diverse means of communicating a single message that are found within a communication code, new ways made be added, and old ways deleted, over time and during unique moments, such as the COVID-19 pandemic.

Achim (2020) noted, for example, the sharp decrease in the sale of cosmetics in the initial stages of masking, at least in China. Over time, however, products for the eyes increased substantially over the point that they had been pre-pandemic. Part of this rise in sales likely had to do with enhancing the one part of the face that could still be seen when people are masked and suggested a desire to still appear attractive or reflect personal identity. It can be argued, however, that emphasizing one's eyes with makeup when they are the only part of the face that can be seen also allows for greater attention to the role that eyes can play in signalling our connection to others. When the movement of our mouths can no longer communicate our feelings towards another, we substituted what we did with our eyes, again showing the equifinality inherent in the non-verbal communication system.

Other products also helped us to engage in behaviours that show our humanity. Masks with clear plastic over the mouth not only allowed hearing-impaired people to still read the lips of others (Fallowfield, 2021; Marler & Ditton, 2020), they also provided the opportunity for some healthcare providers to use their mouths to show kindness and compassion. When this was not available, some hospital employers had their staff wear badges that showed them smiling so that patients could see them in the way that they would normally appear, something that Marler and Ditton also advocated. As well, Fallowfield (2021) reported that "a community children's nurse specialist … was deeply concerned that her chronically sick young patients could not see her face, so she printed off a variety of Memoji stickers to place on her visor" (p. 13) to which she would point to reveal her emotions. She encouraged her patients to do the same to show her how they were feeling. These actions reflect alternative—and creative—means for communicating a message non-verbally when more "traditional" forms are unavailable.

Being able to substitute some cues for others is important in how we relate to others. When certain behaviours, particularly facial expressions, are blocked or absent, the tendency to make decoding errors goes up. In an article by Robert Hotz (2021) in the *Wall Street Journal*, the writer noted that in,

> laboratory experiments published last fall in *Frontiers in Psychology*, psychologist Claus-Christian Carbon at Germany's University of Bamberg found that people readily confused expressions when the lower part of the face was blocked by a surgical mask. Happiness and sadness seemed like neutral poker faces. Signs of anger were especially hard to perceive. Wide-eyed fear, though, came through clearly. "It hampers everyday life," Dr. Carbon said. "It's not just that you can't read the face anymore. You misread it and misinterpret emotions. You also feel yourself a little bit misunderstood." (par. 6)

That people can exchange one set of behaviours for others that are no longer available or are reduced in some way can help counter these concerns.

The Rule-Governed Nature of Communicating Non-verbally

When the circumstances changed because of COVID-19, so did the rules for our use and interpretation of many non-verbal cues. This was most notable for physical distancing. When creating larger proxemic distances first became strongly advised, people often felt the need to explain to others (or at least to themselves) that standing far from someone did not mean what it used to. That is, keeping a larger proxemic distance is typically a way to show someone that we are not as close to them (i.e., it can be a form of relational message) or that, although we are usually close, something has changed (e.g., we are mad at them). Many people in the early days of the pandemic felt uncomfortable with that distance and the lack of closeness it implied. They often apologized or commented on the change to their typical behaviour to help show it didn't mean what it once did (i.e., feeling less closeness). When we believe we need to account for our behaviour, it is usually because we have violated a rule or are afraid that someone else will think that, and our account is a form a repair to explain the rule violation (Goffman, 1963; Robinson, 2016).

That there was this initial need to explain our changed behaviour reveals the extent to which non-verbal action is rule-governed. That is, we learn ways to act in particular ways as we grow up. Such rules exist for proxemics: our use of space to communicate and how far to stand when communicating. As Hall (1966, 2003) noted, most cultures have various proxemic distance zones (intimate, personal, social-consultative, and public) that people use based on the nature of the conversation type and their relationship, and we learn the rules for when and how to use these zones as we grow up. The size of these zones varies by culture, based on the values, norms, and structures of that culture and its communication code, and these factors let us know what certain actions mean and which zones are appropriate in which contexts (Burgoon et al., 2021).

Indeed, though some forms of engagement are based in biological conditions (Buck, 2017; Patterson, 2003), much of our daily behaviour with others can be seen to exist within a set of "rules for engagement" (Goffman, 1971). When those rules are broken, we typically have to repair our "spoiled identity" (Goffman, 1963) as well as ensure that our relational partners do not decode a meaning that we did not intend. At the start of the pandemic, for instance, people would cross the street when they saw someone else was coming. Before this action became normative, people often apologized to others and explained that their behaviour was for safety reasons and not to avoid them for social reasons.

Moreover, the pandemic has helped to show that the communicative code in which non-verbal cues, their use, and their meanings are based can be *expanded*. Some of this includes what can be considered normative at any point. Whereas masks in many parts of the world were used rarely, that changed instantly, and what once looked out of place was now commonplace. Additionally, wearing masks, standing farther away, not shaking hands, and not hugging all took on new meanings (for some, at least). That is, in addition to being protective measures for avoiding the virus, many people also saw in them the meaning of care for others. Memes arose that noted these behaviours were meant to help protect others or at least to send the messages that others' well-being was important. For some, the meaning of the behaviours was an infringement of rights, but, for others, the message that was ascribed was more about the importance of others to them.

These multiple ascribed meanings, particularly for mask-wearing but also for physical distancing, reveals that, within any communication code, there can be co-existing meanings for non-verbal cues. That the same non-verbal cue can be seen to represent a range of meanings is at the heart of saying the non-verbal cues are *polysemous* (Manusov, 2016). That is, wearing a mask can be ascribed as a form of self-protection, a willingness to adhere to norms, and/or a concern for others; not wearing one can be seen as an assertion of independence, dismissal of a particular view of the virus, or selfishness, among other meanings. For pandemic daters, not wearing a mask was also a sign of trust: In her article on the "new rules of dating" in *The New York Times*, Courtney Rubin quoted one person who said that "'[t]here's something psychologically when you like someone, you automatically trust that they don't have the virus,' said Kaley Isabella, 31, who works in public relations in Los Angeles and has been dating a man she met during the pandemic. 'It's crazy. It doesn't make someone safe just because you like them'" (par. 6).

Such meanings can coexist and be applied to behaviour at different times. For example, sometimes a smile can signal happiness; other times, it can signal frustration. The context typically allows for people to determine (with some error, of course) what the behaviour signifies in that moment. But in the case of the meanings for mask-wearing, the diverse interpretations that can be ascribed or "given to" (Goffman, 1967) the behaviour can also be pitted against one another, with different people stating that their interpretation is the "right" one. That is, the meaning for non-verbal behaviours can be contested even within the same communication code (Burgoon et al., 2021). This contestation can occur at a public/social level, such as when Colin Kaepernick kneeled before a football game (a rule violation, as people had come to expect players to stand with their hands over their hearts during the US national anthem; such violations are particularly likely to have meanings ascribed to them). But it can also occur at the relational level, such as when not touching someone can be seen as a lack of love or as an expression of it, with people having very different positions about which definition is accurate.

The Particular Relevance of Haptics

Whereas many non-verbal cues are a part of the rule changes brought about by COVID-19 restrictions, perhaps none has been more discussed than touch. In particular, we have become even more aware of the detriments of not giving or getting the touch that we would normally or that we desire (though, notably, there has also been a rise in *unwanted* touch and other forms of intimate partner violence during the pandemic; Peters, 2020). Grandparents missed the chance to touch their grandchildren; friends missed the touch of friends. People did not even get the touch that professionals, such as hair stylists, provide.

Though applicable to a range of contexts, this concern has been voiced specifically in healthcare contexts. According to an editorial in the *Journal of Nursing* (Durkin et al., 2021), for example,

> [w]hen touch is limited or eliminated, people can develop what is termed touch starvation ... or touch hunger. ... Touch hunger impacts all facets of our health and has been associated with increases in stress, anxiety and depression. ... Nurses and community health workers reported the difficulties caring for patients with Ebola during the outbreak in Liberia when 'no-touch guidelines' were in place. The no-touch guidelines not only made it difficult to diagnose a patient without touching them..., but the isolation faced by Ebola patients was found to compromise the nurses' ability to convey connection and provide comfort to patients in times of distress. ... Such measures, while intended to keep people safe, have concerning short- and longer-term implications on the health of already isolated individuals such as people who are ill, older people ... and people with disabilities. (p. e4)

Not only did we become more aware of the importance of touch; the pandemic revealed something larger about certain cultures: that many of us already had less touch than was optimal for our physical and psychological health. In a *New York Times* article, for example, journalist Maham Hasan (2020) cited,

> Tiffany Field, the director of the Touch Research Institute at the University of Miami, who has a Ph.D. in developmental psychology. Field calls touch "the mother of all senses," and in her 2001 book, "Touch," she argues that American society was already dangerously touch deprived, long before the coronavirus exacerbated it. (pars. 2 & 3)

The same deprivation is also common in British culture, Hasan noted, where cultural rules limit how much people are allowed to touch one another. These touch constraints have been (understandably) exacerbated by concerns coming out of the #MeToo movement and by efforts to help protect children from inappropriate contact.

Hasan interviewed a range of people who all commented on how much they missed touch, and hugging in particular, during this time of greater social isolation. Interestingly, the interviews revealed many of the ways that people "normally" get touch, even in the absence of romantic relationships. Petting dogs while out for walks, high-fives with friends and strangers, and professional massages were all curtailed during the pandemic. As a substitute, people commented on their use of stuffed animals, weighted blankets, and even high-fiving trees as ways to at least partially provide some of the tactile connection that they were wanting. As Durkin et al. (2021) noted,

> increased isolation and absence of touch perhaps partly explains the recent rush on animal sanctuaries who report increases in adoptions … with pet ownership being found to have emotional benefits for people living alone with pets providing love, affection and companionship … and a safe means to give and receive touch. (p. e4)

The Changeable Nature of the Communication Code

These patterns of behaviour that have, for the moment at least, become part of the "new normal" in our larger system of rules that guide how we use non-verbal behaviour. That changes occur to a larger communication code is known, though typically they occur gradually, and the larger system often pushes back on such changes (Burgoon et al., 2021). When younger generations create new means for communicating, for instance, they are often met with resistance, as we come to value "traditional" communicative forms and resist accepting new ones. In the case of the pandemic, however, the changes were abrupt, and they were encouraged by many social institutions (and, of course, discouraged by others).

But they may also be temporary changes, as what the new normal will look like is still unclear. At best, as the *Toronto Star* article noted about non-verbal greeting behavior, "it's going to get awkward before it gets better" (par. 2). At the time that this chapter was written, people were wondering whether cultural patterns, such as shaking hands with strangers and hugging our less close friends, will revert to what they were, given the increased awareness about hygiene and the spread of disease along with concerns about inappropriate forms of touch more broadly. If certain kinds of touch—and particular proxemic distances—are no longer perceived as appropriate, some cues will occur only within certain kinds of love relationships and indeed may become a more clear marker of those relationships than the older rules suggested. For people without romantic relationships, then, touch deprivation may be an even greater concern.

Whereas we do not yet know what things will look like after the pandemic, according to Christian Cotroneo (2020) from Treehugger, they will be different:

> At the onset of the pandemic, Dr. Anthony Fauci, America's top infectious disease expert, only "half seriously" suggested we may never shake hands again. Fauci is probably right. The handshake has outlived its social usefulness. It's now more laden with potential threats than a hidden dagger could ever be. But we've already discovered other ways to physically connect with a stranger—a well-timed elbow bump, for example. (pars. 12 & 13)

Likewise, Taner Morgan (2020), a writer for *Reveille*, suggests that greeting behaviour is likely to remain changed after the pandemic. Even "smeyesing" (i.e., a quick smile while saying "hey") may no longer be the norm for acknowledging someone we know but to whom we are not close. Rather, to avoid certain forms of touch when we greet others, the writer (somewhat facetiously) says that we need to try some alternatives and offers that the foot tap, elbow bumps, bowing, "finger guns," and "jazz hands" (i.e., shaking one's palms in another's direction) could be new behaviours in the US cultural repertoire. Whether serious or not, these suggestions cement the idea that cultural codes change over time and circumstance, and what is considered commonplace and normative may disappear or be replaced with other actions at another point.

The amount that a cue is used, such as touch, or the form that a message takes may both change, but the importance of the communication function that they serve typically will not. By "function," what is meant is that non-verbal cues have utilitarian value for communicators. As Patterson (2003) stated, among other functions, non-verbal cues express "intimacy … [and] can also regulate interaction, provide social control (exercising influence and managing impressions), and facilitate service and task goals" (p. 202). So, for example, even if the form of showing closeness or greeting another alters because of COVID-19 or other factors, the need or desire for the function itself remains, as does the importance of non-verbal cues in fulfilling that function.

The Imperative of Empathy and Compassion

At the same time, however, we may see an *increase* in the importance of certain functions or messages, and this increase may reflect shifting values within our communication code. Of particular note is showing empathy and compassion to others, in part because of our greater awareness of the conditions that people face (Cotroneo, 2020). One study of young people, for example, found that the pandemic created a range of deleterious effects that the participants wanted to be recognized, including "headaches and muscle pain … symptoms of depression, anxiety, and loneliness, longer screen time, and more substance use … increase of family conflicts and disagreements, [and] loss of important life moments, contacts, and social skills" (Branquinho et al., 2020, p. 2740). Women and girls may be particularly likely to suffer negative effects based on the conditions of the pandemic (Mukhtar, 2020), as are immigrants (Falicov et al., 2020) and the elderly (Kotwal et al., 2020), particularly those in care facilities (Yeh et al., 2020). As such, people may require others' non-verbally communicated concern to help them cope. Indeed, receiving messages of verbal and non-verbal support from others has been found to help people cope with the social challenges and stress of the pandemic (Moore & Lucas, 2020).

The recognition of others' challenges during the pandemic may specifically awaken the larger need to both feel and show empathy and compassion going forward. Empathy is the understanding of another's experience, communicating one's understanding, and supporting the relationship we have with them by moving forward in a "helpful style" (Stevens et al., 2020). Compassion is defined as "recognizing suffering, understanding the universality of human suffering, feeling for the person suffering, tolerating uncomfortable feelings, and [the] motivation to act/acting to alleviate suffering" (Strauss et al., 2016, p. 15). It too can be made apparent in our non-verbal cues. Moreover, both empathy and compassion can be considered forms of love for other human beings and what they are experiencing, regardless of the nature of the relationship that we have with them.

The bulk of published academic studies focusing on non-verbal communication in the COVID-19 period has come from healthcare disciplines, given their disciplinary focus on showing care and the related concern when some of the typical means for doing so are not as available (i.e., when masks and other personal protective equipment [PPE] block expressions, limit vocalics, and cease skin-to-skin touch). These studies often centre on the importance of communicating empathy and compassion to patients, particularly when patients' families are not allowed to be with them and, for those hospitalized with COVID-19, because of their experience with the disease.

Stevens et al. (2020) noted specifically that the empathy training that their team provided to hospitals included *reflective listening*, which "involves mindfully paying attention to what the communicator feels and believes, so that an empathic reflective response can be formulated, allowing the speaker to feel understood" (p. 649). This suggestion was a reaction to a sense of compassion for the patients' suffering brought about through such empathy practices. Training is particularly relevant in situations where masking is required as, for instance, "when doctors [wear] a facemask during consultations, this has a significant negative impact on the patient's perceived empathy and diminish[es] the positive effects of relational continuity" (Wong et al., 2013, p. 200). Indeed, COVID-19 patients commented on the importance of receiving compassionate care from their providers for their well-being (Costello, 2020). Likewise, recent research has found that careful attention to decoding brief eye behaviour can help people determine when *another* is suffering (Schmidtmann et al., 2020).

Whereas reflective and other forms of listening involve cognitive processes (e.g., paying attention, including to another's non-verbal cues, interpreting, and remembering what another has said), listening is also a behavioural process, particularly when it occurs in interpersonal interactions and as part of showing care to another (Manusov, 2020). That is, a person typically needs to be seen *as* listening by an interaction partner for listening to function relationally. As with many other cues during the pandemic, however, some of the non-verbal cues that show a person is listening to us (e.g., facial expressions, certain vocal cues) may be limited. Nonetheless, most studies on interpersonal listening have identified cues that are still available.

For instance, Floyd (2014a) discussed Carl Rogers's (1966) view of *empathic listening*, summarizing its elements as including "a concern for accurately reflecting the experiences of the speaker; unconditional positive regard, defined as confirmation or validation of the speaker, rather than necessarily agreement with the speaker's message; 'presentness' to the speaker, including active involvement in the conversation, receptivity, and openness; equality with the speaker, or the avoidance of manipulation or coercion; and [a] nonevaluative stance wherein the listener offers support and withholds value judgments" (p. 5). Tobase et al. (2021) argued that listening empathically is important in the medical context with patients *and* staff, given the level of suffering that both groups experience.

Relatedly, sustained eye contact, though difficult with face shields, is an important reflection of *active-empathic listening* (Bodie et al., 2012). Trees (2000) found that vocal warmth, kinesic (body) and proxemics attentiveness, and movement synchrony are all listener behaviours that are perceived as supportive, and such social support can alleviate some of the stress during periods of self-isolation (Szkody et al., 2020). Likewise, Halone and Pecchioni (2001) reported that good *relational listening* involves noticing the speaker's non-verbal cues (i.e., being a good decoder) and not interrupting. Manusov and Keeley (2015) found that just being physically present and spending time with a dying loved one were important ways to express connection and care, and the same physical and chronemic (time) cues may play a role in helping show empathy and compassion during (and after) the pandemic.

What is central to include here, however, is that certain messages that can be reflected non-verbally may be considered more relevant and indeed "imperative" in times of crisis. COVID-19 thus created a context in which particular behaviours and meanings were encouraged in a way that they were not in more normative times. As such, another feature revealed about non-verbal communication in the present moment is the importance of the larger social conditions for *emphasizing the role of particular messages*. Compassion and empathy, for many at least, were two such messages (Cotroneo, 2020). In support of this, Blauwet et al. (2020) said "[t]hese issues came to the forefront for many of us during the COVID-19 crisis as we all found ourselves in unprecedented and novel personal and professional terrains" (p. 1038).

Conclusion

Marra et al. (2020) asserted that "nonverbal aspects of our communication [were] thwarted, ineffective, and impaired during the COVID-19 pandemic" (p. 297). In this chapter, I have argued instead that the adaptable nature of non-verbal communication allows for their still-important role in relating to others even in the face of greater physical distancing, limited touch, mask-wearing, and social isolation. In particular, when the cues people use more typically to communicate caring and connection to others become less available, the equifinality of the non-verbal communication system allows people to employ other behaviours that help "make up" for what is missing. Moreover, the reason to show empathy and compassion is amplified.

Whereas this replacement of some cues with others may not always "just occur" but, rather, may need to be brought to people's attention, including for friends, family members, and medical professionals, the specific ways in which non-verbal cues function and the types of messages that they help to portray allow for a certain flexibility in times of profound change. Given the role that certain messages of support and care can play in the development of resilience in the face of difficulty (Sannes et al., 2020), that a range of non-verbal cues can be adapted to signify these meanings allows for their benefits to be more likely. Moreover, though not discussed directly, we can sometimes substitute words for the messages we may otherwise send non-verbally, emphasizing that language and non-verbal communication are all part of the same system of engagement.

One behaviour appears to be less replaceable, however. Touch that is desired and that serves to communicate affection, relational closeness, and care remains a core missing element in a time of greater social distancing. Not everyone is on their own physically, and not all people are without touch from others, but most people gave and received less social touch during the pandemic. That so many people look forward to a time when they can, for example, hug in the ways that they once did (assuming that norms do not change for doing so after this period, though they may well do so) shows just how relevant this particular cue is to our sense of life satisfaction and well-being. People can find other ways to show affection. But touch provides a particularly powerful behaviour to do so and provides other benefits tied to our sense of connection with others and to our health. That the rules for touch and other non-verbal cues have changed, nonetheless, highlights that non-verbal behaviour is, by its nature, rule-governed within a larger communicative code. It also shows that these rules and norms evolve—or in some cases change abruptly—given the larger set of conditions within a cultural system.

This chapter used existing research on non-verbal communication, the small body of already-published academic work on non-verbal cues during COVID-19, as well as popular sources to make a set of larger claims about the nature of non-verbal communication as it is revealed in this historical era. When we cannot use the cues on which we have relied to show how we feel about others, the adaptive capacity of our communication code and the embeddedness of non-verbal cues within it reveal further their relevance in our personal and social lives. Being less able to show and receive love when certain behaviours are lost to us, at least temporarily, reveals just how much we rely on non-verbal communication of love, belonging, and our shared sense of humanity. It also reflects how quickly we learn new ways to communicate these central messages so that we can continue to support and stay connected to others. Love in the time of COVID-19 remains strong.

References

Achim, A.-L. (2020, June 22). Have Chinese beauty consumers changed after the COVD-19 outbreak? *Jing Daily*. https://jingdaily.com/have-chinese-beauty-consumers-changed-after-the-covid-19-outbreak/

André, N. (2020). Covid-19: Breaking bad news with social distancing in pediatric oncology. *Pediatric Blood & Cancer, 67*(9), E28524-N/a. https://doi.org/10.1002/pbc.28524

Aziz, S. (2020, March 30). Why 'physical distancing' is better than 'social distancing'. Coronavirus pandemic News. *Al Jazeera*. https://www.aljazeera.com/news/2020/3/30/why-physical-distancing-is-better-than-social-distancing#:~:text=%E2%80%9CPhysical%20distance%20is%20measured%20in%20metric%20metres%20or,was%20important%20to%20differentiate%20between%20the%20two%20terms

Blauwet, C. A., Brashler, R., Kirschner, K. L., & Mukherjee, D. (2020). Vulnerability, interdependence, and trust in the COVID-19 pandemic. *Physical Medicine and Rehabilitation, 12*(10), 1038–1044. https://doi.org/10.1002/pmrj.12480

Bodie, G. D., St. Cyr, K., Pence, M., Rold, M., & Honeycutt, J. (2012). Listening competence in initial interactions I: Distinguishing between what listening is and what listeners do. *International Journal of Listening, 26*, 1–28. https://doi.org/10.1080/10904018.2012.639645

Branquinho, C., Kelly, C., Arevalo, L. C., Santos, A., & Gaspar de Matos, M. (2020). "Hey, we also have something to say": A qualitative study of Portuguese adolescents' and young people's experiences under COVID-19. *Journal of Community Psychology, 48*(8), 2740–2752. https://doi.org/10.1002/jcop.22453

Buck, R. (2017). Spontaneous communication and infant imitation. *The Behavioral and Brain Sciences, 40*, E385. https://doi.org/10.1017/S0140525X16001850

Burgoon, J. K., Buller, D. B., Hale, J. L., & deTurck, M. A. (1984). Relational messages associated with nonverbal behaviors. *Human Communication Research, 10*, 351–378. https://doi.org/10.1111/j.1468-2958.1984.tb00023.x

Burgoon, J. K., & Hale, J. L. (1984). The fundamental topoi of relational communication. *Communication Monographs, 51*, 193–214. https://doi.org/10.1080/03637758409390195

Burgoon, J. K., Manusov, V., & Guerrero, L. K. (2021). *Nonverbal communication* (2nd ed.). Routledge.

Burgoyne, N., & Cohn, A. S. (2020). Lessons from the transition to relational teletherapy during COVID-19. *Family Process, 59*(3), 974–988. https://doi.org/10.1111/famp.12589

Chatterjee, P., & Yatnatti, S. K. (2020). Intergenerational digital engagement: A way to prevent social isolation during the COVID-19 crisis. *Journal of the American Geriatrics Society, 68*(7), 1394–1395. https://doi.org/10.1111/jgs.16563

Chu, C. H., Donato-Woodger, S., & Dainton, C. J. (2020). Competing crises: COVID-19 countermeasures and social isolation among older adults in long-term care. *Journal of Advanced Nursing, 76*(10), 2456–2459. https://doi.org/10.1111/jan.14467

Costello, M. (2020). Expressions of compassion during COVID-19 pandemic. *International Journal of Caring Sciences, 13*(3), 1788–1793.

Cotroneo, C. (2020, April 4). What happens when humans are not allowed to touch each other? *Treehugger.* https://www.treehugger.com/physical-contact-touch-humans-covid-4859440

Docan-Morgan, T., Manusov, V., & Harvey, J. (2013). When a small thing means so much: Nonverbal cues as turning points in relationships. *Interpersona: An International Journal on Personal Relationships, 7*, 110–124. https://doi.org/10.5964/ijpr.v7i1.119

Durkin, J., Jackson, D., & Usher, K. (2021). Touch in times of COVID-19: Touch hunger hurts. *Journal of Clinical Nursing, 30*(1–2), E4–E5. https://doi.org/10.1111/jocn.15488

Falicov, C., Niño, A., & D'Urso, S. (2020). Expanding possibilities: Flexibility and solidarity with under-resourced immigrant families during the COVID-19 pandemic. *Family Process, 59*(3), 865–882. https://doi.org/10.1111/famp.12578

Fallowfield, D. L. (2021). Enhancing your 'webside' manner: Communication during COVID-19. *Trends in Urology & Men's Health, 12*(1), 12–15. https://doi.org/10.1002/tre.784

Floyd, K. (2014a). Empathic listening as an expression of interpersonal affection. *International Journal of Listening, 28*(1), 1–12. https://doi.org/10.1080/10904018.2014.861293

Floyd, K. (2014b). Relational and health correlates of affection deprivation. *Western Journal of Communication, 78*(4), 383–403. https://doi.org/10.1080/10570314.2014.927071

Floyd, K. (2019). *Affectionate communication in close relationships*. Cambridge University Press.

Floyd, K., Hesse, C., & Haynes, M. T. (2007). Human affection exchange: XV. Metabolic and cardiovascular correlates of trait expressed affection. *Communication Quarterly, 53*, 285–303. https://doi.org/10.1080/01463370600998715

Floyd, K., Mikkelson, A. C., Tafoya, M. A., Farinelli, L., La Valley, A. G., Judd, J., Haynes, M. T., Davis, K. L., & Wilson, J. (2007). Human affection exchange: XIII. Affectionate communication accelerates neuroendocrine stress recovery. *Health Communication, 22*, 123–132. https://doi.org/10.1080/10410230701454015

Goffman, E. (1963). *Stigma: Notes on the management of spoiled identity*. Prentice-Hall.

Goffman, E. (1967). *Interaction ritual: Essays on face-to-face behavior*. Anchor/Doubleday.

Goffman, E. (1971). *Relations in public: Microstudies of public order*. Basic Books.

Guerrero, L. K. (2016). Proxemics. In C. R. Berger & M. E. Roloff (Eds.), *International encyclopedia of interpersonal communication*. Wiley-Blackwell and the International Communication Association. https://doi.org/10.1002/9781118540190.wbeic128

Hajek, A., & König, H.-H. (2021). Social isolation and loneliness of older adults in times of the COVID-19 pandemic: Can use of online social media sites and video chats assist in mitigating social isolation and loneliness? *Gerontology, 67*(1), 121–124. https://doi.org/10.1159/000512793

Hall, E. T. (1966). *The hidden dimension* (2nd ed.). Anchor/Doubleday.

Hall, E. T. (2003). Proxemics. In S. M. Low & D. Lawrence-Zuniga (Eds.), *The anthropology of space and place: Locating culture* (pp. 51–73). Blackwell.

Halone, K. K., & Pecchioni, L. L. (2001). Relational listening: A grounded theoretical model. *Communication Reports, 14*, 59–71. https://doi.org/10.1080/08934210109367737

Hasan, M. (2020, October 7). What all that touch deprivation is doing to us. *The New York Times*. https://www.nytimes.com/2020/10/06/style/touch-deprivation-coronavirus.html

Hotz, R. L. (2021, January 18). Covid face masks are disrupting a key tool of human communications, new research shows. *The Wall Street Journal*. https://www.wsj.com/articles/covid-face-masks-are-disrupting-a-key-tool-of-human-communications-new-research-shows-11610989200

Kotwal, A. A., Holt-Lunstad, J., Newmark, R. L., Cenzer, I., Smith, A. K., Covinsky, K. E., Escueta, D. P., Lee, J. M., & Perissinotto, C. M. (2020). Social isolation and loneliness among San Francisco Bay area older adults during the COVID-19 shelter-in-place orders. *Journal of the American Geriatrics Society*. https://doi.org/10.1111/jgs.16865

Lindsay, J. A., Hogan, J. B., Ecker, A. H., Day, S. C., Chen, P., & Helm, A. (2021). The importance of video visits in the time of COVID-19. *The Journal of Rural Health, 37*(1), 242–245. https://doi.org/10.1111/jrh.12480

Manusov, V. (1991). Perceiving nonverbal messages: Effects of immediacy and encoded intent on receiver judgments. *Western Journal of Speech Communication, 55*, 235–253. https://doi.org/10.1080/10570319109374383

Manusov, V. (2016). Nonverbal communication. In K. B. Jensen & R. T. Craig (Eds.), *International encyclopedia of communication theory and philosophy*. Wiley-Blackwell and the International Communication Association. https://doi.org/10.1002/9781118766804.wbiect096

Manusov, V. (2020). Interpersonal communication. In D. L. Worthington & G. D. Bodie (Eds.), *The handbook of listening* (pp. 103–119). Wiley-Blackwell. https://doi.org/10.1002/9781119554189.ch7

Manusov, V., & Keeley, M. P. (2015). When family talk is difficult: Making sense of nonverbal communication at the end-of-life. *Journal of Family Communication, 15*, 387–409. https://doi.org/10.1080/15267431.2015.1076424

Marler, H., & Ditton, A. (2020). "I'm smiling back at you": Exploring the impact of mask wearing on communication in healthcare. *International Journal of Language & Communication Disorders*. https://doi.org/10.1111/1460-6984.12578

Marra, A., Buonanno, P., Vargas, M., Iacovazzo, C., Ely, E. W., & Servillo, G. (2020). How COVID-19 pandemic changed our communication with families: Losing nonverbal cues. *Critical Care, 24*(1), 297–298. https://doi.org/10.1186/s13054-020-03035-w

Marston, P. J., Hecht, M. L., & Robers, T. (1987). True love ways: The subjective experience and communication of romantic love. *Journal of Social and Personal Relationships, 4*(4), 387–407. https://doi.org/10.1177/0265407587044001

Moore, K. A., & Lucas, J. J. (2020). COVID-19 distress and worries: The role of attitudes social support, and positive coping during social isolation. *Psychology and Psychotherapy*. https://doi.org/10.1111/papt.12308

Morgan, T. (2020, August 30). Coping with COVID: Nonverbal mask-friendly greeting alternatives. *Reveille*. https://www.lsureveille.com/entertainment/socially-distant-salutations-nonverbal-mask-friendly-greeting-alternatives/article_2d8e2572-e954-11ea-b54e-6fa06fdd0eb9.html

Mukhtar, S. (2020). Feminism and gendered impact of COVID-19: Perspective of a counselling psychologist. *Gender, Work and Organization, 27*(5), 827–832. https://doi.org/10.1111/gwao.12482

Murphy, J. (2020, August 26). How to smize (smile with your eyes) when you're wearing a mask; Service employees in the Covid era practice a modeling move coined by Tyra Banks to show customers a happy face. *The Wall Street Journal*. https://www.wsj.com/articles/smize-mask-coronavirus-pandemic-covid-tyra-banks-reopen-restaurants-11598463705

Patterson, M. L. (2003). Commentary: Evolution and nonverbal behavior: Functions and mediating processes. *Journal of Nonverbal Behavior, 27*(3), 201–207. https://doi.org/10.1023/A:1025346132037

Peters, G. (2020). *What a "stay home, stay safe" order means when home isn't safe: The impact of the COVID-19 pandemic on survivors of intimate partner violence and IPV service providers*. Master's thesis, University of Washington. https://digital.lib.washington.edu/researchworks/handle/1773/46187

Philipsen, G. (1992). *Speaking culturally: Explorations in social communication*. State University of New York Press.

Robinson, J. (2016). *Accountability in social interaction*. Oxford University Press.

Rogers, C. R. (1966). Client-centered therapy. In S. Arieti (Ed.), *American handbook of psychiatry* (pp. 183–200). Basic Books.

Sannes, T. S., Yeh, I. M., & Gray, T. F. (2020). Caring for loved ones with cancer during the COVID-19 pandemic: A double hit risk for social isolation and need for action. *Psycho-Oncology, 29*(9), 1418–1420. https://doi.org/10.1002/pon.5466

Schmidtmann, G., Logan, A. J., Carbon, C.-C., Loong, J. T., & Gold, I. (2020). In the blink of an eye: Reading mental states from briefly presented eye

regions. *I-Perception, 11*(5), 2041669520961116. https://doi.org/10.1177/2041669520961116
Sternberg, R., & Sternberg, K. (2006). *The new psychology of love*. Yale University Press.
Stevens, S. K., Brustad, R., Gilbert, L., Houge, B., Milbrandt, T., Munson, K., Packard, J., Werneburg, B., & Siddiqui, M. A. (2020). The use of empathic communication during the COVID-19 outbreak. *Journal of Patient Experience, 7*(5), 648–652. https://doi.org/10.1177/2374373520962602
Strauss, C., Lever Taylor, B., Gu, J., Kuyken, W., Baer, R., Jones, F., & Cavanagh, K. (2016). What is compassion and how can we measure it? A review of definitions and measures. *Clinical Psychology Review, 47*, 15–27. https://doi.org/10.1016/j.cpr.2016.05.004
Szkody, E., Stearns, M., Stanhope, L., & McKinney, C. (2020). Stress-buffering role of social support during COVID-19. *Family Process*. https://doi.org/10.1111/famp.12618
Tobase, L., Cardoso, S. H., Rodrigues, R. T. F., & Peres, H. H. C. (2021). Empathic listening: Welcoming strategy for nursing professionals in coping with the coronavirus pandemic. *Revista Brasileira de Enfermagem, 74*(1), E20200721. https://doi.org/10.1590/0034-7167-2020-0721
Toronto Star. (2020, August 10). Way forward for non-verbal greetings is a touch unclear; Hugs, handshakes may have to evolve in post-pandemic world. B10. https://search.proquest.com/newspapers/way-forward-non-verbal-greetings-is-touch-unclear/docview/2431733741/se-2?accountid=14784
Trees, A. R. (2000). Nonverbal communication and the support process: Interactional sensitivity in interactions between mothers and young adult children. *Communication Monographs, 67*, 239–261. https://doi.org/10.1080/03637750009376509
van der lee, M., & Schellekens, M. P. J. (2020). Bridging the distance: Continuing psycho-oncological care via video-consults during the COVID-19 pandemic. *Psycho-Oncology, 29*(9), 1421–1423. https://doi.org/10.1002/pon.5468
Vrach, I. T., & Tomar, R. (2020). Mental health impacts of social isolation in older people during COVID pandemic. *Progress in Neurology and Psychiatry, 24*(4), 25–29. https://wchh.onlinelibrary.wiley.com/doi/pdf/10.1002/pnp.684
Wong, C. K. M., Yip, B. H. K., Mercer, S., Griffiths, S., Kung, K., Wong, M. C.-S., Chor, J., & Wong, S. Y.-S. (2013). Effect of facemasks on empathy and relational continuity: A randomised controlled trial in primary care. *BMC Family Practice, 14*(1), 200–207. https://doi.org/10.1186/1471-2296-14-200

Yeh, T.-C., Huang, H.-C., Yeh, T.-Y., Huang, W.-T., Huang, H.-C., Chang, Y.-M., & Chen, W. (2020). Family members' concerns about relatives in long-term care facilities: Acceptance of visiting restriction policy amid the COVID-19 pandemic. *Geriatrics & Gerontology International, 20*(10), 938–942. https://doi.org/10.1111/ggi.14022

Yuko, E. (2020, February 29). Use nonverbal cues to make your point when wearing a face mask. *Lifehacker*. https://lifehacker.com/use-nonverbal-cues-to-make-your-point-when-wearing-a-fa-1845215241

11

Non-verbal Communication: From Good Endings to Better Beginnings

Stephen Nowicki and Ann van Buskirk

Human beings can't help but form relationships. We have them with cars, clothes, watches, teddy bears, dogs, cats, goldfish; you name it, and we can have a relationship with it. And thank goodness we have both the motivation for and the skill to connect with objects both inanimate and animate, because the truth is that without relationships we could not survive infancy and childhood or have a life worth living as adults.

What we seek most, being close to others in meaningful romantic relationships and friendships, turns out to be a struggle for many of us. Some of us are better at relating to our stuffed toys or attractive cars than we are to people. Frustratingly, we often create barriers to connecting even when we believe it would be in our best interest.

Non-verbal language and communication play a crucial role in the resolution of this struggle. Relationships follow a dynamic process

S. Nowicki (✉)
Department of Psychology, Emory University, EU, Atlanta, GA, USA
e-mail: snowick@emory.edu

A. van Buskirk
Emory University, EU, Atlanta, GA, USA

R. J. Sternberg, A. Kostić (eds.), *Nonverbal Communication in Close Relationships*,
https://doi.org/10.1007/978-3-030-94492-6_11

repeatedly cycling through choosing, beginning, deepening, and ending phases. The four-phase relationship model we present here provides a framework for understanding how relationships develop and how to deal with the inevitable endings in a way that allows them to provide the information we need to make our future connections better. In such a system, closeness is not as a static goal to attain but rather a constantly moving target that often needs re-negotiating between participants.

Sternberg's Approach to Relationships

Perhaps no one person has done more to further our understanding of "relationship" than Robert Sternberg. Sternberg's triangular theory of love (Sternberg, 1986, 2019) has provided clinicians and researchers a viable framework for understanding the distinct yet interrelated components of love—intimacy, passion, and commitment. Intimacy involves feelings of connection, closeness, and trust and is heavily dependent on effective communication between partners. Passion integrates excitement, desire, and sexual attraction and may involve obsessive thoughts or a strong need to be with a partner—the feeling of "Can't get you off of my mind." Commitment, the only element Sternberg describes as conscious and intentional, involves a decision to stop looking for other partners followed by an ongoing choice to continue the relationship.

Combinations of intimacy, passion, and commitment result in eight different types of love. *Consummate love*, strong and enduring, encompasses all three elements and is described by Sternberg as rare. Intimacy and commitment lead to *companionate love*. The presence of intimacy alone yields *friendship*. *Infatuation* describes a relationship built solely on passion. A relationship built solely on *commitment* and devoid of intimacy or passion is referred to as "empty love." Intimacy and passion combine to create *romantic love*. Passion and commitment without intimacy yield "fatuous" or "*foolish love*." Sternberg describes relationships in which none of the components are present as "*non-love*."

Since the introduction of his relationship theory, Sternberg has been interested not only in the components of love, but also how love develops over time. While the triangular theory of love describes the structural nature of love, for Sternberg, the development of love is best understood within the context of story. According to Sternberg, each of us has a set of stories about love which guide how we think about relationships and our expectations for how those relationships play out. Often these stories are out of our awareness yet include predefined roles that we unknowingly assign to ourselves and partners. For example, roles in the fairy-tale story may involve a prince and a princess (Sternberg, 1995).

Sternberg's duplex theory of love combines the triangular and love as a story models and suggests that exposure to multiple love stories leads us to form our own. Many themes of our stories come from childhood experiences with our parents, siblings, and friends, and these stories are expanded as we incorporate experiences from our adolescence. The stories influence our perception of the actions of others as well as impacting our own actions as we try to shape our relationships to fit our own stories (for an extensive description and examples see: https://lovemultiverse.com/understanding-love/different-kinds-of-love-stories/).

The stories we seek to live out are related to many factors—what we observed growing up, how our needs for affection were met (or not), our relationships with friends and family members when we were children, and the impact of our culture and community, including the media we read and watched. Sternberg (2019) lists 26 stories, based on analysis of love stories in literature, previous psychological research, and anecdotal case material. Although the stories Sternberg and his colleagues analysed were from people in the United States, they were similar to stories found across cultures (Sorokowski et al., 2021). Sternberg suggests we form our own stories of love and then seek to fulfil them by finding partners who fit our narrative expectations. He and his colleagues have noted that we are most likely to succeed in close relationships with people whose stories of love are most like our own. We gravitate to those who embrace similar stories about love yet seek out partners who fulfil the complementary role within our love story.

For most of us, the love we long for is what Sternberg describes as Consummate love. Consummate love involves the intimate communication of a soulmate, the sexual passion of a lover, and loyal, unshakeable commitment, as in "til death do us part." Sternberg has noted that consummate love is sought by many and achieved by few. In his conceptualization of relationship process, when passion decreases, the consummate love relationships ends and the choice may be made to "settle for" a less vibrant connection he terms companionate love, or perhaps to leave the relationship in search of a different partner.

The possibility of ending a consummate love relationship in the service of recreating consummate love again intrigues us. We are most interested in this re-creation when it involves doing the work to allow the rebirth of an even stronger and better relationship *with the same person*. By focusing on the flow of dyadic love, we have noted that many relationships "end" multiple times, with the lessons learned and incorporated from those endings offering an opportunity to draw closer.

Interpersonal Perspective on Relationships: The Four-Phase Model

When asked what relationships they seek and value, most adults are likely to mention two—a loving spouse/romantic partner and a "best" or close friend. Recent data from YouGov finds that over half (56%) of US adults believe in the idea of soulmates (Ballard, 2020). Much energy is put in the pursuit of finding that soulmate, romantic or platonic.

In the 1970 film "Love Story," based on the book of the same title by Erich Segal, Oliver says to his terminally ill wife Jenny, that "love means never having to say you're sorry." The novelist Lauren Kate writes, "true love never says goodbye." While this makes for great movie making and best-selling books, the reality of what it takes to achieve long-lasting close relationships is different. Such examples give the mistaken impression we should put most of our relationship effort into finding and connecting with the "right" person because if we find him or her, then we'll be "set" for life. Attaining relationship closeness, according to this view, is much like an Alpine skier who after finishing the difficult turns and twists around the poles of the giant slalom race, goes into the "tuck position" and effortlessly glides to the finish line.

There is a difference in theoretical expectation between "close relationships" and "closeness in relationships." *Close relationships* suggest a stationary state we strive to attain and once we have, we try to "hang on to." In contrast, *closeness in a relationship* reflects the idea that closeness ebbs and flows with the changing needs of those in a relationship. This idea positions love as more like a never-ending slalom that continues to have poles and standards to navigate, rather than a few challenges to conquer before "gliding" to the finish line of a close relationship.

Attaining and maintaining relationship closeness is a task that takes persistent and continuous effort. We drop in and out of closeness with others and must constantly communicate with one another to create balance. When we lose closeness, we must re-negotiate our wants and needs to re-acquire intimate connections. While the successful development of relationship closeness requires skill in choosing with whom to begin, we suggest that it depends to an even greater extent on how well we handle relationship endings and what we learn about ourselves and how we relate during that process.

Based on this conception of ever-changing levels of closeness, we assume any long-lasting relationship in which we experience closeness will have not one, but a series of endings, as well as new choices, beginnings, and deepenings, leading up to endings. While this conception suggests attaining and maintaining successful relationships may require more work than we realize, the good news is that every time we end, we are presented with a new opportunity to learn from the relationship in its entirety. When we allow ourselves to acknowledge relationship endings, we grant ourselves the birds-eye view to see not only where we are, but where we've been and how we got from there to here. We can view the relationship from its early beginnings and remind ourselves of how our interactions lead or didn't lead to closeness. At the same time, we experience what is happening now as the relationship draws to a close. In this conception of how relationships operate, ending is an extraordinarily crucial time for us, filled with emotions and stressors but also rich with possibilities of learning what we are good at and what we may lack in relating well to others.

Nowicki–Duke Four-Phase Relationship Model (4-PRM)

Emphasizing relationship endings aligns with the theoretical structure of the four-phase model or 4-PRM (Duke & Nowicki, 1982; Nowicki & Duke, 2012, 2016) that places relationship ending at the very core of functioning successfully with others. The 4-PRM provides a framework for describing and understanding how closeness develops across the "lifetime" of a relationship. In this model, dyadic intimacy develops as part of a dynamic interpersonal process in which relationships move through the four phases of choosing, beginning, deepening, and ending. Meaningful relationships that continue over the years will experience a number of these sequences.

The origins of the 4-PRM are found in the writings of interpersonal theorists beginning with Harry Stack Sullivan (1953, 1954), who was among the first to suggest there was more to human behaviour than the interplay of intrapsychic id, ego, and superego processes described by Freud (1936). Emphasizing the importance of non-verbal communication, Sullivan theorized that who we are and how we behave is a consequence of our interpersonal rather than intrapsychic interactions.

To understand how we navigate towards closeness as adults, it is helpful to examine how our ability to connect with others develops. Interpersonal communication begins in infancy, where we use the reflected non-verbal appraisals of significant others to begin forming a rudimentary self-concept. When parents or caregivers largely relate to us through encouraging non-verbal messages in the form of reassuring touch, smile, warm tone of voice, we are likely to view ourselves more positively. If, on the other hand, the non-verbal messages we perceive are primarily disapproving in tone, in the form of rigid touch, frowns, angry voices, then we are likely to develop a largely negative self-concept. Our self-concept develops in the presence of the anxiety we experience early in life. Sullivan believed that a major way we reduced anxiety was to interact with others whose interpersonal messages agreed with how we perceived ourselves to be, our self-concept. As we grow older, anxiety reduction continues to motivate our social behaviour, and our self-concept will become more stable and more resistant to change as verbal reflections are added to non-verbal input from others.

For Sullivan, interacting with someone whose behaviour confirms how we see ourselves reduces anxiety. As in Sternberg's love as a story model, we are motivated to interact more often and more deeply with those who behave in ways to confirm how we view ourselves and to avoid the anxiety generated by interacting with those who don't. According to Sullivan, we learn to develop personality styles to "pull" reactions from others that confirm our self-concepts. While open to modification at any age, the personality style we develop at a young age lays the groundwork for how we navigate relationships throughout our life.

The Circumplex Theory

Timothy Leary (1957) undertook the first large-scale scientific study of Sullivan's concepts, analysing thousands of therapeutic interactions of individuals involved in a Kaiser Permanente mental health project. Leary's research produced scientific support for Sullivan's clinical and theoretical ideas, His analysis suggested two major orthogonal dimensions described the messages being sent between people when they interacted. The first, *Status*, is anchored at one end by Dominance and at the other by Submission. The second independent dimension, *Affiliation*, has Friendliness at one end and Hostility at the other. Carson (1969) accepted the idea of two independent dimensions of Status and Affiliation and went a step further to suggest it would be helpful to cross the two dimensions to form a Circumplex Model of Interpersonal Behaviour. The resulting quadrants reflected four major interpersonal styles: *friendly/dominant (FD)*, *friendly/submissive (FS)*, *hostile/dominant (HD)*, and *hostile/submissive (HS)*. Consistent with Sullivan's theory, Carson reported evidence that interpersonal styles are learned modified through interactions with important people in our lives and are calculated to pull behaviours from others to confirm self-concept, reducing anxiety and motivating us to stay connected in relationships that do so.

In the circumplex model, the Status dimension is governed by the *rule of opposites*; that is, dominance pulls for submission and submission pulls for dominance. In contrast, the Affiliation dimension follows the *rule of similarity*; that is, friendliness begets friendliness and hostility begets hostility. Applying the "rules" governing the interpersonal effect of each style helps us understand what behaviours are being solicited from others to confirm our self-concept. Individuals behaving in a friendly dominant manner are asking others to be similar in affiliation but opposite in status, in other words, act in a friendly submissive manner.

When two people conform to what each is "asking" for interpersonally they are in a ***complementary*** interaction. In complementary relationships self-concept is validated and anxiety is reduced, leading to a comfort conducive to producing intimate relationships. There is significant support for the positive impact of complementary relationships. (see Altenstein et al., 2013; Dermody et al., 2017; Estroff & Nowicki, 1992; Hopwood et al., 2020; Kiesler, 1999; Pincus, 2005; Pincus & Ansell, 2013; Rosen et al., 2012).

When we interact with someone who does not agree with us on the friendly dimension, but instead presents as hostile, yet is similar to us on the status dimension by being dominant, we find ourselves in an ***anti-complementary*** relationship. Because the other person's interpersonal style does not offer any confirmation of our own self-concept on either dimension, it produces uncomfortable feelings of anxiety and our relationship will likely terminate as soon as possible.

Between these two extremes lie those relationships described as ***mixed complementarity***, in which there is agreement on one of the two dimensions, but disagreement on the other. For example, if we offer our friendly dominant style in an interpersonal situation and find the other person to be either friendly dominant or hostile submissive, we are left with a decision as to be influenced more by the positive confirmation on one dimension or the negative confirmation on the other. Often individuals who are in mixed complementary relationships will stay for a while, to see if they can negotiate change to produce complementarity and increase opportunities for closeness to develop.

The dynamics of complementarity operate the same way on the hostile side of the circumplex as they do on the friendly side. That is, the complement for hostile dominance is hostile submissive. Hostile complementary dyads also tend to continue even though they are governed by hostile affect. Hostile complements are most often found to be effective in promoting positive outcomes in competitive but not cooperative situations whereas friendly complements seem to be more effective in cooperative situations (Estroff & Nowicki, 1992; Nowicki et al., 1997). Non-verbal communication plays a significant role in the expression of interpersonal styles described in the circumplex model, especially when verbal and non-verbal messages differ and are incongruent.

Non-verbal Communication

Non-verbal social behaviour includes all human responses which are not overly manifested in words (either spoken or written) and that convey meaning (Hall & Bernieri, 2001), including facial expressions, paralanguage or prosody, body movement or kinetics, gestures/postures, touch, and proxemics (Harper et al., 1978). Non-verbal social skills "include … abilities to encode and decode cues of emotion … to control and regulate emotional displays, as well as the management of conversations (Riggio, 1992, p. 3).

Kiesler (1999) emphasized that "The vehicle for human transactions is communication; the verbal and nonverbal. … Since nonverbal messages predominate in emotional and relational communication, understanding of interpersonal behavior requires simultaneous study of both the linguistic and nonverbal levels of human communication" (p, 5). Simply put, we should place more emphasis on the experience of what we see, what we feel, and the way in which words are communicated than on the words themselves.

Interest in the role non-verbal communication plays in our relationships is nothing new. Over 50 years ago, Ekman and Friesen (1969) described non-verbal communication as a "relationship language" with unique characteristics that could be depended on to "signal" changes in ongoing interpersonal interactions. They speculated that non-verbal behaviour represented the most valid type of communication, providing more reliable indicators of "unconscious' attitudes and beliefs than words. The view that non-verbal is predominant over verbal communication in relationships continues to be widely held (Kiesler, 1999).

As with verbal skills, we have both receptive and expressive non-verbal processing abilities, although research results suggest they are not highly correlated (Elfenbein et al., 2010). That is, we can be skilled in identifying nonverbal cues in others, but relatively unskilled in sending our own nonverbal messages and vice versa. Receptive skills are learned earlier than expressive ones (Feldman et al., 1991; Johnson & Myklebust, 1967). Non-verbal communication, like its verbal counterpart, develops with age and is assumed to mature into a learned organized sign system relied on in social interaction. That is, like words are signs and signals of meaning, so too are non-verbal cues. Some suggest there are pre-wired connections enabling the use of nonverbal behaviours that have evolved phylogenetically because of their usefulness for survival of the individual and the species (Wellman et al., 1995). Others, however, emphasize that though the rudimentary aspects of non-verbal communication may be biologically present and required, it is primarily cultural and social experiences that shape this skill for our everyday use (Manstead, 1995). We believe it is likely that both biological factors and social experiences contribute to the maturing of our non-verbal language system.

Challenges in Non-verbal Communication

Non-verbal communication differs from its verbal counterpart, in ways that make it particularly relevant for social competence and successful relating (Duke et al., 1996; Ekman & Friesen, 1975; Nowicki & Duke, 2012). First, non-verbal communication is more continuous than its verbal partner. Individuals may stop talking when in proximity to others, but they cannot stop sending emotional cues in their facial expressions, gestures, postures, personal space, and the like. Watzlawick, Beavin, and Jackson (1967) summarized this difference in the now classic statement, "You cannot not communicate nonverbally."

Next, non-verbal communication is more likely to take place out of awareness. Because we are less aware of what is transpiring non-verbally, we are also more likely to be unaware of our non-verbal communication's strengths and weaknesses (Friedman, 1979). Ammirati (2013) found, for example, that participants lacked awareness of their own skill in recognizing emotions in the facial expressions of others, overestimating their accuracy by an average of 25%, even after being given empirical feedback of their strengths and weaknesses.

In addition to differing from verbal communication in terms of continuousness and awareness, non-verbal messages are more likely have a negative emotional rather than a negative intellectual impact (Nowicki & Duke, 2012). Standing too close to someone who is a stranger will likely make that person uncomfortable and perhaps even anxious, while using the wrong grammar when speaking to them may leave an impression of intellectual shortcomings, but not generate much of an emotional response. Humans tend to be more tolerant of intellectual rather than emotional shortcomings.

Nowicki and Duke (1994) have suggested that these three characteristics of non-verbal communication create a difficult social scenario for those who lack non-verbal skills and highlighted the negative interpersonal impact of what they term "dyssemia" (dys = inability, semia = signs: an inability to process non-verbal signs). Because of the very nature of non-verbal communication, those with non-verbal skill deficits are likely to produce negative emotional impacts on others continuously, leading to ongoing challenges in forming and maintaining relationships. Those who are dyssemic typically are unaware of the negative impact of their erroneous non-verbal messages and their significant role in creating social difficulties. Dyssemias have the potential to be detrimental during any phase of the relationship process be it at choosing, beginning, deepening, or ending.

Non-verbal communication is learned differently than how we usually become skilled with words. Non-verbal skills are learned indirectly and informally while verbal skills are directly taught, first at home, and then later at school. We learn non-verbal cues primarily by observing others and modelling their behaviour (Johnson & Myklebust, 1967). Unfortunately, in this kind of learning, we receive little direct feedback about the "correctness" of our learning which stands in stark contrast to the clear, direct, and continuous feedback we receive about our verbal skills both at home and at all levels of education.

Because non-verbal behaviour is the primary vehicle for communicating emotions in social interactions it should be no surprise that it is associated with social competence (Hall & Bernieri, 2001; Saarni 1999). The association between social competence and non-verbal skills exists, at least in part, because non-verbal cues provide information regarding emotions necessary for effective and successful social regulation and interaction. Non-verbal communication has greater power to convey emotional messages, overriding verbal messages when they differ. When our non-verbal and verbal emotional communications are in opposition, described by Kiesler as "incongruence," we are more likely to believe the non-verbal message (Bugenthal et al., 1970). For example, when interacting with others who "say" they are not anxious their words will not carry nearly as much weight as how they present themselves non-verbally. Shaking hands, wavering voice, and tapping feet override the words, "I'm not worried about this at all."

The 4-PRM Process

Choice

We don't have much freedom in deciding with whom to interact when it comes to family or preordained social situations such as office parties. However, when we do have the flexibility to choose with whom to interact, our choice can take place in seconds. Because the decision takes place so quickly, in fact before we or others utter a word, it is primarily determined by what is being communicated in the non-verbal cues especially facial expressions. Psychology Today (2019) reported we only take about seven seconds to form an opinion about another person using only their posture, facial expression, and perhaps tone of voice. Although our evaluations can sometimes be wrong, we tend to stick to them even when evidence to the contrary is presented.

Although choosing takes place quickly, it is by no means a simple task. It turns out we have to sift through a vast number of non-verbal cues in making our choices. In fact, Pei (2015 suggests there are well over 75,000 different discriminable non-verbal signs. Some non-verbal cues are hard-wired and physically determined, such as the shape of our head and face, which may make us look more masculine or feminine (Hobgood, 2017) or more or less mature (Gorvett, 2016). While we can't change physical aspects rooted in biology, we can become more aware of their potential impact on our interactions during the early stages of relating to others.

In contrast, although many non-verbal signals are under our control, including posture, gestures, appearance, and facial expressions, most of the time we usually are unaware of the subtle and quick non-verbal calculations being made to decide whether to begin a relationship with someone. Despite research suggesting otherwise, we tend to think we are accurate in reading non-verbal cues (Ammirati, 2013). As mentioned earlier, we tend to overrate our accuracy, which can make our beginnings more problematic. Future interpersonal difficulties brought about by our unfounded confidence in our non-verbal abilities can be even greater in those with dyssemia (Nowicki & Duke, 2012; Nowicki et al., 2009), individuals who already are more prone to make more mistakes reading or expressing non-verbal cues; mistakes that can stop a relationship before it even starts.

Love Is a Garden: An Application of the 4-PRM

A popular story provided by Sternberg's theory is the Garden story, embracing the "view that relationships need to be continually nurtured and tended to" (Sternberg, 2019). Let's examine the role non-verbal behaviour plays within this narrative as it develops in the Choice, Beginning, Deepening, and Ending phases of the Nowicki–Duke model, through the lens of our gardeners, "Joe" and "Joan," imaginary characters drawn from our own personal and professional experiences.

Joan greeted Joe at the door wearing a red soft terry cloth dress, the same one that had caught his eye earlier that day between high school classes. She hadn't been sure he'd be coming by that day, but Joe had asked her at school if he could stop by sometime and confirmed her address. Just in case, Joan was ready – the curls of her 1980's perm unbrushed and lip gloss applied at a lower level to create an illusion of casualness. Tilting her head and dropping one shoulder she smiled encouragingly from the doorway. Shy Joe had a way of blinking rapidly when attracted to someone – and his long-lashed brown eyes began blinking now. When he asked her for a date, she reached up to twirl a curl and said, "yes."

In the Choice phase, our gardener/lovers survey the landscape, seeking a fertile and welcoming plot of land to tend. The garden of love is perhaps viewed as a third entity, with the gardeners focusing not only on each other but on the relationship as something to be tended by both of them. Visual cues are critical in the choice phase, including frequent and increasingly prolonged gaze, appearance including dress and use of color as tools to signal interest (Pazda et al., 2012; Wen et al., 2014) and gestures such as tilting heads or leaning forward with interest. Physical appearance is important in this phase, as are facial expressions and openness of posture.

Beginning

While typically anecdotal or informal advice is offered when *choosing* someone with whom to begin, we receive more structured and direct help in what to do when *beginning* with another once we have made our choice. From childhood on we are taught how to begin by using a widely accepted and overlearned set of rules called "manners" (Nowicki et al., 2009, Nowicki & Duke, 2012). Manners include verbal and non-verbal skills. We smile, we offer our hand for a handshake, and we say something polite about being pleased to meet the person. We offer similar behaviours to everyone we meet. This partnership of verbal and non-verbal communication typically is followed by what is colloquially called "small talk," conversation about some innocuous topic like the weather.

Because of the overlearned and reflexive nature of beginnings, neither complementarity nor incongruence is thought to play a major role in the success or failure of a relationship in this phase. From Kiesler (1999) and Duke and Nowicki's (1982) perspective, "the negotiation of relationship definition is not essential in the earliest stages of a relationship but becomes more important as the interaction continues over time. … Complementary transactions ought to determine relationship valence only when interactions continue past the initial stage" (Kiesler, p. 50).

Joe was nervous as he pulled into Joan's driveway to pick her up for the prom. Placing his trembling hands in his pockets, he stood tall and walked confidently to the door to ring the bell. At dinner before the dance, they discussed the beauty of spring weather in Atlanta, asked about each other's pets, and were careful to use the right fork for salad. They sat across from each other at the restaurant, but at the prom moved closer, standing nearer even when not dancing. By the end of the evening, Joe and Joan were holding hands. Dancing slowly, they had eyes only for each other, gazing for long stretches as Joe tried to be sure not to step on Joan's feet, and Joan kept her heels on all night. At the end of the evening, they kissed, and Joan brushed Joe's cheek gently with her hand before leaving. They kissed once more, Joe's hand sliding down Joan's back before making plans for breakfast the next morning, both impatient for 6 hours to pass quickly until they were together again.

The beginning phase in a relationship is marked by the passion of newness, akin to the joy the gardeners experience as they survey a plot of richly turned soil ripe with possibilities. The gardeners dream of colorful flowers, satisfying food, verdant trees and bushes. In this fresh beginning stage, touch plays a greater role. Just as gardeners speak a language all their own, using phrases like "testing soil ph levels" and "monitoring for invasive pests," the new lovers may develop a paralanguage all their own, marked my cooing and sighs. The first seeds of love sprout tenderly, unspoiled by disease or outside pests. In the beginning phase the gardeners are absorbed with their relationship and each other, listening carefully, acting in unity, touching frequently and excited by the possibilities. As gardeners take care to plant complementary plants the partners take care to curate their shared experiences in ways that lead to closeness and connection.

Deepening

The "real" work of getting closer to someone starts after we have made a choice of with whom to begin and moved past "small talk." Theorists and researchers are intensely interested in understanding what occurs during this time to foster successful progress toward relationship closeness. Some suggest progress is the result of an orderly progression of stages from initial concrete observations of physical appearance to a more important evaluation of shared values (e.g., Murstein & Azar, 1986). For these investigators, the key to the development of a closer relationship resides in the ability to decipher the cues that reflect the underlying values, and if acceptable, use them to deepen the connection.

Others offer an incremental approach, suggesting that rather than movement through discrete stages, relationships gradually tend to become closer over time if intimacy also increases (Altman & Taylor, 1973). The development of closeness in this view is dependent on the success of a process of reciprocating self-disclosures to build intimacy and trust.

Regardless of our perspective on the progression of relationships we embrace, it is likely that out of the estimated 75,000 people we will meet in our lifetime (Anna Vital, Adioma Founder, 2020), most will remain stalled at the beginning stage and characterized by culturally determined structured interactions. Only a few will progress further, deepen, and become meaningful "close" relationships.

Joe and Joan continued to spend increasing amounts of time with each other. They developed pet names that appeared silly to others, including "Fraise" (strawberry) for Joan and "Punky" for Joe. Although they came from different religious backgrounds, the values they shared led them to work together on political campaigns during college and engage in volunteer work together with Big Brothers and Big Sisters following graduation. They enjoyed spending time hiking and talking about movies they watched together on Friday nights, sitting next to one another with legs intertwined and Joan's head on Joe's chest. Unspoken rules and patterns of interactions emerged, with Joan often creating meals and Joe doing dishes and cleaning up afterwards. They developed the ability to signal across the room with the raise of an eye-brow and tilt of the head when one of them was ready to leave a party. All was not perfect in their relationship, and at times Joe wondered if he had made a mistake by choosing to commit to a monogamous relationship at such a young age. Still, they married the summer after graduation and moved to a town not far from extended family and friends.

As the garden grows in the deepening phase, the weeds of stressful life events and the pests of jealousy, fatigue, or boredom with the daily chores may threaten the beauty of the garden. The gardeners unite in defending their love, engaging in rituals that signal commitment and focus on their garden to the exclusion of cultivating other plots. Like scarecrows planted in a garden to warn away the unwanted invasion of strange birds or markers indicating what flowers will soon bloom, these signals may involve the wearing of certain items (wedding rings, for example), extending gazes to each other while decreasing eye contact with others, engaging in public affection involving dance, hand holding, hugging, kissing and intimate touches to the face. Couples develop non-verbal cues easily deciphered (a raised eyebrow while talking in a group may refer to a private understanding: "See what I mean about him?". A look across the room to a partner followed by a glance toward the door may convey, "Hey, are you ready to get out of here and go have some fun?").

Interpersonal theory suggests some possible reasons for *why* some relationships become closer and others don't, and the circumplex construct provides some promising explanations for *how* closeness develops. While similarity in age, physical appearance, activities and the like is as a basis for continuing to relate earlier in relationships, when considering deepening a relationship, the interactive process becomes more demanding and complex. With increasing closeness being the payoff, according to the 4-PRM, we undertake an evaluative search for those who will interact with us in ways to confirm our own self-concept. We use our own favoured interpersonal style that was developed to act as a bid for others to behave in ways to make us comfortable by confirming our self-concept. Leary (1957) suggested that in this manner we were responsible for creating the interpersonal world we live in. "You are mainly responsible for your life situation. You have created your own world. Your own interpersonal behavior has, more than any other factor, determined the reception you get from others. Your slowly developing pattern of reflexes has trained others and yourself to accept you as this kind of person—to be treated in this kind of way. You are the manager of your own destiny" (p. 117).

When two people have moved past the beginning phase of interacting, they engage in the exchange of verbal and non-verbal information necessary in deciding whether a complementary relationship consistent with the principles of the circumplex construct is possible. This already difficult task is further complicated by the fact that the four general interpersonal styles described in the circumplex model (Friendly Dominant, Friendly Submissive, Hostile Dominant, and Hostile Submissive) are communicated via two different languages: verbal language, which is expressed and received within our awareness, and non-verbal language, used more often out of our awareness. When both verbal and non-verbal languages deliver a similar interpersonal style message, communication is congruent; however, when they differ, the message becomes incongruent, presenting a complex interpersonal problem for us to solve. The problem is that incongruence elicits different behavioural responses from others; one in awareness using words and the other out of awareness communicating non-verbal cues. Not only are non-verbal messages more out of awareness, but they also are assumed to have more emotional impact than verbal ones and hence can pull "unexpected" responses creating relationship problems.

Shantae, a friend of Joe and Jane, has completed the "small talk" beginning phase of a new relationship and wants to find out if the person she's met is a good candidate for a deeper relationship. Shantae believes she has a friendly dominant style and uses words reflecting that style to "pull" for a complementary friendly submissive response. Unfortunately, unknowingly, and simultaneously, she was also sending quite a different hostile submissive message non-verbally, a message asking for a complementary response of hostile dominance in return. Because past research shows the non-verbal message will have a greater emotional impact than the verbal one, rather than the hoped for friendly dominant reaction, she received a more confusing hostile dominant response.

Non-verbal Behavior Associated with Closeness

Research identifying non-verbal behaviours associated with relationship closeness has offered few surprise findings. Guerero and Floyd (2006); Guerero and Wiedmaier (2013) has identified a variety of non-verbal behaviours found with relationship closeness, which she also describes as "intimacy." Intimacy results from interpersonal interactions using both non-verbal and verbal communications that lead us to "feel" closer to another. Although some non-verbal cues have direct and nearly universal meaning, context is often critical in determining the meaning of the emotional message being conveyed.

Not surprisingly, touch is often used to indicate how close we feel about one another, although it is less frequently employed in the United States than elsewhere. The onset of a global pandemic in the spring of 2019 has further reduced the opportunity and experience of touch at all points along the relationship process. Lack of experience with touch during childhood and adolescence may lead to struggles in expressing our feelings through touch or difficulties interpreting touches from others in adulthood. Touch is a complex channel composed of a variety of types (pat, poke, punch), applied with different degrees of intensity on various parts of the body. Jones and Yarbrough (1985) have identified and mapped out areas of our physical bodies that are "non-vulnerable," such as hands, arms, elbows, and "vulnerable" includes face, thigh, and waist and especially areas "inside" legs and arms. Vulnerable touching areas are usually reserved for close relationships that have moved into the deepening phase.

Personal space is also often used to convey closeness. When the decision is up to us and not predetermined by the situation (elevators and other public spaces), emotional closeness determines how close we physically choose to be with each other. Hall (1966) suggests that 0 to 18 inches of physical distance is the space for the transmission of "intimate" verbal and non-verbal communication. Physical proximity has the added benefit in that it allows for other non-verbal channels to come into play, such as facial expressions especially involving smiling and eye contact and tone of voice, to convey a greater or lesser desire to be close (Floyd & Ray, 2003).

Although less often considered, chronemics also can reflect closeness in our relationships. The amount of time we spend with others often is synonymous with our evaluation of our relationship with them, with more time indicating greater intimacy. Time provides opportunities for interactions to happen and the rhythm and flow of non-verbal information to take place.

As shown below, learning to read the nonverbal behaviour of your partner is essential to the process of drawing close in the extended deepening phase of relationships.

Joan moved rigidly past Joe in the kitchen, gripping the orange juice bottle tightly as she opened the refrigerator door, her mouth set in a tight and silent line. "Are you mad at me because I asked if you wanted more juice and you thought that was my way of telling you to put the bottle back in the fridge?" Joan didn't answer, continuing to move about the kitchen for a few more minutes in silence. Wiping off her hands she came up behind Joe, who was washing dishes at the sink, embracing him in a tight hug. Joe looked up and saw the prescription bottle on the counter. "I'm sorry you're in so much pain," he said, turning to embrace Joan. What Joe had initially read as irritation was an expression of Joan's physical suffering. Years spent reading non-verbal cues allowed them to avoid misunderstanding and to quickly move from distance to comfort.

Just as gardeners carefully examine plant leaves for health and look closely at buds for indications of the prized fruit to come, the deepening phase involves a willingness to examine the relationship more closely and attend to the needs found, even if that nurturing involves hard work. Commitment is a critical component of the deepening phase, creating a safe garden space, and intimacy grows with shared experiences, feelings of connection, dependability, and bondedness. Just as gardeners make peace with the lack of perfection in their greener world, couples in the deepening phase acknowledge the lack of perfection in their relationship while communicating love through physical presence, use of time, daily and yearly rituals, tangible gifts, and touch.

Ending

Relationships end for many reasons. Whether we describe the ending as positive or negative, when a relationship has run its course, we have an opportunity to look back to examine, and evaluate the "life" of that relationship. Non-verbal behaviour not only plays a significant role in determining whether relationships deepen into closeness or stop at the acquaintance level but also contributes to how well we end our relationships.

Because it often operates without our awareness, special effort is required to examine how non-verbal communication affected all aspects of our relationship when we end with someone. Although we don't like goodbyes, and tend to shy away from self-examination that can be painful at this time, we can gain valuable relationship information by looking back that can be used to increase our chances of success in our future choosing, beginning, and most importantly, deepening and ending.

While touch, personal space, tone of voice, and time can be relatively direct indicators of closeness in the deepening phase of relating to others, their meaning becomes more complex to interpret as we end our relationships. We need to know more than we do about how non-verbal communication operates in determining a "good" or "bad" ending. While we clearly want to get "closer" to others in the deepening phase, emotions can be more mixed about ending with them. We may wish to stay or regain closeness while also experiencing a desire to end the current relationship. This dynamic may produce incongruent communications between what we say and what we do. Take the example of chronemics. Our tendency to get "busy" with other activities when we face endings, means we take time away from the very relationships we have valued. More research is needed to further our understanding of why this occurs, as it is unclear whether the tendency to avoid the anxiety and pain often associated with ending leads to spending less time or if our allocation of time to this phase suggests a disconnect between the value we placed on the relationship and our non-verbal behaviour.

People report facing a relationship ending is like getting a root canal. "Pain" and "painful" are often used words to describe endings. We so dislike endings we will avoid them if we can. More than one out of two surveyed in a study admitted to breaking up with someone using a text message (*Bustle* magazine). If ending by texting is too personal, we can even hire someone to end for us. The "Breakup Shop" proudly proclaims it is as easy to end a relationship in the age of Tinder as it is to begin one with a first date. And for a fee, they will take care of both for us (as presented on NPR, 2015).

While endings are typically characterized by psychological and emotional loss, Bridges and Bridges (2017) suggest they can also be a positive experience. They describe a three-stage transitional process in which we must first acknowledge an ending is taking place before we can move into a "neutral" zone. We spend time in the "neutral zone" disconnecting ourselves from past people and events so that we can be free to consider what comes next by "reorienting" ourselves. According to Bridges and Bridges, if done correctly, reorientation transitions into a third stage, a "new beginning," where we apply what we learned about ourselves during the time we spent in the neutral zone.

Others also believe endings can be positive. Van Gennep (1960, 2019) suggests that we can learn much about ourselves during "liminality," a period he identified lying between ending and beginning anew. Liminality is defined as a transitional period or a rite of passage where past social status and/or rank are no longer important. While in this period of liminality, we can explore who we have been, who we are, and who we want to be. Van Gennep describes three states, beginning with separation from past relationships, followed by the liminality period for self-exploration, and finally a re-assimilation back to reality with what was learned during the liminality time.

Although not yet supported by empirical research, the ending theories of Bridges and van Gennep are relevant for gaining a better understanding of the "life" of a relationship from an interpersonal theory perspective because they emphasize the possibility of growth resulting from a well-handled ending transition. However, their emphasis is on what follows endings rather than what precedes them. In contrast, the 4-PRM model suggests that better relating in the future springs from greater awareness of every aspect of our endings, including the interactions across each phase prior to saying goodbye.

Schworer, Krott, and Oettingen (2019) provided empirical support for the idea that effectively using the time before ending or what they called "well rounded" endings, will lead to more positive future outcomes. Using a variety of methodologies including self-report, observation, and controlled experiments, they found that the more individuals reported they had done everything they could to end well, the "happier," the less regretful they were afterwards. What the researchers called a "well-rounded" ending appeared to provide a foundation for future positive emotional, interpersonal, and professional growth.

We continually experience endings throughout our lives. Some are unpredictable, such as injuries or accidents which bring an end to activities we have previously been able to do. We can't do much to prepare for them, but that's not the case for the many predictable endings we will experience. Graduations from preschool to graduate school represent the ending of a distinct phase, involving rituals that include certain costumes (kindergarten cap and gown, doctoral robes and hoods), ceremonies with special music and marches, and the conveying of a "transitional object" in the form of a "diploma." Marriage, the birth of a child, and retirement also fall into the category of predictable endings, each representing an opportunity to end well enough to increase chances of better future relationships.

Joe and Joan gazed down the red and wrinkled newborn, their son cradled against Joan's chest. Joe had climbed up into the hospital bed of the delivery room to lie next to Joan. They couldn't take their eyes off of the sleeping seven-pound miracle, their synchronized breath punctuated by occasional sighs of joy and fatigue, Joe reached over to brush a damp strand of hair out of Joan's eyes, thinking "This changes everything." An hour earlier Joan had been holding his hands with vice-like strength, eyes locked with focused connection as he panted through a contraction with her. Joe's eye contact with Joan was unwavering, even when she vomited on his shirt midway through labour. Now their gaze was directed at the sleeping infant. Immersed in the early stages of infant infatuation washing over them like a tidal wave, Joe and Joan would spend hours looking at little Antonio, not giving much thought, if any, to how their gaze had shifted. It would be weeks before they came up for air.

Even with endings that we know are coming, we aren't very good at taking the time to attend to the past relationship we've had and what can be learned from it. Instead, more of our attention is on the future and thinking about the next relationship or phase will bring. Endings and new beginnings like graduations or marriages are characterized by speeches and predictions about what is to come next, with only brief reflections on the past. Good endings take time and involve a process rather than a single event. The perfect wedding or graduation day does not predict relationship success. Spending time examining what we did right or wrong interpersonally leading up to the moment of ending and comparing our verbal and non-verbal behaviour to what we have we have exhibited in previous relationships is more likely to set the stage for learning what is needed to develop closeness.

Some predictable endings are determined by age. Developmental psychology has broadened in recent years to include research on adult development, providing greater understanding of how adults continue to grow and change. Levinson (1986, 1989) provides research to suggest we go through a somewhat orderly process of stability and change as we age, the stable times more often occurring between the decimal markers of decades; with transitions at 20, 30, 40, 50, and so on and stability more likely to be present between the two-decade markers such as 22–28, or 52–58.

Implications of Adult Life Development for Relationships

As we continue to develop and change throughout our life, so will our relationships. The relationship we choose at 20 may be different from what we want and need at 50. For our relationships to be satisfying across our lifetime, we must be open to changing ourselves and the way we interact. Although age transitions are part of the naturally occurring developmental process, they are often characterized by the feelings of anxiety or discomfort that are part of any transition.

Individuals who are not aware of the rhythm of adult life developmental periods may misread their diminished comfort during transitions as a sign that their current relationship is not working. Rather than staying and learning about how to end and begin again with the same person at an even better place, they may leave their partner to begin another relationship. Learning from our previous decade of interactions requires us to slow down and become more aware of how we relate, perhaps asking for feedback from people with whom we have previously been in relationship. Examining these transitions carefully positions us to experience greater closeness in relationships as we move forward into the next decade.

Rather than rushing our way through our endings, it is important to make a conscious effort to revisit what we have experienced in previous relationships. Reflection, while at times painful, brings insight that allows for behavioural changes that can lead to greater opportunities for closeness with others. Although the conversations can be awkward, gathering feedback from partners and friends regarding the impact our behaviour, especially our non-verbal behaviour, has had on our relationships with them may increase our awareness of what we need to change in order to be more successful in the future.

Dyssemic individuals, who experience the more significant challenges because of their deficit in one or more non-verbal channels, may benefit from assessment of their abilities and supportive training to improve their non-verbal communication skills. Work with a trusted therapist can assist them in reflecting on how they engage others at each phase of their relationships, allow them to safely examine endings that may be painful, and facilitate their insight leading to better relationships in the future, with the hope of finding consummate love.

References

Altenstein, D., Krieger, T., & Grosse Holtforth, M. (2013). Interpersonal microprocesses predict cognitive-emotional processing and the therapeutic alliance in psychotherapy for depression. *Journal of Counseling Psychology, 60*, 445.

Altman, I., & Taylor, D. A. (1973). *Social penetration: The development of interpersonal relationships*. Holt, Rinehart & Winston.

Ammirati, R. (2013). *Self-assessed emotion recognition skill and social adjustment among college students.* Unpublished doctoral dissertation, Department of Psychology, Emory University.

Ballard, J. (2020). Most Americans believe in soulmates. Published online in *YouGovAmerica.*

Bridges, W., & Bridges, S. (2017). *Managing transitions. 25th anniversary edition.* Da Capo Lifelong books.

Bugenthal, D. E., Kaswan, J. W., & Love, L. R. (1970). Perception of contradictory meanings conveyed by verbal and nonverbal channels. *Journal of Personality and Social Psychology, 16*, 647–650.

Carson, R. C. (1969). *Interaction concepts of personality*. Aldine.

Dermody, S. S., Thomas, K. M., Hopwood, C. J., Durbin, E., & Wright, A. G. C. (2017). Modeling the complexity of dynamic, momentary interpersonal behavior: Applying the time-varying effect model to test predictions from interpersonal. *Journal of Research in Personality*. https://doi.org/10.1016/j.jrp.2017.03001

Duke, M. P., & Nowicki, S., Jr. (1982). A social learning theory analysis of interactional theory concepts and a multi-dimensional model of human interaction constellations. In J. C. Anchin & D. J. Kiesler (Eds.), *Handbook of interpersonal psychotherapy* (pp. 78–94). Pergamon.

Duke, M. P., Nowicki, S., Jr., & Walker, E. (1996). *Teaching your child the language of social success*. Peachtree Publishers.

Ekman, P., & Friesen, W. V. (1969). The repertoire of nonverbal behavior: Categories, origins, usage, and coding. *Seminotica, 1*, 49–98.

Ekman, P., & Friesen, W. V. (1975). *Unmasking the face*. Prentice-Hall.

Elfenbein, H. A., Foo, M. D., Mandal, M., Biswal, R., Eisenkraft, N., Lim, A., & Sharma, S. (2010). The relationship between displaying and perceiving nonverbal cues of affect: A meta-analysis to solve an old mystery. *Journal of Personality and Social Psychology, 98*, 301–318.

Estroff, S. R., & Nowicki, S., Jr. (1992). Interpersonal complementarity, gender of interactants and performance on puzzle and word tasks. *Personality and Social Psychology Bulletin, 18*, 351–363.

Feldman, R. S., Philippot, P., & Custrini, R. (1991). Social competence and nonverbal behavior. In R. S. Feldman & B. Rimé (Eds.), *Fundamentals of nonverbal behavior* (pp. 107–137). Cambridge University Press.

Floyd, K., & Ray, G. B. (2003). Huan affection exchange: IV. Vocalic predictors of perceived affection in initial interactions. *Western Journal of Communication, 67*, 56–73.

Freud, S. (1936). *The problem of anxiety*. Norton.

Friedman, H. S. (1979). Nonverbal communication between patients and medical practitioners. *Social Issues*. https://doi.org/10.1111/j.1540-4560.1979.tb00790.x

Gorvett, Z. (2016). BBC Future Blog. https://www.bbc.com/future/article/20160809-why-it-pays-to-be-grumpy-and-bad-tempered

Guerrero, L. K., & Floyd, K. (2006). *Nonverbal communication in close relationships*. Lawrence Erlbaum, Associates.

Guerero, L. K., & Wiedmaier, B. (2013). Nonverbal intimacy: affectionate communication, positive involvement and flirtation. In J. A. Hall & M. L. Knapp (Eds.) Nonverbal communication (577–612). Walter de Gruyter GmbH, Berlin/Boston.

Hall, E. T. (1966). *The hidden dimension*. Doubleday.

Hall, J. A., & Bernieri, F. J. (Eds.). (2001). *Interpersonal sensitivity: Theory and measurement*. Erlbaum.

Harper, R. G., Wiens, A. N., & Matarazzo, J. D. (1978). *Nonverbal communication: The state of the art*. Wiley.

Hobgood, T. (2017). Blog - Hobgood Facial Plastic Surgery. https://www.toddhobgood.com›

Hopwood, C. J., Harrison, A. L., Amole, M., Girard, J. M., Wright, G. C., et al. (2020). Properties of the continuous assessment of interpersonal dynamics across sex, level of familiarity and interpersonal conflict. *Assessment, 1*, 40–56. https://doi.org/10.1177/1073191118798916

Johnson, D. J., & Myklebust, H. R. (1967). *Learning disabilities: Education principles and practices*. Gruen and Stratton.

Jones, S. E., & Yarbrough, E. A. (1985). A naturalistic study of meanings of touch. *Communication Monographs, 52*, 19–56.

Kiesler, D. J. (1999). *Contemporary interpersonal theory research*. Wiley.

Leary, T. F. (1957). *Interpersonal diagnosis of personality*. Ronald.

Levinson, D. J. (1986). A conception of adult development. *American Psychologist, 41*, 3–14.

Levinson, D. J. (1989). *Seasons of a woman's life*. Knopf.

Manstead, A. S. R. (1995). *Everyday conceptions of emotion: An introduction to the psychology, anthropology and linguistics of emotion*, J. A. Russell, J-M. Fernandez-Dols, A. S. R. Manstead, & J. C. Wellenkamp (Eds.). NATO, ASI, Book Series.

Murstein, B. I., & Azar, J. A. (1986). The relationship of exchange-orientation to friendship intensity, roommate compatibility, anxiety, and friendship. *Small Group Behavior, 17*(1), 3–17. https://doi.org/10.1177/104649648601700101

Nowicki, S., Jr., & Duke, M. P. (1994). Individual differences in the nonverbal communication of affect: The diagnostic analysis of nonverbal accuracy scale. *Journal of Nonverbal Behavior, 18*(1), 9–36.

Nowicki, S., Jr., Duke, M. P., & van Buren, A. (2009). *Starting kids off right*. Peachtree Publishers.

Nowicki, S., Jr., Fost, L., & Naik, M. (1997). Performance in mixed-sex groups as a function of a competitive or cooperative situation. *Journal of Research in Personality, 31*, 512–522.

Nowicki, S., & Duke, M. P. (2012). *Will I Ever Fit In?* Peachtree Press.

Nowicki, S., & Duke, M. P. (2016). Foundations of locus of control. In J. W. Reich & F. J. Infuma (Eds.), *Perceived control: Theory, research and practice in the first 50 years*. https://doi.org/10.1093/acprof:oso/9780190257040.003.0007

Pazda, A. D., Elliot, A. J., & Greitemeyer, T. (2012). Sexy red: Perceived sexual receptivity mediates the red-attraction relation in men viewing women. *Journal of Experimental Social Psychology, 48*(3), 787–790.

Pei, M., & cited in Axtell, R. E. (2015). *Gestures: Do' and taboos of body language around the world.* Wiley.

Pincus, A. L. (2005). A contemporary integrative interpersonal theory of personality disorders. In J. Clarkin & M. Lenzenweger (Eds.), *Major theories of personality disorder* (2nd ed., pp. 282–331). Guildford Press.

Pincus, A. L., & Ansell, E. B. (2013). Interpersonal theory of personality. In J. Suls & H. Tennen (Eds.), *Handbook of psychology* (Vol. 5, pp. 141–159). Wiley.

Riggio, R. E. (1992). Social interaction skills and nonverbal behavior. In R. S. Feldman (Ed.), *Applications of nonverbal behavioral theories and research* (pp. 3–30). Lawrence Erlbaum Associates, Inc.

Rosen, D. C., Miller, A. B., Nakash, O., Halperin, L., & Alegria, M. (2012). Interpersonal complementarity in the mental health intake: A mixed-methods study. *Journal of Counseling Psychology, 39*, 185–196.

Saarni., C. (1999). *Development of emotional competence.* Guilford Press.

Schworer, B., Krott, N. R., & Oettingen, G. (2019). Saying goodbye and saying it well: Consequences of a (not) well-rounded ending. *Motivation Science.* https://doi.org/10.1037/mot0000126

Sorokowski, P., Sorokowska, A., Karowski, M., et al. (2021). Universality of the triangular theory of Love: Adaptation and psychometric properties of the triangular love scale in 25 countries. *The Journal of Sex Research, 58*(1), 106–115. https://doi.org/10.1080/00224499.2020.1787318

Sternberg, R. J. (1986). The triangular theory of love. *Psychological Review, 93*, 119–135.

Sternberg, R. J. (1995). Love as a story. *Journal of Social and Personal Relationships, 12*(4), 541–546.

Sternberg, R. J. (2019). When love goes awry (part 1): Applications of the duplex theory of love and its development to relationships. In R. J. Sternberg & K.S. (Eds.), *The new psychology of love* (2nd ed., pp. 280–289). Cambridge University Press.

Sullivan, H. S. (1953). *Conceptions of modern psychiatry.* Norton.

Sullivan, H. S. (1954). *The psychiatric interview.* Norton.

van Gennep, A. (1960, 2019). *The rites of passage* (2nd ed.). University of Chicago Press.

Vital, A. (2020). Adioma Foundation. https://blog.adioma.com/author/anna-vital/

Watzlawick, P., Beavin, J. H., & Jackson, D. D. (1967). *Pragmatics of human communication.* Norton.

Wellman, H., Harris, P. L., Banjaree, M., & Sinclair, L. (1995). Early understanding of emotion: Evidence of natural language. *Cognition and Emotion, 9*, 117–149.

Wen, F., Zuo, B., Wu, Y., Sun, S., & Liu, K. (2014). Red is romantic, but only for females: Sexual dimorphism moderates red effect on sexual attraction. *Evolutionary Psychology, 12*(4), 719–735.

12

The Functions and Consequences of Interpersonal Touch in Close Relationships

Martin S. Remland and Tricia S. Jones

Primary Functions of Touch in Social Interaction

Touch Can Serve As a Form of Paralanguage

Early attempts to develop a vocabulary for the language of touch tended to focus on common types of touch such as patting, squeezing, stroking, brushing, pinching, shaking, and the like (Argyle, 1975; Nguyen et al., 1975), or on the intimacy of a touch, ranging from professional touching to sexual touching (Heslin & Alper, 1983).

M. S. Remland (✉)
Department of Communication and Media, West Chester University of Pennsylvania, West Chester, PA, USA
e-mail: MRemland@wcupa.edu

T. S. Jones
Communication and Media, Temple University, Philadelphia, PA, USA
e-mail: tsjones@temple.edu

R. J. Sternberg, A. Kostić (eds.), *Nonverbal Communication in Close Relationships*,
https://doi.org/10.1007/978-3-030-94492-6_12

Of all the attempts to classify touch signals, Stanley Jones and Elaine Yarbrough (1985) sought to give us a comprehensive vocabulary for understanding the meanings of touch; that is, how touch can take the place for the use of verbal expressions. As a research assignment they instructed students in their classes to keep diaries of how often they were touched and what was said by the other person when they were touched. Based on the data obtained from these diaries the researchers identified the five most meaningful categories:

1. *Positive affect touches*—These touches signal some degree of liking towards another person and include expressions of appreciation, support, affection, sexual interest, and so forth.
2. *Playful touches*—Playful touches signal a non-serious, joking, or teasing attitude towards another person either in the form of mock aggression or quasi-affection, and include tickling, punching, grabbing, pinching, shoving, and so on.
3. *Control touches*—These touches are intended to influence another person in some way, such as getting someone's attention or compliance.
4. *Ritualistic touches*—These touches are an integral part of certain rituals, such as greetings and departures.
5. *Task-oriented touches*—These touches occur while trying to accomplish a particular task (inspecting someone's clothing, handing someone a telephone, helping someone out of a car, etc.).

Touch Can Encourage Prosocial Behavior and Gain Compliance

For decades, researchers have been conducting experiments to determine whether or not the use of touch alters the likelihood that others will say yes when we ask for assistance. In nearly all of these experiments, researchers place one or more individuals (confederates) into an ordinary situation in which they must ask strangers (participants) for help. Varying their use of touch according to the researcher's specifications (the confederates might be instructed to touch some participants but not others) the confederates approach randomly selected individuals (participants in the study) and ask each for some type of assistance (to give money, participate in a survey, mail a postcard, donate money, sign a petition, etc.). With the exception of the touch variable, the confederates try to keep their actions constant from one encounter to another. Recording how many participants comply with the request, researchers compare rates of compliance (e.g., touching the participant compared to not touching the subject).

In one of the earliest field studies on the practical effects of touch, the researchers selected a restaurant environment as an appropriate place for their study. Specifically, they were interested if customer reactions and tipping behaviour were affected in some observable and measurable way by the brief touch of a waitress. So, the researchers instructed the waitresses to briefly touch a customer on the hand or shoulder when returning the customer's change after receiving payment for the check. Although touching on the hand or shoulder made no difference, customers who were touched left a bigger tip than did the customers who were not touched (Crusco, & Wetzel, 1984).

In a review of 13 field studies, Segrin (1993) found positive effects for touch: lightly touching people on the forearm or shoulder increased their compliance with requests to sign a petition, return money, score questionnaires, volunteer time for charity, participate in a market survey, and the like. In one study, confederates asked passersby if they would look after a large and excited dog for ten minutes, a request more demanding than those made in most previous studies. When touched, 55% agreed; when not touched, compliance dropped to 35% (Guéguen & Fischer-Lokou, 2002). In another study, researchers found a post-compliance effect: After complying with a request to participate in a survey, respondents who were touched on the arm worked harder completing the questionnaire than did those who were not touched (Nannberg & Hansen, 1994). Psychologist Nicolas Guéguen discovered that touch can lead to compliance in a courtship context. One experiment found that a male confederate approaching women in a French nightclub had more success when asking women to slow dance with him when he touched the women on the arm while asking them to dance than when he didn't touch them. And a second experiment found that a male confederate approaching women on the street and asking them for their phone numbers obtained more phone numbers when he touched the women on the arm than when he didn't (Guéguen, 2007). In instances such as these, one explanation for the effect of touch is that its use may have created a brief social bond leading to a closer relationship than if touch had not been used in the same set of circumstances.

But touch doesn't always help and may depend on the context. In one study, for instance, touching people at an airport while asking them to mail a postcard produced no more compliance than did not touching them at all (Remland & Jones, 1994). In another study, a female confederate asked individual shoppers ahead of her in the checkout lines of a discount store if she could move ahead of them. Her verbal justification varied from a low justification ("Excuse me. Do you mind if I get ahead of you in line?") to a high justification ("Excuse me. I just volunteered to drive my neighbor to the hospital for a lab appointment. Do you mind if I get ahead of you in line?"). Whereas the confederate's justification made a difference to the shoppers, her use of touch did not (Bohn & Hendricks, 1997). Sometimes, compliance depends on the gender of the person making the request, as it did in a study where male bus drivers were only more likely to go along with a person's request to ride the bus for less than the full payment, if the person was a woman who used a slight touch while making the request (Guéguen & Fischer-Lokou, 2003). Identifying homophobia as the most likely cause, a series of experiments actually found that men touched by a man were *less* likely to comply with a request than if they were not touched by the man (Dolinski, 2010). Perhaps in certain environments, with certain kinds of requests, and with certain individuals touch may not matter, and may even be counterproductive. Future research may help determine the conditions under which touch is most likely to facilitate compliance and prosocial behaviour.

Touch Can Reflect the Intimacy of a Relationship

Social psychologist Richard Heslin (1974) devised a taxonomy of touches based on the context in which touching takes place. The categories range from distant and impersonal to intimate and highly personal:

Functional/professional—This kind of touching takes place in the context of a professional relationship, in which physical contact of some sort is part of the task. Examples include a doctor touching a patient, a ski instructor touching a student, a hair stylist touching a customer, and so forth.

Social/polite—The common, ritualistic touches prescribed by cultural norms suggesting how, when, where, and whom one should touch. The various forms of touch that occur during greetings and departures are good examples.

Friendship/warmth—We often touch others to express warm feelings and positive regard. These are the touches that are most likely to be misinterpreted as more intimate than intended and that occur more regularly in some cultures than in others. In addition, the incidence of these touches is affected by differences in gender, personality, and age (see identification section in this chapter).

Love/intimacy—The most personalized kind of physical contact, these touches convey strong feelings of affection or represent close emotional ties. Certain types of touch are not appropriate and will arouse considerable discomfort if initiated by non-intimates. Various hand-to-head and hand-to-body touches fall in this category.

Sexual arousal—This kind of touching, which usually targets the erogenous zones, is used primarily for sexual stimulation, even though the parties involved may perceive love/intimacy connotations.

The context in which touching occurs is also a sign of intimacy, which explains why, for example, there is a lot of interpersonal touching at airports than at other locations. As Tiffany Field (2014) suggests, "[m]ore touch may occur in airports because closely related people are more often separated at airports" (p. 34). Not surprisingly, flirting contexts produce more touching than other contexts. Anthropologist Helen Fisher's (1992) five-stage model of the courtship ritual, for instance, highlights the important role of mutual touching as a pivotal sign of romantic interest that takes place during the latter part of the courtship ritual. In her view, touching is one of the universal stages that occur when one individual is interested in another individual as a romantic partner.

We can also distinguish between touching that is non-reciprocal and touching that is mutual. Non-reciprocal touch is initiated by one person but not returned by the person who is touched. This concept is important because of what one-sided touching can tell us about the nature of the relationship (e.g., intimacy or differences in status). With respect to married couples in particular, one study found that married couples were more likely than dating couples to reciprocate their partner's use of touch (Guerrero & Andersen, 1994). Reciprocity is also important because many social touches are not meant to be returned. The touch may complement what someone says (e.g., "Thanks"), it may take the place of words (e.g., "Don't worry, it'll be okay"), or it may be initiated to gain compliance with a request (e.g., "Excuse me, could you watch my bag for a couple of minutes?"). But mutual touch is also revealing. One special category of mutual touches that focuses on the symbolism of physical contact is known as tie signs (Morris, 1977). A tie sign is a public display of togetherness between two persons. Ranging from casual to very intimate, these social touches include handshakes, arm links, embraces, handholds, kisses, and more. They advertise to onlookers that some sort of bond exists between the touchers. Another important characteristic of most tie signs is that the touch usually lasts longer than other kinds of social touching. In a study, comparing differences in the use of touch tie signs between opposite-sex friends and dating partners, researchers found that the latter used more waist and shoulder embraces, and body supports, than did the former (Afifi & Johnson, 1999).

As Field (2014) notes, the greatest percentage of touch occurs among couples in romantic relationships compared to the amount that occurs in less intimate relationships. But systematic observations of interpersonal touching show how outward signs of mutual attraction often peak and then decline as couples become increasingly intimate. One study suggested this curvilinear relationship between public displays of affection and relational intimacy. Guerrero and Andersen (1991) recorded the number of times opposite-sex partners standing in line at a public zoo and at movie theatres touched each other. They found that couples that were seriously dating or marriage-bound touched the most—much more than either married couples or couples who were casually dating. In another field study of touching in public, McDaniel and Andersen (1998) found additional support for a curvilinear relationship between physical displays of affection and relational intimacy. They observed opposite-sex couples from Asian, European, and Latin American countries, as well as the United States, at the international terminal of a major US West Coast airport. The least amount of touching occurred among strangers and acquaintances, as expected, but there were no more touches among spouses and family members. The most touching took place among close friends and lovers.

Touch Can Express Affection and Emotional Support

There is some evidence that intentional acts of touch alone can signal specific emotions. In one series of studies, for example, participants in Spain and in the United States were able to guess with much better than chance accuracy, whether an instance of touch alone expressed anger, fear, disgust, love, gratitude, or sympathy (Hertenstein et al., 2006). Studies on the uses of touch confirm that physical contact communicates affection and emotional support. For instance, when asked to describe how they would react non-verbally to a situation in which a close same-sex friend tells them that he or she just ended a romantic relationship, college students in two separate surveys largely agreed on what they would do. Overall, hugging emerged as the number one response, but the men in both surveys were much less likely than the women to say they would hug their troubled friend. Other high-ranking responses included being attentive, concerned facial expressions, increased touch, and eye contact. Some responses depended mainly on the respondent's gender: men were more likely to pat their friend on the arm or shoulder; women were more likely to use a wider variety of comforting touches (Bullis & Horn, 1995; Dolin & Booth-Butterfield, 1993). Another study found that embraces are seen as more expected for women than for men (Floyd, 1999). This coincides with other studies suggesting that women are more likely than men to use touch for giving and receiving emotional support (Upenieks & Schafer, 2021).

In general, however, there is a great deal of research that most forms of touch, particularly those that occur in the context of helping someone, convey and elicit strong positive emotions (Jones, 1994; Montagu, 1986). According to Field's (2014) research there is a strong connection between expressions of love and the use of touch. Specifically, she includes touches such as holding hands, hugging, kissing, cuddling, caressing, and massaging as the primary examples of romantic touch.

Does touch between individuals in close relationships improve the success of their relationship, and, if it does, how does it contribute? In one study, the researchers recruited 102 romantic couples that had been dating for at least three months and asked the couples to make entries in an e-diary four times a day for one typical week. The researchers found strong support for the claim that interpersonal touch is associated with positive feelings of closeness and intimacy in the relationship. Moreover, with partners who reported touching them more frequently experienced higher levels of well-being six months later (Debrot, Shoebi, Perrez, & Horn, 2013).

The positive impact of touching, particularly in close relationships, is influenced by both biological and social processes, as we will discuss in the next sections. For instance, touch in close relationships can stimulate the release of chemicals in the brain, such as oxytocin, that reduce stress and promote comfort and intimacy (Goleman, 2006). Moreover, the effects of touch may depend on socialization processes that reflect the influence of culture, gender, and other environmental factors.

Biological and Social Influences on Interpersonal Touch

Studies confirm that some effects of interpersonal touch or touch deprivation are universal and result from a variety of biological processes. These studies focus on the social-psychological and health-related consequences of touch and touch deprivation. But there is also a considerable body of research on how people differ in their need for touch, their reactions to touch, and their interpretations of touch. This latter body of research focuses largely on cultural, gender, personality differences, and other factors arising from the development and transmission of rules, norms, and stereotypes attributed to socialization.

The Benefits of Touch and the Consequences of Touch Deprivation

Although not taken seriously for most of this century, the need for touch is now firmly established. In his pioneering book, *Touching: The Human Significance of the Skin*, Ashley Montagu (1986) traces the scientific work that has transformed our thinking about the biological significance of touch. Decades of scientific study show the devastating consequences of touch deprivation and the existence of a "skin hunger" for touch. Studies of non-human primates, for instance, show that touch-deprived monkeys suffer an array of physiological, psychological, and emotional problems. Compared to their comforted counterparts, they experience brain damage, immune system deterioration, depression, aggressiveness, and poor social functioning. One of the most widely cited of these studies is Harry Harlow's experiments on rhesus monkeys in which infant monkeys were able to maintain contact with two surrogate mothers: one made of terry cloth and another made of wire mesh. In some cases, the terry cloth surrogate also provided milk and in other cases the wire mesh surrogate provided milk. Harlow discovered that the monkey infants preferred the cloth mother without the milk over the wire mother with milk, suggesting that the monkeys would rather receive tactile comfort more than the milk provided by the wire mesh mother (research reported in Field, 2014).

There is a great deal of research that most forms of touch, particularly those that occur in the context of close relationships, produce an array of benefits that include conveying and eliciting strong positive emotions, decreasing the likelihood of depression, reducing stress, lowering blood pressure, decreasing inflammation, promoting empathy, decreasing the chances of cardiovascular disease, improving the quality of sleep, increasing tolerance to pain, strengthening the immune system, decreasing domestic violence, and more (Field, 2014; Jones, 1994; Montagu, 1986; Thomas & Kim, 2021). For example, in a study at Carnegie Mellon University, researchers interviewed 404 healthy adults over 14 consecutive evenings to find out how much social support they thought they received from others, which included how many hugs they received. Then the participants were exposed to a common cold virus and were monitored in quarantine to assess infection and signs of illness. The researchers discovered that both perceived social support and hugs reduced the risk of illness. (Cohen, et al., 2015).

Although there are many factors that may contribute to these potential benefits, one factor that has been receiving a great deal of attention in recent years is the notion that touches, especially in close relationships, can stimulate the release of chemicals in the brain, such as oxytocin (Field, 2014; Goleman, 2006). Oxytocin is a hormone produced in the hypothalamus of the brain and released in the pituitary gland. Research suggests that it can contribute to some of the benefits noted above, particularly in facilitating improved social relations (e.g., greater empathy, less stress, more positive emotions, and so forth). In general, studies of touch in close relationships show that touch not only contributes to the release of oxytocin but that the release of oxytocin also increases the desire for more physical contact, thus demonstrating the interdependent relationship between touch and oxytocin.

In one experiment, for example, researchers found that intranasal administration of oxytocin to the man or woman in romantic couples enhanced the pleasantness of the gentle touch they received, when they believed they were being touched by their partner, even when they were actually being touched by a stranger but were not aware of that. In the same study, perceived partner touch was also correlated positively with their evaluation of the quality of their relationship (Kreuder, et al., 2017). In another experiment, researchers discovered that the touch of a loving romantic partner, along with increased levels of oxytocin, were effective in reducing the unpleasantness of electric shocks (Kreuder et al., 2018). In another experiment, researchers found that, after intranasal oxytocin treatment, gentle human touch heightened participants' sensitivity to facial expressions of emotion, so that frowning faces were perceived as less friendly and attractive, whereas smiling faces were rated as more friendly and attractive (Ellingsen et al., 2014).

The Development and Influence of Rules, Norms, and Stereotypes

Young children are guided by the rules they learn about touch from their parents, siblings, peers, and other significant people in their lives. One general finding from this developmental research is that the overall frequency of touch declines steadily from kindergarten through the sixth grade (Willis & Reeves, 1976). Beginning in preschool and well into adolescence, same-sex touching is more common than is opposite-sex touching (Berman & Smith, 1984). These patterns reflect societal norms regarding the use of touch; they suggest that rules are being learned, such as "touching other people can be rude" and "boys and girls shouldn't touch each other."

In many ways our use and interpretation of touch depends on where we are, who we are with, what we are doing, and when we are doing it. This is because we learn to follow rules. We learn what is and is not appropriate or meaningful in a particular context. But not everyone learns the same set of rules, and sometimes the rules change. Despite what may be a universal need for touch, a touch can often send the wrong message. Laws against sexual harassment, and more frequent reporting of child abuse cases, for example, have combined in recent years to change dramatically the climate in which social touching occurs. In the modern workplace, touches that in the past may have been ignored are now often seen as crude and ill-mannered. Examples of this new intolerance are common and widespread. In El Paso County, Colorado, an undersheriff was fired for violating departmental policy on sexual harassment by hugging several lower-level employees ("Undersheriff fired for hugging," 1999). In New Zealand, issuing a statement that his intentions were irrelevant, the government found a naval instructor guilty of sexual harassment and fired him for hugging a former student, touching her hair, calling her "darling" and telling her she was beautiful ("Navy issues warning," 2002). In Singapore, school principals, counselors, and social workers have been warned to avoid physical contact with children, unless it is absolutely necessary. They have been told that it is okay to shake hands or pat a child on the back, but hugs are not allowed ("No hugging or kissing," 2002). Another example of changing norms concerns sexual touching, which at one time was taboo outside marriage. Perhaps the most dramatic illustration of our shifting sensibilities regarding the use of touch involves the way parents touch their children. Not long ago, parents were cautioned against the use of touch with their children; such indulgences pediatricians warned would spoil the child and create a condition of excessive dependency. Today we generally shun such advice. But consider the words of then-professor of psychology at Johns Hopkins University, John Watson, who wrote in his 1928 textbook, *Psychological Care of Infant and Child:*

> There is a sensible way of treating children: Never hug and kiss them, never let them sit in your lap. If you must, kiss them once on the forehead when they say good night. Shake hands with them in the morning. Give them a pat on the head if they have made an extraordinarily good job of a difficult task. Try it out. In a week's time you will find how easy it is to be perfectly objective with your child and at the same time kindly. You will be utterly ashamed of the mawkish, sentimental way you have been handling it. (quoted in Montagu, 1986, p. 151)

The Influence of Culture

It happened "innocently" enough at an HIV-AIDS news conference in New Delhi, India. Movie actor Richard Gere, in a moment of unbridled enthusiasm, embraced and kissed one of Bollywood's most popular actresses, Shilpa Shetty. A photograph of the kiss made the front page of newspapers across the country amid protests condemning the act as disgraceful and obscene. Outraged protesters beat burning effigies of Gere and set fire to photographs of Shetty (Robinson, 2007). India is one of many countries in the world where large numbers of people frown on public displays of affection. In 2007, Pakistan's tourism minister said she feared for her life after clerics at a radical mosque issued an edict accusing her of committing a great sin by hugging her French parachute instructor at a fund-raising event (Jan, 2007).

Incidents like these should remind us of an important principle: the meaning and significance of non-verbal communication, in this case a kiss or a hug, can vary dramatically from culture to culture. What may be routine and expected in one culture, can be taboo and alarming in another. Anthropologist Edward Hall's (1959, 1966) research on cultural differences in the use of space raised our consciousness about the existence of these norms. Among his findings was the observation that some cultures rely on tactile (touch) and olfactory (smell) modes of communication more than other cultures do. Members of these "contact cultures" (e.g., Arab, Latin American, and Southern European nations) use more touch and less personal space than do members of so-called non-contact cultures, who prefer the visual mode of communication (e.g., North American, Asian, and Northern European nations). These differences underscore the arbitrary nature of an approach–avoidance signaling system that relies as much on nurture as it does on nature.

In several studies of cultural differences in Europe, Remland, Jones, and Brinkman (1991, 1995, 1999) found that southern Europeans were more inclined to use touch than northern Europeans. Brief observations of nearly 1000 couples at numerous train stations in 15 countries revealed differences in the percentages of couples in which one person touched the other. For example, among countries with at least 50 observed couples, the highest incidence of touch occurred for those in Greece (32%), Spain (30%), Italy (24%), and Hungary (23%). The lowest was found in the Netherlands (4%), Austria (9%), England (11%), Belgium (12%), and Germany (16%).

Some researchers report cultural differences in public displays of affection. Tiffany Field (1999) observed peer interactions among adolescents in Paris, France and Miami, Florida. She found that American adolescents spent less time leaning against, stroking, kissing, and hugging their peers than did the French adolescents. Compared to the French, the Americans also displayed more self-touching and more aggressive physical behaviour. In another study, a team of researchers observed male–female couples walking on a college campus. They found no differences in hand-holding when comparing Latino couples with Asian couples, but arm embracing was much more prevalent among the Latinos than it was among the Asians (Regan et al., 1999). In another study, researchers observed the most male–female affectionate touching (hugging, kissing) in Italian dance clubs and the least in American dance clubs (DiBiase & Gunnoe, 2004).

The meaning of touch often depends on one's culture. In some Middle and Near-Eastern countries, shaking hands is an act of bargaining rather than a form of greeting. In much of the Middle East, holding hands is a sign of friendship (unlike in the West, where such an act between men implies homosexuality) and is a common practice among male friends. In fact, same-sex touching in public is more acceptable in many Asian and Middle Eastern countries than is opposite-sex touching (Jones, 1994). Some forms of touch have meanings that are unique to a particular culture. In Saudi Arabia, for example, an individual will sometimes kiss the nose of another person after an argument to say, "I am sorry" (Morris, 1994).

The Influence of Gender and Personality

Jones (1994) points out that women are more apt than men to exchange affectionate touches such as hugs and kisses (Derlega et al., 1989), and to use touch when offering social support (consoling, complimenting, etc.). In contrast, men are more likely to exchange playful touches (mock aggression, teasing, etc.). Studies also suggest that men and women interpret touch differently. Overall, women tend to find it more pleasant than men do (Hall, 1984), but their reactions depend on how well they know the toucher. For men, touch often carries sexual overtones and, as a result, their reactions seem to depend on whether the toucher is male or female (Heslin & Alper, 1983; Heslin et al., 1983). In fact, researchers mainly attribute the fact that men, compared to women, avoid same-sex intimate forms of touch and possess a more negative attitude about such touching to homophobic attitudes (Derlega et al., 1989). After observing same-sex couples and recording how often they touched, one team of researchers found that those who touched least scored the highest on a questionnaire measuring negative attitudes towards homosexuals (Roese et al., 1992). Recent research also supports the claim that homophobia in men produces negative judgements of certain kinds of touching between men (Floyd, 2000).

In addition, observations of the way men and women touch in public (i.e., tie signs) often reveal that men get the upper hand (e.g., guiding and directing). In fact, researchers have confirmed the idea that men literally get the upper hand when men and women hold hands in public. Observations of more than 15,000 couples showed that men had the "dominant" hand position, even when taking into account male–female differences in height (in couples with a taller woman more men than women still had the upper hand). Moreover, the finding seems to hold up across cultures. Men had the upper hand in Asian, African-American, Hispanic, and Japanese couples as well as European American couples (Chapell & Beltran, 1999).

Some researchers claim that men touch women more than women touch men and that touch-initiation in these cases constitutes a status reminder (Henley, 1973, 1977, 1995). But many observations of touching in opposite-sex interactions have failed to corroborate this. Researchers find that women initiate touch more than men do (Jones, 1994; Stier & Hall, 1984; Willis & Dodds, 1998). One extenuating circumstance may be the age of the couple. One study of couples in public places found that men initiated more touch than women did in younger couples, whereas women touched more in older couples (Hall & Veccia, 1990). Another related factor is the kind of touch one uses. Research shows that males initiate more hand touches, whereas women tend to initiate more non-hand touches, such as hugs and kisses (DiBiase & Gunnoe, 2004). One possible explanation is that touch in these situations may be a status reminder—signaling possessiveness—in less secure relationships. In addition, if touch does count occasionally as a status reminder, it probably makes more sense to investigate how touch is used instead of how often. A touch that attempts to control (i.e., directing someone), for example, seems more indicative of status than is a touch that is meant only to show concern or affection. Another explanation offered by some researchers is that differences in the use of touch between men and women reflect an evolutionary model of reproductive strategies: men use touch for sex and women use touch to maintain resources and parental involvement. This theory may explain why researchers sometimes find that men who are dating or newly married are much more likely to initiate touch than men who have been married longer than a year. But for women, there are no reported differences in the use of touch between courting and married couples (Willis & Briggs, 1992; Willis & Dodds, 1998).

Surveys suggest that women share a more positive attitude towards same-sex touch than men do (Andersen & Leibowitz, 1978; Willis & Rawdon, 1994). And studies comparing males and females in their use of touch usually show more frequent touching between females than between males (Hall, 1984; Hall & Veccia, 1990; Roese et al., 1992), although these gender differences don't always show up when researchers observe people in other countries (Remland et al., 1995). As for the amount of touch that occurs in opposite-sex encounters, it depends primarily on the couple's relationship (Guerrero & Andersen, 1991; McDaniel & Andersen, 1998). In one study, for example, persons who initiated touch were regarded as more dominant, assertive, and expressive than were those who received touch (Major & Heslin, 1982).

Perhaps the most common form of touch is the handshake. One recent study confirms the importance of hand shaking as an expression of personality and as a behaviour that influences first impressions. Examining the importance of a "firm" handshake, which depends on the strength, duration, vigour, and completeness of the grip (along with the use of eye contact), researchers found that women who used a firm handshake had different personalities than women who didn't. The firm handshakers were more extroverted, expressive, liberal, intellectual, and open to new experiences. They also made a better first impression. As the authors conclude, "Our results provide one instance in which women who exhibit a behavior (a firm handshake) that is more common for men and that is related to confidence and assertiveness are evaluated more positively than are women who exhibit a more typical feminine handshake" (Chaplin et al., 2000, p. 115).

Almost instinctively, we seem to know how to comfort people in need. Indeed, the experience of giving and receiving emotional support goes back to the earliest of our infant–parent interactions, setting the stage for what we crave in the years to come. Comforting encounters begin in infancy with parental communication that involves the use of gentle touch and patterns of mutual influence, in which infant and parent engage in synchronized movement, mirroring, reciprocity, and the like.

One of the consequences of these early experiences is the insecurity a child develops over the prospect of forming close relationships. Extending the basic principles of attachment theory (Bowlby, 1973, 1980), which regards attachment to others as a human need activated during moments of distress, researchers have been studying differences in attachment styles. These styles are relatively stable interpersonal orientations, developed in childhood, which reflect beliefs we have about whether we are worthy of receiving care and affection from others and whether others can be counted on to provide it (Bartholomew, 1990). A negative view of others results in avoidant attachment styles: Not wanting closeness because one is overly self-reliant (low anxiety and high avoidance) creates a dismissive style; whereas not wanting closeness because of apprehension (high anxiety and high avoidance) creates a fearful style. A positive view of self and others results in a secure attachment style. Secure persons (low anxiety and low avoidance) are comfortable with intimacy, confident and optimistic about close relationships, but self-sufficient to the point of not being overly dependent on others. In contrast, a preoccupied style, which includes a negative view of self and a positive view of others (high anxiety and low avoidance), results in a lack of self-confidence, combined with a desire for intimacy. Preoccupied persons may be "clingy" in their close relationships with others (Bartholomew & Horowitz, 1991; Schachner et al., 2005).

Studies show that attachment security or insecurity is like a filter in the communication process that blocks a person's sensitivity to certain nonverbal messages and discourages the expression of certain messages as well (Noller, 2006). For example, people who have a secure attachment style are the most likely to seek comfort from others when they need it (Ognibene & Collins, 1998), and the best equipped to comfort others, offering more reassurance and physical comfort than persons with other attachment styles (Becker-Stoll et al., 2001; Feeney & Collins, 2001; Guerrero, 1996; Tucker & Anders, 1998). For instance, research shows that anxious and avoidant individuals are less tolerant of close interpersonal distances, a behavioural tendency that would make it difficult for them to offer "contact comfort" and emotional support to others (Kaitz et al., 2004; Yukawa et al., 2007).

Future Implications: Effects of Social Media and the Pandemic

Well before the COVID-19 pandemic, people worldwide were carrying on most of their interpersonal interactions on various social media platforms. In short, nearly everyone has been using social media in the digital age. More specifically, about 88% of American adults aged 18–29; 78% ages 30–49; 64% age 50–64; 37% ages 65 and over have been communicating across multiple social media platforms, multiple times a day (Smith & Anderson, 2018). Reliance on social media technologies has been growing. According to recent data, adults were spending over 11 hours per day listening to, watching, reading, or generally interacting with media (Nielsen, 2018), resulting in half of their day dedicated to consuming or sharing media content. New technologies have proven their social utility as "mostly a good thing", with 40% of users stating that it would be hard to give up social media (Smith & Anderson, 2018). Usage extends across all ages, gender, race, and socioeconomic status. But with social media there are also far fewer opportunities to convey messages of intimacy and to build close relationships by means of physical contact. In face-to-face interactions, we connect with others in the moment with various forms of touch: handshaking, hugging, conversational touch, kissing, and the like (Remland, 2017). Insofar as we have been relying even more than ever on social media during the pandemic, we have been touching each other less.

Since March 2020, the world has experienced a perfect storm of conditions for touch deprivation brought to bear by the COVID-19 pandemic and the resultant social isolation and social upheaval that has marked our "new normal" as one of anxiety, loneliness, and all too often, grief (Petry et al., 2021). The new "normal" includes social distancing, wearing masks, travelling restrictions, schools closed, and the inability to be with our loved ones in healthcare and elderly care situations—even in death and in paying respect to their memories (Clements-Cortes, 2020). As Doreen Dodgen-Magee expressed in her recent *Psychology Today* article (2020, pp. 1–2):

> This is a marathon, not a sprint, and our nerves are becoming frayed, the unknown is taking its toll, and none of us are at our best ... lack of physical connection, and a profound sense of existential aloneness are real. In each of these settings, the lack of both intimate and casual, social physical touch is becoming a source of agitation and sadness. ... It turns out that touch deprivation is experienced by many people much like dehydration is experienced by the marathon runner. If it goes unaddressed, it can take us out.

The extent of our loss of the most foundational sense—the sense of touch as Aristotle adeptly explained (Sigley, 2020)—means a self-inflicted adverse impact on mental, physical, and emotional health and well-being that may last long into the future (Smith & Bilbo, 2021).

In this final section of our chapter, we discuss the impacts of COVID-related touch deprivation on children, adults in intimate relationships, and healthcare workers. We explore the costs and benefits of the forced and increasing reliance on social media as a means of creating and maintaining connection more conventionally and effectively met by access to human touch. And we review the ideas for addressing touch deprivation through positive practices and innovative technologies.

The Effects of COVID-Related Touch Deprivation

Effects on Children

As explained earlier in this chapter, touch deprivation is debilitating for anyone but is critically dangerous to children. And, the experiences in this pandemic have confirmed that sad reality. As Bebler et al. (2019) remind us, touch deprivation for younger children is most harmful because their developmental processes are so accelerated and at risk. Thus, we see severe touch deprivation in early childhood resulting in difficulty learning to use language and develop speech competence. Not having touch means unfulfilled emotional needs and senses of safety that increase aggressiveness and emotional instability. The cycle of touch deprivation disrupts sleep behaviour, making it difficult for brain development to continue as needed. The longer and more intense the touch deprivation – the more serious and potentially irreversible the consequences, especially for children with developmental delays or disabilities (Asbury et al., 2021).

Given that most touch provision for young children comes from a loving parent or caretaker, touch deprivation also has damaged the emotional attachments to caregivers; with lack of attachment often translating to significantly lower cognitive development (Clark, 2020). Clements-Cortes (2020) notes that during COVID children have been separated from grandparents or other family members who were part of their regular social circles due to the need for older adults to be cautious about who they interact with. We hear of grandparents waiting for over a year to be in the presence of their grandchildren and, even then, not feeling safe enough to touch, hug, or kiss their grandchild. Children have missed out on taken-for-granted social celebrations with full family; the birthday celebrations, kindergarten graduations, sports events, holidays, etc., where essential memories of a safe and supportive family environment are created.

Effects on Intimate Adult Relationships

The stresses on adults in intimate and partnership relationships have not received as much attention in the COVID literature, but touch deprivation is also a reality for them. Naruse and Moss (2021, p. 450) reported that:

> [e]xternal stressors such as economic strain, confinement, and isolation can create a context that decreases couples' ability to give responsive support, affection, and warmth to each other because of the depletion of personal resources and self-regulation.

They emphasize that touch deprivation creates further anxiety and emotional distance that can result in domestic violence, separation and even divorce. Ironically, even though couples may be "sheltering in place" together and have even more opportunity for supportive and/or intimate touch, many couples are too stressed to provide that support to each other. In their study of 1746 participants surveyed for intimate, friendly, and professional touch experiences during COVID-19-related restrictions, researchers discovered that intimate touch deprivation during COVID-19-related restrictions was associated with higher anxiety and greater loneliness even though this type of touch was still the most experienced during the pandemic (von Mohr et al., 2021). They concluded that the more the lack of intimate touch (but not friendly or professional), the worse the self-reported anxiety and feelings of loneliness.

One variable of note is the degree to which individuals "long" for touch. Bebler and her colleagues (2019) argued that not everyone has the same felt need for touch and that the impact of touch deprivation should be measured in terms of the gap between a person's need and the amount of touch they experienced. They developed the Longing for Interpersonal Touch Picture Questionnaire [LITPQ] and used it to test the relationship of longing for touch, touch deprivation and mental health. For 72.7% of the participants, their touch wish exceeded the reported touch frequency. Participants currently in a relationship didn't differ significantly from those who were single regarding their LITPQ scores, touch frequencies and degree of touch wish. Nor were there differences between females and males. However, unfulfilled longing for touch was significantly related to negative mental health.

Effects on Healthcare Workers

During the pandemic there have been numerous acknowledgements of the emotional labour healthcare workers must expend to provide treatment for COVID patients without being able to provide a "healing touch" (Mehta-Lee, 2020). Dhananjaya Sharma (2020, p. 1), an Indian surgeon, shared this professional and personal difficulty in this statement:

> 'Empathy' and 'compassion' were the quintessence of my code of honour as a physician, inculcated on patients' bedside more than four decades ago as a zealous medical student. And now I suddenly find their simple expression towards my patients—the human 'touch'—is gone. It was not called the healing touch for nothing, so it hurts to lose the 'touch'.

The *Journal of Clinical Nursing* (2020) published an editorial about the personal and professional challenges of restricted touch for nurses and other healthcare professionals during COVID. Within healthcare, touch is used to send messages of care, comfort, and compassion. It is critical to building strong relationships with patients that, in turn, feed compliance with healthcare practices. But due to social distancing rules the personal touch is no longer a part of their practice. They compare it to when healthcare workers were caring for victims of Ebola.

Effects on Adolescents: The Dual Impact of Touch Deprivation and Social Media

Social media permeates the personal and professional lives of most people, but it is particularly compelling and encompassing for teens. So, when we consider the impact of COVID touch deprivation on teens it is best understood in light of how much social media shapes their connection with the world. The ubiquity of social media is now a fact of life. As Kutok (2020, p. xx) reports:

> However, the risk of exposure to COVID-19 has led many teens to turn to social media and technology to fulfill their social interaction. Around 95% of adolescents in the United States have access to a smartphone, and 97% reported having a social media profile, the most popular apps being YouTube, Instagram, and Snapchat. … Social media has been the bridge that connects us during times of isolation, and while it is by no means a replacement for in person interactions, 81% of adolescents have said that social media helps them feel more connected to friends, and 68% have said that it allows them to access social support during tough times.

In weighing the benefits (Sigley, 2020) and disadvantages of social media, the scales are tipping towards the disadvantages. Sherry Turkle, the MIT professor who has made contributions in our understanding of the impact of social media on children's emotional and social development (2011, 2015) has raised a number of concerns over the research indicating that social media use is negatively related to development of empathic response. Indeed, she suggests that overall the research indicates as much as a 40% decrease in teen's ability to take the emotional perspective of another.

The connection between Turkle's warning and touch deprivation is alarming. As mentioned earlier in this chapter, touch is one of the means through which empathic connection is achieved. If COVID-related touch deprivation leads to increased dependence on social media, which in turn, decreases empathic response, the possibility for even more severe degradation of empathic ability is strong. In an editorial in the journal, *Child and Adolescent Mental Health* (2019, p. e4), the editors reported on a 2018 event by the Royal College of Psychiatrists in which they asked young people about social media and its place in their lives:

> One young person held up his smartphone and stated 'this is my heroin – it's the heroin of our generation'. In contrast, another young person argued 'I don't agree – this is my life line, I am a looked after child, living on my own, and it's the only way I have of keeping in touch with my family and friends'. And therein lies the conundrum.

When social media becomes the only or primary lifeline to others for teens, as has been obvious in the COVID period, we see more harmful effects of screen media, especially for teens who are vulnerable to negative online interactions. There's a strong chance for experiencing rejection online, and "young people who feel rejected online are particularly vulnerable to heightened feelings of depression, anxiety, reduced self-esteem, online bullying and isolation" (p. e5). Supporting this, a recent study reported that the more time adolescents spend on social media and watching television, the more severe their symptoms of depression become (Boers et al., 2019). What we have is a fairly vicious cycle. A final irony is discussed in a report by the European Union (2021, p. 4):

> Sadly, many people now feel like they live in the society described in the 1990s science fiction movie Demolition Man, where physical contact is prevented and heavily sanctioned. The increased virtualisation of our social interactions feeds our hunger for touch, the lack of which can have profoundly negative consequences.

Positive Programmes and Alternatives to Address Touch Deprivation

The good news, in addition to the hoped-for success of vaccines to release us from social distancing restrictions, is that enterprising problem-solvers have been developing ways to help reduce the effects of touch deprivation. The following are some suggestions for children and for adults.

For Children

Many of the ideas for how to help children find positive replacements for personal touch come from the United Kingdom (UK). The focus of several organizations has been on developing positive practices that allied health workers and educators can use with children to "replace" personal touch to some degree (Clark, 2020). In July 2020, the All- Party Parliamentary Group (APPG) report on Fit and Healthy Childhoods argues that methods involving positive touch should become an established component of therapeutic working with children, embedded within training and continuous professional development. Some of these positive touch techniques were explained by Jean Barlow, a counselor working with primary and secondary school children in the UK:

- Child-to-child peer massage is a short daily practice that aims to manage stress and improve communication.
- Mirroring early bonding and attachment techniques—including eye contact, body movement and posture, gesture and facial expressions—alongside enthusiastic and emphatic voice tones to fully engage in their clients' process.

For Adults

Doreen Dodgen-Magee (2020, para. 6, 11, 12, & 13) suggests the following alternatives for adults to address touch hunger.

- **Explore and become comfortable with self-touch**. Skin-to-skin contact, even from our selves, can be helpful when touch from others is limited. The key is to be intentional and to direct our attention to the feeling of our skin on our skin.
- **Increase the attention to all the senses of the body.** Touch is but one of our many senses. When the body is starving for one kind of sensory stimulation that is not easily accessible, we can comfort the longing by tending to it in other ways. Offering ourselves new flavours and sounds, stimulating our sense of smell, and providing interesting things to look at can all help. Given our current reliance on the auditory and visual senses to connect us to others via the digital realm, tending to our sense of smell and taste can be particularly effective.
- **Stimulate the skin with textures and temperature**. Gather up a diverse range of textured fabrics from your clothing or linen closet. Place these in locations where you can feel them regularly. Run them over your arms or legs or place them between your hands and make circular motions. Do the same thing with heat and cold, using water, ice packs, or heating pads to stimulate the sensory receptors in your skin. When you are outside, feel the texture of the sidewalk or grass. Pay attention to the feeling of wind, rain, and sun on your skin.
- **Apply gentle weight or resistance**. This is the time in life when nearly everyone would benefit by owning a weighted blanket or compress of some kind.

Pet therapy is extremely helpful (Pierce, 2020). Increased isolation and absence of touch perhaps partly explains the recent rush on animal shelters who report increases in adoptions. Animal shelters around the world have reported spikes in adoption rates during lockdown, and data suggest, at least in the United States, that shelters are running out of animals to put up for adoption. Pets provide emotional benefits for people living alone by providing love, affection and companionship and a safe means to give and receive touch. Even exchanging touch with a pet can be hugely beneficial. Unlike with cuddle parties, the affection of a pet has some genuineness—they are getting something out of it too, rather than it being a transaction between two strangers (Park, 2020).

Technological Innovations

We would be remiss if we didn't give a nod to how science is tackling the problem of touch deprivation in the pandemic. A development of new haptic technologies and use of robot touch offer exciting possibilities.

- TOUCHLESS, a new project supported under the European Union's Horizon 2020 EIC Pathfinder funding programme, proposes innovation in haptic technologies used in virtual social interactions. It could help people who cannot fulfil their need for touch, for example, because of social distancing. They are developing the next generation of touchless haptic technologies using neurocognitive models and a novel artificial intelligence (AI) framework. Without having physical contact with any device, users will receive digital touch sensations that evoke not only a functional response (i.e., receptor response), "but also an experiential one (i.e., affective, social and cognitive)." The 48-month project started in January 2021. Dr. Diego Martinez Plasencia, from the Touchless team said: "This project is exciting because we will not only develop new mid-air touch-mimicking using ultrasound, heat or electrostatic stimulation. We will go deeper than ever, understanding how they help us bond, feel attached and engaged during touch interaction, and developing neuro-cognitive models to help us bring back these missing touch related aspects when creating mid-air, touchless experiences" (European Union, 2020).
- ROBOT TOUCH—Researchers Hoffmann and Kramer (2021) have been developing different kinds of robot touch and testing the degree to which robot touch can meet the touch needs of humans. Since interpersonal touch research has demonstrated that touch has several positive behavioural (e.g., reduced stress, better immune functioning) as well as evaluative consequences (e.g., better evaluation of the initiator of touch), the question arises whether touch from a humanoid robot, the body of which is somewhat similar to that of a human, can evoke similar effects. Previous research on robot touch suggests that it can reduce loneliness in elderly people, provide comforting touch for patients in hospitals, and fulfil similar emotional needs of human touch.

References

Afifi, W. A., & Johnson, M. L. (1999). The use and interpretation of tie signs in a public setting: Relationship and sex differences. *Journal of Social and Personal Relationships, 16*, 9–38.

Andersen, P. A., & Leibowitz, K. (1978). The development and nature of the construct touch avoidance. *Environmental Psychology and Nonverbal Behavior, 3*, 89–106.

Argyle, M. (1975). *Bodily communication*. Methuen.

Asbury, K., Fox, L., Deiz, E., Code, A., & Toseeb, T. (2021). How is COVID-19 affecting the mental health of children with special educational needs and disabilities and their families. *Journal of Autism and Developmental Disorders, 51*, 1772–1780. https://doi.org/10.1007/s10803-020-04577-2

Bartholomew, K. (1990). Avoidance of intimacy: An attachment perspective. *Journal of Social and Personal Relationships, 7*, 147–178.

Bartholomew, K., & Horowitz, L. M. (1991). Attachment styles among young adults: A test of a four-category model. *Journal of Personality and Social Psychology, 61*, 226–244.

Bebler, R., Bendas, J., Sailer, U., & Croy, I. (2019). The "Longing for Interpersonal Touch Picture Questionnaire": Development of a new measurement for touch perception. *International Journal of Psychiatry, 55*(3), 446–455. https://doi.org/10.1002/ijop.12616

Becker-Stoll, F., Delius, A., & Scheitenberger, S. (2001). Adolescents' nonverbal emotional expressions during negotiation of a disagreement with their mothers: An attachment approach. *International Journal of Behavioral Development, 25*, 344–353.

Berman, P. W., & Smith, V. L. (1984). Gender and situational differences in children's smiles, touch, and proxemics. *Sex Roles, 10*, 347–356.

Boers, E., Afzali, M. H., & Newton, N. (2019). Association of screen time and depression in adolescence. *JAMA Pediatrics*, 173, 853–859.

Bohn, J. K., & Hendricks, B. (1997). Effects of interpersonal touch, degree of justification, and sex of participant on compliance with a request. *The Journal of Social Psychology*, 4, 460–469. https://doi.org/10.1080/00224549709595462

Bowlby, J. (1973). *Attachment and loss: Separation, anxiety and anger*. Basic Books.

Bowlby, J. (1980). *Attachment and loss: Sadness and depression*. Basic Books.

Bullis, C., & Horn, C. (1995). Get a little closer: Further examination of nonverbal comforting strategies. *Communication Reports, 8*, 10–17.

Chapell, M. S., & Beltran, W. (1999). Men and women holding hands II: Whose hand is uppermost? *Perceptual and Motor Skills, 89*, 537–549.

Chaplin, W. F., Phillips, J. B., Brown, J. D., Clanton, N. R., & Stein, J. L. (2000). Handshaking, gender, personality, and first impressions. *Journal of Personality and Social Psychology, 19*, 110–117.

Clark, H. (2020, October). The power of touch. *Community Practitioner*, 48–49.

Clements-Cortes, A. (2020). The impact of COVID-19 on children and educators. *Canadian Music Educator, 50*.

Cohen, S., Janicki-Deverts, D., Turner, R. B., & Doyle, W. J. (2015). Does hugging provide stress-buffering social support? A study of susceptibility to upper respiratory infection and illness. *Psychological Science, 26*, 135–147.

Crusco, A. H., & Wetzel, C. G. (1984). The Midas touch: The effects of interpersonal touch on restaurant tipping. *Personality and Social Psychology Bulletin, 10*, 512–517.

Debrot, A., Shoebi, D., Perrez, M., & Horn, A.B. (2013). Touch as an interpersonal emotion regulation process in couples' daily lives: The mediating role of psychological intimacy. *Personality and Social Psychology Bulletin, 39*, 1373–1385.

Derlega, V. J., Lewis, R. J., Harrison, S., Winstead, B. A., & Costanzo, R. (1989). Gender differences in the initiation and attribution of tactile intimacy. *Journal of Nonverbal Behavior, 13*, 83–96.

Dibiase, R., & Gunnoe, J. (2004). Gender and culture differences in touching behavior. *The Journal of Social Psychology, 144*, 49–62.

Dodgen-Magee, D. (2020, April 28). Physical touch in the time of COVID-19: Physical distancing has reduced our ability to touch. Here's how to help. *Psychology Today*. https://www.psychologytoday.com/us/blog/deviced/202004/physical-touch-in-the-time-covid-19

Dolin, D. J., & Booth-Butterfield, M. (1993). Reach out and touch someone: Analysis of nonverbal comforting responses. *Communication Quarterly, 41*, 383–393.

Dolinski, D. (2010). Touch, compliance, and homophobia. *Journal of Nonverbal Behavior, 34*, 179–192.

Editorial. (2019). Screen time, social media and developing brains: A cause for good or corrupting young minds? *Child and Adolescent Mental Health, 24*(3), 203–204. https://doi.org/10.1111/camh.12346

Editorial. (2020). Touch in times of COVID-19: Touch hunger hurts. *Journal of Clinical Nursing, 30*, e4–e5. https://doi.org/10.1111/jocn.15488

Ellingsen, D., Wessberg, J., Chelnokova, O., Olausson, H., Laeng, B., & Leknes, S. (2014). In touch with your emotions: Oxytocin and touch change social impressions while others' facial expressions can alter touch. *Psychoneuroendo—crinology, 39*, 11–20.

European Union. (2021, January 22). *A new research fights against touch deprivation.* https://ec.europa.eu/programmes/horizon2020/en/news/new-research-fights-against-touch-deprivation

Feeney, B. C., & Collins, N. L. (2001). Predictors of caregiving in adult intimate relationships: An attachment theoretical perspective. *Journal of Personality and Social Psychology, 80*, 972–994.

Field, T. (1999). American adolescents touch each other less and are more aggressive toward their peers as compared with French adolescents. *Adolescence, 34*, 753–758.

Field, T. (2014). *Touch*. MIT Press.

Fisher, H. (1992). *Anatomy of love*. Fawcett- Columbine.

Floyd, K. (1999). All touches are not created equal: Effects of form and duration on observers' interpretations of an embrace. *Journal of Nonverbal Behavior, 23*, 283–299.

Floyd, K. (2000). Affectionate same-sex touch: The influence of homophobia on observers' perceptions. *Journal of Social Psychology, 140*, 774–788.

Goleman, D. (2006). *Social intelligence: The new science of human relationships*. Bantam Books.

Guéguen, N. (2007). Courtship compliance: The effect of touch on women's behavior. *Social Influence, 2*, 81–97.

Guéguen, N., & Fischer-Lokou, J. (2002). An evaluation of touch on a large request: A field setting. *Psychological Reports, 90*, 267–269.

Guéguen, N., & Fischer-Lokou, J. (2003). Tactile contact and spontaneous help: An evaluation in a natural Setting, *The Journal of Social Psychology, 143*(6), 785–787, https://doi.org/10.1080/00224540309600431

Guerrero, L. K. (1996). Attachment-style differences in intimacy and involvement: A test of the four-category model. *Communication Monographs, 63*, 269–292.

Guerrero, L. K., & Andersen, P. A. (1991). The waxing and waning of relational intimacy: Touch as a function of relational stage, gender, and touch avoidance. *Journal of Social and Personal Relationships, 8*, 147–165.

Guerrero, L. K., & Andersen, P. A. (1994). Patterns of matching and initiation: Touch behavior and touch avoidance across romantic relationship stages. *Journal of Nonverbal Behavior, 18*, 137–153.

Hall, E. T. (1959). *The silent language*. Anchor/Doubleday.

Hall, E. T. (1966). *The hidden dimension*. Anchor/Doubleday.

Hall, J. A. (1984). *Nonverbal sex differences: Communication accuracy and expressive style*. Johns Hopkins University Press.
Hall, J. A., & Veccia, E. M. (1990). More "touching" observations: New insights on men, women, and interpersonal touch. *Journal of Personality and Social Psychology, 59*, 1155–1162.
Henley, N. M. (1973). Status and sex: Some touching observations. *Bulletin of the Psychonomic Society, 2*, 91–93.
Henley, N. M. (1977). *Body politics: Power, sex, and nonverbal communication*. Prentice Hall.
Henley, N. M. (1995). Body politics revisited: What do we know today? In P. J. Kalbfleisch & M. J. Cody (Eds.), *Gender, power, and communication in human relationships* (pp. 27–62). Lawrence Erlbaum.
Hertenstein, M., Keltner, D., App, B., Bulleit, B., & Jaskolka, A. (2006). Touch communicates distinct emotions. *Emotion, 6*, 528–533.
Heslin, R. (1974). *Steps toward a taxonomy of touching*. Paper presented at the annual convention of the Midwestern Psychological Association, Chicago.
Heslin, R., & Alper, T. (1983). Touch: A bonding gesture. In J. M. Weimann & R. P. Harrison (Eds.), *Nonverbal interaction* (pp. 47–75). SAGE.
Heslin, R., Nguyen, T. D., & Nguyen, M. L. (1983). Meaning of touch: The case of touch from a stranger or same-sex person. *Journal of Nonverbal Behavior, 7*, 147–157.
Hoffmann, L., & Kramer, N. C. (2021). The persuasive power of robot touch. Behavioral and evaluative consequences of non-functional touch from a robot. *PLoS One, 16*(5), e0249554. https://doi.org/10.1371/journal.pone.0249554
Jan, S. (2007, April 16). *Pakistan tourism minister fears for her life after clerics say she sinned by hugging man*. https://www.seattletimes.com/life/travel/pakistan-tourism-minister-fears-for-her-life-after-clerics-say-she-sinned-by-hugging-man/
Jones, S. E. (1994). *The right touch: Understanding and using the language of physical contact*. Hampton Press.
Jones, S. E., & Yarbrough, A. E. (1985). A naturalistic study of the meanings of touch. *Communication Monographs, 52*, 19–56.
Kaitz, M., Bar-Haim, Y., Lehrer, M., & Grossman, E. (2004). Adult attachment style and interpersonal distance. *Attachment and Human Development, 6*, 285–303.
Kreuder, A., Scheele, D., Wassermann, M., Wollseifer, M., et al. (2017). How the brain codes intimacy: The neurobiological substrates of romantic touch. *Human Brain Mapping, 38*, 4525–4534.

Kreuder, A., Wasserman, L., Wollseifer, M., Ditzen, B., et al. (2018). Oxytocin enhances the pain-relieving effects of social support in romantic couples. *Human Brain Mapping, 40*, 242–251.

Kutok, E. (2020, August 7). *Social distancing vs. social media: Can social media mitigate the effects of social deprivation in adolescents?* Brown Medical School. https://digitalhealth.med.brown.edu/news/2020-08-07/social-distancing-social-media

Major, B., & Heslin, R. (1982). Perceptions of cross-sex and same-sex nonreciprocal touch: It is better to give than to receive. *Journal of Nonverbal Behavior, 6*, 148–162.

McDaniel, E., & Andersen, P. A. (1998). International patterns of interpersonal tactile communication: A field study. *Journal of Nonverbal Behavior, 22*, 59–75.

Mehta-Lee, S. S. (2020). Touch in the era of coronavirus pandemic. *BJOG, 127*, 1053–1054.

Montagu, A. (1986). *Touching: The human significance of the skin* (2nd ed.). Harper & Row.

Morris, D. (1977). *Manwatching: A field guide to human behavior*. Harry N. Abrahms.

Morris, D. (1994). Body talk: The meaning of human gestures. Crown.

Nannberg, J. C., & Hansen, C. H. (1994). Post compliance touch: An incentive for task performance. *Journal of Social Psychology, 134*, 301–307.

Naruse, S. M., & Moss, M. (2021). Positive massage: An intervention for couples' wellbeing in a touch-deprived era. *European Journal of Investigation in Health, Psychology and Education, 11*, 450–467. https://doi.org/10.3390/ejihpe11020033

Navy Issues Warning on the Dangers of Hugging. (2002, May 25). *The Dominion* (Wellington), p. 6.

Nguyen, M. L., Heslin, R., & Nguyen, T. (1975). The meaning of touch: Sex differences. *Journal of Communication, 25*, 92–103.

Nielsen. (2018). *Time flies: U.S. adults now spend nearly half a day interacting with media.* Retrieved November 15, 2018, from https://www.nielsen.com/us/en/insights/news/2018/time-flies-us-adults-now-spend-nearly-half-a-day-interacting-with-media.print.html

No Hugging or Kissing—They're Counsellors. (2002, May 16). *The Straits Times* (Singapore), p. 15.

Noller, P. (2006). Nonverbal communication in close relationships. In V. Manusov & M. L. Patterson (Eds.), *The Sage Handbook of Nonverbal Communication* (pp. 403–420). Sage.

Ognibene, T. C., & Collins, N. L. (1998). Adult attachment styles, perceived social support, and coping strategies. *Journal of Social and Personal Relationships, 15*, 323–345.

Park, W. (2020, July 7). Why human touch is so hard to replace. *BBC.com*. https://www.bbc.com/future/article/20200706-why-human-touch-is-so-hard-to-replace

Petry, S. E., Hughes, D., & Galanos, A. (2021). Grief: The epidemic within an epidemic. *American Journal of Hospice & Palliative Medicine, 38*(4), 419–422. https://doi.org/10.1177/1049909120978796

Pierce, S. (2020, May 15). *Touch starvation is a consequence of COVID-19's physical distancing*. https://www.tmc.edu/news/2020/05/touch-starvation/

Regan, P. C., Jerry, D., Marysia, N., & Johnson, D. (1999). Public displays of affection among Asian and Latino heterosexual couples. *Psychological Reports, 84*, 1201–1202.

Remland, M. S. (2017). *Nonverbal communication in everyday life*. Thousand Oaks, CA: Sage.

Remland, M. S., & Jones, T. S. (1994). The influence of vocal intensity and touch on compliance gaining. *Journal of Social Psychology, 134*, 89–97.

Remland, M. S., Jones, T. S., & Brinkman, H. (1991). Proxemic and haptic behavior in three European countries. *Journal of Nonverbal Behavior, 15*, 215–232.

Remland, M. S., Jones, T. S., & Brinkman, H. (1995). Interpersonal distance, body orientation, and touch: Effects of culture, gender, and age. *Journal of Social Psychology, 135*, 281–298.

Remland, M. S., Jones, T. S., & Brinkman, H. (1999). *Use of touch as a function of culture*. Unpublished manuscript, West Chester University, West Chester, Pennsylvania.

Robinson, S. (2007, April 17). *Richard Gere's scandalous smooch*. http://content.time.com/time/world/article/0,8599,1611428,00.html

Roese, N. J., Olson, J. M., Borenstein, M. N., Martin, A., & Shores, A. L. (1992). Same- sex touching behavior: The moderating role of homophobic attitudes. *Journal of Nonverbal Behavior, 16*, 249–260.

Schachner, D., Shaver, P. R., & Mikulincer, M. (2005). Patterns of nonverbal behavior and sensitivity in the context of attachment relations. *Journal of Nonverbal Behavior, 29*, 141–169.

Segrin, C. (1993). The effects of nonverbal behavior on outcomes of compliance gaining attempts. *Communication Studies, 44*, 169–187.

Sharma, D. (2020). Losing the 'touch'. *Indian Journal of Surgery, 82*(6), 1316. https://doi.org/10.1007/s12262-020-02629-6

Sigley, I. (2020). It has touched us all: Commentary on the social implications of touch during then COVID-19 pandemic. *Social Sciences & Humanities Open, 2*(1), 100051. https://doi.org/10.1016/j.ssaho.2020.100051

Smith, A., & Anderson, M. (2018). *Social media use in 2018.* Pew Internet Research Center. Retrieved November 15, 2018 from http://www.pewinternet.org/2018/03/01/social-media-use-in-2018/

Smith, C. J., & Bilbo, S. D. (2021). Sickness and the social brain: Love in the time of COVID. *Frontiers in Psychiatry, 12*, 633–664. https://doi.org/10.3389/fpsyt.2021.633664

Thomas, P. A., & Kim, S. (2021). *Journals of Gerontology: Social Sciences, 76*, e111–e115.

Tucker, J. S., & Anders, S. L. (1998). Adult attachment style and nonverbal closeness in dating couples. *Journal of Nonverbal Behavior, 22*, 89–107.

Undersheriff Fired for Hugging. (1999, December 18). *Rocky Mountain News*, p. 7A.

Upenieks, L., & Schafer, M. H. (2021). Keeping "in touch": Demographic patterns of interpersonal touch in later life. *Research on Aging, 44*, 22–33.

von Mohr, M., Kirsch, L. P., & Fotopoulou, A. (2021). Social touch deprivation during COVID-19: Effects on psychological wellbeing and craving interpersonal touch. *Royal Society of Open Science, 8*, 210287. https://doi.org/10.1098/rsos.210287

Willis, F. N., & Briggs, L. F. (1992). Relationship and touch in public settings. *Journal of Nonverbal Behavior, 16*, 55–63.

Willis, F., & Dodd, R. (1998). Age, relationship, and touch initiation. *The Journal of Social Psychology, 136*, 115–123.

Willis, F. N., & Rawdon, V. A. (1994). Gender and national differences in attitudes toward same-gender touch. *Perceptual and Motor Skills, 78*, 1027–1034. https://doi.org/10.1177/003151259407800364

Willis, F. N., & Reeves, D. L. (1976). Touch interactions in junior high students in relation to sex and race. *Developmental Psychology, 12*, 91–92.

Yukawa, S., Tokuda, H., & Sato, J. (2007). Attachment style, self- concealment, and interpersonal distance among Japanese undergraduates. *Perceptual and Motor Skills, 104*, 1255–1261.

13

Nonverbal Skills in Relationships: Too Little or Too Much May Be a Bad Thing

Ronald E. Riggio and Alan Crawley

There is little doubt that possession of skills in nonverbal communication is a good thing. Even casual observation of people in social settings suggests that there are vast individual differences in people's abilities to communicate nonverbally. As social animals, we use nonverbal communication skills in our everyday lives to establish social relationships with others, to strengthen and maintain those relationships, and to form social groups in order to accomplish the tasks of daily living (Friedman, 1979; Guerrero & Floyd, 2006). There is a general assumption that when it comes to nonverbal skill, more is better. Possessing more of a particular skill in nonverbal communication seems to be a good thing; however, we argue in this chapter that possessing too much of a particular nonverbal skill may not always be advantageous. For example, if someone is

R. E. Riggio (✉)
Kravis Leadership Institute, Claremont McKenna College, Claremont, CA, USA
e-mail: Ronald.Riggio@claremontmckenna.edu

A. Crawley
Universidad del Salvador, Buenos Aires, Argentina

R. J. Sternberg, A. Kostić (eds.), *Nonverbal Communication in Close Relationships*,
https://doi.org/10.1007/978-3-030-94492-6_13

exceptionally skilled in emotional decoding skill, they may become overwhelmed by others' emotional expressions—experiencing what is called the *emotional contagion* process of vicariously experiencing the same emotion that the other person is expressing. You cry, and it makes me cry. We intend to explore the complex relationships among the various dimensions of nonverbal skill.

This idea that *both* too little or too much of an individual characteristic is not unique to skills in nonverbal communication. Aristotle (Ameriks & Clarke, 2000), in discussing possession of cardinal virtues, argued that possessing too much or too little of a virtue was problematic. For example, regarding courage, Aristotle claimed that too little courage led to cowardice, while too much courage made an individual reckless and foolhardy. More recently, psychologists have begun to argue that personality traits may also have curvilinear (inverted-U) relationships with important outcomes such as social behavior and well-being—the "too much of a good thing" phenomenon (Grant & Schwartz, 2011; Pierce & Aguinis, 2013). Of course, it may be even more complicated than just the curvilinear relationship for possession of a particular nonverbal skill, because these skills interact with one another, creating very complex interactions affecting social behavior and interpersonal relationships, as we will see.

Nonverbal/Emotional Skills: A Model

Much of the research on nonverbal skill focuses on particular skills, such as nonverbal decoding skill/nonverbal sensitivity (Hall & Bernieri, 2001; Hall et al., 2016; Schmid Mast & Hall, 2018), emotional/nonverbal encoding skill (Buck et al., 1980; Buck & Powers, 2013), skill in successful deception (Riggio et al., 1987; Feldman et al., 1999), or ability to regulate and control emotional expressions (Friedman & Miller-Herringer, 1991; Chervonsky & Hunt, 2017). Riggio and colleagues (Riggio, 1986; Riggio & Carney, 2003) attempted to construct a basic model for conceptualizing and assessing basic skills in nonverbal communication, consisting of skill in decoding, encoding, and regulating nonverbal/emotional skills within the larger Social Skills Model (Riggio, 2006). In essence, this model argues that these three basic skills represent the core of interpersonal communication at the emotional/nonverbal level. These are some of the important skill "building blocks" of initiating and maintaining interpersonal relationships.

Nonverbal/Emotional sensitivity is the term given to basic ability to decode and identify nonverbal cues of emotion, but also decoding of cues of dominance, positivity-negativity, personality traits, group membership, and the like. A great deal of research has been conducted on nonverbal sensitivity, with at least one entire volume dedicated to its role in interpersonal relationships (Hall & Bernieri, 2001), as well as a book covering the various forms of nonverbal sensitivity (Hall et al., 2016). This ability to decode nonverbal and emotional messages sent by others is a core element of conceptualizations of emotional intelligence (see Elfenbein et al., 2002; Riggio, 2010). Nonverbal sensitivity is a key component of the ability to be empathic, for it is necessary that an individual recognize and accurately decode another's emotional state in order to empathize.

Nonverbal/Emotional Expressiveness The flip side of emotional decoding is emotional encoding skill, or the ability to easily and accurately express emotions and other nonverbal cues to others. Emotional expressiveness includes both the ability to pose clear emotional expressions on cue, as well as to be spontaneously expressive (Friedman et al., 1980). Nonverbal expressiveness is particularly important in initiating high-quality social interactions because it allows for an early emotional "connection" with others. Research on emotional expressiveness suggests that it is related to making a more positive impression on strangers (Friedman et al., 1988), having larger social networks (Riggio, 1986), and experiencing less social anxiety and loneliness (Riggio et al., 1990). Nonverbal/ Emotional Control Ability to regulate and control emotional displays is the third basic nonverbal/emotional skill. Emotional control comes into play in stifling unwanted emotional expressions and assists, along with emotional expressiveness, in posing specific emotions. Emotional control, for example, allows the individual to not express a negative emotion and to cover that felt emotion with a different emotional mask. An example would be covering felt anger with a pleasant, smiling face. Emotional regulation and control is a complex process, and there are clear individual differences in this ability (John & Gross, 2007). In addition to the nonverbal/emotional skills, the Social Skills Model also outlines their verbal/social counterparts—ability to express oneself verbally in social interaction, skill in decoding verbal messages and social situations, and controlling one's social behavior. For the purposes of our discussion, however, we will focus exclusively on the nonverbal/emotional skills in the model.

Measuring Nonverbal/Emotional Skills

Ideally, the best way to measure possession of emotional skills is through performance-based methods. For example, to assess emotional sensitivity/decoding skill, respondents are presented with photos or videoclips of actors expressing specific emotions and a decoding score is derived from the number of emotions that are correctly identified. Three such early measures of nonverbal decoding skill are the Profile of Nonverbal Sensitivity (PONS; Rosenthal et al., 1979), the Communication of Affect Receiving Ability Test (Buck, 1976), and the Diagnostic Analysis of Nonverbal Accuracy (DANVA; Nowicki & Duke, 1994). To assess nonverbal/emotional encoding skill, respondents are videotaped while expressing specific emotions. These clips are then shown to judges who try to determine the emotions being enacted. A score is determined based on how accurately the judges are able to detect the posed emotions. Another measurement strategy is to have trained judges observe and assess someone's nonverbal skill. An obvious drawback to both performance-based and observational measures of nonverbal skill is the amount of time and cost involved in obtaining these assessments.

A more convenient strategy for measuring nonverbal skill is the use of self-report measures. These assessments require individuals to report on their ability to communicate via different nonverbal channels, and/or report on their skill-related social behaviors (e.g., reporting on whether people can read their emotions, or whether they can decode others' emotions easily). The nonverbal/emotional skill model that was just presented typically uses the Social Skills Inventory (SSI; Riggio & Carney, 2003) to assess the three core skills. The SSI items ask respondents to report on their success using various nonverbal and emotional cues in social interaction, and has been well-validated. Of course, there are the usual limitations of self-report methodology, which include self-enhancement biases and the like.

Certain nonverbal skills are very difficult to assess through performance-based or observational measures and thus require the use of self-report methodology. For example, measuring emotional control/regulation is very difficult because it requires knowing whether a person is actively inhibiting their reactions to, and expression of, emotions. As a result, emotional regulation and control is routinely measured via self-reports (e.g., Gross & John, 2003; Riggio, 1986). For the reader interested in the assessment of nonverbal skills and nonverbal behaviors more generally, there is a terrific sourcebook of nonverbal measures (Manusov, 2005).

The Role of Emotional/Nonverbal Skills in the Formation and Maintenance of Interpersonal Relationships

Initial Encounters and Relationship Formation

Typically, in our culture, personal relationships only develop because some form of attraction occurs to bring people together. It may be common interests, a common purpose, or simply liking that pulls us together in a relationship. Furthermore, much of the formation of a new personal relationship takes place via nonverbal channels—we like the way a person looks or behaves and we engage in conversations that are full of both verbal and nonverbal cues. In short, when it comes to the formation of interpersonal relationships, possession of nonverbal skills is particularly important.

Persons who are high on nonverbal/emotional sensitivity are open to connecting with other people and they are empathic. As a result, it is no surprise that there is a consistent, positive correlation between emotional sensitivity and the size and depth of one's social network (Riggio, 1986). Related to emotional sensitivity is the construct of *empathic accuracy*, which is defined as the ability to read others' feelings and thoughts (Ickes, 1997). There is some speculation that more sensitive and empathically accurate individuals may play an important role in deciding whether or not an initial encounter with a stranger should move forward into the development of a relationship (Colvin et al., 1997).

There is quite a bit of research which suggests that emotional expressiveness is particularly advantageous in the formation of new relationships. Emotionally expressive persons tend to make positive first impressions and are judged as more likable in initial encounters (Friedman et al., 1988; Gallaher, 1992). Why is nonverbal expressiveness so impactful even in brief, initial encounters? There is evidence that nonverbal expressiveness is related to appearing more attractive to others (Riggio et al., 1991) and expressive people tend to engage in more intimate greetings and initial conversations in first encounters (Riggio et al., 1981).

Emotional control and regulation of emotions are critical skills primarily in established relationships, but can also come into play during initial encounters and in the development of interpersonal relationships. For example, skill in controlling negative emotions is particularly important. Expressions of irritation or anger can interfere with relationship development ("s/he's a hothead"), although expression of sadness might stimulate an empathic response in another person.

Emotional Skills in Friendships and Romantic Relationships

Emotional skills are particularly important as relationships deepen, and they play a major role in the maintenance of both friendships and romantic relationships (Guerrero & Floyd, 2006). For example, expressive skill allows partners to share felt emotions. It is this emotional communication that deepens relationships.

There is considerable evidence that expression of positive emotions (joy, happiness, affection) serves to strengthen relationships. This is particularly true in romantic relationships. A study of married couples found that more satisfied couples expressed more positive emotions than did dissatisfied couples (Karney & Bradbury, 1995). On the other hand, expression of negative emotions, particularly anger, disgust, and disliking, can tear a relationship apart. Gottman (1994) found that when in conflict situations, romantic couples who expressed more positive than negative expressions were more likely to stay together. In these "happy" marriages, the ratio of positive to negative expressions was 5-to-1. Unhappy couples expressed a 1-to-1 ratio of positive to negative expressions.

Emotional sensitivity is also critical for maintaining close relationships. For example, Maatta and Uusiautti (2013) suggest that the accuracy, speed, and efficiency by which partners decode the other's emotional states is key to a quality relationship. Noller (1980) found that husbands with poor nonverbal decoding skills were more likely to be in distressed marriages, perhaps due to husbands' inability to read their partners' emotions (although the causal direction is unclear).

In friendships, there is evidence that ability of friends to detect the other's subtle facial expressions of emotion differentiated close friends from acquaintances (Parmley & Zhang, 2015). Moreover, emotionally sensitive individuals reported that their social networks provided more social support during stressful times—likely because they are reciprocating their friend's empathy when they are distressed (Riggio & Zimmerman, 1991).

It is important to note that women score higher, on average, in possession of skill in both emotional expressiveness and sensitivity. For example, in married couples, wives display more emotions—and particularly more positive emotions—than do husbands (Guerrero & Floyd, 2006). However, when husbands are more accurate in decoding their wives' emotions, there is higher relationship satisfaction (e.g., Koerner & Fitzpatrick, 2002).

The role of emotional control in relationships is also important, although it is complicated. While women tend to possess greater emotional expressiveness and sensitivity, men tend to score higher on emotional control. Emotional control is critical in regulating the expression of emotions—particularly negative emotions. It also is associated with ability to cover up felt emotional states, often by expressing neutral affect, or posing a different emotional expression (e.g., "putting on a happy face" to cover irritation or sadness). Indeed, Buck and Powers (2013) have argued that appropriate control over emotional displays is necessary for effective and healthy social functioning. Emotional control is a particular advantage when a relationship is experiencing stress or emotional volatility, but it can also lead to perceptions that the emotionally controlled individual is distant and uncaring (Shaver & Mikulincer, 2007). We will explore this potential downside in more depth later in this chapter.

Emotional Skills and Relationships at Work

There are many and varied relationships that occur in the workplace—relationships between coworkers, with supervisors/leaders, with customers/clients, and with outside stakeholders (e.g., suppliers, vendors). Emotional skills facilitate the formation and maintenance of these relationships, and because coordinating and collaborating with other persons at work is so important, can lead to improved work performance. For example, there is a great deal of research which suggests that emotional sensitivity leads in predictable ways to higher performance. Research on salespeople suggest that nonverbal emotion recognition is associated with greater sales (Byron et al., 2007). Supervisors who are more emotionally sensitive receive higher performance ratings (Byron, 2007; Hall & Halberstadt, 1994). Physicians who are more accurate at reading the emotional states of their patients attract more patients and receive higher evaluations from their patients (DiMatteo et al., 1979). Emotional sensitivity is also critically important for leaders in order for them to sense when organizational members are distressed in order to take action (Rubin et al., 2005; also see Riggio, 2014, for a review).

Emotional expressiveness is also associated with workplace success. For instance, there are consistent relationships between emotional expressiveness and salesmanship (Friedman et al., 1980; Riggio, 1986). Emotional expressiveness is particularly important for effective leadership in organizations (and politics). Emotional expressiveness is a key component of charismatic leadership (Awamleh & Gardner, 1999; Bass & Riggio, 2006). Leaders use emotional encoding/expressiveness as a way of inspiring and motivating organizational members (see Darioly & Schmid Mast, 2014, for a review).

Likewise, control and regulation of emotions is critically important for success in the workplace, and particularly for leaders. Emotional outbursts in the workplace can lead to poor performance evaluations and can damage relationships at work. Leaders, under conditions of crisis or stress, need to control their emotions and appear calm and collected in order to avoid increasing the anxiety level of organizational members. Riggio (2005) reviews the myriad ways that nonverbal communication skill come into play in business settings, including such critical interactions as job interviews, performance evaluations, coaching sessions, and virtual/online interactions.

Nonverbal Skill Deficits and Relationships

Given that much of the evidence that we have presented for possession of nonverbal skills suggests that more skill is better, it makes sense that possessing emotional-skill deficits is problematic. For example, difficulty in decoding a partner's emotions (as expressed by empathic accuracy) is associated with greater levels of psychological and physical aggression in couples (Cohen et al., 2015). Exploring this further, Schweinle and Ickes (2007) suggest that men who aggress against their partners may be misreading emotional cues and infer that they are being criticized or rejected by their partners. In short, deficits in nonverbal decoding skill lead to a person having difficulties in deepening existing relationships because of the person's inability to empathize and make an emotional connection.

Lack of nonverbal/emotional expressiveness can also affect relationships as the unexpressive person may have difficulties in initiating interpersonal relationships. For example, in a study of initial encounters, strangers who scored low on nonverbal expressiveness were rated as less likable by their partners (Friedman et al., 1988). Moreover, in a study of lonely individuals, it was found that there was an inability to return positive emotions to another (inability to smile when the partner smiles), but not in returning expressions of negative emotions (Arnold et al., 2019). In intimate relationships, lack of expressiveness can make an individual seem cold, distant, and unfeeling. There may be little sharing of emotions, combined with lack of emotional decoding skill; it is extremely difficult for low-skilled persons to have the necessary level of emotional communication in order to keep a romantic relationship flourishing.

Inability to regulate and control emotional expressions can be problematic in relationships as the partner expresses feelings that might best be regulated. This is particularly true as inability to control the expression of negative emotions, which can put a great deal of stress on a relationship. For example, expression of contempt, a strong emotion of dislike, is related to incidence of divorce in married couples (Carrère et al., 2000). Indeed, a lack of expressive control may lead to an individual appearing emotionally "needy" and tax a partner's resources for dealing with the other's ongoing emotions. John and Gross (2004) argue that emotional regulation and ability to suppress negative emotions is critical to healthy social functioning. Indeed, Perez and Riggio (2003) argue that persons with certain psychopathological disorders lack specific nonverbal and emotional skills.

Nonverbal Skill Deficits in the Workplace

When it comes to nonverbal skills, relationships at work are just like any other relationships—possession of nonverbal skills is a distinct advantage. Inability to decode the subtle nonverbal cues of others in the workplace can lead to decreased performance, particularly in areas where one's job requires attentiveness to the emotional reactions of others, such as in sales, customer service, and positions of leadership (see DePaulo, 1992). For example, it has been argued that success in sales requires sensitivity to meet a customer's needs and concerns, in what is labeled *adaptive selling* (Spiro & Weitz, 1990).

Lack of nonverbal expressiveness is another job-related disadvantage. In fact, research shows that more expressive, outgoing persons receive more favorable evaluations in hiring interviews, so lack of emotional expressiveness may even be a barrier to employment (Riggio & Throckmorton, 1988). Persons in a supervisory or leadership position often use nonverbal expressiveness to show who is in charge (cues of dominance), and to motivate and inspire team members (see Riggio, 2014), so lack of expressiveness could handicap leaders.

In a similar vein, inability to control and regulate nonverbal and emotional cues is also problematic for leaders, particularly in crisis situations. Leaders need to dampen the expression of negative emotions—keeping a "cool head" under stressful circumstances, or when dealing with emotionally charged situations, such as when disciplining employees.

Another workplace situation that requires emotional control and regulation is outlined in the research on *emotional labor*, which is the ability to control emotional expressions in jobs that require serving the public, particularly under stressful circumstances, such as customer service, healthcare, and law enforcement (Grandey, 2000). Emotional control (coupled with emotional expressiveness) allows the worker to display positive emotions even when feeling negative emotions such as anger or stress.

Emotional Skill Surplus and Relationships (Too Much of a Good Thing)

This brings us to the main theme of this chapter. While there is voluminous research that suggests that possessing more nonverbal skill is beneficial for all kinds of social relationships, and skill deficits are problematic, it may also be true that too much of a particular nonverbal skill creates problems. We will explore the relevant research.

Can someone be too emotionally sensitive? Research on multiple forms of empathy suggests that a problem with emotional decoding skill is that some people may vicariously feel another's expressed emotion—the emotional contagion process mentioned earlier. Why might this be problematic? Davis (1983) maintains that there are different types of empathy, including what he terms *Empathic Concern* and *Personal Distress.* Empathic concern involves reading another's nonverbal emotional cues and expressing concern and support. Personal distress, on the other hand, creates a sympathetic experience of the other's sent emotion. You cry, it makes me cry. You laugh, I also feel happy. While there may not be a problem in vicariously experiencing another's positive emotions, negative emotions might lead to a "pity party"—both members are flooded with negative emotions. Schlegel (2020) also notes that high levels of emotional sensitivity can have both positive and negative outcomes, particularly if the relationship partners are in a negative and stressful environment. The sensitive individual can become "flooded" with negative emotions, and unless the person possesses good emotional regulation skills, this can be problematic.

Ickes (2003) also suggests that too much emotional sensitivity (based on his Empathic Accuracy Model) may create problems in relationships. For instance, knowing nearly everything that a partner is feeling or thinking might lead to the partner feeling "intruded upon," violated, and lacking a sense of privacy in regard to feelings. In married couples, too much empathic accuracy from one partner put additional strain on the relationship when the couples were undergoing a problem (Simpson et al., 2003). Likewise, too much sensitivity may lead one partner to overanalyze every emotional cue the partner emits, leading to a sort of "suspicious minds" phenomenon that could put strain on the romantic relationship (Ickes et al., 2003).

Too much sensitivity may also be problematic in the workplace. Elfenbein et al. (2002) explored this "eavesdropping effect," showing that highly sensitive workers received lower ratings from supervisors and peers, presumably because their oversensitivity to others' emotional cues led to greater interpersonal conflicts. Similar to what occurs in romantic relationships, a work colleague who is too accurate at decoding others' nonverbal cues may harm rapport with colleagues—again, too much "eavesdropping" may lead to a sense of privacy intrusion and rudeness (Pucinelli & Tickle-Degnen, 2004).

Can too much nonverbal and emotional expressiveness also cause problems? The obvious issue with possessing high levels of emotional expressiveness is that whatever emotion the individual is feeling gets immediately expressed. As a result, emotionally expressive persons are an easy emotional "read" as they "wear their hearts on their sleeve." This can be problematic in relationships as it creates an "emotionally charged" relationship. If the other partner is particularly emotionally sensitive and empathic, this could put a strain on the partner who has to always deal with the expressive person's emotional outbursts. Another issue may be that in an imbalanced relationship, with one highly expressive partner, and the other relatively inexpressive, the expressive partner may dominate the emotional aspects of the relationship. In larger social settings the overly expressive individual gets all of the emotional attention and sympathy from others.

While there is quite a bit of evidence that suggests that emotional expressiveness is an advantage in the workplace, too much expressiveness may be problematic. For example, research on salespersons suggests that expressive individuals have higher sales outcomes, but if the seller becomes too exuberant and excited customers may react negatively (Puccinelli et al., 2010). Similarly, expressive individuals have an advantage in job interviews, but too much expressiveness may lead to negative impressions. In one study, too much smiling led to lower evaluations when candidates were applying for positions in business and education. Overly expressive individuals were assumed to be too unprofessional for the job (Ruben et al., 2015). Buck and Powers (2013) suggest that overly expressive individuals may be seen as trying to be the center of attention, leading to disapproval.

While emotional control is important for dampening strong emotional expressions, too much is not a good thing. Highly controlled individuals can appear cold and emotionally distant. Butler et al. (2003) argue that emotional regulation can stifle social discourse and cause stress in the overcontrolling person, but also for the interaction partner. Some evidence exists that too much suppression of emotions not only leads to difficulty in relationships, but may be associated with lower levels of psychological well-being (Chervonsky & Hunt, 2017). Gross and John (2003) have argued that emotional suppressors—those who tend to overcontrol emotional expressions—experience and express fewer positive emotions and experience more negative emotions. There is some evidence that too much emotional control may interrupt the interactional synchrony that is so important for feeling connected to a relationship partner (Lakin, 2013). In addition, there is evidence that having too much suppression of emotional expressions somehow inhibits one's sensitivity to other's emotions (Schneider et al., 2013). In the workplace, high levels of emotional control may hamper the development of good relationships with peers. When a leader/supervisor is too high on emotional control, team members may feel that the leader is distant and emotionally unavailable.

Emotional Skill Balance and Relationships

While too much of a particular nonverbal/emotional skill may be problematic, the reality is that nonverbal skills interact in complex, and sometimes subtle, ways. For example, combine high levels of emotional control/regulation with very low levels of emotional expressiveness and the person seems emotionally unreachable—what is sometimes referred to as the "poker face" (Schneider et al., 2013). Alternatively, a highly expressive person who lacks emotional control can come on too strong and never "turn it off." Think of the late comedian, Robin Williams, who had difficulty controlling his highly emotional banter, even to the point of being unable to sit down for a structured interview.

Possessing high levels of emotional sensitivity with low levels of emotional control and expressiveness could lead a person to become flooded by others' emotional expressions, without the ability to regulate and send back one's own emotional reactions. Indeed, to be truly empathic, it may take a combination of emotional sensitivity coupled with the ability to express emotional concern back to the other party. In fact, there is evidence that skill in emotional sensitivity has a positive correlation with emotional expressiveness (Riggio, 1986).

In order to get a rough estimate of the balance among the different nonverbal/emotional skills (as well as additional social skills), the Social Skills Inventory includes an *Equilibrium Index* that calculates levels of imbalance among the various skills to provide a notice to look more closely at the combinations of the various skill dimensions for interpretation of someone's communication skill profile (see Riggio & Carney, 2003). In one study of former patients diagnosed with mental illness, the imbalance score provided by the equilibrium index correlated with reports of illness-related problems—more "imbalanced" individuals had greater levels of psychopathology (Perez et al., 2007).

Conclusions and Future Research and Practice

In summary, there is growing evidence that the relationship between possession of nonverbal/emotional skills is not necessarily linear—more of a particular skill may not necessarily be better. This is in line with research looking at extremes of personality traits, virtues, and even too much intrusive parenting behavior (e.g., Liu et al., 2019). What is suggested by our "more may not be better" hypothesis is that successful nonverbal communication in human relationships is really all about balance and regulation (but not *overregulation*) of nonverbal skills. Interestingly, a review of research on emotional intelligence has come to a similar conclusion (Davis & Nichols, 2016).

So, where do we go from here? From a research perspective, we can draw some firm conclusions. First, it is important to explore the nonlinear relationships between possession of nonverbal skills and relationship outcomes (e.g., quality of relationship, relationship continuance, etc.). If there is an optimal level of a particular nonverbal skill, we need to know what that is. Furthermore, we need to better understand how specific nonverbal skills interact with one another to produce positive (or negative) outcomes. Some combinations of nonverbal skills may be more advantageous (or disadvantageous). Finally, with the available advanced technology, we should be able to find more accurate, performance-based ways to measure possession of nonverbal skills.

It is also important to bear in mind the fact that skills in nonverbal communication are trainable—although it is not easy to develop these skills (e.g., Costanzo, 1992; Riggio & Merlin, 2011). Indeed, an entire "industry" has developed to help coach and train people to become more nonverbally and socially skilled. There has been a particular emphasis on applying these skills in the workplace, such as in job interview training, or training leaders to be more nonverbally skilled and charismatic (see Antonakis et al., 2011; Towler, 2003 for research on charisma training efficacy). These practitioner-trainers need to bear in mind the central theme that "more may not necessarily be better." An important lesson learned during the assertiveness training craze in the 1970s was that being too assertive led to perceptions of "pushiness." An important part of using nonverbal skills successfully is knowing when and how to use the skills, and knowing how to modulate them.

References

Ameriks, K., & Clarke, D. M. (2000). *Aristotle: Nicomachean ethics*. Cambridge University Press.

Antonakis, J., Fenley, M., & Liechti, S. (2011). Can charisma be taught? Tests of two interventions. *Academy of Management Learning & Education, 10*(3), 374–396.

Arnold, A. J., Winkielman, P., & Dobkins, K. (2019). Interoception and social connection. *Frontiers in Psychology, 10*, 2589.

Awamleh, R. A., & Gardner, W. L. (1999). Perceptions of leader effectiveness and charisma: The effect of vision content, delivery, and organizational performance. *The Leadership Quarterly, 10*, 345–373.

Bass, B. M., & Riggio, R. E. (2006). *Transformational leadership* (2nd ed.). Lawrence Erlbaum Associates.

Buck, R. (1976). A test of nonverbal receiving ability: Preliminary studies. *Human Communication Research, 2*, 162–171.

Buck, R., Baron, R. M., Goodman, N., & Shapiro, B. (1980). Unitization of spontaneous nonverbal behavior in the study of emotion communication. *Journal of Personality and Social Psychology, 39*(3), 522.

Buck, R. W., & Powers, S. R. (2013). Encoding and display: A developmental-interactionist model of nonverbal sending accuracy. In J. A. Hall & M. L. Knapp (Eds.), *Nonverbal communication* (pp. 403–440). De Gruyter Mouton.

Butler, E. A., Egloff, B., Wlhelm, F. H., Smith, N. C., Erickson, E. A., & Gross, J. J. (2003). The social consequences of expressive suppression. *Emotion, 3*(1), 48–67.

Byron, K. (2007). Male and female managers' ability to read emotions: Relationships with supervisor's performance ratings and subordinates' satisfaction ratings. *Journal of Occupational and Organizational Psychology, 80*(4), 713–733.

Byron, K., Terranova, S., & Nowicki, S., Jr. (2007). Nonverbal emotion recognition and salespersons: Linking ability to perceived and actual success. *Journal of Applied Social Psychology, 37*(11), 2600–2619.

Carrère, S., Buehlman, K. T., Gottman, J. M., Coan, J. A., & Ruckstuhl, L. (2000). Predicting marital stability and divorce in newlywed couples. *Journal of Family Psychology, 14*, 42–58.

Chervonsky, E., & Hunt, C. (2017). Suppression and expression of emotion in social and interpersonal outcomes: A meta-analysis. *Emotion, 17*(4), 669–683.

Cohen, S., Schulz, M. S., Liu, S. R., Halassa, M., & Waldinger, R. J. (2015). Empathic accuracy and aggression in couples: Individual and dyadic links. *Journal of Marriage and Family, 77*(3), 697–711.

Colvin, C. R., Vogt, D., & Ickes, W. (1997). Why do friends understand each other better than strangers do? In W. Ickes (Ed.), *Empathic accuracy* (pp. 169–193). Guilford.

Costanzo, M. (1992). Training students to decode verbal and nonverbal cues: Effects on confidence and performance. *Journal of Educational Psychology, 84*(3), 308–313.

Darioly, A., & Schmid Mast, M. (2014). The role of nonverbal behavior in leadership: An integrative review. In R. E. Riggio & S. J. Tan (Eds.), *Leader interpersonal and influence skills: The soft skills of leadership* (pp. 73–100). Routledge/Psychology Press.

Davis, M. H. (1983). Measuring individual differences in empathy: Evidence for a multidimensional approach. *Journal of Personality and Social Psychology, 44*(1), 113–126.

Davis, S. K., & Nichols, R. (2016). Does emotional intelligence have a "dark" side? A review of the literature. *Frontiers in Psychology, 7*.

DePaulo, P. J. (1992). Applications of nonverbal communication research in marketing and management. In R. S. Feldman (Ed.), *Applications of nonverbal behavioral theories and research* (pp. 63–87). Lawrence Erlabum Associates.

DiMatteo, M. R., Friedman, H. S., & Taranta, A. (1979). Sensitivity to bodily nonverbal communication as a factor in practitioner-patient rapport. *Journal of Nonverbal Behavior, 4*(1), 18–26.

Elfenbein, H. A., Marsh, A. A., & Ambady, N. (2002). Emotional intelligence and the recognition of emotion from facial expressions. In L. F. Barrett & P. Salovey (Eds.), *The wisdom in feeling: Psychological processes in emotional intelligence* (pp. 37–59). The Guilford Press.

Feldman, R. S., Tomasian, J. C., & Coats, E. J. (1999). Nonverbal deception abilities and adolescents' social competence: Adolescents with higher social skills are better liars. *Journal of Nonverbal Behavior, 23*(3), 237–249.

Friedman, H. S. (1979). The concept of skill in nonverbal communication: Implications for understanding social interaction. In R. Rosenthal (Ed.), *Skill in nonverbal communication* (pp. 2–27). Oelgeschlager, Gunn & Hain.

Friedman, H. S., & Miller-Herringer, T. (1991). Nonverbal display of emotion in public and in private: Self-monitoring, personality, and expressive cues. *Journal of Personality and Social Psychology, 61*(5), 766–775. https://doi.org/10.1037/0022-

Friedman, H. S., Prince, L. M., Riggio, R. E., & DiMatteo, M. R. (1980). Understanding and assessing nonverbal expressiveness: The affective communication test. *Journal of Personality and Social Psychology, 39*, 333–351.

Friedman, H. S., Riggio, R. E., & Casella, D. (1988). Nonverbal skill, personal charisma, and initial attraction. *Personality and Social Psychology Bulletin, 14*, 203–211.

Gallaher, P. E. (1992). Individual differences in nonverbal behavior: Dimensions of style. *Journal of Personality and Social Psychology, 63*(1), 133.

Gottman, J. M. (1994). *What predicts divorce? The relationship between marital processes andmarital outcomes*. Lawrence Erlbaum.

Grandey, A. A. (2000). Emotional regulation in the workplace: A new way to conceptualize emotional labor. *Journal of Occupational Health Psychology, 5*(1), 95–110.

Grant, A. M., & Schwartz, B. (2011). Too much of a good thing: The challenge and opportunity of the inverted-U. *Perspectives on Psychological Science, 6*, 61–76.

Gross, J. J., & John, O. P. (2003). Individual differences in two emotion regulation processes: Implications for affect, relationships, and well-being. *Journal of Personality and Social Psychology, 85*, 348–362.

Guerrero, L. K., & Floyd, K. (2006). *Nonverbal communication in close relationships*. Routledge.

Hall, J. A., & Bernieri, F. (Eds.). (2001). *Interpersonal sensitivity: Theory and measurement*. Lawrence Erlbaum Associates.

Hall, J. A., & Halberstadt, A. G. (1994). Subordination and sensitivity to nonverbal cues: A study of married working women. *Sex Roles, 31*(3–4), 149–165.

Hall, J. A., Mast, M. S., & West, T. V. (Eds.). (2016). *The social psychology of perceiving others accurately*. Cambridge University Press.

Ickes, W. (Ed.). (1997). *Empathic accuracy*. Guilford.

Ickes, W. (2003). *Everyday mind reading: Understanding what other people think and feel*. Prometheus.

Ickes, W., Dugosh, J. W., Simpson, J. A., & Wilson, C. L. (2003). Suspicious minds: The motive to acquire relationship-threatening information. *Personal Relationships, 10*, 131–148.

John, O. P., & Gross, J. J. (2004). Healthy and unhealthy emotion regulation: Personality processes, individual differences, and life span development. *Journal of Personality, 72*, 1301–1333.

John, O. P., & Gross, J. J. (2007). Individual differences in emotion regulation. In J. J. Gross (Ed.), *Handbook of emotion regulation* (pp. 351–372). Guilford.

Karney, B. R., & Bradbury, T. N. (1995). The longitudinal course of marital quality and stability: A review of theory, methods, and research. *Psychological Bulletin, 118*(1), 3–34.

Koerner, A. F., & Fitzpatrick, M. A. (2002). Toward a theory of family communication. *Communication Theory, 12*(1), 70–91.

Lakin, J. L. (2013). Behavioral mimicry and interpersonal synchrony. In J. A. Hall & M. L. Knapp (Eds.), *Nonverbal communication* (pp. 539–576). De Gruyter Mouton.

Liu, Z., Riggio, R. E., Day, D. V., Zheng, C., Dai, S., & Bian, Y. (2019). Leader development begins at home: Over-parenting harms adolescent leader emergence. *Journal of Applied Psychology, 104*(10), 1226–1242.

Manusov, V. (Ed.). (2005). *The sourcebook of nonverbal measures*. Lawrence Erlbaum.

Maatta, K., & Uusiautti, S. (2013). Many faces of love. Rotterdam, The Netherlands, Sense.

Noller, P. (1980). Misunderstandings in marital communication: A study of couples' nonverbal communication. *Journal of Personality and Social Psychology, 39*(6), 1135–1148.

Nowicki, S., Jr., & Duke, M. P. (1994). Individual differences in the nonverbal communication of affect: The diagnostic analysis of nonverbal accuracy scale. *Journal of Nonverbal Behavior, 18*, 9–35.

Parmley, M., & Zhang, F. (2015). Your face says it all. Closeness and perception of emotional expressions among females. *The Journal of Social Psychology, 155*(2), 127–142.

Perez, J. E., & Riggio, R. E. (2003). Nonverbal social skills and psychopathology. In P. Philippot, E. J. Coats, & R. S. Feldman (Eds.), *Nonverbal behavior in clinical settings* (pp. 17–44). Oxford University Press.

Perez, J. E., Riggio, R. E., & Kopelowicz, A. (2007). Social skill imbalances as indicators of psychopathology: An exploratory investigation. *Personality and Individual Differences, 42*, 27–36.

Pierce, J. R., & Aguinis, H. (2013). The too-much-of-a-good-thing effect in management. *Journal of Management, 39*, 313–338.

Puccinelli, N. M., Motyka, S., & Grewal, D. (2010). Can you trust a customer's expression? Insights into nonverbal communication in the retail context. *Psychology and Marketing, 27*(10), 964–988.

Pucinelli, N. M., & Tickle-Degnen, L. (2004). Knowing too much about others: Moderators of the relationship between eavesdropping and rapport in social interaction. *Journal of Nonverbal Behavior, 28*, 223–243.

Riggio, R. E. (1986). Assessment of basic social skills. *Journal of Personality and Social Psychology, 51*, 649–660.

Riggio, R. E., & Zimmerman, J. A.* (1991). Social skills and interpersonal relationships: Influences on social support and support seeking. In W.H. Jones & D. Perlman (Eds.), *Advances in personal relationships* (Vol. 2), (pp. 133–155). London: Jessica Kingsley Press.

Riggio, R. E. (2005). Business applications of nonverbal communication. In R. E. Riggio & R. S. Feldman (Eds.), *Applications of nonverbal communication research* (pp. 119–138). Lawrence Erlbaum Associates.

Riggio, R. E. (2006). Nonverbal skills and abilities. In V. Manusov & M. Patterson (Eds.), *The SAGE handbook of nonverbal communication* (pp. 79–95). Sage Press.

Riggio, R. E. (2010). Before emotional intelligence: Research on nonverbal, emotional, and social competences. *Industrial and Organizational Psychology: Perspectives on Science and Practice, 3*, 178–182.

Riggio, R. E. (2014). A social skills model for understanding the foundations of leader communication. In R. E. Riggio & S. J. Tan (Eds.), *Leader interpersonal and influence skills: The soft skills of leadership* (pp. 31–49). Routledge/Psychology Press.

Riggio, R. E., & Carney, D. C. (2003). *Manual for the social skills inventory* (2nd ed.). MindGarden.

Riggio, R. E., Friedman, H. S., & DiMatteo, M. R. (1981). Nonverbal greetings: Effects of the situation and personality. *Personality and Social Psychology Bulletin, 7*, 682–689.

Riggio, R. E., & Merlin, R. K. (2011). *Social skill training guide: A resource guide for social skill training and development*. Mindgarden.

Riggio, R. E., & Throckmorton, B. (1988). The relative effects of verbal and nonverbal behavior, appearance, and social skills on evaluations made in hiring interviews. *Journal of Applied Social Psychology, 18*, 331–348.

Riggio, R. E., Throckmorton, B., & DePaola, S. (1990). Social skills and self-esteem. *Personality and Individual Differences, 11*(8), 799–804.

Riggio, R. E., Tucker, J., & Widaman, K. F. (1987). Verbal and nonverbal cues as mediators of deception ability. *Journal of Nonverbal Behavior, 11*(3), 126–145.

Riggio, R. E., Widaman, K. F., Tucker, J. S., & Salinas, C. (1991). Beauty is more than skin deep: Components of attractiveness. *Basic and Applied Social Psychology, 12*, 423–429.

Rosenthal, R., Hall, J. A., DiMatteo, M. R., Rogers, P. L., & Archer, D. (1979). *Sensitivity to nonverbal communication: The PONS test.* Johns Hopkins University Press.

Ruben, M. A., Hall, J. A., & Schmid Mast, M. (2015). Smiling in a job interview: When less is more. *The Journal of Social Psychology, 155*(2), 107–126.

Rubin, R. S., Munz, D. C., & Bommer, W. H. (2005). Leading from within: The effects of emotion recognition and personality on transformational leadership behavior. *Academy of Management Journal, 48*, 845–858.

Schlegel, K. (2020). Inter- and intrapersonal downsides of accurately perceiving others' emotions. In R. J. Sternberg & A. Kostic (Eds.), *Social intelligence and nonverbal communication* (pp. 359–395). Palgrave Macmillan.

Schmid Mast, M., & Hall, J. A. (2018). The impact of interpersonal accuracy on behavioral outcomes. *Current Directions in Psychological Science, 27*(5), 309–314.

Schneider, K. G., Hempel, R. J., & Lynch, T. R. (2013). That "poker face" just might lose you the game! The impact of expressive suppression and mimicry on sensitivity to facial expressions of emotion. *Emotion, 13*(5), 852–866.

Schweinle, W. E., & Ickes, W. (2007). The role of men's critical/rejecting overattribution bias, affect, and attentional disengagement in marital aggression. *Journal of Social and Clinical Psychology, 26*(2), 173–198.

Shaver, P. R., & Mikulincer, M. (2007). Adult attachment strategies and the regulation of emotion. In J. J. Gross (Ed.), *Handbook of emotion regulation* (pp. 446–465). Guilford.

Simpson, J. A., Oriña, M. M., & Ickes, W. (2003). When accuracy hurts, and when it helps: A test of the empathic accuracy model in marital interactions. *Journal of Personality and Social Psychology, 85*(5), 881–893.

Spiro, R. L., & Weitz, B. A. (1990). Adaptive selling: Conceptualization, measurement and nomological validity. *Journal of Marketing Research, 27*, 61–69.

Towler, A. J. (2003). Effects of charismatic influence training on attiudes, behavior, and performance. *Personnel Psychology, 56*(2), 363–381.

14

Non-verbal Communication in Relationships as a Link between Affect and Social Intelligence

Robert J. Sternberg

All of the authors represented in this book believe in the importance of non-verbal communication in close relationships. Otherwise, they probably would not have agreed to contribute! In reading the chapters, I have asked myself whether there are points of universal agreement among them. There may be many, but here are 12 that I came up with in reading the essays:

1. Non-verbal communication is important in close relationships.
2. Non-verbal communication is not only important; often it is more important than verbal communication; when non-verbal signals belie verbal ones, people often believe the non-verbal ones over the verbal ones.

R. J. Sternberg (✉)
Department of Psychology, College of Human Ecology, Cornell University, Ithaca, NY, USA

Department of Psychology, University of Heidelberg, Heidelberg, Germany
e-mail: robert.sternberg@cornell.edu

R. J. Sternberg, A. Kostić (eds.), *Nonverbal Communication in Close Relationships*,
https://doi.org/10.1007/978-3-030-94492-6_14

3. Non-verbal communication is a language, indeed, as much a language as is expressed through verbal communication.
4. Non-verbal communication has two main aspects—encoding (transmission of signals) and decoding (receipt of non-verbal signals)—which are distinct although related abilities (or, relatedly, skill sets).
5. Non-verbal abilities have some domain-specificity. For example, one may be adept at receiving non-verbal signals in a work setting but not in a personal setting, or vice versa.
6. Non-verbal communication is often transmitted preconsciously—without conscious awareness of the signals one is transmitting.
7. Thus, much, although certainly not all of non-verbal communication is unintentional.
8. Sometimes people try to manipulate non-verbal communication to make it appear as though a signal that is intentional is unintentional (e.g., repeated glances at someone to attract their attention).
9. Non-verbal communication is transmitted through all of the senses. One can communicate non-verbally visually (e.g., gestures), of course, but also through audition (e.g., tone of voice), touch (e.g., affectionate touches), smell (e.g., bodily odours and perfuming of various kinds), and even taste (e.g., kissing).
10. Non-verbal communication often provides an indirect window to see one's own or others' internal states, as, for example, when one can see another person's blood pressure rising.
11. Mistaken interpretation of non-verbal communications can lead to serious impairments or breakup of close relationships.
12. Channels of non-verbal communication may not only contradict verbal communication; they also may contradict each other, as when tone of voice is inconsistent with facial expressions.

These 12 principles suggest that non-verbal communication, like verbal communication, can be viewed as an ability (Archer & Akert, 1977; Barnes & Sternberg, 1989; Friedman et al., 1980; Riggio et al., 1987; Rosenthal et al., 1979; Sternberg & Smith, 1985), perhaps as an aspect of social intelligence (Kihlstrom & Cantor, 2020). If that is indeed the case, it may be that non-verbal communication provides a link between skill in close relationships and the social intelligence needed to make them succeed.

The situation with non-verbal communication is even more complex than it appears to be at first.

First, non-verbal communication is not just one language, but many different languages corresponding to the different channels. Each channel uses different kinds of communicative symbols to convey messages.

Second, the situation may be even more complicated than that because, even within a channel, the communications legitimately may have different interpretations. For example, someone may smile because they enjoy making another person happy or because they make the other person miserable. The smile may be different, but then, it may not be. What the smile means can be ascertained only contextually. This, of course, also is often true for verbal communication, as when someone says, "That's just great!" The person may mean it is truly great or that it is truly terrible. The tone of voice may or may not differ between the two meanings.

In the case of close relationships, I believe my duplex theory of love is relevant to interpretation of non-verbal signals.

Duplex Theory of Love

My duplex theory of love (Sternberg, 2006, 2021) posits that love consists of stories and triangles that the stories generate.

Theory of Love As a Story

I have proposed in my work on love that all actions in all intimate relationships are filtered through stories (Sternberg, 1998b). Each story has two roles, one for each partner. The stories are formed over a period of many years and correspond to what each partner's ideal of love looks like. Stories are arranged hierarchically. Some are more preferred, others less preferred. Individuals thus have profiles of stories. Couples tend to be most satisfied when their profiles of stories match, at least, approximately, to each other (Sternberg et al., 2001).

As an example, one story is a fantasy story, where two partners view themselves as characters in a fairy tale—a prince and a princess, or a knight in shining armour and the princess to whom the knight is pledged. Another example of a story is a business story, according to which the two partners in a close relationship are like business partners enacting the roles that a relationship needs in order to transact the business of daily life, such as owning house, caring for children, paying bills, and so forth. A third example, less fortunate, is a horror story, which is a story of violence with a perpetrator and a victim. A fourth example is a travel story, in which two partners travel together through time, attempting to stay on the same path.

Social intelligence is involved in encoding and decoding of non-verbal signals for these stories.

First, one has to make the connection between the feelings one has and the signals to express it. These signals will depend upon the story one has. Signals that would communicate intense passion, for example, would differ between a fantasy (fairy-tale) story and a horror story.

Second, one has to decode the other's feelings to know what the other partner is trying to express.

Third, in both encoding and decoding, one may have to do some "translation." If the partner has a different story from one's own, then one needs to decode in a way that fits the other person's story and encode in a way that the other person will understand what you are encoding in terms of their own story. The language the partner will use will depend in part upon the story or stories that the other has. Without some translation, there may be continual misunderstandings.

Triangular Theory of Love

The triangular theory of love (Sternberg, 1998a) posits that love comprises three components: intimacy, passion, and commitment. Intimacy is a matter of closeness, caring, communication, compassion; one has a friendship. Passion is a matter of excitement, enthusiasm, and even addiction; one cannot imagine living without the partner. Commitment is a matter of a decision; one decides that one is in the relationship for good.

Each member of a couple has a triangle for the love relationship. The triangles of the two partners are not likely to be identical. Almost certainly, one partner will feel somewhat more or less intimacy, passion, and commitment than the other.

Very few people are going to say that they are deliberately changing their triangle toward their partner. That is, they are unlikely to say, "I have decided to dial down the intimacy" in our relationship, or "The passion part is over for me," or "I think we should stay together for now but let's forget the lifelong commitment part." Rather, the communication of such desires is more likely to be non-verbal, but not necessarily any less clear.

There are many ways to communicate these ideas non-verbally. With regard to intimacy, one keeps more of a distance from one's partner, or smiles less, or frowns more, or adopts a harsher tone of voice, or just speaks less, or of less consequential matters. With regard to passion, one simply becomes less available sexually, or acts more rigid or less enthusiastic during sexual communion, or stops buying surprise presents, or touches one's partner less. With regard to commitment, one may act less certain of the future, or stop wearing a wedding ring, or even have an affair or a relationship with another individual that, while not an affair, has elements of one, whether sexual or not.

Non-verbal communication can introduce an element of ambiguity that is harder to introduce when the communication is verbal. There is always an element of ambiguity, as there is no definitive dictionary of what constitutes the meaning of a particular non-verbal communication. Thus, using non-verbal communication can provide the opportunity to convey a message but at the same time retain a measure of deniability with respect to the way the message is intended to be interpreted.

Social intelligence, on the present view, is involved in encoding and decoding of signals of intimacy, passion, and commitment.

First, one may feel a certain way, but for a close relationship to succeed, one needs to be able to communicate—to *encode*—one's feelings of intimacy, passion, and commitment accurately and in a persuasive way. Two potential suitors who, in theory, felt the same way, might have unequal success with a potential mate if one of the potential suitors were better able than the other to communicate their feelings.

Second, a potential suitor would be more adaptive if they were able accurately to *decode* signals of intimacy, passion, and commitment from the potential mate so that they recognized whether that potential mate was romantically interested in them. If they discovered interest, they would know it is worthwhile to pursue the potential mate; if they discovered lack of interest, they would not waste their time.

Third, a potential suitor would likely be more successful if they could recognize from the non-verbal signals they receive from a potential mate whether the potential mate's interest, in terms of the love triangle, matches their own. If the potential suitor is looking for commitment but the potential mate is not, the suitor is better off not wasting their time on the potential mate. Or if they are looking for passion but the potential mate is not emitting non-verbal signals consistent with someone looking for passion, then the potential suitor would fare better looking elsewhere.

Application of the Duplex Theory to Non-verbal Communication

Imagine a situation of two people speaking to each other. They use similar, even often the same words, similar grammar, similar sentence structure. On the surface, they have no trouble understanding each other. But as time goes on, their relationship begins to degenerate. They are not quite sure why. They feel that they no longer are "communicating." Perhaps they try harder to communicate, but their efforts are not rewarded. They still are not communicating. Eventually, the relationship may go seriously downhill.

Why might this happen? Of course, there are many possible reasons. The two partners may believe they are speaking the same language, but they are not. From the standpoint of the essay, the most important word might be "love" and the most important declaration, "I love you." What could be simpler than that? But suppose that, instead, it was complex. Suppose that, although each partner is using the same word, "love," they mean entirely different things by the word, both in terms of its denotation, or exact meaning, and in terms of its connotation, or associated meanings. Then, over time, they might realize that something is wrong without necessarily realizing exactly what it was.

The reason they mean different things by *love* is that they have different stories of love. Each views their story not merely as a story, but rather, as what love is. So, for example, consider something as extreme as one partner hitting the other partner. What, exactly, does this non-verbal signal mean? If one has a fantasy, fairy-tale type of story, or indeed, most stories, this story would be interpreted as negative physical contact: The first partner is angry, perhaps furious at the second partner. But if the partners have a horror story, the slap might be interpreted as a sign of love. As a reader, this may sound utterly ridiculous and shameful to you. But that is the point: What one individual or couple views as obviously meaning one thing, another individual or couple may interpret as obviously meaning something else. Partners who have stories of abuse as love may view the abuse as a sign of love.

Let's take a far less extreme example. A partner goes on business trips that bring in money and support the family. On the one hand, if the other partner has a sewing and knitting story, the partner may interpret the trips as the travelling partner trying to help knit together a relationship that strengthens the fabric of the family. On the other hand, if the other partner has a police story, and the other partner is in the role of the police officer, that other partner may suspect that the travelling partner is using the trips to engage in illicit activity, whether intimate, financial, or otherwise. Of course, one does not need a police story to be suspicious. But if one has that story, the chances are elevated that one will indeed be suspicious.

Now consider a third example, something as innocuous as a very fancy birthday present of expensive jewelry. The present could indicate love, and in a fantasy story, may indicate that the prince is bestowing valuable jewels upon the princess (or vice versa). But if one has suspicions of any kind—for example, that whatever story the couple has—there has been a betrayal, then the gift may be interpreted as an attempt by the gift-giving partner as an attempt to throw one off the scent. The odd thing is that a betrayal does not necessarily mean that the gift-giving partner has been suspected of being intimate, or potentially intimate, with someone else. The betrayal may be an unexpected and possibly unwelcome change either of story or of love triangle. That is, the partner may be dialing down (or up) the level of intimacy, passion, or commitment without involving the other partner in the decision to change the level.

In each case, part of social intelligence as applied to relationships is understanding the partner's actions not just from the standpoint of one's own triangle and story of love, but also from the partner's. This means being able to discern, at some level, how the partner conceives of the relationship, and putting oneself in the place of the partner. And this, again, involves social intelligence.

Relation to Other Chapters in the Book

The social-intelligence/ability aspect of non-verbal communication in close relationships as well as its connection to strong feelings of love, attachment, or desire are reflected in many of the chapters in this volume. Consider some examples:

"After all, popular discussions about the use of eyes in communication seem to focus exclusively on the role of eye contact, missing other key elements of oculesic behaviours that may in fact impact our ability to send and receive relational messages using our eyes" (Bowman & Compton, Chap. 1, this volume).

"These stages are in turn succeeded by the attainment of mature *Theory of Mind* (ToM) on the part of the child, along with the cognitive skills of attribution and perspective-taking. This results in the maturation of the ability accurately to read the thoughts and intentions of others, or cognitive empathy" (Buck, Chap. 2, this volume).

"In our opinion, the general characteristic *social sensitivity* can become a skill in the context of the subject of *the leader*, in terms of the person's awareness of the importance of, and the corresponding ability to control, the manifestation of non-verbal signals" (Francěško & Nedeljković, Chap. 3, this volume).

"They attributed the inability of these babies to thrive as a product of not being lifted, fondled, or cuddled as frequently as babies in non-institutional settings" (Givens & White, Chap. 5, this volume). Here, lack of non-verbal signalling received in the early years impedes people's ability to survive later on.

"Thanks to their multi-signal ability, faces "speak" to us about experienced, suppressed, or simulated emotions" (Kostić, Pejičić, & Chadee, Chap. 8, this volume).

"The ability to substitute some cues for others to send the same messages reveals that non-verbal cues have *equifinality* (i.e., the same messages can be communicated in different ways)" (Manusov, Chap. 9, this volume).

"[T]hree characteristics of nonverbal communication create a difficult social scenario for those who lack non-verbal skills and highlighted the negative interpersonal impact of what they term 'dyssemia' (dys = inability, semia = signs: an inability to process nonverbal signs)" (Nowicki & vanBuskirk, Chap. 10, this volume).

"If COVID-related touch deprivation leads to increased dependence on social media, which in turn, decreases empathic response, the possibility for even more severe degradation of empathic ability is strong" (Remland & Jones, Chap. 11, this volume).

"Non-verbal sensitivity is a key component of the ability to be empathic, for it is necessary that an individual recognize and accurately decode another's emotional state in order to empathize" (Riggio & Crawley, Chap. 12, this volume).

Thus, non-verbal communication in close relationships, as viewed in this book, may provide an important link between affect in close relationships, on the one hand, and social intelligence, on the other hand. Liking and loving are separate from social intelligence, but their success may depend in large part on the application of social intelligence in the context of these relationships.

References

Archer, D., & Akert, R. M. (1977). Words and everything else: Verbal and nonverbal cues in social interpretation. *Journal of Personality and Social Psychology, 35*(6), 443–449. https://doi.org/10.1037/0022-3514.35.6.443

Barnes, M. L., & Sternberg, R. J. (1989). Social intelligence and decoding of nonverbal cues. *Intelligence, 13*, 263–287.

Friedman, H. S., Prince, L. M., Riggio, R. E., & DiMatteo, M. R. (1980). Understanding and assessing nonverbal expressiveness: The Affective Communication Test. *Journal of Personality and Social Psychology, 39*, 333–351.

Kihlstrom, J. F., & Cantor, N. (2020). Social intelligence. In R. J. Sternberg (Ed.), *Cambridge handbook of intelligence* (2nd ed., pp. 756–759). Cambridge University Press.

Riggio, R. E., Tucker, J., & Widaman, K. F. (1987). Verbal and nonverbal cues as mediators of deception ability. *Journal of Nonverbal Behavior, 11*(3), 126–145.

Rosenthal, R., Hall, J. A., DiMatteo, M. R., Rogers, P. L., & Archer, D. (1979). *Sensitivity to nonverbal communication: The PONS test.* Johns Hopkins University Press.

Sternberg, R. J. (1998a). *Cupid's arrow: The course of love through time.* Cambridge University Press.

Sternberg, R. J. (1998b). *Love is a story.* Oxford University Press.

Sternberg, R. J. (2006). A duplex theory of love. In R. J. Sternberg & K. Weis (Eds.), *The new psychology of love* (pp. 184–199). Yale University Press.

Sternberg, R. J. (2021). The ups and downs of love – What makes love go well, or badly? In A. Kostić & D. Chadee (Eds.), *Current research in positive psychology* (pp. 177–192). Palgrave Macmillan.

Sternberg, R. J., & Smith, C. (1985). Social intelligence and decoding skills in nonverbal communication. *Social Cognition, 2*, 168–192.

Sternberg, R. J., Hojjat, M., & Barnes, M. L. (2001). Empirical aspects of a theory of love as a story. *European Journal of Personality, 15*(3), 199–218.

Index[1]

[1] Note: Page numbers followed by 'n' refer to notes.

R. J. Sternberg, A. Kostić (eds.), *Nonverbal Communication in Close Relationships*,
https://doi.org/10.1007/978-3-030-94492-6

CPSIA information can be obtained
at www.ICGtesting.com
Printed in the USA
LVHW020830050423
743532LV00003B/319